This copy of

D.M. Bennett: The Truth Seeker

was donated by the

James Hervey Johnson

Charitable Educational Trust

D. M. BENNETT

D. M. BENNETT

THE TRUTH SEEKER

RODERICK BRADFORD

Prometheus Books

59 John Glenn Drive
Amherst, New York 14228-2197

Published 2006 by Prometheus Books

Inquiries should be addressed to
Prometheus Books
59 John Glenn Drive
Amherst, New York 14228-2197
VOICE: 716-691-0133, ext. 207
FAX: 716-564-2711
WWW.PROMETHEUSBOOKS.COM

10 09 08 07 06   5 4 3 2 1

Library of Congress Cataloging-in-Publication Data

Bradford, Roderick.
    D. M. Bennett, the truth seeker / Roderick Bradford.
        p. cm.
    Includes bibliographical references and index.
    ISBN-13: 978-1-59102-430-9 (hardcover : alk. paper)
    ISBN-10: 1-59102-430-7 (hardcover : alk. paper)
    1. Bennett, De Robigne Mortimer, 1818-1882. 2. Freethinkers—United States—Biography. I. Title.

BL2790.B46B72 2006
211'.4092—dc22
[B]   2006012115

Printed in the United States of America on acid-free paper

To those who continue the work he left unfinished . . .

CONTENTS

8   Contents

ACKNOWLEDGMENTS

"I am well aware it has many defects, like all I do," D. M. Bennett confessed while presenting one of his books to a friend. "I have a long road before me to reach perfection," he added—as does this writer.

In writing this biography, I have had the encouragement and support of several generous individuals. I am grateful to Bonnie Lange and William B. Lindley, who believed in the Bennett biography from its inception. I am especially thankful and indebted to Linda Osman, who, like Mary Wicks, is a gentle and generous soul whose attentiveness, enduring empathy, and patient proofreading has decidedly diminished this book's—and hopefully some of my—"many defects."

I wish to thank Ken Burchell for reading the manuscript at various stages of development, sharing his Thomas Paine research, and providing invaluable suggestions and steadfast support throughout the years. I would also like to express my gratitude to the following persons for their assistance and cooperation in the preparation of this biography: Mary A. Read, Professor Mark Lause, Randy Zilinskas, Sonja Headley, Mary Cronin-Lamonica, Howard H. Urban, Regine Schmidt, Nancy Melton, Jeff McDonald, Paul Eisner, and John Vanderby at the San Diego Public Library. Special thanks goes to Sarah Louise Mullin, a bright young freethinker, for her meticulous proofreading. In addition, I would also like to thank Jerry Grant, librarian, at the Shaker Museum and Library, Old Chatham, New York. I am grateful to Tom Flynn, editor of *Free Inquiry* magazine, and the Council for Secular Humanism. Above all, I am especially appreciative to Kevin Munnelly, trustee of the James Hervey Johnson Charitable Educational Trust, who provided a generous grant for the research, completion, and publication of *D. M. Bennett: The Truth Seeker*.

NOTE TO THE READER

The basic source for this biography of DeRobigne Mortimer
Bennett is his own writings. Fortunately, all of his writing
that was published in the *Truth Seeker* is preserved on microfilm.
I own a full run of the *Truth Seeker* on microfilm from 1873
through 1884. During my research, I also examined the *Truth
Seeker* periodical on microfilm through 1911. Several of Bennett's
books are extremely rare and only available to the public at the
New York Public Library and the Library of Congress, which I
have visited on several occasions. I also spent time at the Shaker
Museum and Library in Old Chatham, New York. Bennett's
Shaker years are chronicled in the illuminative Shaker manuscripts available on microfilm, which include his extensive
journal entries written while he was a ministry-appointed scribe.
I have tried to quote the Shaker-journalists' entries as accurately
as possible and did not think it necessary to interject [*sic*] in order
to point out errors in spelling, grammar, or punctuation. The

Library of Congress provided the New York Society for the Prevention of Vice papers on microfilm. A most invaluable and comprehensive source of information about D. M. Bennett, the freethought movement, and the history of the *Truth Seeker* is George E. Macdonald's *Fifty Years of Freethought: Story of The Truth Seeker from 1875.* Clarence Darrow wrote the foreword and commended the "rare production, to all who want to know something about the struggle for truth and freedom in America, and the devoted men who made it."

Each paragraph of *D. M. Bennett, The Truth Seeker* is numbered and the source of the information is provided in the endnotes for each chapter.

ABBREVIATIONS EMPLOYED IN NOTES

TS—The *Truth Seeker*
GM—*Fifty Years of Freethought*
WSIT—*The World's Sages, Infidels and Thinkers*
TSAW—*A Truth Seeker around the World*
SP—*Four Hundred Years of Freethought*
DAB—*The Dictionary of American Biography*
EB—The *Encyclopaedia Britannica*

INTRODUCTION

Mr. Bennett brought to our philosophical Liberalism a smack of human nature; he poured into it the freshness and vigor of the soil . . . He was our Thomas Paine, and he spoke words of thrilling common sense.

           —Samuel P. Putnam

"Mr. Bennett was a *deeply religious* man," a close friend declared at the dedication of the monument erected to honor the freethinking founder, publisher, and editor of the *Truth Seeker*. The woman went on to explain her assertion by quoting Thomas Paine's motto: "To do good is my religion." "If that was Paine's *highest* work, it made it his religion," she maintained. "It is in this sense that Mr. Bennett was a religious man; and if we measure his religion by the measure of his devotion to his work, he was a *deeply religious* man."[1]

DeRobigne Mortimer Bennett (1818–1882) was the most

revered *and* reviled publisher-editor during the Gilded Age. In 1873 he founded the *Truth Seeker* and devoted it to science, morals, freethought, and human happiness. He opposed dogmatic religion and took great pride in debunking the Bible, exposing hypocritical clergymen, and reminding Americans that the government of the United States was *"not in any sense founded on the Christian religion."* He argued that Abraham Lincoln and many of the founding fathers were, like his hero Thomas Paine, deists or infidels; the most noteworthy being Benjamin Franklin, Thomas Jefferson, and George Washington. The editor and many of his fellow freethinkers were former devout Christians who retained a good deal of the religion's moral spirit.[2]

In the nineteenth century the United States was predominantly orthodox Christian. The church had overwhelming power and influenced or controlled nearly every aspect of American citizens' lives. There were still blasphemy laws on the books in some states (though seldom enforced) and anyone courageous enough to question religion, let alone criticize *in print* the ubiquitous and powerful Christian institutions or their influential leaders, was regarded as an enemy of God and/or peculiar. Opponents of religion were referred to by a variety of names: atheists, agnostics, infidels, or, as they preferred, liberals or freethinkers, and were often ostracized and occasionally persecuted.[3]

The period from 1776 to the late nineteenth century was a paradoxical era in the United States. Americans boasted about their freedom for all citizens but tolerated slavery. A country proclaiming law and order, it often suffered violent mob rule. A nation proudly hailing its freedom of speech, it enforced puritanical laws and church-sponsored censorship. America was home to a minority of reform-minded citizens trying to enlighten and change the rigid and intolerant religionist majority still clinging to archaic superstitions.[4]

Throughout his life (he lived to be nearly sixty-four), Bennett was involved with controversial movements, but it was only in his last decade that he became a lightning rod for controversy while publishing the *Truth Seeker*. He spent the first half of his life as a member of the United Society of Believers in Christ's Second Appearing, more commonly known as the Shakers. Bennett was a ministry-appointed journalist and physician during the celibate sect's most intense spiritualistic period, the Era of Manifestations.[5]

After Bennett's apostasy from the Shakers, he discovered the writings of Thomas Paine, the radical English-American author whose inspirational *Common Sense* pamphlet helped win the Revolutionary War. Thomas Paine, who died in 1809, nearly a decade before D. M. Bennett was born, was one of the most widely read and iconoclastic writers of the late eighteenth century. The "Apostle of Freedom" as Paine has been called, was the first to advocate absolute freedom for the United States. But when Paine expressed his opposition to slavery and criticized religion, he found himself persona non grata in America, even among some of the founding fathers.[6]

Thomas Paine was praised for his *Crisis* papers, *Common Sense*, and *Rights of Man*, but his *Age of Reason*—the book that enlightened D. M. Bennett—offended America's Christian majority; they in turn assailed Paine and disregarded his contribution to the United States. Although Paine was in fact a deist who believed in God, clergymen vilified him, and he was often characterized in the American press as an "outrageous blasphemer" and falsely accused of being a drunkard and an immoral atheist. The patriotic author-hero who named the United States of America was denied the right to vote in New Rochelle and was refused a burial plot in a Quaker cemetery.[7]

Inspired by Thomas Paine, D. M. Bennett denounced religion and he, too, was misunderstood, maligned, and persecuted for his beliefs or lack thereof. His life spanned the greater part of the nineteenth century and reflected the young nation's evolutionary character—a period in America's history of enormous social, political, and economic change. And, along with the century, Bennett evolved.[8]

"Without doubting," Charles Darwin declared, "there can be no progress." In the 1870s freethinkers asserted that doubt was the first step to knowledge. They believed science was the only acceptable method of discovering truth and that evolution destroyed the creation hypothesis. Freethinkers found the universe to be neither moral nor immoral and that man's morals and ethics did not arise from a belief in a supreme being or future life, but from "man's actions towards his fellow-man as he advances in the march of human progress." Freethinkers were convinced that man's well-being was best served by rationalism and total separation of church and state.[9]

At the same time that D. M. Bennett began publishing the *Truth Seeker*, free speech came under attack by Anthony Comstock, America's self-appointed arbiter of morals. Comstock was a "special agent" for the US Post Office and secretary and chief vice hunter for the New York Society for the Suppression of Vice, an organization that was part of the social-purity crusade. A religious zealot, Comstock waged war on "obscene" books (including some classic works of literature), freethinking writers, and publishers. Some of the country's most powerful and pious citizens backed Comstock, who bragged about driving fifteen people to suicide in his Christian-sanctioned mission to "save the young."[10]

There was little protest against the ill-defined Comstock Laws in the nation's newspapers and magazines. Like the politicians, most publishers felt that opposing the vice hunter and his "fight for the young" might be interpreted as tolerating crime. Censorship and church hypocrisy, however, were two of Bennett's favorite subjects. In Comstock and his "Vice Society," as the editor dubbed it, he found both. While other periodicals occasionally scolded Comstock, Bennett persistently scrutinized, ridiculed, and challenged "Saint Anthony" and his wealthy supporters in books, pamphlets, and countless pages of the *Truth Seeker*.[11]

The *Truth Seeker* was the official organ of the National Liberal League, an association of freethinkers devoted to complete separation of church and state. Founded a century after the American Revolution, the National Liberal League held its first national convention in Philadelphia in 1876. Numerous distinguished authors, abolitionists, suffragists, and scholars were members of the NLL. D. M. Bennett was a vice president along with America's most famous orator, Robert G. Ingersoll, "the Great Agnostic."[12]

Organized freethinkers in America were an articulate, eclectic, and vociferous group. Although there are no reliable numbers available, it has been estimated that during the late nineteenth century—known as the Golden Age of Freethought—there were approximately thirty thousand to forty thousand freethinkers and one hundred thousand active sympathizers. About a twelfth of the population was opposed to organized religion. New scientific and philosophical discoveries, most importantly Darwin's theory of evolution (descent with modification by means of natural selection), were beginning to take hold in the public consciousness.[13]

The *Truth Seeker* was not the only freethought periodical in the late nineteenth century, but it was the most successful. After Bennett moved his little prairie monthly from Paris, Illinois, to New York City in 1874, it became the most widely read reform journal in America. The *Truth Seeker* had fifty thousand readers and several illustrious subscribers, including Robert Ingersoll, Mark Twain, and Clarence Darrow. (It continued publication in New York for nearly a century.) The *Truth Seeker* was popular because of the editor's understanding of his subscribers' education level and their desire for a more accessible, tabloid-style weekly instead of the scholarly or "cultured" (as he called them) liberal periodicals. And while some of Bennett's fellow liberals found his harsh criticism of Christianity offensive, his sentiments struck a chord with the common man. Bennett argued that his hero Thomas Paine was also accused of being "uncultured."[14]

Opinions about Bennett were diverse. To his supporters he was an "American Voltaire" and "Nature's Nobleman." His opponents expressed their limitless hate by calling him the "Devil's Own Advocate." His hard-fought battle for free speech was praised by liberals and assailed by religionists. Anthony Comstock declared the editor "everything vile in blasphemy and infidelism."[15]

In the 1870s many Americans believed that one had to be religious, preferably Christian, to be a moral person. Bennett's religious adversaries tried to link freethought to immorality and labeled him a free-love advocate. The *Christian Union*, edited by Lyman Abbott and Henry Ward Beecher, two of America's most prominent religious leaders, publicized a pastor's inflammatory editorial that expressed the prevalent Christian sentiment toward Bennett and his supporters: "There is a sort of nervous communication among the ganglia of vicious Infidelity scattered through the country that constitutes them one system—a church of Antichrist or synagogue of Satan."[16]

D. M. Bennett's publications were censored by religionists and prohibited from the mail and newsstands long before the phrase "banned in Boston" was heard. The enterprising editor popularized the Darwinian discoveries, sold birth control books, and was the first editor in the world who routinely reported immoral and criminal behavior of Christian clergymen and published "black-collar crimes" in *Sinful Saints and Sensual Shepherds*. Bennett was a prolific and provocative writer who promoted his publications *and* himself with the lecture "An Hour with the Devil" and articles titled "An Open Letter to Jesus Christ" and "Was Christ a Negro?"[17]

The year before his death, Bennett traveled around the world exploring different cultures and investigating Buddhism, Druidism, and Theosophy. Some of his more skeptical subscribers were surprised when he traveled to India to learn about the mystical Theosophical Society. Bennett, however, was a spiritualist decades before it became the rage of the Gilded Age, and it made perfect sense for "the truth seeker," as he was known, to inquire into new philosophical movements, especially Theosophy, whose motto is: "There is no religion higher than truth."[18]

When D. M. Bennett was convicted and imprisoned for sending "obscenity" through the US mail, tens of thousands of supporters—including Shakers—came to his defense, sending money, signing petitions, and writing personal letters to President Hayes. (It was the largest protest of its kind in nineteenth-century America.) Bennett's loyal supporters provided funds for his yearlong tour around the world, and their unwavering devotion and generosity continued after his death when they donated to the impressive memorial honoring the Defender of Liberty and Its Martyr—still standing today in Brooklyn's Green-Wood Cemetery.[19]

NOTES

"thrilling common sense.": TS Jan. 13, 1883

1. *"deeply religious* man.": Asenath Chase Macdonald, TS June 28, 1884.

Although Bennett rarely used the term *atheist*, there is at least one instance on record where he referred to himself as an atheist. In a reply to a man (William H. Pindar) who questioned Bennett's beliefs, the editor advised the man to read "some sound Atheistic works," and went on, with signature candor, to state his views on religion. He wrote:

> We readily believe in everything that we are convinced has an existence. When proofs are placed before us of the existence of a God, we shall at once believe in him. Up to this time we have received no such proof, and consequently we are an unbeliever. We believe in the universe because we see it everywhere around us. Its material and its powers and forces are made apparent to us every hour of our lives. It is not so with God, whether he be called Brahm, Jupiter, or Mumbo Jumbo. . . . Nobody has ever seen him, and nobody knows the first thing about him. What men think they know about him has come from what somebody told them, and that somebody obtained it from somebody else, and all were equally ignorant. . . . Our friend will be entirely justified in counting us an *Atheist* [italics mine].
>
> Yes, numerous religions existed in the world before the Jewish Bible was written, and to say the least they were quite as good as the religion practiced by the believers of that book. . . . Our doubts as to the inspiration of the Bible arise from a want of proof. It is not enough for us that somebody says it was written by the finger of God, or that he dictated it. Something more convincing is necessary. Before it can be accepted as the work of God it must be shown superior to what man can accomplish. If gods can do no better than men, they are entitled to no higher credit. The Bible presents no evidence of being superior to human power, but, on the other hand, it is so full of errors and imperfections of many kinds that we are forced to the conclusion that it was produced by crude, ignorant, and unscientific minds. Some of its poetry does very well considering the age in which it was written, but it has been surpassed in later years. Its narratives, its history, its science, and its morals are very defective. We simply

take it just as it is and accord no more credit to it than it deserves. It is unjust to apply the "eye of faith" or any other instrument to magnify it into something that it really is not. In many respects it has been surpassed by the bibles of other nations, some of which were written at an earlier date. If it is liable to be distorted and perverted by translators, transcribers, and printers it is another proof that it is not unlike other human productions. If God took the trouble to write it or to dictate it, it would seem but reasonable that he should look after it a little, and keep men from changing it and spoiling it.

All religions are fallible, all contain myths, fables, and superstitions which are held up to the world as divine truths. All religions are of human production. . . . There is not in existence the slightest proof that a god ever had anything to do with any of them. . . . It is quite natural for every one to think his own a little the best; but on some accounts the Christian religion is not the happiest. It has the most angry and cruel God, the meanest and most malicious devil, and the hottest and most everlasting hell. There may be some religions worse than Christianity, but it is hard to find them. There are evidently some that have been better, far less tyrannical, bloodthirsty, and murderous. As truth is far better than falsehood, it is always greatly preferred. Even if truth is called Infidelity, it is greatly superior to superstition and blind delusion. There is no man happier in his belief than he who discards fables, mysticisms, and the supernaturalisms, and accepts the truths of the universe and lives in obedience to its laws—who regards humanity as the highest intellect and who does all in his power to improve it.

Christianity has shed far more blood and taken far more life than all the other religions combined. It has made a hell here upon earth in every deed. . . . We fail to see where Christians have any advantage over Infidels. The belief that men and women are going to heaven upon the merits of another individual is a fallacious one, and in the sequel will undoubtedly prove so. The Infidel who depends upon his own good deeds and in living a good life occupies the safer ground, whether in life or at the hour of death. Infidels have far less fear of death and the devil than have Christians, and consequently they are happier. The greatest horror in the world is the continuous dread of an unmerciful God, a torturing devil and an ever-yawning, ever-burning hell. These are the Christian's portion, and he is entirely welcome to them if he wants them. The Infidel has no use for anything of the kind.

We hope Mr. Pindar may be able to come out of the darkness of superstition and error into the broad sunlight of science, reason, and truth. Let him continue to inquire and to investigate; we will cheerfully try to know such questions as he may wish to ask.

TS June 1, 1878 & July 29, 1878.
    2. "and human happiness.": TS Sept. 1873. "the Christian religion.": TS April 14, 1877.
Bennett acknowledged that Franklin, Jefferson, and Washington were *not* atheists. However, "They were unbelievers in the divinity of Jesus and in supernatural and revealed religion." Bennett cited Franklin's "creed" in which the statesman wrote: "There is one supreme, most perfect Being, author and father of the gods themselves. He is infinite and incomprehensible. He does not expect nor desire the worship of man; he is above it." Bennett bolstered his argument about Franklin's unbelief by quoting James Parton's *Life and Times of Benjamin Franklin* (1864): "Parton tells us that Franklin was in the habit of amusing his friends at the expense of Bible admirers by opening the Bible and pretending to read from it parables and stories that conflicted with the usual Christian opinions." Regarding Thomas Jefferson, Bennett had numerous "radical extracts from Jefferson's writings" that expressed his infidelity. The editor cited Jefferson's *Notes on Virginia* that contained the following passage: "Difference of opinion is advantageous to religion. The several sects perform the office of *censor-morum* over each other. Is uniformity attainable? Millions of innocent men, women, and children since the introduction of Christianity have been burnt, tortured, fined, imprisoned yet we have not advanced one inch towards uniformity. What has been the effect of coercion? To make one half the world fools and the other half hypocrites; to support error and roguery all over the earth." TS March 10, 1878.

I am well aware that Christian biographers and pious adulators have made great efforts to show that Washington was a Christian; that he was a sanctimonious man, and that he preceded his engagements on the battle-field by prayer; that it was discovered that upon a certain occasion he retired into a thicket to pray; but the stories lack confirmation, and are too much like the Sunday-school story about the cherry tree and his little hatchet, in which it was impossible for him to tell a lie—a story, by the way, first told by a clergyman.

The truth is, Washington has been so far deified by an admiring American people, and we have grown up from our infancy with the impressions implanted upon our minds that he was a model man, a great and good personage, far superior to any other who lived at the same time, that he is exalted into a demi-god who could not tell a lie, who could not use a profane word, and who was almost perfection itself. This is all an error. The truth is, he had his faults and failings like other men. He could not only use duplicity and strategy when necessary, but he could swear "like a trooper." Those who were well acquainted with him pronounced him a profane man who often gave way to passion, who was aristocratic and almost unapproachable to his inferiors, and who often showed a species of tyranny and cruelty. Still, the eminent services which he rendered this country should be duly acknowledged and remembered, but not on the false ground that he was a Christian.

Humphrey-Bennett Discussion. The Services of Infidelity and Christianity to American Liberty. TS April 14, 1877.

Jane Mahan was one of a party of prisoners of war released by the British in Canada in 1782 as the Revolutionary War was winding down. Coming through New York, the party was invited to dine with George Washington. Much later, in 1841, she reported: "Hugh [Henry Brackenridge] was in the army as preacher. Washington used to send for the young preachers, to come and preach to the army. I heard him laugh hearty, and say Brackenridge was one of their greatest preachers for the army. He would tell the soldiers if they died in battle, they would be sure to go to heaven. To be valiant in the cause, & died in battle. . . . Washington was then at New Windsor. . . ." William B. Lindley, Draper Manuscripts 11CC28, 33–35.

3. Sidney Warren. *American Freethought, 1860–1914.*

The freedoms declared in the Bill of Rights were not used to constrain state governments until the twentieth century.

4. Ibid.

5. WSIT.

6. Jack Fruchtman Jr. *Thomas Paine: Apostle of Freedom.*
"With the publication of *Common Sense* in January 1776," John C. Miller asserted in his *Origins of the American Revolution*, "Tom Paine broke the ice that was slowly congealing the revolutionary movement." Quoted in Philip S. Foner's introduction to *The Age of Reason*, Citadel Press-Kensington Publishing Corp., 1988. Another eminent historian of the Revolutionary period, Evarts B. Greene, assessed the importance of Paine's fifty-page pamphlet in his *The Revolutionary Generation*, writing: "Thomas Paine's *Common Sense*, more than any other single piece of writing, set Americans to thinking of the possibility and desirability of an independent place among the nations." Ibid.

In one of the earliest (1775) and best attacks upon slavery in America, Paine equated the bondage of blacks on the same level with "murder, robbery, lewdness, and barbarity," and implored Americans to immediately "discontinue and renounce it, with grief and abhorrence." Ibid.

"Of all the tyrannies that affect mankind," Paine wrote in his *Letter to Erskine*, "tyranny in religion is the worst; every other species of tyranny is limited to the world we live in; but this attempts to stride beyond the grave, and seeks to pursue us into eternity." Ibid.

7. Ibid.

8. Warren.

9. SP.

10. Heywood Broun and Margaret Leech. *Anthony Comstock: Roundsman of the Lord.*

11. Ibid. and TS.

12. Anthony Comstock. *Frauds Exposed; or How the People are Deceived and Robbed, and Youth Corrupted.* Howard Brown, N.Y. 1880.

13. Warren.

14. TS June 1, 1878.

15. "Devil's own advocate.": Warren. "blasphemy and infidelism.": The New York Society for the Suppression of Vice arrest blotter, Library of Congress.

16. "synagogue of Satan.": TS Aug. 7, 1879.

17. An Hour with the Devil": lecture Dec. 5, 1875. "An Open Letter to Jesus Christ": TS Nov. 1, 1875. "Was Christ a Negro?": TS Jan. 8, 1876.

18. TSAW.

19. *Hayes: The Diary of a President, 1875–1881*. Edited by Harry T. Williams. David McKay Company Inc., N.Y. 1964.

The indignation, protest, and petition campaign in support of Bennett had no modern parallel in America except for the execution of Francisco Ferrer, the Spanish educator in 1909, and the Sacco-Vanzetti murder case in 1927. GM v. 1 p. 247.

1

THE BELIEVERS

I have understood from those who knew him intimately that he was thoroughly upright, of apparently strong religious convictions and sensitive to spiritual influences.

— Catherine Allen

DeRobigne Mortimer Bennett was born ahead of his time on December 23, 1818, in Springfield, New York. His advent should have occurred two months later in February, but after his eighteen-year-old mother strained herself lifting a Dutch oven, he was born prematurely two days before Christmas, weighing only four pounds. Near the end of his life, Bennett provided an amusing account of his birthday in comparative biblical terms:

[O]n an extremely rough and stormy day, the snow flying and blowing most furiously, so that roads were so blocked that few or none, even of neighbors, could be present at his advent. It is not believed that any angels troubled themselves to sing to shepherds or unfortunate travelers on that occasion, and the event passed off just the same as though no remarkable affair had taken place. Nature was not reversed; the sun, it is true, was somewhat darkened by the blinding clouds of snow, but rocks were not rent, and the moon did not change to blood.[1]

Springfield is a hamlet about sixty miles west of Albany, New York, on the northern tip of Lake Otsego between the rolling hills of the Catskill Mountains and the Mohawk Valley. Lake Otsego extends about nine miles south to the village of Cooperstown and is surrounded by unspoiled wilderness and protected on both sides by mountains. The surface of the lake is unaffected by the predominate winds out of the west, and the tranquil body of water is home to flocks of aquatic birds. The placid highland lake and the foreboding primeval forest served as both inspiration and setting for James Fenimore Cooper's Leatherstocking series of novels, which have become classics in American literature.[2]

James Fenimore Cooper (1789–1851) was America's first great professional novelist. His best-known work, *The Last of the Mohicans*, was first published in 1826. The author's father, William Cooper, established the village of Cooperstown in 1786, and James enjoyed a wealthy and privileged childhood. James spent his carefree youth playing in the forest near Lake Otsego, which he later christened "Glimmerglass." DeRobigne Mortimer Bennett also spent his childhood near the calm waters of Lake Otsego, but his early years were anything but serene—he lived in abject poverty and constant turmoil.[3]

John and Betsey Bennett were poor farmers living on a rented farm when DeRobigne, the first of their three children, was born. One of DeRobigne's earliest memories was when his "young and giddy" mother abruptly weaned him and took a journey to visit relatives in Massachusetts. She left him at home with a bottle and a "strange woman"—a maternal indiscretion that, along with other painful memories, he would remember for the rest of his life. Besides being poverty-stricken, his parents were incompatible and fought continually. John Bennett was an honest and humble farmer with a good disposition, but he could barely read or write. Betsey Bennett was an educated, showy, and spirited woman who constantly criticized her husband for the family's many misfortunes.[4]

Three years after DeRobigne's birth, his father, who was not much of a farmer or businessman, decided to buy a farm in the adjoining town of Middlefield. A daughter, Letsey Ann, was born in 1821. John Bennett struggled to feed his growing family and although he worked every day and into the night, he always managed to get into debt. His horses were constantly sick and dying of some malady, and during a period of only a few years he lost fifteen of his livestock to disease. He became increasingly sensitive to his wife's nagging, and they failed to agree on almost everything, especially religion.[5]

Betsey Bennett was a devout Christian who dressed in her finest clothes every Sunday and, with her children in tow, attended Methodist services. DeRobigne remembered standing along the bank of a country stream watching his mother being baptized by a minister. DeRobigne faithfully memorized twenty to thirty verses of the New Testament each week in order to recite them for his Sunday school teacher. Although his father was a very moral man, he never went to church or cared for religion. Incompatible as the Bennetts were, the couple had yet another daughter when DeRobigne was ten years old, and the family became even more destitute.[6]

After seven hard years of struggle, John Bennett was forced to sell the farm and all the family's worldly possessions. A sheriff's auction was held, attended by a hundred or so unsympathetic neighbors who bought the family's treasures for next to nothing. DeRobigne witnessed his mother bitterly weep as she watched furniture, heirlooms, and quilts made by her own hands get sold and carried off in the arms of strangers. This was a tearful scene that he never forgot, and it would give him the compassion he had for unfortunate people for the remainder of his life.[7]

The family moved to Cooperstown where John got a job as a laborer at the printing establishment of H. & E. Phinney. Ten-year-old DeRobigne attended the district school where he received a basic education lasting a short four years. John Bennett remained only a year or two at the printing profession and then returned to his favorite occupation, teaming, driving a wagon pulled by horse. At the age of twelve and weighing only fifty-two pounds, DeRobigne got a job at H. & E. Phinney working as a roll-boy or "printer's devil" as they were called. At the time of his employment, H. & E. Phinney was one of the largest publishing firms in the country; a substantial part of their business was the printing of Bibles. These were primitive days of printing and everything was done on hand presses. DeRobigne's job was to apply ink with composition rollers to the stereotype plates and later wash them in lye and put them away. He dutifully took home his weekly wage of a dollar and a half and gave it to his mother, suddenly a single parent after his father left the family to live in another part of the state. About this time, DeRobigne's youngest sister died.[8]

DeRobigne's career as a printer's devil soon ended after an apparatus was invented that eliminated the roll-boy's job. He worked briefly at one of Cooperstown's local weekly newspapers and later got a job in a wool-carding business. Years earlier his uncle promised to make a doctor of him when he was old enough. Betsey Bennett decided to take her brother up on his offer and sent her fourteen-year-old son to his uncle's home in Berkshire County, Massachusetts. With only four years of formal education and weighing just seventy pounds, the young man set out for his new life.[9]

When DeRobigne arrived at his uncle's home, the doctor took notice of the diminutive youth's size and had a change of heart but agreed to fulfill his promise of making him a doctor when the young man became a little older and bigger. Before returning home to his mother and sister in Cooperstown, DeRobigne detoured a few miles away to make a short visit at the home of his father's uncle. Two friendly Shakers were staying at the home, and they offered to give him a ride as far as they were going. DeRobigne accepted and joined the Shakers on the twenty-five-mile journey to their home in New Lebanon, New York.[10]

THE SHAKERS

The Shakers were a communitarian and celibate sect officially called The United Society of Believers in Christ's Second Appearing or The Millennial Church. The group originated in England and was an offshoot of the Quakers. Because of the spiritualistic sect's ecstatic and often violent shaking contortions during their religious services, they were derided as Shaking Quakers. Eventually they were commonly called Shakers, although some of its founders preferred the name Alethians—as they considered themselves children of the truth.[11]

The Shakers, who would become known more for their furniture craftsmanship than their religious beliefs, came to America in 1774. That year Ann Lee (1736–1784), an English religious visionary, and her followers arrived from England. Although Lee believed in celibacy, she had married in England at her parents' insistence and had four children; all died in infancy. She joined the Wardleys, a group of former Quakers who encouraged their followers to attack sin and preach publicly of the second coming of Jesus Christ. It was subsequently believed that in Ann Lee the promise of the second coming was fulfilled. Lee became the religious sect's charismatic leader and was imprisoned for dancing, shouting, and blasphemy on the Sabbath. She reportedly miraculously escaped death on several occasions and claimed to be able to speak in tongues. Her followers referred to her as "Mother in spiritual things," and she called herself "Ann, the Word." In 1774 she received a "revelation" instructing her to take a select group of Shakers to America.[12]

The Shakers first settled in an isolated area outside of Albany, New York, called Niskeyuna, later known as Watervliet. Their pacifism drew scorn, and they were persecuted during the American Revolution. Ann Lee was imprisoned for a few months in 1780. That year a group of curious New Light Baptists from New Lebanon came to investigate the strange new religious group and later joined the society. Lee died on September 8, 1784, but her followers continued to grow in numbers and flourish. A second settlement formed in New Lebanon that would be the first of many. The first meetinghouse for worship at New Lebanon was raised in 1785. Although New Lebanon was the second community, it became the hub of Shakerdom because of its access to New England, where most of the other communities would be located. The Shakers became the most successful communitarian society in America.[13]

When fourteen-year-old DeRobigne Bennett arrived on September 12, 1833, the Society of Believers at New Lebanon numbered nearly five hundred men, women, and children. The settlement was the largest of the sixteen villages located in eight states. New Lebanon served as a model for other Shaker communities and was home of the government or central ministry. New Lebanon was the Jerusalem of Shakerism. In an autobiographical sketch, Bennett described the society, its charismatic leader, and their beliefs:

> The Shakers have a peculiar religion and lead peculiar lives. They believe that in Ann Lee, an English married woman, the wife of a dissipated blacksmith, over one hundred years ago, Jesus Christ made his second appearance, and made known the true and only plan of salvation. To her was revealed that the fall of man, in the persons of Adam and Eve, consisted in premature and unauthorized sexual connection and that through the indulgence in the passion of lust from that early day all the sin and misery which has since existed came into the world. She taught her followers that to become the true disciples of Christ they must lead virgin lives and wholly abstain from the pollution of the sexual embrace. Marriage is accordingly prohibited among them. They dance and march for worship, and hold all their property in common, each family by themselves.
> They are industrious, frugal and honest people, and so far

as religion is concerned they probably have an article that is as practical, as useful and as sincere as any in the world.

The objections to them are, they are somewhat intolerant towards the faith of others. Their creed is narrow, and they hold that Nature is wrong and must be subdued and entirely overcome. They are Unitarians, or rather Duotarians, believing God consists of two persons or elements—male and female—"Power and Wisdom." Jesus and "Mother Ann" are regarded as human representatives of the Father and Mother deities or principles, and were chosen as special messengers to bring special tidings to the world. Their original exclusiveness and intolerance has become greatly modified in late years. The great law of evolution has been working with them as well as other believers in the various religious systems of the world.[14]

A few years before Bennett arrived at New Lebanon, James Fenimore Cooper visited the community and wrote that he had never seen any "villages as neat, and so perfectly beautiful, as to order and arrangement, without, however, being picturesque or ornamented, as those of the Shakers." However, Cooper also declared the Believers as "deluded fanatics," albeit clean and orderly. Another distinguished visitor was Charles Dickens who was critical of the manner in which the Shakers gained members and wrote: "[T]hey take as proselytes persons so young that they cannot know their own minds, and cannot possess much strength of resolution in this or any other respect." The four Shaker virtues were Christian communism, virgin purity, separation from the world, and confession of sin, which one had to perform to become a member. The teenage Bennett might well have been one of the proselytes that Dickens thought was too young to know his own mind. Nevertheless, considering the young man's impoverished background, it is understandable that his first impression of New Lebanon was favorable: "I was most kindly received in a family of some 75 genial kindhearted Brethren and Sisters who lived happily on the community plan with plenty around them on every side."[15]

After a visit of ten days DeRobigne decided to join the

Shakers. He fulfilled the first requirement of joining by confessing his sins that he later described as "not a very black list at
the time." A Shaker journal entry recorded the event: "DeRobigne
Bennett opened his mind and set out with Believers." Soon after
joining, he wrote to his mother and sister inviting them to come
to New Lebanon. DeRobigne spent the next thirteen years
"acknowledging the correctness of their faith and believing they
were living more acceptable to God than any others of the children of men."[16]

On April 13, 1834, DeRobigne's mother and sister arrived at
New Lebanon. Betsey Bennett's commitment to the society, however, was not as firm as her children's. Her behavior was erratic,
according to several journal entries, and she periodically left the
community. Since the Shakers were celibate, they depended on
converts (sometimes orphans) from "the world." The society had
something to offer almost anybody, at least temporarily. New-
comers joined for different reasons and were Believers of varying
degrees of commitment. Some "bread and butter" Believers and
"winter Shakers" arrived and stayed for brief periods only to take
advantage of the food and shelter, while others stayed longer but
did not participate wholeheartedly and eventually apostatized.[17]

Some converts arrived with their whole families. One such
family was the Wickses from Reading, New York, a village in
Steuben County west of the Catskill and Adirondack Mountains.
The constant religious crusades in that locale and the peculiar
religious beliefs held by many of its residents caused the area to
be called the Burned-over District, drawing on the western
analogy between forest fires and those of the soul. In the summer
of 1824, fifty-year-old Job Wicks arrived at Watervliet and
"opened his mind." Two months later he returned with his wife
and ten children. In the early 1830s, two of the children died, and
several of the others, including Job, left the Shakers. One of the
girls, Mary, born April 28, 1819, joined the Shakers when she was
five years old. Besides attending school, sisters performed routine
chores and became apprentices to a skill or trade. Mary Wicks was
trained as a hat liner, basket maker, and was adept at sewing and

weaving. In addition to other duties, Mary was a beloved teacher and caretaker of the children at New Lebanon.[18]

Relationships and intimate contact with the opposite sex were forbidden, and both male and female Believers nearly always remained separated. They never shook hands or touched, and spent their days and nights in a communal social order. Some interaction and a few wholesome diversions were permitted but always limited and closely monitored. The males were each assigned to a female member who mended the brethren's clothes, informed him when new items were needed, and reminded him if he was not orderly. Evenings were spent at worship meetings or family meetings where elders read excerpts aloud from periodicals, books, and even newspapers. Some evenings were spent learning new hymns and singing. Their busy schedule left no time for contemplation or loneliness, and church elders strongly believed that an idle mind was the devil's workshop.[19]

At least once a week "union meetings" were held in which both the males and females were afforded the opportunity to be together, in a group and under close scrutiny. Sisters would enter the brethrens' quarters, sit across the room, and engage in light conversation mostly confined to society matters. Any instances of a "special liking" or "sparking" between individual members of the opposite sex were monitored and likely reported to an elder. A Shaker described a union meeting as follows:

> In fact to say "agreeable things about nothing," when conversant with the other sex, is as common here as elsewhere. . . . Nevertheless, an hour passes away very agreeable and ever rapturously with those who there have a chance to meet an especial favorite; succeeded soon however, when soft words and kind, concentrated looks become obvious to the jealous eye of a female espionage, by the agonies of a separation. For the tidings of such reciprocity, whether true or surmised, is sure before the lapse of many hours, to reach the ears of the elders; in which case the one or the other party would be subsequently summoned to another circle of colloquy and union.[20]

Bennett spent his first winter at New Lebanon attending a school for boys that ran from November through March. "He was possessed of marked individuality and more than average intellectual ability," a journal entry noted. It was a common practice for the youth to be teamed with an older "brother" who served as a mentor. At the end of the school year, he was placed to work in the seed gardens with Charles Crosman, a painter, seedsman, and caretaker of the boys. The garden-seed business was a principal industry for the Shaker communities. Seeds were produced and packaged by the Shakers and marketed to farmers by seed agents who traveled around America in horse-drawn wagons. Occasionally Bennett would join Crosman for trips to other Shaker communities. In 1836 Crosman edited a gardener's manual that sold for six cents a copy and was the first of its kind. Sixteen thousand copies were printed and sold to garden-seed dealers.[21]

The Shakers were the first group in America to grow herbs for the burgeoning pharmaceutical market. Wild herbs and medicinal plants were gathered and grown at New Lebanon as early as 1800. Some of the many herbs the society raised were boneset, catnip, horehound, mandrake, sage, spikenard, wormwood, and skunk cabbage. The plants and herbs were dried, pressed, and powdered, making it a very labor-intensive process. Many of the sisters and some of the children were needed for the business of making extracts, ointments, pills, and syrups. While spending several years in the medical environment, Bennett became familiar with the sciences of botany and chemistry. He worked as an herbalist and community physician. On December 30, 1839, the twenty-one-year-old signed the Shaker covenant and formally became a partner in the society. Three decades later, he wrote in an autobiographical sketch:

> He was finally appointed physician to the Society. He attended no medical college nor course of lectures. He had the use of a very fair medical library and the experience of an old physician who had been retired. Bennett continued this profession two years or more. The system pursued was the eclectic. The sick were promptly attended to, and the success was usually very good.[22]

ERA OF MANIFESTATIONS

In the late 1830s a revival of spiritualistic activity occurred among the Shakers. The Shakers were spiritualists decades before the modern spiritualism movement began in 1848. In a sense, the Shakers were the forerunners of the spiritualism movement that became popular in America and, later, Europe. The Shakers were the first religion in America to acknowledge channeling (although the word was not known in their time). Ann Lee and the other founding members believed in spirits apart from the human body and that they could and did communicate with them and receive revelations.[23]

The Era of Manifestations or "Mother Ann's Work" as it was known, began in 1837 and lasted until 1844; it was a period filled with messages and visions from the spirit world. The spiritualistic outburst preoccupied the Shakers for nearly a decade and both revitalized and weakened the society. Shaker historians have compared the period favorably with the first century of Christianity. It was an intense charismatic epoch in Shaker history that attracted much attention. The phenomenon was similar to the spirit communication experienced by Ann Lee and other founders of the society. Although these "gifts" often caused derision from outsiders, they also attracted converts including Frederick W. Evans, who became a leading Shaker and spokesman: "It was by spiritual manifestations . . . that I, in 1830, was converted to Shakerism. In 1837 to 1844, there was an influx from the spirit world, 'confirming the faith of many disciples' who had lived among Believers for years, and extending throughout all the eighteen societies."[24]

By the mid-1830s most of the original members in the society were dead, and the church elders felt that the Shakers were becoming removed from Ann Lee's initial vision and wisdom. With a declining membership and a growing number of apostasies, mostly young Shakers, the society's elders welcomed the restoration of the charismatic gifts. Although numerous accounts of spiritual manifestations occurred during the 1830s, including inspired dreams, prophetic visions, and speaking in tongues, it was not until 1837 that the church elders declared a new Era of Manifestations. This began during a worship service at Watervliet, New York, when a group of ten- to fourteen-year-old girls exhibited unusual trancelike behavior. Some spoke in tongues, while others saw visions and communicated with angels in heavenly places. Others, as if possessed by spirits, shook, jerked, and twirled about. Some talked to Mother Ann and other first-generation leading Shakers and were given songs, dances, drawings, rituals, and revelations to share with their fellow Believers. Those individual Shakers who received "gifts" were called visionists or instruments. The Shakers believed the instruments were their connection to the celestial sphere where Ann Lee and other founding members of the society existed.[25]

Shaker instruments played an important role during the Era of Manifestations. The ministry designated as official some instruments whom they felt were divinely inspired. Because of their sacred calling and personal sacrifices, instruments were separated from the other Believers. And because of their unique abilities, they were influential and slightly controversial. In some ways Mother Ann's work helped revitalize the society; in other ways it widened the generation gap that already existed.[26]

During the Era of Manifestations, Shaker journalists carefully recorded the inspired gifts. The first year (1837) of the Era of Manifestations was the same year that Bennett began his three years' duty as an official journal keeper, recording, collecting, and transcribing the society's most important communications and revelations. These manuscripts were of immense importance and were believed to be divinely inspired. The same meticulous attention to detail that the Believers paid to their business records, building a chair or laying out a garden, was given to the important documents. A holy celebration could last eight hours, and the transcription could fill a small booklet.[27]

Bennett was mindful of the importance of his status as a journalist. In a self-effacing statement made on January 1, 1840, he promised to be "more brief" in the journal that he had been keeping for three years, which he "kept considerable of a full & minute account of the work of God & the movings of the spirit among us." But, he added, "when there is particular inspiration or revelation or anything that will be considered most worthy to be recorded, I shall endeavor to give as comprehensive a description as my feeble abilities will allow." He ended these introductory remarks with: "If my labors in recording the gifts of our heavenly parents & some of the great displays of a wise providence, meet the approbation & continence of my friends & prove to be any satisfaction to those now living, or to those who may hereafter come upon the stage, my most ardent wishes will be fully realized. It is all I want, it is all I desire in this respect."[28]

During the Era of Manifestations, every year seemed to present new and more intense developments. In 1841 Holy Mother Wisdom spoke through a chosen instrument. Bennett recorded that the feminine deity's visit lasted over a week, examining members and speaking "love and blessing." Another unusual incident was the appearance of a mysterious object in the sky in May 1842. Bennett and several other Shakers spotted the "sign" and a journal entry documented the event and included a rare depiction of the object.

> Sat 21 Last night—about 1 o clock AM a wonderful sign was seen in the heavens a large cross appearing across the moon, a large ball or body of light on each side of the moon, or at the end of the cross & then a bow, over the moon, connecting these two lights together. This was seen by Derobigne B. & B. Coates & Joseph Baker & two or three at the 2nd order, but for some reason they neglected to awake others to see it.[29]

The most delightful and discernible spiritualist gifts were drawings and paintings rendered by Shaker artists while under the inspiration of the spirits. These inspired instruments or image makers, as they were known, produced unworldly religious pictures that were important to the Believers, a community that in the past forbade any type of "superfluous" pictures, portraits, images, engravings, or likeness of any kind—especially art. The

visionary artworks were presented to older members for their
devoted service to the society. One of the revered image makers
was Mary Wicks, who together with another Shakeress produced
a drawing titled "A Sacred Sheet, Sent for Holy Mother Wisdom
by Her Holy Angel of Many Signs for Daniel Bowler."[30]

Rare gift images were especially powerful because of their
simple yet abstract and intricate detail that could be subcon-
sciously appealing. Although outsiders were admitted to the
Shaker meetings, the general public was never allowed to view
the visionary drawings and paintings. Their abstract quality
would have surely confused even the most aesthetically aware art
connoisseur in the mid-nineteenth century. Perhaps only a fellow
instrument like Philemon Stewart, an insider who understood
Shaker myth, history, and iconography, could accurately describe
the merit and importance of gift images, messages, and visions:

> The mighty manifestations of God to his chosen people are
> truly wonderful, very wonderful; far beyond any thing ever
> before revealed on earth. It has often seemed as though the
> Heavens and earth had come together, and that we were in
> reality surrounded by heavenly hosts; yet these heavenly and
> divine manifestations, with which we have so often been
> favored, are not understood by the world of mankind; nor can
> they understand them except by revelation from God, or faith
> in the testimony of his appointed agents.[31]

In 1842, at the height of the Era of Manifestations, the lead ministry instructed each village to prepare a sacred site for an outdoor
feast and ritual activity. These sites, chosen by instruments under
inspiration, were believed by Shakers to be the holiest places on
earth. The sacred feast ground at New Lebanon was at the top of
a mountain, within walking distance of the community. Beginning in May 1842 this Holy Mount would be the site of the
society's most sacred and important celebrations. Bennett, the
twenty-three-year-old community scribe, chronicled the seminal
first meeting on the mount. He collected and transcribed the religious devotion that day in his "Statement of the First Meeting

Held on the Holy Mount," a twenty-five-page official document. On May 1, 1842, at 5 AM, he wrote that the members of the Church Order gathered together "in the meeting room to receive the blessing of the Ancients [oldest Shakers] who were not going upon the Mount." The historical significance of the day was expressed by a fellow journalist, who wrote, "This is a memorable day & long to be remembered, being a day lately instituted by divine authority to be observed a feast or Passover, to be kept yearly, sacred to Holy & Eternal Wisdom. The Church, (Except some of the aged & those unable to go), all marched up the mountain, to the Holy consecrated ground, & assembled there to perform religious devotion."[32]

Bennett's written account of these esoteric religious rituals is a fascinating document filled with descriptions of peculiar phenomena and inspirational messages. The day began with the members singing "Feast of Lord" followed by the Believers kneeling and being blessed by the Ancients. The instruments were identified, including John Allen who "was Instrument for the Savior & spoke for him in most cases." Another instrument, Philemon Stewart, read from the fourth chapter of the Prophet Micah that everyone "united in repeating." Other instruments included Giles Avery, who spoke of "a fountain of wine." The members "partook of the wine after which [they] sung & danced joyfully." Most of the activity that day consisted of playful worship and elaborate mime. One of the "messages," however, revealed a subconscious discontent among some instruments. While under inspiration, John Allen came forward and stated, "Who has doubts? What doubts? saith the Prophet (Isaiah). Many answered & said they had none. Well said the Prophet I have doubts. The Instrument was then taken under violent operations, thrown on the ground & rolled over. He was then raised up, & the P'[Prophet] said I guess I shall get rid of them now."[33]

THEY HAVE FALLEN!

Bennett's duties as an herbalist and physician included leaving the New Lebanon society on business trips. These local day trips afforded him an opportunity to interact with fellow Shakers, some of whom decided to leave the society. Journal entries for the period disclose an increased number of departures and the reproachful attitude of the Shaker journalists. As the apostasy rate increased, the journal entries included more pointed remarks regarding the apostates. DeRobigne gave a ride to two departing Shakers who, a journalist wrote, "choose rather to live among the world than with us." One entry noted that two sisters made their choice "to go away into the wide world of sin." Another Shaker, "loving his own way much better than the gospel," was determined "to have a swing in the world of pleasure & sin."[34]

By the mid-1840s Believers began to lose interest in spiritual gifts and communications. Messages from deceased Shaker leaders were replaced by revelations from historical figures such as George Washington, Thomas Jefferson, and Christopher Columbus. Some instruments claimed to have received spiritual communications from American Indians. Shaker leaders were finding it increasingly difficult to determine the authenticity of the spiritual "gifts" that were beginning to border on the absurd. A sister brazenly informed elder Frederick Evans of her revelation from Ann Lee that the society should discontinue celibacy! An atmosphere of cynicism bordering on anarchy developed among many of the younger members and several of the important official instruments. The relations between the sexes became troublesome for the church elders. The Shakers were only human, and occasionally a love affair or sparking occurred within the community. These taboo relationships often began during union meetings or while brethren and sisters worked in close proximity. In 1837 a Believer from the Harvard community testified, "The worst snare that Satan has to decoy souls from the way of God is to lead them into carnal fleshly affections. These affections are often created by sympathizing with each other in times of sickness and weakness. . . . When you are obliged to be together at such times you ought to be as careful as you would be if you was at work among powder with fire."[35]

During this period, the intensity and fervor of the revival known as Mother Ann's Work began to dissipate even though the communal rules and regulations that were part of the gifts of spirit manifestations (felt by many younger members to be petty) were continued. The strict Millennial Laws of 1845 were severe, even for Believers who were accustomed to a rigid coexistence among the sexes. One of the new rules was designed to limit further the familiarity between males and females that was becoming a formidable problem for the church elders. One regulation declared, "Sisters must not mend, nor set buttons on brethren's clothes while they have them on."[36]

In the mid-1840s the New Lebanon society began losing members, instruments from the church family among them. In 1846 the rate of apostasy was nearly 15 percent in the Church Family, the most devout Shakers in the New Lebanon community. "In the summer of 1846 a spirit of dissatisfaction and discontent overspread the minds of many of the young folks in the society," Bennett recalled, "and the faith in the Shaker religion had lessened."[37]

On September 12, 1846—thirteen years to the day of his arrival at New Lebanon—Bennett and three other Shakers, including his sister, eloped. It was the most shocking apostasy in the history of the Shakers. The backsliders were John Allen, DeRobigne Bennett, Letsey Ann Bennett, and Mary Wicks. George Allen, John's brother, would join them a few days later. The society's dismay was expressed in the Shaker journals of the day:

An astonishing & awful event this day occurs, by the sudden & unsuspected absconding of four our number, viz—John Allen, Derobigne M. Bennett, Mary Wicks & Letsey Ann Bennett!!!!— They had very privately concerted the plan, agree with a man at the pool to come with a carriage & take them, which he did, coming up the round by the gristmill, as far as the house below the burying ground. The 4 walked off not far distant from each other pretending to be going on some common business, no one suspected them, tho they were seen, excepting in one or two cases, when too late. They all went to the pool where some of our Deacons afterward went to settle with them.[38]

Peter L. Edward F. Samantha F & Hannah Ann T. went up to the Pool, with the baggage of said deserters, & settle fully with them. Some of them felt very uncomfortable.[39]

George Allen having made up his mind to follow the late deserters to destruction was taken to the Rail R by Peter Long.[40]

The story concerning John and George Allen, Derobigne & Letsey Ann Bennett & Mary Wicks is true. They have fallen! And they fell as did the Angels, by rebellion against the order of God! And tho they went voluntarily and without the knowledge of the Elders, yet they went as tho they were driven out by a whirlwind! John was their leader & drove on the rebellion and apostasy.[41]

That their hell has already begun, for they reflect on themselves for the sad condition in which they have plunged themselves, & they accuse John Allen of being the instigator of the whole plan. They shed a flood of tears when too late, John was more braced for a time, but he finally bust forth almost in torrents. Poor Mary Wicks could hardly find words to express how awful it felt to lose her state of innocency which she had been brought up in. She said if some one would dig a hole in the ground & bury her therin it would be a heaven to her!!![42]

It is unknown when DeRobigne Bennett and Mary Wicks began their relationship. Shaker leaders suspected that the apostates planned their departure during a union meeting. Elder Thomas Damon announced that the elopements were the first to be contracted at the New Lebanon Church Family. One month following their apostasy, Elder Damon declared, "[T]he time had come for particular union to be abolished, and a general union to be substituted in its place . . . it went into effect last sabbath."[43]

Catherine Allen (no relation to the Allen brothers), a reform-minded Shaker spokesperson, noted that following the Era of Manifestations, "a sudden reversion of thought and feeling encompassed [Bennett's] being, radically changing his view points in life." Like Bennett, Allen, a ministry-appointed scribe, declared, "He not only became infidel to the teachings of the Shaker Church but, I am told, one of the rankest atheists—hence excessively irreverent and I have heard *blasphemous*." And prior to leaving New Lebanon, she added, "[H]e courted & took with him a very nice young sister, Mary Wicks & married her."[44]

The Allen-Bennett apostasy was a traumatic event that had diverse and lasting effects on the participants and remaining members of the society. All five of them had been Shakers since childhood, and Bennett later recalled, "The parting from the home and friends of so many years was a severe trial. It seemed almost like 'pulling the heartstrings.'"[45]

Shaker historians wrote at length about the harmful impact caused by the Allen-Bennett apostasy. Some Shaker leaders were glad to see the rebellious deserters' banishment because of their deleterious influence over devoted Believers. Elder Rufus Bishop expressed the society's dismay and his suspicions about John Allen. He wrote,

> This feels awful beyond description, & has caused many tears & is such an occurrence as this family never experienced before since we began to gather in the year 1787.[46]

> [John Allen] had some beautiful gifts when he yielded obedience; but the most remarkable one seemed to be about himself. This was while the church were marching up the Holy Mount, and while assembled there on the Holy ground. He was then an Instrument, and spoke for the Savior. Both on the way, and while at the feast ground, he, with another Instrument (?) frequently went aside & knelt and wept bitterly; and asked if there could ever be any mercy for Judas? He said there was a Judas on the Holy Ground! And that he, from whom the word came, would yet betray the Son of God!! And many expressions to the same effect.[47]

Some of the remaining Believers at New Lebanon were less judgmental and wondered if the apostates were to be blamed. A poignant poem by Anna Dodgson, who grew up with Mary Wicks and Letsey Ann Bennett, expressed her sentiments about her departed friends *and* the fate of the society:

Ah fond recollection comes stealing upon me,
Unmindful the tears of affection do flow,
As my heart wanders back to my former companions
Who with me refused yet longer to go.
But ah! can it be that it will be eternal,
That this separation must always be made?
It will and it must, it can never be altered,
They've made their own choice and they cannot be saved . . .
O hear me my God for my soul is in anguish,
When but for a moment I take a review
Of the sorrow and grief and the sore tribulation
That we have been called in times past to go thro'.
Could this be the end of these days of affliction,
I'd willingly live to be threescore and ten,
But my spirit does murmur when all the predictions
Do firmly declare it is but just begun.[48]

Although the Shakers are recognized mainly for their beautifully designed and practical furniture, they were also known for their simplicity, humility, order, peace, and simple goodness. And while their strict rules of celibacy, strange modes of worship, and separatism eventually caused their demise, they certainly attracted men and women with integrity, personality, and virtue. In studying their lives and reading their words, it is difficult to believe that such intelligent individuals were only "deluded fanatics." During an age of seeking, a Shaker historian wrote, "Shakerism was a clear answer to the question: What shall I do to be saved? It offered a discipline and a means of service. And in the end it bore fruit of abundance. . . . And as the world slowly absorbs another dissident faith, much remains to record the seeking, and in some measure the finding, of truth, and beauty, and light."[49]

NOTES

"to spiritual influences.": Catherine Allen (attachment) to the back cover of Bennett and Youngs, "Journal of Inspired Meetings," WRHS 77 VIII: B-138. (Three pages by Shaker Catherine Allen examining Bennett's activities and character prior to and after leaving the Shakers.)

1. WSIT. "change to blood": TS Nov. 18, 1882.

2. Alan Taylor, *William Cooper's Town: Power & Persuasion on the Frontier of the Early American Republic*, Knopf 1995.

3. WSIT. DAB.

4. Ibid.

5. Ibid.

6. Ibid.

7. Ibid.

8. Ibid.

9. Ibid.
   The *Watch Tower* (A Cooperstown newspaper).

10. Ibid.

11. EB.

12. E. D. Andrews, *The People Called Shakers: A Search for the Perfect Society*. Dover Publications, Inc. N.Y. 1963

13. Ibid.

14. TS Nov. 18, 1882.

15. "of the Shakers": James Fenimore Cooper, Quoted by Andrews, pp. 126–27. "deluded fanatics": Cooper, *Notions of the Americans Picked up by a Traveling Bachelor*, 1828 2 328–31 917.35, vols. 1 and 2. "any other respect.": Charles Dickens, "American Notes for General Circulations." 1822 217–220 storage 917.3. "virtues.": EB. "on every side.": WSIT.

16. "at the time.": WSIT. "out with Believers.": "A Brief Journal kept by R[ichard] Bushnell [North Family, New Lebanon, N.Y., 1829–1857]." Shaker Museum, Old Chatham, N.Y. 12136 #10,346. "children of men.": WSIT.

17. April 13, 1834 Betsey's arrival. Stein.

18. Whitney R. Cross, *The Burned-Over District*. Chapter 1, "The Great Revival." Wicks arrival and Mary's training: Daniel W. Paterson, *Gift Drawing and Gift Song, A Study of Two Forms of Shaker Inspiration*, The United Society of Shakers, Sabbathday Lake, Maine 1983.

The Mormons (Latter-day Saints) were founded in 1830 at Manchester, New York, a vicinity in the burned-over district. The *Book of Mormon*, or *Golden Bible* was claimed by Joseph Smith to have been written on golden plates by an angel called "Moroni." EB.

19. Charles Nordhoff, *Communist Societies of the United States: From Personal Visits and Observations*. Hillary House N.Y. 1960.

20. "sparking": Nordhoff, p. 179.

"colloquy and union": Hervey Elkins, *Fifteen Years in the Senior Order of Shakers*, 1853. Quoted by Flo Morse in *The Shakers and the World's People*. University of New England Press 1987.

21. "average intellectual ability.": Catherine Allen. Seeds: Andrews.

22. "herbalist," and "physician": "A List of the names of all who resided in the Church on the first day of January 1845. With their age, a hint of their Occupation." See N-13500 and Domestic Journal of Daily Occurrences, Isaac Youngs Roll A-FM 76 New York Shaker Museum.

A notation in the Shaker journal that records their age and "hint" of their occupation reflects the Society's meticulous attention to detail: "All were measured with shoes on. [Bennett was five foot and seven eighths of an inch.] Brethren's shoes raise them one half or three quarters of an inch & sisters about one and one quarter." See Shaker manuscripts for additional accounts of Bennett's activities and day trips.

Bennett "signed" December 30, 1839, "Covenant or Constitution of the Church of the United Society in the Town of New Lebanon. Come and let us join ourselves to the Lord in a perpetual Covenant that shall not be forgotten.—Jeremiah." New York Public Library MS #50. "usually very good.": WSIT p. 1040.

23. EB.

Shaker "instruments" prophesied the modern spiritualism movement that began in Hydesville, New York, in 1848. Some believe the Shakers were the precursors of the modern spiritualism movement in America. Andrews, p. 175.

The Shakers were intrigued with modern spiritualism. Shaker Elder Giles B. Avery wrote: "What the extent or end of these things will be, time must determine, but they are surely very interesting and useful to the spiritually minded." Salley M. Promey, *Spiritual Spectacles: Vision and Image in Mid-Nineteenth Century Shakerism*, pp. 115–16. Indiana University Press, 1993.

In 1878 George Albert Lomas, the editor of the *Shaker Manifesto*, reported that Mount Lebanon might "become a Mecca for those who are now materialistic unbelievers in truths of spirit returns and physical embodiments." Lomas asserted that since "scores of Shaker spirits" had materialized under "Shaker supervision" at Mount Lebanon, the visitations could not be attributed to fraud.

Stein, p. 321.

24. "the eighteen societies.": Stephen Stein, *The Shaker Experience in America*. p. 53 F. W. *Evans Autobiography of a Shaker and Revelation of the Apocalypse*, N.Y.: American News Company 1869.

25. Stein.

26. Ibid.

27. Ibid.

28. Bennett's "Introductory Remarks": Jan. 1, 1840.

29. "others to see it." May 21, 1842, Domestic Journal of Daily Occurrences, Isaac Youngs Roll A-FM 76, New York Shaker Museum.

30. Promey, p. 137. Daniel W. Patterson, *Gift Drawings and Gift Songs, A Study of Two Forms of Shaker Inspiration*, The United Society of Shakers, Sabbathday Lake, Maine, 1983.

31. Philemon Stewart (*Sacred Roll and Book*, p. 373), Quoted by Promey.

Philemon Stewart received a series of revelations in the spring of 1842 that were subsequently published by the Shakers in 1843 as *A Holy, Sacred and Divine Roll and Book*. According to Stewart, an angel directed him to the Holy Fountain at New Lebanon, where for fourteen days he transcribed "the sentences of [the] Eternal God and Creator." The source of the spirit communications was the deceased founder Ann Lee. The book admonished Believers to remain humble and threatened them with the wrath of God if they disobeyed divine commands. The *Sacred and Divine Roll and Book* was regarded by the Shakers as equal to the Bible and was sent to prominent political and religious leaders in America and around the world. The two-volume book of over four hundred pages was read in its entirety at several Shaker communities by Stewart and Giles Avery. The process in which Stewart received the *Sacred and Divine Roll and Book*, together with his assertions regarding its importance, elicited comparison with another new "bible" that was also "received" in New York state and published over a decade earlier, the *Book of Mormon*. And, like the *Book of Mormon*, the *Sacred and Divine Roll and Book* was criticized, derided and denounced by outsiders to such a degree that the Shakers withdrew it from public circulation prior to the end of the decade. Stein.

32. "going upon the mount.": "A Statement of The First Meeting held on the Holy Mount when The Whole Church assembled there. May 1, 1842. Collected and Transcribed by DeRobigne M. Bennett." Acc. # 12323 Shaker Museum, Old Chatham, N.Y. 12136. "perform religious devotion.": Domestic Journal of Occurrences, Isaac Youngs Roll A-FM 76 New York Shaker Museum.

33. Ibid.

34. Domestic Journal of Daily Occurrences, Isaac Youngs, Roll A-FM 76.

35. "powder with fire.": Brother Abijah Worster of Harvard Testified in 1837, Bathrick comp. Testimonies, pp. 347–49.

36. "have them on.": Lawrence Foster, *Religion and Sexuality: Three American Communal Experiments of the Nineteenth Century.*

37. Apostasy rate: Patricia J. Brewer. *Shaker Communities, Shaker Lives.* University Press of New England, Hanover and London 1986. "religion had lessened.": WSIT.

38. Domestic Journal of Daily Occurrences Isaac Youngs, roll A-FM 76.

39. Ibid.

40. "by Peter Long.": V:B-61 (Jerry Grant)

41. "rebellion and apostasy.": "Copies of the principal Letters of the Ministry at New Lebanon to other Societies of Believers East and West; Written by Rufus Bishop, Began July 16, 1833." Western Reserve Historical Society IV:B-Q Journal of Passing Events, Sept. 12, 1846.

42. "heaven to her!!!": New York Public Library, 58-M-140, vol. 2, entry for Sept. 12, 1846, Quoted by Patterson in *Gift Drawings* "Bishop, Daily Journal of Passing Events, September 12, 1846."

43. "effect last sabbath.": Green, "Biographic Memoir," pp. 38, 1846.

44. "and married her.": Bennett and Youngs "Journal of Inspired Meetings," WRHS 77 VIII: B-138, Catherine Allen.

45. WSIT p. 1040.

46. "the year 1787.": Rufus Bishop, Quoted by Stein p. 184.

47. "the same effect.": Rufus Bishop, Domestic Journal of Daily Occurrences, Isaac Youngs Roll A-FM 76.

48. "but just begun.": Ann Dodgson poem "Dye House Journal": Quoted by Brewer in *Shaker Communities, Shaker Lives.*

49. Andrews, pp. 239–40.

2

SEEDS OF DOUBT

Who never doubted never half believed.
Where doubt there truth is—'tis her shadow.

—Philip James Bailey

After a brief stay with relatives in Cooperstown, New York, the two young couples—"clad as they were in the plain Shaker garb," Bennett later recalled—were married. The double ceremony, performed by a Methodist minister, took place at a cousin's home on the evening of October 19, 1846. The local newspaper, the *Freeman's Journal*, announced, "MARRIED—Mr. DeRobine [*sic*] M. Bennett and Miss Mary Wicks. Also, on the same occasion, Mr. Geo. W. Allen to Miss Letsey Ann Bennett; all late of the society of Shakers at New Lebanon."[1]

The truant members of the United Society of Believers in Christ's Second Appearing were now in the *world*. And there was no turning back. Having spent most of their lives free from

49

making important decisions, suddenly the five young rebels needed to decide where to go and what to do to survive. The former Shakers, who went into the world in September 1846 in search of a new life, were not alone. In the 1840s the country was in transition and many Americans were on the move. It was a period in the nation's history that one historian christened as "one of restless ferment." Nearly every American seemed to be on an endless search for paradise in a country full of promise—but hardly Eden.[2]

Manifest Destiny

The concept of progress inherent in the nation's character was, in 1846, being superseded by the aggressive philosophy of Manifest Destiny. The term was coined the previous year when John O'Sullivan, a political leader and magazine editor, wrote of "our manifest destiny to overspread the continent allotted by Providence for the free development of our yearly multiplying millions." The phrase caught on with the entire country and within a year politicians were espousing "the right of our Manifest Destiny to spread over the whole continent."[3]

The term *Manifest Destiny* might have been new in the 1840s, but the genesis of the arrogant Christian attitude of spiritual superiority had been around for centuries. In 1819 Reverend Heman Humphrey of the Congregational Church in Pittsfield, Massachusetts, articulated the Christian imperialist doctrine during a missionary ordination sermon. The pastor proclaimed, "As the land of Canaan belonged to Israel, in virtue of a divine grant, so does the world belong to the church; and as God's chosen people still had much to do, before they could come into full and quiet possession of the land, so has the church a great work to accomplish, in subduing the world 'to the obedience of Christ.'"[4]

Manifest Destiny has traditionally been presented as an economic and political (i.e., secular) proposition; the legend of struggling pioneers who heroically fought the enemies of progress to introduce civilization to savages in the wilderness. But the popular doctrine was founded on the European theory of the right of discovery that, one historian declared, "derived from the ancient claim that Christians were everywhere entitled to dispossess non-Christians of their land." This assumption reflected *vacuum domicilium*: a tradition that claimed any land not occupied or settled was obtainable to any "civilized" or Christian person. Naturally, the Christian was granted the right to determine whether or not the land was occupied or settled. Manifest Destiny was in truth a *religious* concept. It asserted that Christians (sanctioned by God) had a divine mandate and legitimate right to the land. Manifest Destiny provided incentive and justification for the nation's westward expansion, the massacre of Native Americans, and war with Mexico.[5]

During this era of "boundless optimism" there seemed to be opportunities in almost every direction. For dissatisfied easterners there was the lure of the expanding West and its silver, gold, and limitless natural resources. The nation's struggling farmers, tired of hard times and constant toil, could relocate to the growing cities that offered factory jobs and excitement. Americans who desired to live, work, and worship in a more structured society could seek sanctuary in one of the many utopian communities flourishing in the country; an option chosen by some individuals who believed all was not well in America.[6]

The "right" of Manifest Destiny, however, was not for all Americans. It was not for the continent's native citizens who would have to become God-fearing or be eliminated because they were in the way of progress. It was not an option for the country's slaves who were a long way from becoming Americans with *any* rights. In the final analysis, Manifest Destiny was a racist as well as religious doctrine. Many of these Americans who believed they were chosen people, were humble, generous, compassionate individuals. Nevertheless, the preferred-by-God principle also bred contempt, conceit, piousness, and bigotry—all the ingredients of institutional racism.[7]

In the mid-1840s the nation's inequities were coming into

focus and giving impetus to reform movements covering education, women's rights, and slavery; issues that would divide the "great experiment," cause doubts in its institutions, and create a loss of innocence as well as a million human lives. And although the Civil War was not to be fought for another fifteen years, the slavery issue was a growing concern. The mounting tension between the North and South served to further expose the problem and stir political discourse. In 1835 Alexis de Tocqueville, a French aristocrat, noted prophetically: "The most dreadful of all the evils that threaten the future of the United States arises from the presence of the blacks on its soil. When one seeks the cause of present troubles and future dangers to the Union, from whatever point one departs one almost always arrives at this first fact."[8]

IN THE WORLD

The former Believers decided to face the world together. John Allen, who according to some Shaker accounts was responsible for the apostasy, instigated their next move. Allen met a man who claimed to have a thriving nursery business in Brandenburg, Kentucky. The man offered jobs to the Allen brothers and Bennett, assuring them he had "the facilities for rendering all comfortable and prosperous." It sounded like a lucrative idea. They accepted the offer and set out for Kentucky a few days after the wedding. The long and arduous journey began by canal from New Lebanon to Buffalo, where they boarded a boat for Toledo, Ohio. At Toledo, they took the Miami canal to Cincinnati, and boarded a steamboat on the Ohio River for their final destination: Brandenburg, forty miles south of Louisville.[9]

Brandenburg was an active port where large quantities of agricultural products, including corn, hay, and tobacco, were shipped. The small town on the Ohio River was in a prosperous fruit-growing region known for producing the world's finest apple brandy. Brandenburg survived the great flood of 1832 when for many days homes on Main Street were tied to flatboats. In November the former Shakers arrived in Brandenburg while the Kentucky port town was engulfed in another kind of storm. A local murder trial was about to begin that would gain national importance and subsequently generate interest in the antislavery movement sweeping the country.[10]

On November 3, 1846, a jury was impaneled for possibly the most ignoble and infamous trial ever to be heard in Meade County, Kentucky. Lucy, a slave girl, was accused of murdering her master. Two years later, Lucy was found guilty and sentenced "to be hung on a gallows erected on a public road leading from the town of Brandenburg." Several thousand people attended her execution. Slave owners brought their slaves to witness the penalty for killing masters. Lucy was dressed for the gallows and seated on her own coffin when she arrived by ox cart at the oak hanging tree. She was carrying her baby that was born in jail— fathered by her dead master. Lucy's hanging and the death of another slave woman in nearby Irvington fueled the abolitionist movement throughout the nation. It would take decades, however, before this part of the country abolished slavery. In the 1860 election Abraham Lincoln received only four votes from all of Meade County.[11]

The naive Yankees soon learned that coming to Brandenburg was the wrong move. Within a few days of their arrival, the Allen-Bennett party realized the region had little to offer them. "It was in the days of slavery, and all new arrivals from the east were looked upon as Abolitionists and natural enemies," Bennett wrote. "[And we] found the world here presented wholly different from [our] quiet Shaker home, and it is not strange that a home-sick feeling settled over the party." The promises made by the man who persuaded them to come to Brandenburg were groundless. Brandenburg turned out to be "a most uninviting locality," Bennett recollected. With winter approaching and their nest egg vanishing, Bennett and his brother-in-law went to Louisville looking for work. With his Shaker medical experience he was able to obtain a clerk position in a drugstore. Bennett and his bride moved to Louisville to "commence housekeeping in a single room upon the most frugal and economical plan, and save every cent they could."[12]

After working in the drugstore for one year, Bennett made a commercial tour selling drugs throughout the Kentucky and Tennessee regions. With his savings and a two-hundred-dollar inheritance left to Mary from a deceased brother, they were able to purchase a stock of drugs and open their own drugstore. His shop on Preston Street in Louisville was "conducted eight years, meeting with fair success." The bottles used for medicines were blown from green glass and lettered by a private mold that advertised: *D. M. Bennet—Druggist and Chemist—Louisville, Ky.*[13]

While living in Louisville, Bennett made a few unwise business investments in property and buildings. It was during this period in Kentucky that the Bennetts suffered their most grievous misfortune. They lost their only child, a daughter who died at birth. It was also around this time when the two former Shakers, who had lived in the inhospitable world for five years, made their first of many sentimental pilgrimages back to New Lebanon. "There are many persons still living there whom we remember with fondness, and whom we like to see as often as we can make it convenient to visit the old grounds," Bennett wrote. Their visit was recorded by a Shaker journalist, who wrote that Bennett "and his wife Mary came to the office & wished to stay over night; they are from Louisville, Kentucky." The couple would subsequently return every five years or so to the home of their "youth."[14]

THE AGE OF REASON

In 1848, two years after leaving the Shakers, Bennett read his first infidel publication. The material jarred his confidence in the truth of the Bible and Christianity, his religion since childhood. Since only a few infidel or freethought publications existed in America, he likely read either the *Boston Investigator* published since 1831, or the *Beacon*, a New York monthly published by

Gilbert Vale, a British navigation teacher. Gilbert Vale (1788–1866) was possibly America's most devoted Thomas Paine enthusiast. He authored the book *The Life of Paine* and erected a monument in 1839 at Paine's historical farm site in New Rochelle, New York. Vale's "motto of liberalism" read: "He who will not reason is a bigot; he that cannot is a fool; and he who dares not is a slave." Sometime in 1850, Bennett traveled to New York and bought approximately twenty volumes of freethought literature from Vale. Among his purchase was Thomas Paine's *The Age of Reason* that Bennett found "unanswerable." Paine's cogent argument transformed Bennett from being a devoted Christian (who prayed twice daily and at meals) into becoming a freethinker or infidel, as unbelievers were known at that time.[15]

Thomas Paine (1737–1809) was the most radical writer and revolutionary figure of the eighteenth and early nineteenth centuries. A colleague of Benjamin Franklin and Thomas Jefferson, Paine was an enlightened thinker on the level of Goethe and Voltaire. His pamphlet *Common Sense*, published in 1776, sparked the American Revolution. Although Thomas Paine gave the United States its name, by the mid-nineteenth century, his momentous role in America's independence became obscured by his provocative *Age of Reason*, published in 1794. The *Age of Reason* was an iconoclastic and eloquent attack on the Bible and organized religion. Religious leaders and their followers (who probably never read it) found *The Age of Reason* so shocking that it blinded them to the revolutionary hero's extraordinary patriotic accomplishments. Paine's radical assertion that the Bible was filled with lies and was not the word of God elicited the brand of infidel and atheist.[16]

Although Thomas Paine was routinely condemned and vilified from pulpits around the country, he was very much a deist. "It was not true, as many in the nineteenth century charged and as some unenlightened people still affirm, that Paine was an atheist," a freethought historian asserts. "Almost the opening words of *The Age of Reason* are: 'I believe in one God, and no more; and I hope for happiness beyond this life.'"[17]

A Thomas Paine biographer contends that the author-hero's religiosity was pantheistic rather than solely deistic: "[H]e believed in a universal, ubiquitous God, who infused the world with his power and spirit, but human beings were sufficiently independent of him to make the world better or worse in their lifetime."[18]

The more rigorously clergymen and politicians assailed Thomas Paine, the larger his legend and legacy grew among free-thinking Americans. By the mid-nineteenth century the revolutionary author-hero was the central and luminous figure in the flourishing freethought movement. Freethinkers virtually venerated the author of *The Age of Reason*, and the book became their favorite reading.[19]

Bennett's gradual conversion to freethought was similar to those of other inquiring Americans of the time. This period witnessed several seminal developments that reflected the doubts of questioning individuals who once possessed the nation's long-held religious beliefs. While Bennett continued to operate his drugstore and read the rationalistic works of Thomas Paine and the French author-philosopher Voltaire, events were taking place around the nation that were disrupting and threatening orthodox religion as never before in American history.[20]

In 1848 the first women's rights assembly was held in Seneca Falls, New York. The Seneca Falls Convention's two main organizers, Lucretia Mott and Elizabeth Cady Stanton, were both freethinkers who publicly criticized the Bible. Mott, Stanton, and other leading suffragists believed Christianity was the root cause for their disenfranchisement and the Bible and the church were in the way of women's emancipation. In her address, Stanton assailed the clergy and chastised devout Christian women, a theme she would continue for decades. She reprimanded the Christian women who worked all day in the "Education Society" in order to pay to train a "strong, lazy man" for the ministry; a man who would later denounce the same women from the pulpit. Stanton's "immaculate priesthood" remarks, as well as the event itself, drew the wrath of clergymen from all over the country.[21]

Another development that fractured orthodox religion was the birth of the spiritualistic movement. It began in 1848 in Rochester, New York, when two sisters, Margaret and Kate Fox, reported hearing mysterious rappings in their home. Within months, half a dozen spiritualist publications were in print helping launch what became a pseudoscientific national craze. Communicating with spirits acted as a surrogate religion for many Americans fearful of the vast changes in American life. Spiritualists had no need for dogma or ministers in their communications with the unseen and the deceased. It eliminated the middleman, the clergy.[22]

Andrew Jackson Davis was the leading proponent of spiritualism in America. Referred to as the Poughkeepsie Seer, Davis was born the son of an illiterate, alcoholic shoemaker and a clairvoyant mother in Blooming Grove, New York. Because his poverty-stricken family moved so frequently, the young Davis attended school for only five months and claimed to have read only a single book in his life. In 1843 Davis, who was influenced by Swedenborg and the Shakers, developed his own clairvoyant powers and allegedly cured disease using his supernatural gift.[23]

Andrew Jackson Davis presented lectures around Manhattan while in states of trance and in 1847 published them as *The Principles of Nature, Her Divine Revelations, and a Voice to Mankind.* His popular harmonial philosophy asserted that certain people are drawn to one another because of spiritual auras, making them natural mates. His theories were especially popular with women who were beginning to assert their individualism. Most of the *mediums* involved in the spiritualism movement were this same type of woman; those who were finally gaining a sense of freedom and adventure and the courage to speak up and take action. Some claimed that the spirits' mission was to further women's rights. Thus, during this time, a link was established between feminism, spiritualism, and other social reforms.[24]

One of the most controversial and extraordinary events of this period was the Hartford Bible Convention of 1854. The meeting was attended by a diverse group of outspoken and preeminent abolitionists, suffragists, atheists, agnostics, and spiritualists. The convention was open to "all who are friendly to free discussion . . . for the purpose of freely and fully canvassing the origin, authority and influence of the Jewish and Christian Scriptures." The four-day meeting was called to order by Andrew Jackson Davis who stated, "Resolved, that each mind, by virtue of its endowments, rights, and liberties, should 'prove all things and hold fast to that which is good.'"[25]

The Poughkeepsie Seer's genteel opening remarks were followed by some of the most inflammatory rhetoric ever heard by the American public. One of the speeches that created a huge sensation throughout the orthodox New England area was made by firebrand atheist Ernestine L. Rose who boldly declared, "My sisters, the Bible has enslaved you; the churches have been built on your subjugated necks. Do you wish to be free? Then you must trample the Bible, the church, and the priests under your feet." Her accusations caused pandemonium among the theological students who were whistling, hissing, and stamping their feet in the gallery. Even the dimming of the gaslights and the tumultuous cries of "Go on, go on," could not stifle the petite woman's radical lecture that she finished amid deafening applause. Her daring assertion of religion's impediment to women's rights was a recurring theme among suffragists.[26]

Ernestine Rose's sentiment was repeated by William Lloyd Garrison, America's leading abolitionist and founder of the *Liberator*, the Boston antislavery weekly. Garrison's speech was of the same tenor as Rose's, as were the words of Parker Pillsbury, the most forceful speaker at Hartford that June. Pillsbury was an abolitionist, publisher, editor, labor reformer, and women's rights activist. Ralph Waldo Emerson proclaimed Pillsbury "The strongest man, intellectually, of the earlier Abolitionists."[27]

While describing his religious training, Pillsbury, a former seminarian, recited extracts from "The Day of Doom," a popular and enormously influential pre-Revolutionary war poem. The poem was written by Michael Wigglesworth, a Puritan clergyman who raised an entire family of ministers and theologians. His poem was a realistic and frightful expression of the preponderant Calvinistic theology as well as the most church-endorsed rhyme ever written. The country's schoolchildren were required to read and memorize the theological poem in the colonial period. The excitement, horrors, and terror of the verse were still remembered by Americans living in the mid-1850s. The poem's full title was "The Day of Doom; or, A Poetical Description of the Great and Last Judgment." The poem echoed the Puritan belief that children who died at birth were sent to hell. Freethinkers found this Christian judgment from God expressed in "The Day of Doom" to be horrid doggerel. Pillsbury's passionate recitation elicited "immense sensation" when he read the punishment for children:

> Yet to compare your sin with theirs
> Who lived a longer time,
> I do confess yours is much less,
> Though every sin's a crime.
> A crime it is, therefore, in bliss
> You cannot hope to dwell;
> But unto you I shall allow
> The easiest rooms in hell.[28]

In their opposition to slavery, freethinkers who attended the Hartford Bible Convention, or only read about it, were uniting in their distrust and dislike for the religious institutions in America. Parker Pillsbury's incisive speech included the resolution:

> Resolved, That if men are to prove all things and only hold fast to that which is good, then any Bible or religion, church or ministry, that defends or apologizes for slavery, war, oppressive government, or any form of despotism or tyranny, secular or spiritual, governmental or individual, is to be specially examined and discussed, and approved or condemned according as those sins or systems which they defend shall be found at variance with the nature of man and destructive of the happiness of the universe.[29]

DR. BENNETT'S FAMILY MEDICINES

In 1855 Bennett sold his drugstore in Louisville and moved to Rochester, New York, where his sister, Letsey Ann, and her husband had settled. After engaging in the business of selling trees and shrubbery with his brother-in-law and losing $4,000 when a shipment froze solid, Bennett became a traveling salesman for a large Rochester seed firm. He traveled around the country as far away as Wisconsin, Iowa, and Illinois.[30]

In 1859 the Bennetts bought a drugstore in Cincinnati, Ohio, where they lived for the next nine years. The Cincinnati years were a prosperous and intellectually stimulating period in Bennett's life. He resumed his patent medicine production and with his practical knowledge of medicinal herbs began a large-scale preparation and distribution of his "family medicines." With only a single wagon, Bennett distributed his products among farmers and others throughout the country. By the time the Civil War erupted in 1861, he had fifteen wagons in operation. According to Bennett, his medicines were very profitable and they "became well known in thousands of families and gave uniform satisfaction." Some years he made a profit of $10,000. Besides carrying a general line of drugs, Bennett marketed several of his own concoctions:

- Dr. Bennett's Bronchial Tablets
- Dr. Bennett's Golden Liniment "For Man and Beast"
- Dr. Bennett's Magnetic Quick Cure—"The Greatest Family Medicine Ever Offered to the Public"
- Dr. Bennett's Sure Death to Rats, Mice, Roaches and Vermin
- Dr. Bennett's Root and Plant Pills
- Dr. Bennett's Worm Lozenges[31]

Bennett's family medicines were sold in a relatively primitive period in pharmaceutical research and according to historian James Harvey Young, "[M]edical science and ethics were on unsure foundations and the line was hard to draw between the legitimate and the quack." Young asserts that many Civil War–period nostrum promoters were not unscrupulous rogues but honest and kindly men "though their handiwork might be hazardous to their customers." Possibly Bennett's most effective product was his Sure Death to Rats, Mice, Roaches and Vermin, which was still being sold in 1874. Young calls the era's patent medicine makers "gullible entrepreneurs" and recalls Dr. Oliver Wendell Holmes who said "it was difficult to tell a mushroom from a toadstool."[32]

From 1860 through 1868 the Bennetts lived at various locations in Cincinnati, and his occupations included druggist, apothecary, sealing-wax manufacturer, and finally, physician. It is unknown whether he was still practicing the Eclectic system that he had learned at the New Lebanon Shaker community. The name *Eclectics* was given to a classification of medical practitioners by a prominent botanist. The Eclectics were a significant part of American medicine in the nineteenth century and established medical schools. Their school of medicine attained substantial professional respectability and was described as "those who select and adopt in practice whatever is beneficial, and who change their prescriptions according to emergencies and acquired knowledge."[33]

Bennett was influenced by one of his closest friends, Charles Winterburn. A former Methodist clergyman from England, Dr. Winterburn lived in Cincinnati and practiced homeopathic medicine. Although it was a popular medical movement, homeopathic doctors were considered by "regular" physicians to be charlatans. Homeopathy relied on the healing power of nature that appealed to the public. It was fervently advocated by Louisa May Alcott, Daniel Webster, Harriet Beecher Stowe, Nathaniel Hawthorne, Henry James, Henry Wadsworth Longfellow, and other members of America's intelligentsia.[34]

RADICAL AND SCIENTIFIC DISCOURSE

Remembering his years in Cincinnati, Bennett wrote, "Dr. Winter-burn very often visited my place of business, where we passed scores of hours . . . in the aggregate . . . in radical and scientific discourse." Together they attended the radical lectures of Mon-cure Conway, the clergyman and author. Conway was also an out-spoken abolitionist who was influenced by Ralph Waldo Emerson. After listening to the Transcendentalist speak, the two often "compared notes, exchanged views and mutually enlight-ened each other."[35]

Moncure Conway authored several books, contributed to the *Atlantic Monthly,* and edited his own liberal periodical, the *Dial,* a magazine dedicated to literature, philosophy, and religion. Conway not only advocated antislavery, but was also an impas-sioned defender of Cincinnati's Jewish population toward which there was a growing prejudice. Since childhood, Conway was aware of the vehement sentiments the clergy expressed about Thomas Paine and stated, "I could not help being interested in a writer whom Jehovah was said to have chosen for the object of his special wrath." Conway saw parallels between the prejudice against Jews and the vilification of Thomas Paine. In his "unprej-udiced investigation" into Paine's reason, Conway attended meetings held by Cincinnati's small group of infidels.[36]

"In listening to the freethinkers in their humble hall I became aware of the large mythology grown and growing around Thomas Paine," Conway wrote. "Through their exposure of the traditional calumnies of Paine I discovered that in his legend there were traces of the old folktales of the wandering Jew and of Faust. These clerical fictions also reminded me that towers may be measured by the shadows they cast." Upon further investigation, Conway discovered the important role Paine played in the Amer-ican Revolution and the country's independence.[37]

Conway decided to devote a sermon to his research on Thomas Paine, but feared that his sermon "might incite some opposition in [his] congregation." Before moving to Cincinnati he caused division among the members of his Unitarian church in Washington, DC, because of his radical antislavery discourses. Conway's sermon on Paine's birthday, January 29, 1860, was well received and his discourse was published with the title "Thomas Paine, A Celebration." Among freethinkers, Conway became a respected minister and speaker who subsequently wrote the definitive biography of Thomas Paine.[38]

In 1859 Charles Darwin published *On the Origin of Species*, an iconoclastic book that stunned the conventional Victorian society, shocked intellectuals, and infuriated religionists. Samuel Putnam, an author, publisher, and prominent freethinker, believed that Charles Darwin contributed more to human knowledge (in the history of the world) than any other man. "No one man has so changed the outlook of the human race, so changed its morality, its religion, its hope, its intellectual and practical motive, as Darwin." The Darwinian theory of evolution gave ammunition to freethinkers who now had scientific evidence to support their attack on the Bible's account of creation. In 1860 the *Boston Investigator* optimistically predicted that "[i]f the progress of infidelity for the next hundred years was as great as that of the preceding century, infidelity and not Christianity would in all probability be in the ascendancy."[39]

In the years preceding the Civil War, infidels met periodically and began to organize. In 1857 the Infidel Association of the United States held a convention in Philadelphia. These convention halls were often decorated with banners quoting the Treaty of Tripoli: "As the government of the United States of America is not in any sense founded on the Christian religion." Often the most prominent words displayed were Thomas Paine's principle of faith: "The world is my country, to do good my religion."[40]

Although there were about twenty-five local infidel chapters during this period, the association's existence was relatively brief. The organization annoyed the religious and secular press. American newspapers often erroneously associated freethought with free love. In the article "The Harmony of Infamy," the *New York Times* bitterly assailed the Infidel Association, writing,

Report says that a National Infidel Convention was held in Philadelphia; that it sat for a week presided over by Horace Seaver of Boston, and that its proceedings were very harmonious. We should like to know why it should not be? When a parcel of blatant noodles, whom God permits to live as the highest possible evidence that His mercy is mightier than His justice, have persuaded their foolish selves that there is no such thing as a devil and that he isn't trying to steal their shadow every time they walk out in the sunshine, what but the most delightful idiotic harmony could we expect? One thing, however, has always puzzled us, viz: when these Infidels and free loving people have legislated God out of existence, got rid of Satan and destroyed society, when theft, lust, and murder hold jolly saturnalia on earth, when everybody has run away with somebody's wife or cut somebody's throat, what are the rest going to do for amusement?[41]

While living in Cincinnati, Bennett became interested in politics. He was an ardent Republican in 1856 when the party nominated their first presidential candidate, John C. Frémont, an opponent of slavery. "We sometimes took active interest in political campaigns, and spent time and money to secure the election of our candidates," he later recalled. "This was particularly the case in the election of Lincoln. We believed the salvation of our country depended upon his election, and we worked for it as earnestly as we ever worked for our own daily bread."[42]

Soon after developing his line of family medicines, Bennett was forced to affix revenue stamps on his products indicating that tax had been paid. The stamps increased operating expenses so enormously that his business was dramatically curtailed. That same year he sold his entire business at a loss. His estate was now worth $30,000, a sum that in 1865 was, he lamented, "enough to render him independent for life had he put it in bonds or at interest."[43]

The middle-aged entrepreneur embarked on several business ventures that he confessed all "proved unfortunate." His investments included spring planting beds, chromolithography, and an ill-advised building endeavor in Cincinnati. Out-of-state investments recorded Sonora mining land, insurance stock, and oil-and-mineral lands in Tennessee. After all the investments failed, the Bennetts suffered a heavy loss totaling over $32,000. Sad and depressed, the couple entered a state of poverty. After two unsuccessful years he tried a new enterprise but failed again. In 1868 Bennett's last year in Cincinnati, he described his occupation as simply *physician*.[44]

In the next five years the couple moved nearly as many times. In 1868 when they left Cincinnati, Bennett made another unwise business decision and purchased a drug store in Kansas City. Within a few months he was forced to sell out taking a heavy loss. Later, when a boyhood friend persuaded him to join him in the brick-manufacturing business, the couple moved to Long Island. His friend turned out to be financially broke, forcing him to take on other partners. The New York partnership turned into yet another failure. Three miles east of Northport, Long Island, Bennett, the ever-industrious entrepreneur, constructed buildings, opened a brickyard, and even invented an apparatus for drying bricks outside of the mill. The invention required fifty tons of iron and, unfortunately, some construction defects caused another disaster. After losing $1,000 and six months' worth of labor, Bennett returned to Rochester and worked as a traveling salesman. He also tried his hand at selling proprietary medicines but was only moderately successful.[45]

SUNSHINE

In the post–Civil War period, some of the country's greatest minds were declaring their independence from conventional religion. Freethought gained popularity and respect when leading citizens (authors, doctors, lawyers, suffragists, reformers, scientists, and clergymen) began defining themselves as freethinkers. Following the signing of the Emancipation Proclamation by Abraham Lincoln in 1863, many of the dedicated men and women who worked for decades to end slavery joined the ranks of freethought. These admired abolitionists believed that slavery was not only "the greatest misery, the greatest wrong, the greatest curse to white and black alike that America has ever known," but asserted that it was also supported by the Christian church. Like Thomas Paine, William Lloyd Garrison attacked the Bible and its authority. America's leading antislavery agitator dubbed the unholy alliance between the church and slave owners the "sum of all villainies." And like Paine, Garrison was called infidel from the pulpit—or the "coward's castle" as he described it. Samuel P. Putnam, a Civil War veteran, depicted the church's role in slavery:

> It supported it, defended it, gave it the sanction of its own Bible, and persecuted and excommunicated those who were in favor of freedom. The attitude of the American church in regard to slavery has branded it with eternal shame. If freedom had been left to the tender mercies of the church it would have perished amid the clanking chains of millions. It was the Infidel who kindled the fires of opposition; who stirred the people and made them see the wrong; and it is true, beyond question, that Infidelity has been the salvation of American Liberty.[46]

Freethinkers were often called infidels, defined by Webster in the 1870s as "the prefix *in* means not; *fides*-faith; the two mean literally not faith—not faithful—not full of faith. The accepted definition is unbelief; unbelief in revelation and especially in the divine origin of Christianity." Freethought is all thought independent of religious dogma.[47]

Most freethinkers adopted the name of liberal, replacing infidel, which had become pejorative. The definition of liberal in the Reconstruction Period was "one who does not acknowledge the authority of the Bible or admit the supernatural character of the Christian system." Freethought was not limited to extreme left-wing atheism, but included widely diverse views as free religion and agnosticism. Thomas Huxley coined the term "agnostic" in 1869, but the attitude it described was common with freethinkers since the 1840s. Agnosticism flourished after Huxley and his fellow

English philosopher Herbert Spencer formalized it as a coherent and definite pattern of thought. By the 1870s Spencer and Huxley were known and admired by much of the American public.[48]

After the Civil War, several distinguished abolitionists who had educated the North about the evils of slavery gave their time and money for the dissemination of freethought. Arthur B. Bradford, Lucy N. Colman, Stephen Pearl Andrews, Amy Post, and Elizur Wright were among those freethought lecturers who promoted their emancipated views. Others like Parker Pillsbury became publishers who, together with Susan B. Anthony and Elizabeth Cady Stanton, published the *Revolution*. Freethinkers were proud of the fact that three of America's suffragist leaders, Susan B. Anthony, Matilda Joslyn Gage, and Elizabeth Cady Stanton, were agnostic or atheist.[49]

A few lesser-known freethinkers also decided to invest their time and money to promote freethought. After Bennett was offered a contract to operate a drugstore in Paris, Illinois, the couple moved again. They arrived in Paris in 1870, but remained in the drugstore for only about fifteen months before deciding to get back into the seed business. Bennett planted fifty acres for cultivation the first year and seventy-five the second year. The combination of extremely dry weather and an "unharmonious" partnership spelled disaster. Although his goal was met, he lost $2,000 on the endeavor. "We feel that they have cruelly wronged us to the extent of a few thousand dollars and two years' hard toil," Bennett wrote. These "supporters of orthodoxy," he concluded, were "staunch believers in the 'Holy Book' and have at least carried out one portion of it with us, we were a stranger and *'they took us in.'*"[50]

Another unfortunate incident occurred in the summer of 1872 that nearly killed the fifty-three-year-old farmer. Bennett was returning home on horseback after checking his seed crop about fifteen miles outside of town. After stopping to close a gate, he proceeded to remount his horse but the animal suddenly bolted. Because he only had time to put one foot in the stirrup, the spooked horse ran a lengthy distance dragging him alongside until his foot finally disengaged. Bennett lay unconscious for several hours until a group of hunters found him. With a concussion and broken rib, he was lifted onto the hunters' wagon and taken home to Paris.[51]

In the summer of 1873 another drought caused seventy-five acres of seeds to be unprofitable, and the question of praying for rain became a topic of discussion. The struggling seed farmer was drawn into a debate with two Paris clergymen over the efficacy of prayer that was carried in the local newspapers. In addition to the subject of prayer, several Bible points were discussed, including the divine leadership of Moses. When one of the papers refused to print Bennett's rejoinder because they felt it was too radical, he felt slighted.[52]

Bennett signed his articles "D. B. Mortimer" and "A Liberal Thinker," until one of the ministers questioned him about his real name. He responded: "My name? Why do you wish to know? What difference does it make to you whether my mother ever gave me a name, unless you wish to hurl your anathemas at me from the pulpit? In case you should wish to condescend to this, call me Sunshine."[53]

Although D. M. Bennett considered himself a freethinker since 1850, starting his own publication never occurred to him prior to his inability to get his views published in the local press. It was at this juncture that Bennett decided to start his own paper with the intent of giving equal voice to advocates of all sides. He listed fifty possible names and showed them to Mary, who selected—the *Truth Seeker*.[54]

NOTES

"tis her shadow.": Philip James Bailey (1816–1902) author.

1. WSIT. Reverend B. W. Gorham, M. E. Church.

2. Alice Felt Tyler, *Freedom's Ferment*, Harper & Brothers, N.Y., 1944.

3. *U.S. Magazine and Democratic Review*, vol. xvii, p. 5. "Manifest Destiny": Forrest G. Wood, *The Arrogance of Faith: Christianity and Race in America From the Colonial Era to the Twentieth Century*. Alfred A. Knopf, Inc., N.Y., 1990.

4. Ibid.

5. Ibid.

6. Tyler.

7. Wood.

8. Alexis de Tocqueville, *Democracy in America* (1835, 1840), Alfred A Knopf, Inc. 1994.

9. WSIT.

10. Early Brandenburg and Early Meade County, W. M. Boling, *The Meade County Messenger*, April 11, 18, 1946; June 28, July 5, 12, 1962. "comfortable and prosperous": WSIT.

11. Ibid.

12. Ibid. "cent they could.": WSIT.

13. Ibid.

14. child's death: TS Nov. 25, 1882. "the old grounds.": TS July 31, 1880. "from Louisville, Kentucky.": "Domestic Journal of Important Occurrences," WRHS 32 V:B-61. "youth.": TS July 31, 1880.

15. TS Dec. 16, 1882.

16. Fruchtman.

Regarding the Bible, Thomas Paine wrote: "Whenever we read the obscene stories, the voluptuous debaucheries, the cruel and torturous executions, the unrelenting vindictiveness, with which more than half the Bible is filled, it would be more consistent that we called it the word of a demon than the Word of God. It is a history of wickedness that has served to corrupt and brutalize mankind; and, for my part, I sincerely detest it as I detest everything that is cruel." Thomas Paine, *The Age of Reason*.

17. Warren, pp. 193–98.

"I believe in the equality of man;" Paine continues, "I believe that religious duties consist in doing justice, loving mercy, and endeavoring to make our fellow creatures happy. . . . I do not believe in the creed professed by the Jewish Church, by the Roman Church, by the Greek Church, by the Turkish Church, by the Protestant Church, nor by any church that I know of. My own mind is my own church. All national institutions of churches, whether Jewish, Christian or Turkish, appear to me no other than human inventions, set up to terrify and enslave mankind, and monopolize power and profit."

Thomas Paine, *The Age of Reason*, p. 50.

18. Fruchtman, p. 138.

19. Warren.

20. WSIT.

21. "Address Delivered at Seneca Falls Convention and Rochester.": Quoted in *Women Without Superstition: "No Gods—No Masters." The Collected Writings of Women Freethinkers of the Nineteenth & Twentieth Centuries.* Edited by Annie Laurie Gaylor. Freedom From Religion Foundation, Madison, Wisconsin, 1997.

22. Fox sisters: EB v. 25, pp. 705–708.

23. A. J. Davis: EB v. 7, pp. 865–66.

24. Ibid.

25. SP.

26. Ibid.

27. GM.

28. EB.

29. Ibid.

30. WSIT

31. WSIT.

32. James Harvey Young, *The Toadstool Millionaires: A Social History of Patent Medicines in America before Federal Regulation.* Princeton University Press, Princeton, N.J., 1961.

33. WSIT. "and acquired knowledge.": C. S. Rafinesque.

The Williams Cincinnati City Directory for 1860 included the listing—"Bennett D. M., druggist and apothecary, s.w.c. Chestnut and W. Row." The Hamilton County census records indicate Bennett's "value of personal estate" at $1,000. In 1863 and again in 1864, the city directory lists—"Bennett Derobigne M. Druggist and Apothecary, Proprietor of Bennett's Family Medicines, and Manufacturer of Sealing Wax, &c., s.w.c. Central Av. and Chestnut, h. 21 Chestnut." The Cincinnati city directory of 1868, Bennett's last year there, listed him as "physician."

34. Winterburn obituary: TS Jan. 29, 1881.

35. EB. "and scientific discourse.": TS May 1, 1880.

36. EB. "his special wrath": Moncure Conway, *The Wandering Jew.* 1881, (microfilm) University of California at San Diego.

37. Ibid.

38. Ibid and EB.

39. "any other man.": SP. "in the ascendancy.": Warren.

40. Ibid.

The Treaty of Tripoli was a legal document written in the late 1700s that revealed the sentiments of the founding fathers and secular character of the United States. The Treaty, signed by John Adams and officially ratified and proclaimed in Philadelphia, PA, on June 10, 1797. Article X1 reads as follows: "As the government of the United States of America is not in any sense founded on the Christian Religion,—as it has in itself no character of enmity against the laws, religion or tranquility of Mussulmen, [Moslems]—and as the said States never have entered into any war or act of hostility against any Mohammedan nation, it is declared by the parties that no pretext arising from religious opinions shall ever interrupt the harmony existing between the two countries.": Sherman D. Wakefield, *Progressive World*, Dec. 1955. Reprinted in *Freethought Today*, June/July 1997.

41. "do for amusement.": As quoted by Warren from the *Boston Investigator*, Nov. 2, 1859.

42. "own daily bread.": TS July 17, 1880. "or at interest.": WSIT.

John Charles Frémont (1813–1890), a heroic western explorer and major general, was supported by radical Republican antislavery congressmen during this political era.

43. TS Nov. 25, 1882.

The Revenue Act of 1862, enacted by the 37th Congress, imposed a one-cent tax on each proprietary retailing at 25 cents or less. He contacted authorities in Washington and had a private die engraved for his stamp that was first issued in 1865. A proof from this die was approved in the office of the Hon. Joseph J. Lewis, Commissioner of Internal Revenue, on February 10, 1865. This amount is equivalent to nearly a half-million dollars in today's market.

44. "proved unfortunate.": TS Nov. 25, 1882. The Cincinnati City Directory, 1868.

45. TS Nov 25, 1882.

46. SP.

47. Webster's "infidel" definition quoted in WSIT.

48. Warren.

49. Ibid.

50. TS Dec. 1873.

51. WSIT.

52. TS Nov. 25, 1882.

The *Gazette*, the *Beacon*, and the *Blade*. Reverend William Holt/Paris Christian Church. Reverend R. D. Van Deursen/Paris Presbyterian Church.

53. TS Sept. 1873.

54. TS Nov. 25, 1882.

3

The Truth Seeker

[Bennett's] journalism was of the sort called personal.
The Truth Seeker was Bennett, and in advertising himself he advertised the paper.

—George E. Macdonald

D uring the Civil War, Americans started to routinely read newspapers with enthusiasm in order to follow battle details, learn information about loved ones, and keep abreast of the ever-changing status of the wartime conflict. After the war, the country saw a proliferation of publications catering to a diverse group of readers with disparate interests involving local and national events. Nearly every Christian denomination in America had its own newspaper or journal, and the overwhelming majority of the nation's secular daily newspapers were also owned and edited by Christians. Although there was substantial freethought activity in the second half of the nineteenth century, the country's newspapers and periodicals rarely accepted articles or editorials written by infidels expressing their irreligious or blasphemous views. About the only way freethinkers could counteract the ubiquitous Christian doctrine constantly printed in the religion-dominated press was to publish their own periodicals.[1]

One of the earliest, most successful, and most courageous freethought publishers in America was Abner Kneeland, a former Universalist minister. Kneeland gained the expertise in publishing inexpensive, hardball polemical journalism during his twenty-five years as an editor and publisher of periodicals that advocated Universalism. After renouncing Christianity in 1831, Kneeland moved from New York City to Boston where he started publishing the *Boston Investigator* with a hope "to improve the condition of Man." He also pledged to "expose vice . . . oppose all monopolies . . . advocate a general system of education . . . the abolition of slavery, the abolishment of imprisonment for debt . . . particularly espouse the cause of the laboring and producing classes; and . . . advocate the rights of women." In addition to his extensive prospectus, Kneeland allotted columns (space permitting) in the *Investigator* for poetry and "articles of light reading."[2]

The *Boston Investigator* was founded during a period of freethought that saw agnosticism replacing deism. The "religion of nature" advocated by many of America's Founding Fathers was considered too conservative by a new generation of more aggressive freethinkers. Abner Kneeland's weekly was extremely radical for the middle of the nineteenth century. The editor promoted everything from birth control to homeopathic medicine, regulation of child labor, and other progressive reforms. Many of Kneeland's subscribers were living in the Christian hinterlands and the *Investigator* became their only forum to share new ideas. Kneeland also published freethought books including Voltaire's *Philosophical Dictionary* with blank pages for readers to record marriages, births, and deaths. The *Boston Investigator* thus served as the freethinker's family bible.[3]

PUBLISHING, POLITICS, AND FREETHOUGHT
1865–1873

After the Civil War, freethought speakers began traveling the lecture circuit to preach their emancipated views to anybody willing to listen. People came from miles away to their local forums to hear freethinkers like Benjamin F. Underwood, an articulate speaker who promoted and helped popularize the scientific discoveries of Charles Darwin and Herbert Spencer. Another inveterate liberal lecturer was Octavius B. Frothingham, a Free Religionist. Frothingham welcomed the increase in doubt and unbelief that he attributed to science, philosophy, social progress, and "unquestioning indifference to ideal things, that is almost peculiar to our generation and our people." The most popular and adored speaker during the post–Civil War period was Robert G. Ingersoll, a former colonel in the Illinois Cavalry, whose resplendent oratory was spreading the gospel of freethought as no one had ever done before—or since.[4]

Robert Green Ingersoll (1833–1899), known as the Great Agnostic, was the most acclaimed orator in America during the second half of the nineteenth century. Ingersoll was one of the leading lawyers of his generation, served as attorney general in Illinois, was on friendly terms with three presidents, and was backed by some of the most important men in the Republican Party. After making numerous brilliant political stump speeches for fellow Republicans, Ingersoll hoped to be appointed United States attorney general. However, his agnosticism held him back from gaining the federal office. Many believed Ingersoll could have been president if he only stifled his antireligious rhetoric. And while he never held an elected public office, Ingersoll's personal life and devotion to family were beyond reproach. His popularity, magnificent presence, and massive physique were often fodder for cartoonists. Envious religionists tried relentlessly to uncover any fragment of scandal or skeleton in the colonel's closet in an attempt to dishonor his character—but they found nothing.[5]

Soon after Ulysses S. Grant won the 1868 election (with Ingersoll's help), the colonel returned his attention to law. By late 1869 he realized that he would never be eligible for, appointed to, or elected to public office. The thirty-six-year-old attorney chose to never pursue a political office—a decision he would vacillate on for the rest of his life. In the early 1870s he was America's foremost freethinker, but he had not always been an unbeliever. A native of New York State, Ingersoll was the son of a penniless, itinerant clergyman. Reverend John Ingersoll was an abolitionist who believed that slavery was a national sin. His fervent anti-slavery remarks from the pulpit were not always welcomed. Robert resented how his father was treated by proslavery congregations and recalled that the church of his childhood was gloomy and cold. As a youth he dreaded Sundays, which in the Ingersoll home began on Saturday night. "When the sun fell below the horizon," he wrote, "there was a darkness fell upon the house ten thousand times deeper than that of night. Nobody said a pleasant word; nobody laughed; nobody smiled; the child that looked the sickest was regarded as the most pious. That night you could not even crack hickory nuts."[6]

Like many children in the nineteenth century, every Sunday Robert was forced to attend two religious services filled with Christian hymns, prayers, and long, monotonous sermons. Following the first service and during Sunday school, he and the other children sat listening in the cold to a minister who asked them if they knew that they all deserved to go to hell. "[They] all answered 'Yes.'" Then they were asked if they were each willing to go to hell if it was God's will. "And every little liar shouted 'Yes.'" After a hurried lunch and before the second Sunday service, they all marched out to visit the cemetery to study epitaphs. Robert found "great comfort" in the epitaphs because he thought they were proof that the horrible sabbaths could not last forever. But his hopes were promptly dashed when the congregation sang a hymn with the lines: "Where congregations ne'er break up / And Sabbaths never end." These two lines, he said, "prejudiced me a little against even heaven."[7]

Robert Ingersoll's brother Clark, an Illinois congressman, was defeated for reelection in 1870. The press announced that Clark Ingersoll's defeat was in part "his vulgar brother's" fault. Also aiding in his defeat was a circular diatribe orchestrated by an Illinois clergyman urging the faithful: "The Christian people of this city, almost to a man, feel that the honor, purity and security of the Republican Party, and the interests of Christianity, imperatively demand the defeat of Mr. Ingersoll . . . a thoroughly corrupt man, devoid of moral principle, profane, atheistic."[8]

In the early 1870s Robert Ingersoll had a successful law practice in Peoria, Illinois, but devoted much of his time to his lecture tours. He received as much as $7,000 for his lectures on Shakespeare, Burns, Voltaire, and Thomas Paine. "Shakespeare is my bible, Burns my hymn-book," he was fond of saying. Audiences were not limited to freethinkers; a large portion were God-fearing citizens who were not in attendance to be converted—they regarded Ingersoll as an eloquent and entertaining speaker. Ingersoll was able to translate agnostic philosophical abstractions into comprehensible terms for average Americans. A brilliant and consummate orator, he delivered lectures heard by thousands of people. "He never repeats himself," Bennett wrote after meeting Ingersoll and hearing him speak. "His utterances are always new, sparkling and vigorous. He is the most genial gentleman—full of cheerfulness, earnestness and vivacity. Col. Bob is decidedly a great man. He has few equals in any country, and probably no superiors."[9]

Freethought gained national recognition during the colorful 1872 presidential campaign, but not all of it was positive (Robert Ingersoll did not participate in that campaign). Three freethinkers of varying degrees announced their candidacies for president of the United States. They were Horace Greeley, Victoria Woodhull, and George Francis Train. Each was a publisher or former publisher, and two of them (Woodhull and Train) printed material considered so outrageously antireligious that it shook the Christian community in America. The third, Horace Greeley, was nominated by both the newly formed Liberal Republican Party *and* the Democratic Party.[10]

The two main contestants were the incumbent President Grant and Horace Greeley, antislavery leader, statesman, and editor of the influential *New York Tribune*. Greeley was a reform-minded freethinker, founding member and president of the New York Liberal Club. He coined the phrase, "Go West, young man and grow up with the country." Horace Greeley was displeased with Grant's corrupt administration and became its harshest critic. One of Greeley's supporters was abolitionist and leading freethinker Elizur Wright. "The great question now before the Republican Party, and all the rest of us," Wright stated during the 1872 election, "is whether after our bloody cutting out of cancer [slavery], we are to rot by the cancer of our corruption." Susan B. Anthony, the agnostic suffragist leader, was horrified at the idea of Greeley's candidacy and found him to be "utterly unfitted, by his credulity and lack of judgment," even though she said his "private character is above reproach."[11]

Victoria Woodhull, a provocative feminist firebrand and independent candidate from the Equal Rights Party, dramatically announced her candidacy for president of the United States (Frederick Douglass was her running mate) only a few weeks after publishing the first issue of her *Woodhull and Claflin's Weekly*. Woodhull's speechwriter and intellectual guru was Stephen Pearl Andrews, an eccentric philosopher and utopian romantic whose Long Island community, Modern Times, was possibly the first of its kind in America. His popularity since the 1850s was due mainly to his illustrious three-way debate in the pages of the *New York Tribune* with Horace Greeley and Henry James Sr., the preeminent theological writer. The subject of their publicized discourse was free love, a lifestyle that Andrews championed and reportedly discussed at length with his protégée, Victoria Woodhull. In the nineteenth century, the free-love movement did not encourage promiscuity but promoted a different sexual morality. Free lovers believed marriage was similar to slavery or prostitution and advocated commitment based on individual choice and love, not on legal restraints.[12]

Few Americans took Victoria Woodhull's candidacy seriously

and many perceived it as a publicity stunt to promote her new periodical. She and her younger sister, Tennessee Claflin, were the first female stockbrokers and protégées of Commodore Vanderbilt, one of America's most successful capitalists. In the fall of 1872 the notorious suffragist sisters exposed the Beecher-Tilton Affair, the most talked-about church scandal in the nation's history. Henry Ward Beecher, known as the Great Divine, was America's most famous Congregationalist minister, renowned for his brilliant oratory and crusade against slavery. Theodore Tilton accused his friend Beecher of having an affair with his wife. A sensationalized blackmail trial ensued. The sisters printed intimate details of the affair in their radical weekly to illustrate what they believed was the hypocrisy of the Gilded Age. A notorious loose cannon, Woodhull succeeded in alienating both religionists and freethinkers with her shocking exposé. *Harper's Weekly* cartooned Woodhull as "Mrs. Satan" because of her scandalous free-love beliefs.[13]

Running as the People's Candidate for President was another wealthy eccentric publisher, George Francis Train, a forty-three-year-old shipping magnate who owned a mansion in Newport, Rhode Island. Train financed Susan B. Anthony's weekly, the *Revolution*, during its publication between 1868 and 1870. Train was a man of great ability, who, in 1849 at the age of twenty, had a notable position in the shipping business with an annual salary of $10,000. In addition to creating a fleet of forty sailing ships, he introduced street railways in Europe and organized the Credit Mobilier to finance the Union Pacific Railway in America. Train was a quixotic freethinker who published his *Train Ligue* newspaper with sections of the Old Testament printed under sensational headlines.[14]

At a time when women were not permitted in restaurants unless accompanied by men, the 1872 political campaigns proved to be the most fascinating in American history. The Democratic Party was in such disorder that they endorsed Horace Greeley, who was first nominated by the Liberal Republicans. The Republican Party condemned religious and racial discrimination and proposed granting rights for women. In the first and only presidential ballot ever cast in her life, Susan B. Anthony was arrested after voting for Grant, her fellow Republican. Grant's administration would be one of the most corrupt and scandalous in the nation's history. Furthermore, Grant would carelessly sign into law a fine-tuned obscenity statute that had been around since 1865, giving teeth to an ill-defined hindrance to free speech that would be used to terrorize freethinking authors and publishers.[15]

Soon after the election, the *Catholic World*, a religious periodical, bemoaned that the ungodliness of the age had already produced enough "bitter and deadly fruit." The country's secular newspapers and magazines were also alarmed at the increasing popularity of freethought. Some of the nation's most widely read publications printed articles about the frightening prospects of an irreligious world. *Scribner's Monthly* featured a piece about Abraham Lincoln's rumored illegitimacy and infidelity. The magazine's August 1873 issue began a three-part series titled "Modern Skepticism," reporting the rapid growth of unbelief around the world.[16]

The world was becoming increasingly skeptical, according to the *New York Times*. The Republic, the *Times* opined, or any free government could not exist where religious sentiment does not dominate national thought. The *Times* griped about freethinkers becoming "too successful in enlisting the press as their medium of communication with the public." The sanctimonious newspaper announced that scientists like Charles Darwin and Thomas Huxley were responsible for the menacing increase of freethought. These men, the *Times* asserted, whose "heresies come to us mainly in scientific or philosophical guise," were not merely justifying their own negations, "but burn with a strange and cruel zeal to overturn the very foundation of belief, on the plea of instituting correct modes of thought."[17]

LET US REASON TOGETHER

It was in this "modern" political, philosophical, and ultrareligious climate that D. M. Bennett (the struggling seed farmer from the

Illinois prairie) founded the *Truth Seeker*. There were at least a half dozen liberal publications in the early 1870s. In the premier issue dated September 1873, Bennett gave recognition to the *Index*, the *Boston Investigator*, the *Religio-Philosophic Journal*, *Our Age*, the *Banner of Light*, *Brittain's Quarterly*, and the *Golden Age*.[18]

While Bennett was sensitive about his lack of formal education, he did not let it hinder his mission for his new publication. A letter written to Francis Abbot, the erudite editor of the *Index*, showed his determination. Still using the Seedsmen and Florists, Prairie Gardens business letterhead adorned with a fruity and flowery graphic, Bennett expressed his hopes for his new endeavor. His first letter to Abbot showed his ambitious desire for his new "sheet" but was careful not to overdo the expectations. Bennett informed the New England editor that his small monthly would be "considerably more radical & infidelic than the Index," but assured him that the *Truth Seeker* would not compete with the venerable *Index*. In fact, "Many maybe feel inclined to need both," he wrote. Bennett concluded his cordial letter with a bold request to purchase names from Abbot's subscription list. Abbot replied that the price for the *Index* mailing list was $3,000, an extravagant sum that Bennett could not spare.[19]

By the end of September, Bennett was regularly corresponding with Abbot, using his new letterhead. The *Truth Seeker*'s heading read, "Devoted to Science, Morals, Freethought, Free Enquiry and the Diffusion of Liberal Sentiments." Bennett cobbled together his statement of principles partly from Bible verses, creating the amalgam, "Come now and let us reason together; Let us hear all sides; Let us divest ourselves of prejudice and the effects of early education; Let us prove all things and hold fast to that which is good."[20]

The yearly subscription rate of fifty cents was inexpensive, according to Bennett. He boasted that the eight-page journal was big enough to "embrace, as in one brotherhood, Liberals, Free Religionists, Rationalists, Spiritualists, Universalists, Unitarians, Friends, Infidels, Free Thinkers, and in short all who dare to think and judge for themselves."[21]

The first issue consisted of a reprint of Bennett's "Discussion Upon the Efficacy of Prayer" and the articles, "Virtue and Morality," "Priestcraft and Science Contrasted," "What Christians Are Required to Believe," and "Infidels versus Christians." The premier issue also featured an article titled "Increase in Skepticism," a piece about the modern skepticism article that appeared in *Scribner's*. Bennett wrote the entire issue—about 14,500 words! He also included a reprint of the "Nine Demands of Liberalism" that first appeared in the April 1872 publication of Abbot's *Index*.[22]

THE CHRISTIAN AMENDMENT

Francis Ellingwood Abbot was a former Unitarian pastor, who, together with Octavius B. Frothingham, founded the *Index* in 1870. The *Index* was the official organ of the Free Religious Association, an organization founded by Unitarian ministers. Their mission was to promote the interests of pure religion, encourage the scientific study of theology, and increase fellowship in spirit. Abbot and his fellow Free Religionists rejected the autocratic claims of organized religion and struggled for the complete separation of church and state. "The Spirit of Free Religion," asserted Abbot, "is the Spirit of Science which knows nothing of dogmatic preconception or prejudgment."[23]

In the early 1870s the National Reform Association (NRA), a Presbyterian-sponsored organization founded during the Civil War, was making progress in its crusade to amend the Constitution. The association's mission was to declare America a Christian nation and officially acknowledge "God as the source of all authority and power in civil government" and "the Lord Jesus Christ as the ruler among the nations and his revealed will as of supreme authority." The association also successfully lobbied for stricter Sabbath laws and mandatory Bible instruction in public schools. Some of the country's leading citizens were members of the NRA, including public officials, prominent clergymen, and Justice William Strong of the United States Supreme Court.[24]

By the 1870s some vigilant Americans were alarmed at the NRA's unrestrained power and enforced Christian morality. In 1872 Francis Abbot, who felt that Free Religionists were spending too much time and energy discussing metaphysics, began a campaign to form liberal leagues in opposition to the NRA and for full secularism. Leagues soon flourished throughout America attracting prominent citizens. Abolitionists William Lloyd Garrison, Wendell Phillips, Elizur Wright, Lucretia Mott, and Elizabeth Cady Stanton were members. In 1876 the National Liberal League met for the first time at the centennial celebration in Philadelphia where it honored Benjamin Franklin, Thomas Jefferson, Ethan Allen, and Thomas Paine. One hundred seventy delegates from forty liberal associations attended the meeting and elected their first president, Francis E. Abbot.[25]

The National Liberal League's mission was articulated in the "Nine Demands of Liberalism." The nine demands called for the elimination of army and congressional chaplains, the termination of religious instruction in public schools, the abolition of judicial oaths in courts, elimination of Sunday laws, taxation of church property, and an end to the enforcement of Christian morality. One of the first and most important victories for the NLL was to defeat the National Reform Association's proposed Christian Amendment.[26]

THE CITY OF MAGNIFICENCE AND SQUALOR

Bennett began his publishing career while the country was going through the worst depression it ever experienced, a time when railroads went bankrupt, unemployment was raging, and nearly a thousand papers went out of business. In 1873 the stock exchange crashed for the first time, sparking a recession that would last five long years and cause the seventh decade of the nineteenth century to be called the black seventies.[27]

The first issue of the *Truth Seeker* was printed in Terre Haute, Indiana. Twelve thousand sample copies were sent across the country. Bennett was never above making personal appeals for financial support. "We have learned to think half a dollar is really a good deal of money, in view of the reluctance with which many of our liberal friends seem to part with it," the publishing neophyte wrote in the third issue. "Yes, fifty cents will buy five or six pretty good cigars, or a few ounces of snuff or tobacco, or a dozen or two of oysters, or a ticket to the Negro minstrels and possibly, it is not right we should ask any one to forego either of these pleasures merely to sustain the cause of truth, and have the reading of our paper for a year."[28]

Although subscriptions were slow to come in, the *Truth Seeker* was receiving some complimentary notices. Letters from across the country were arriving, including correspondence from B. F. Underwood, the popular freethought lecturer and one of the first subscribers. A letter from Morris Altman, a wealthy New York merchant, was indicative of the tenor of letters received. Altman, one of the founding brothers of the Altman Department stores in New York, was an early subscriber and became Bennett's loyal friend and benefactor. The merchant wrote,

207 E. 45th Street, New York, Sept 9, 1873

Just received your first number. Think highly of it. Call it a first rate paper. Enclosed is my subscription. Send it regularly. I take all liberal papers, as they are needed—the more the better. The tone of The Truth Seeker is high and sound. Keep it so.

Yours, & co., M. Altman[29]

The venerable *Boston Investigator* printed a notice of the new publication:

The Truth Seeker—this is a good name for a new liberal paper just commenced by the Liberal Association [The Bennetts] of Paris, Illinois. It makes a handsome appearance typographically and contains throughout the right kind of doctrine, as a paper is devoted to science, morals, freethought, free enquiry and the diffusion of liberal sentiments. . . . This is an excellent platform and The Truth Seeker deserves success and we hope it may receive it.[30]

Bennett also received hate mail and "Come to Jesus" letters. He was cognizant of the *Truth Seeker*'s unpopularity among Christians—the majority of the reading public. But these "thousands of pious, self-righteous souls" did not deter the novice publisher who vowed to continue to "fearlessly pursue the even tenor of our way, regardless of snarling dogs and growling wolves." One of these "souls" was a clergyman from Illinois, who, after receiving two copies of the *Truth Seeker*, wrote,

> Sir—You will please keep your infamous, blasphemous, low slang, and slanderous sheet at home; thou enemy of all righteousness; thou child of the Devil. Wilt thou not cease to pervert the right way of the Lord.—*J. W. Riley*[31]

With a growing subscription list and encouraging reviews, the Bennetts decided to relocate. The couple lived in Illinois for three years, but after his partnership in the seed business turned sour, there was no reason to stay. "We trust we part on friendly terms with all save our late partners in the business," Bennett wrote. "We care not for their friendship and part with them without a pang of regret." He was done with partnerships: "If anyone presents us a petition to Congress, to pass an act making it a penitentiary offense for two or more men to form a partnership, we think we shall sign it."[32]

Initially, the couple considered moving to Terre Haute, where the paper was first printed. They also considered Toledo, St. Louis, Chicago, Cincinnati, and Louisville. After he and Mary gave considerable thought to each location, they decided that New York was the place. "It is the metropolis of our country," Bennett stated, "the great center and headquarters for trade, commerce, interchange for the industries of nations, and why should it not be also for progressive and advanced ideas?" There were five hundred newspapers published in New York in 1874, but *Wood-*

hull and Claflin's was the only other freethought periodical in Manhattan and was not a strict liberal periodical. "The harvest is truly great," his business sense told him, "but the laborers are few." And since both he and Mary were natives of the Empire State, it seemed a little like "returning home."[33]

Bennett traveled to New York in late 1873 and spent two weeks investigating the metropolis for his new operation. The first person he visited was Stephen Pearl Andrews, Victoria Woodhull's speechwriter and mentor. He used the Andrewses' home for his headquarters and did his writing there. When Andrews was asked years later *why* Bennett came to see him, he responded:

> Well, the only reason was that for thirty-five or forty years past in New York, I have been in a certain sense a sort of rallying point for radicals and enthusiasts and cranky people of all sorts; my house has always been a sort of cross between a hotel and a university and, somehow or other, I have been known not only in this country, but abroad, so that pretty much everybody of the so-called cranky type that arrived in New York found out where Stephen Pearl Andrews lived, and generally reported pretty early.[34]

Stephen Pearl Andrews was an individualist, anarchist, dynamic reformer, and abolitionist who was in the vanguard of the emancipation of slaves in America. As early as 1843 the agitator traveled to England to enlist the aid of the British Antislavery Society. He hoped to raise money to pay for the slaves in Texas, making the Republic of Texas a free state. Andrews was a brilliant philosopher, pioneer sociologist, lawyer, doctor, and a master in Latin, Greek, and Sanskrit. Three decades earlier he was recognized as the best Chinese scholar outside of China. A philosophical anarchist, Andrews published the first translation in America of Karl Marx's *Communist Manifesto* in *Woodhull and Claflin's Weekly*. Andrews brought shorthand to America. "Other men were known as factors in reforms," the *Truth Seeker* reported; "Andrews was the reform itself."[35]

During Bennett's stay in New York, Andrews tried to explain

the downside of a move to the big city with two and a half million people and 470 churches:

> My spiritual sight wasn't sufficiently open to see in that plain
> countryman the qualities that made D. M. Bennett what he
> proved to be subsequently; and while he consulted me, while
> he told me what he came here for, and what he intended to do,
> I think I said quite as much to discourage him as to encourage
> him. I painted the difficulties. I had known hundreds of
> instances of similar earnest and honest efforts to start this and
> that and the other enterprise in behalf of reform, almost all of
> which had sunk into nonentity; and I didn't sense in Mr. Ben-
> nett any special power that was going to make him the excep-
> tion. I had to learn subsequently, by experience, what, if I had
> had more intuition, I might have known then.[36]

The December issue of the *Truth Seeker* was the last to be
issued from Paris, Illinois. On the front page, Bennett announced
the move to New York and his plans to increase the number of
pages from eight to sixteen. He also explained that when he
started the periodical in September, he was still busily engaged in
other occupations; the *Truth Seeker* was only an experiment, a
"side issue." But plans for the future meant expansion and headquarters in New York, the world's greatest city. At the end of 1873,
the couple moved to New York where their first disappointment
occurred when they were unable to secure an office in the *Sun*
building. Bennett contacted Morris Altman who introduced him
to Eugene Macdonald, a young printer.[37]

Eugene Montague Macdonald was born in Chelsea, Maine,
on February 5, 1855. Eugene and his younger brother George
spent their childhood in New Hampshire. Unlike Bennett who
had a strict religious background, the Macdonald boys were
second-generation freethinkers. Their mother, Asenath Chase
Macdonald, was a remarkable woman for the nineteenth century
or any century for that matter. An enlightened Civil War widow,
Mrs. Macdonald was one of America's first "trained nurses" and
"had a philosophical mind" that her son believed "might have

produced a critique on Kant as abstruse as Kant's critique on reason."[38]

In 1862 after her husband's death (at the second battle of Bull Run), Mrs. Macdonald's main concern was choosing a vocation for her two boys. She knew Horace Greeley, the brilliant editor of the *New York Tribune*, and admired his career that began only modestly but concluded as the country's most famous newspaper editor. Hoping the same for Eugene, Mrs. Macdonald decided to place him (at the age of thirteen) in a printing office "almost against his will," she later recalled.[39]

Eugene served his apprenticeship in New York, and returned home to Keene, New Hampshire, where he worked on local newspapers. At the age of eighteen, Eugene moved permanently to New York where, with the help of his mother, he leased a printing office in lower Manhattan. Bennett hired Macdonald to print the January 1874 issue of the *Truth Seeker*. Macdonald's office at 335 Broadway (corner of West Broadway and Worth Street) became the publication's first home in New York. Bennett was pleased with the location and declared Broadway "the greatest street in the world."[40]

Mrs. Macdonald became concerned after learning that her son used his credit to buy the type needed to print Bennett's journal. She thought Mr. Bennett "might be an honest man, or he might not," since they had previous experience with both kinds. Her first impression of the "editor," whom she found sitting with bag and baggage in their office beside the stove with an unshaven face, unkempt hair, and unpolished shoes, was that he looked more like an elderly farmer and "the farthest possible from a literary man." Her anxiety vanished, however, as soon as Eugene introduced them to each other. "One glance at his kindly, genial face, which spoke so plainly the native goodness of the man," she later recalled, "and a load was lifted from my heart." Mrs. Macdonald was impressed with his "unimpeachable honesty" and "unswavering fidelity" to his own convictions. Her first thought was, "My boy has found a father." She later characterized her first impressions as "almost" prophetic because the two became more like "an elder and a younger brother."[41]

Mrs. Macdonald described Bennett as "a shining example" of Beecher's "man of the future," an individual "so well-born that they do not need to be born again." And she found his generosity another of his foremost traits. "His heart and his pocket were always open. I know whereof I speak. He never refused to help another for the sake of keeping a dollar in his own pocket."[42]

George Everett Macdonald followed in his brother's footsteps and less than two years later began his apprenticeship with the *Truth Seeker*. George started as a printer's devil and worked his way up to proofreading, foreman, and eventually publisher. He would spend over a half century associated with the publication. Like Mary Bennett, Mrs. Macdonald occasionally proofread for the journal, and the *Truth Seeker* became a family affair.[43]

SAGES, INFIDELS, AND THINKERS

At fifty-six, Bennett was still an incredibly vigorous man and described as a "dynamo of nervous energy," awaking religiously at four o'clock and working until 11 PM—eighteen to twenty hours a day, seven days a week. Mrs. Macdonald recalled a time when he fell out of his chair and onto the floor from exhaustion, as if dead. After being revived, the editor went home and rested a few hours only to return and start working again. "Not a full-blooded man was Bennett," George Macdonald wrote, "nor of the sanguineous temperament, but pallid, with a translucent skin; his flesh not very solid nor his physique rugged." Bennett had a deformed foot and walked with a limp. He dressed in a loose gray suit without a tie. Although Bennett was not a man of humor, his eyes twinkled and he was "one who liked to poke the boys in the ribs and crack a joke. No man I ever saw could smile so genially or better appreciate the witticisms of the press." Regarding Bennett's success, Macdonald wrote,

> He owed the popularity he achieved partly to circumstance, and more to his simple and honest nature, his industrious hand, his

capable head, and his courageous heart. His success was all earned and genuine, for he had none of the tricks, either of speech or pen, that deceive the unwary, nor resorted to the "skillful digressions" which appeal to the passions or stir the emotions of the unthinking. He was a likeable man and it did not embarrass him to be praised.[44]

Doctor Bennett, as he was known to his friends, "possessed such a facility as a penman" (a pencil, in his case), George Macdonald said, that he could have easily filled the entire journal every week with his own articles. He always used worn-out lead pencils that the Macdonald brothers suspected were thrown away by the clerks. The editor's writing style was verbose and he was enamored with trios of words, for example, "dogmas, superstitions, and errors," "cruelties, wrongs, and outrages," "persecuted, tortured, and burned," and so on. Bennett's love for phrases of triplets is apparent in the title of his first book, *Sages, Infidels, and Thinkers*, or the revised and enlarged second edition, *Sages, Thinkers, and Reformers*. Some of his contributors also used verbal triplets in an attempt to either follow his style or join the editor in paying homage to the author of the Declaration of Independence, who wrote "life, liberty, and the pursuit of happiness." Bennett's endless supply of words was evident from the *Truth Seeker*'s colossal heading:

> Devoted to Science, Morals, Freethought, Free Discussion, Liberalism, Sexual Equality, Labor Reform, Progression, Free Education, and whatever tends to emancipate and elevate the human race. Opposed to Priestcraft, Ecclesiasticism, Dogmas, Creeds, False Theology, Superstition, Bigotry, Ignorance, Monopolies, Aristocracies, Privileged Classes, Tyranny, Oppression and Everything that Degrades or Burdens Mankind Mentally or Physically.[45]

Bennett published numerous books, tracts, and leaflets written by himself and others. An example of one of his self-written publications is *The Bible in Common Schools*. The lecture is a review of the Bible and its "absurdities, inconsistencies, errors and mistakes." He provided more than a hundred reasons why the Bible should not be used in school. "You can't make it too strong," he used to say when writing against the Bible. For years Bennett had been a "devout believer in the inspiration and absolute truth of the book," wrote Eugene Macdonald, and "he was angry at the deception he had imposed upon himself." Bennett's Liberal and Scientific Publishing House introduced American readers to important works like Viscount Amberley's controversial *Analysis of Religious Belief* and George Drysdale's *The Elements of Social Science* that promoted contraception as a method to increase love and sexual happiness, particularly for women. Bennett was one of the first booksellers in America to furnish readers with the *Bhagavad Gita* and Madame H. P. Blavatsky's *Isis Unveiled*. While his main focus was antireligion material, he also touted new medical, scientific, and technological advances. Similar to *Scientific American*, Bennett often recognized inventors and routinely described new inventions like the typewriter, phonograph, and telephone. The editor promoted cremation, spelling reform, and the Society for Ethical Culture.[46]

In New York, Bennett continued publishing serialized debates with clergymen that were popular with freethinkers and religionists. One of Bennett's most successful endeavors was his debate with Reverend G. H. Humphrey, author of *Hell and Damnation*. Humphrey, a fundamentalist Christian, challenged the editor to a debate that ran through many issues of the journal and was subsequently published in a book titled *The Humphrey-Bennett Discussion*. In the printed encounter, the minister emphasized the immorality of freethinkers; Bennett responded with numerous accounts of the misdeeds of clerics. Although the discourse was very antagonistic, the two became good friends.[47]

A few years later, the minister ran away with his wife's niece and George Macdonald reported that "fragments of the seventh commandment" were in evidence. Thinking that Bennett would enjoy reporting the minister's transgression and hypocrisy, George wrote an article for publication. The editor declined to print the matter and threw the story in the wastebasket. "Bennett had great charity toward human weakness when he knew the circumstances," George observed. Bennett confessed that the temptation to publish the article was just too great. "Why," George asked, "have you seen the young woman?" The editor responded: "No, but I have seen Humphrey's wife."[48]

The Bennett-Teed Discussion was another series of debates published in a book in 1878. Cyrus Romulus R. Teed was an interesting character, but not much of a writer. The discussion ran for many weeks in the *Truth Seeker* and Teed (according to George Macdonald) lost himself "completely in the mists of metaphysical theory and incoherent rhetoric." Teed, or the Prophet Cyrus or Koresh as he alternatively called himself, was a hollow-globe theorist who believed that he was the new messiah. He was also a "doctor" who published a daily paper called the *Herald of the Messenger of the New Covenant.* Teed would later operate his Koreshan colony in Florida and publish the *Flaming Sword,* a magazine that promoted his nonsensical cosmology. His followers believed that he was the second Jesus Christ. "For a man of intelligence and sanity," George Macdonald wrote, "Teed entertained many delusions." Bennett found Teed's system of geology preposterous. But it was the religious fanatic's proposition that "Jesus Christ is not only divine, but is the Lord God, Creator of Heaven and Earth" that Bennett found the most ludicrous and pronounced it "Teed-ious."[49]

Manhattan, in the 1870s, was a vibrant and intellectually stimulating location, especially for freethinkers. The urban island was home to some of the country's most radical and notable liberals. Not since living in Cincinnati five years earlier did Bennett have the opportunity to avail himself of so much organized freethought activity. Dr. Winterburn, his friend from Cincinnati, had also relocated to New York. An association that appealed to the editor was the New York Liberal Club (later renamed the Manhattan Liberal Club). Founded in 1869, the organization met every Friday evening and offered an arena for lectures, debates, the exchange of books, and for the purposes of disseminating information on "Scientific, Social, Political and Religious subjects." Horace Greeley was president for several years and Stephen Pearl Andrews served as vice president. Bennett's closest friends, including the Macdonald family, were members.[50]

In 1875 Eugene Macdonald began contributing articles to the *Truth Seeker* and other freethought publications. One evening while Mrs. Macdonald and Dr. Bennett were walking together to a meeting at the New York Liberal League, the proud mother asked the editor if he thought her son's recently published article in the estimable *Boston Investigator* was "pretty good." "Excellent, excellent," he exclaimed. "I tell you, my mantle will fall on worthy shoulders." Who knew it would have fallen so soon.[51]

NOTES

"advertised the paper.": GM v. 1 p. 326.

1. Warren.
2. Gordon Stein, PhD, editor, *Encyclopedia of Unbelief*.
3. Ibid.
4. Warren.
5. Orvin Larson, *American Infidel: Robert G. Ingersoll*. 1962.
6. Ibid.
7. Ibid.
8. Ibid.
9. "my hymn book.": Ibid. "probably no superiors.": TS Sept. 16, 1873. "earnestness and vitality.": TS Sept. 15, 1874.
10. EB.
11. DAB. "of our corruption.": Lawrence B. Goodheart, *Abolitionist, Actuary, Atheist: Elizur Wright & The Reform Impulse*. Kent State University Press. "is above reproach.": Lynn Sherr, *Failure Is Impossible: Susan B. Anthony in Her Own Words*. N.Y. Random House 1995.
12. Lois Beachy Underhill, *The Woman Who Ran for President: The Many Lives of Victoria Woodhull*, Bridge Works Publishing. Madeline Stern, *The Pantarch: A Biography of Stephen Pearl Andrews*. University of Texas Press. Austin & London 1968.
13. Underhill, Stern, and Broun and Leech.

14. DAB. Broun and Leech.

15. EB.

16. Warren

17. *New York Times*, Sept. 5, 1873.

18. TS Sept. 1873.

19. Letter to Abbot August 12, 1873: The papers of Francis Elling-wood Abbot, (HUG 1101.xx) Harvard University Archives, Pusey Library, Harvard Depository, Cambridge, Massachusetts 02138. $3K for *Index* mailing list: TS May 1880.

20. TS Sept. 1873.

The two Bible verses that Bennett extracted were from Isaiah 1:18 "Come now, and let us reason together, saith the Lord: though your sins be as scarlet, they shall be as white as snow; though they be red like crimson, they shall be as wool," and Thessalonians 5:21 "Prove all things; hold fast that which is good." Bennett's source for "Let us hear all sides; Let us divest ourselves of prejudice and the effects of early edu-cation" is unknown. However, the sentiment expressed is similar to Thomas Jefferson's letter to his nephew Peter Carr who was attending college in 1787. Bennett would subsequently cite Jefferson's letter in an editorial about the statesman's "unbelief." In addition to the similar antireligion creed expressed in the letter, there are two words, *divest* and *prejudices*, that are inserted in Bennett's heading. "In the first place," Jef-ferson advised his nephew, "divest yourself of all bias in favor of nov-elty and singularity of opinion. Indulge them in any other subject rather than that of religion." Later in the letter he states: "On the other hand, shake off all the fears and servile prejudices under which weak minds are servilely crouched. Fix reason firmly in her seat, and call to her tribunal every fact, every opinion. Question with boldness even the existence of God; because, if there be one, he must more approve of the homage of reason, than that of blindfolded fear." Martin A. Larson, *Jef-ferson: Magnificent Populist*. "Notes on Virginia," Thomas Jefferson.

21. TS Sept. 1873.

22. Ibid.

The Nine Demands of Liberalism:

1) We demand that churches and other ecclesiastical property shall be no longer exempt from taxation.

2) We demand that the employment of chaplains in Congress, and in the legislatures, in the navy and militia, and in prisons, asylums, and all other institutions supported by public money, shall be discontinued.

3) We demand that all public appropriations for educational and charitable institutions of a sectarian character shall cease.

4) We demand that all religious services now sustained by the government shall be abolished; and especially that the use of the Bible in the public schools, whether ostensibly as a textbook or avowedly as a book of religious worship, shall be prohibited.

5) We demand that the appointment, by the president of the United States or by the governors of the various states, of all the religious festivals and fasts shall wholly cease.

6) We demand that the judicial oath in the courts and in all other departments of the government shall be abolished, and that a simple affirmation under the pains and penalties of perjury shall be established in its stead.

7) We demand that all laws directly or indirectly enforcing the observance of Sunday as the Sabbath shall be repealed.

8) We demand that all laws looking to the enforcement of "Christian" morality shall be abrogated and that all laws shall be conformed to the requirements of natural morality, equal rights and impartial liberty.

9) We demand that not only in the Constitution of the United States and of the several states, but also in the practical administration of the same, no privileges or advantage shall be conceded to Christianity or any other special religion; that our entire political system shall be founded and administered on a purely secular basis; and whatever changes shall prove necessary to this end shall be consistently, unflinchingly, and promptly made.

23. W. Creighton Peden, *The Philosopher of Free Religion: Francis Ellingwood Abbot, 1836–1903*, p. 71. (American University Studies. Series V, Philosophy; vol. 133) Peter Lang Publishing, Inc. N.Y. 1992.

24. Warren.

25. Ibid.

In 1878, The National Liberal League nominated Francis E. Abbot for vice president and Robert G. Ingersoll for president of the United States. And while their names were never placed on the national ballot, the choice illustrates the important role Abbot played in the American freethought movement.

Peden, p. 170.

26. Warren.

27. Charles P. Kindleberger, *A History of Financial Crisis*. Basic Books, Inc., 1978.

28. TS Nov. 1873.

29. TS Oct. 1873. *100 The First Century: A History of B. Altman & Co.*, John S. Burke Jr. Altman letter: TS Oct. 1873.

30. *Boston Investigator* review reprinted in TS Nov. 1873.

31. Letter: TS Jan. 1874.

32. TS Dec. 1874.

33. TS April 1874.

34. TS June 28, 1884.

35. TS May 29, 1886.

36. TS June 28, 1884. 470 churches: *The Iconography of Manhattan Island, 1498–1909*, Modern City and Island, Chapter v. 111, Arno Press N.Y., 1967.

37. GM.

38. Ibid.

39. Ibid.

40. TS Dec. 1884.

41. A. C. Macdonald reminiscences: TS June 28, 1884.

42. Ibid.

"He [Bennett] could do a favor without preaching a sermon," said George Macdonald. Macdonald remembered a time when he needed to borrow some money and without asking any questions, the editor lent him seventy-five dollars. "He had no bank account; he carried his money in a long pocketbook, which, when I made the touch, he drew forth from an interior pocket, and then counted out the bills without comment." Mrs. Bennett was also helpful and "as motherly as though she had learned the art by raising a family of sons instead of being childless all her life."

GM v. 1 pp. 200–201.

43. TS June 28, 1884.

44. "of nervous energy.": TS Sept. 1, 1923. "to be praised.": GM.

45. "pursuit of happiness.": GM. "Mentally or Physically.": TS masthead.

46. "of the book.": TS Oct. 19, 1889. *Isis*: TS Sept. 15, 1877. TS Jan. 12, 1878.

47. GM.

48. Ibid.

49. Ibid.

50. SP and TS.

51. TS June 28, 1884.

4

The American Inquisition

Worse than all other mean acts are those performed by hypocrites under the cloak of purity and virtue.

—D. M. Bennett

Laws against blasphemy, though seldom prosecuted, were first introduced in the American colonies in the early seventeenth century. The Massachusetts and Virginia colonies passed blasphemy laws and provided the death penalty as punishment. In Massachusetts, numerous Quakers—men and women—were stripped and brutally flogged for their "Anti-Christian" religion and "monstrous *blasphemies.*" The Massachusetts authorities ruled that the Quaker religion was not only "blasphemous," but also "blasphemously heretical." In 1659/60, four Quakers defied banishment in the Massachusetts Bay Colony and were hanged for their religion. The Puritan authorities informed King Charles II that the executed Quakers had in essence committed suicide.

Although they were all "capitall blasphemers, open seducers from the glorious Trinity . . . the Quakers died, not because of their other crimes, how capitoll soever," but because they returned to Massachusetts knowing they would be hanged.[1]

At various times in the American colonies the meaning of blasphemy became vague and nearly indistinguishable from sedition, treason, profanity, sacrilege, idolatry, heresy, nonconformity, and obscenity. Most blasphemy prosecutions had more to do with religious and political dissent than with heresy. As early as 1711 the colony of Massachusetts—infamous for its blasphemy laws—passed a statute that regulated both religious and secular material. The law prohibited the writing, printing, or publishing of any "filthy, obscene or profane song, pamphlet, libel or mock-sermon, in imitation of preaching." The law stated that such "evil communication" and "wicked, profane, impure, filthy and obscene songs, composures, [and] writings . . . do corrupt the mind and are incentive to all manner of impurities and debaucheries."[2]

After the United States Constitution was ratified in 1788, the First Amendment and most state constitutions prohibited the establishment of an official religion. Nevertheless, some states, Massachusetts in particular, continued to pass laws and prosecute persons for blasphemy against Christianity. Although no one was ever executed in the United States for the crime of blasphemy (speaking evil of sacred matters), the offender could be punished by a severe whipping, heavy fine, or both. The only man ever imprisoned in Massachusetts for blasphemy during the nineteenth century was Abner Kneeland, the freethinking founder of the *Boston Investigator*. Kneeland was indicted in 1834 for "unlawfully and wickedly" publishing a "scandalous, impious, blasphemous and profane libel" of and pertaining to God. The indictment was brought against the editor using a blasphemy statute passed in 1782. The *Commonwealth v. Kneeland* case lasted four years and remains one of the most important blasphemy prosecutions in America.[3]

Abner Kneeland, whom Christian enemies called the Apostle of Satan, was indicted on three counts of blasphemy. The first two counts were for articles (written by others and published in the *Investigator*) regarding the "miraculous conception" of Jesus Christ and an irreverent piece that ridiculed prayer. The third count addressed a letter to a Universalist editor wherein Kneeland expressed his views on Universalism, the religion in which he had preached the word of God for three decades. Kneeland was a scriptural scholar renowned for his iconoclasm and series of lectures titled "A Review of the Evidences of Christianity." He still believed in God, but not the Universalists' version. "The whole story concerning him [Christ] was as much a fable and fiction as that of the god Prometheus," Kneeland wrote. "I am not an Atheist but a Pantheist," he confessed in the letter to the Universalist editor. "I believe that it is in God we live, move, and have our being; and that the whole duty of man consists . . . in promoting as much happiness as he can while he lives." Leonard W. Levy, the Pulitzer Prize–winning author and historian, has asserted that "Kneeland's creed was as spiritual as that of the Transcendentalists." According to historian Kenneth Burchell, Kneeland had far more consonance with Thomas Paine who wrote: "Practical religion consists in doing good: and the only way of serving God is that of endeavoring to make His creation happy. All preaching that has not this for its object is nonsense and hypocrisy."[4]

Abner Kneeland's political views had more to do with his prosecution and conviction than his trenchant remarks on religion. In the pages of the *Boston Investigator*, Kneeland not only characterized the Holy Bible as a pack of lies and the clergy as hypocrites, but he also scoffed at the sacredness of marriage, promoted sex education, railed against the rich, and identified with farmers, working men, and organized labor. He was a Democrat and a popular speaker; his lectures attracted thousands of listeners in Boston and New York. His political enemies accused him of hosting "infidel orgies" and being a leader of the "Democratic radicals." One of his lawyers was a former state attorney general and important member of the Massachusetts Democratic Party. During one of his trials, a prosecuting attorney warned jurors that the *Boston Investigator* was inexpensive and popular among the poor. "A lava stream of blasphemy and obscenity which blast the vision and gan-grenes the very soul of the uncorrupted reader" is how a political enemy described the paper. It was plain to Kneeland why his liberal periodical engendered so much animosity: "Birds do not generally flutter much till they are hit."[5]

After four trials and a conviction, Kneeland's case was heard in the Massachusetts Supreme Judicial Court. Kneeland represented himself in front of Chief Justice Lemuel Shaw, "the greatest magistrate" in American history according to Oliver Wendell Holmes. The erudite editor was well informed on legal matters and an experienced public speaker. Kneeland proved himself a worthy opponent of Shaw. Nevertheless, Shaw upheld the editor's conviction and delivered the opinion. Blasphemy, wrote Shaw, the son of a minister, is "speaking evil of the Deity with an impious purpose to derogate from the divine majesty, and to alienate the minds of others from the love and reverence of God . . . [and] purposely using words concerning God, calculated and designed to impair and destroy the reverence, respect, and confidence due to him. . . . It is a willful and malicious attempt to lessen men's reverence of God." The statute, declared Shaw, prohibited a "willful denial of God."[6]

Shaw's judgment was called into question by many of New England's intellectuals and reformers. Richard Henry Dana, a notable author, attorney, and member of the Massachusetts legislature, described Shaw as a "man of intense and doting biases." Marcus Morton, the only judge who dissented from Shaw's opinion, found his fellow jurist's decision disturbing. According to Morton, the "operations of the human mind especially in the adoption of its religious faith [are] entirely above all civil authority." Religious truths, Morton believed, did not require the "dangerous aid" of legislation. Every person "has a constitutional right to discuss the subject of God, to affirm or deny his existence," Morton declared. "I cannot agree that a man may be punished for willfully doing what he has a legal right to do." Kneeland's conviction, Morton concluded, "rests very heavily upon my mind."[7]

The controversy that surrounded Abner Kneeland's freedom of

the press advocacy increased the *Boston Investigator*'s circulation. His written account of his blasphemy trial, conviction, and imprisonment was popular with his readers. Kneeland earned the respect of Boston's intellectuals and reformers including William Lloyd Garrison. The foremost abolitionist admired the editor who offered the use of his building after every Christian church in Boston denied him and his followers a place to meet. Abner Kneeland believed himself to be, as did others, a harbinger of free thought. Freethinkers revered Kneeland as a free-speech martyr, especially D. M. Bennett, who, in 1876, praised the *Boston Investigator* editor in his book *The World's Sages, Infidels, and Thinkers*. "A brave independent thinker" is how Bennett described Kneeland. "He was a man of moral worth and would have had the friendship of all who became acquainted with him had he not had the temerity to avow his honest convictions upon theological subjects."[8]

After serving two months in jail, Kneeland entrusted the *Boston Investigator* to J. P. Mendum and Horace Seaver and moved to Iowa with fellow members of his First Society of Free Enquirers. In Iowa, Kneeland involved himself in Democratic politics and founded Salubria, a utopian community. Kneeland's fight for freedom of the press had an important effect on civil liberties, and the *Commonwealth v. Kneeland* case continues to be the most frequently cited authority on blasphemy laws in America. In 1842, two years before Abner Kneeland's death, the United States Congress passed the first federal law prohibiting the importation of "obscene or immoral" pictures and prints. Two decades later during the Civil War, Montgomery Blair, the postmaster general, set the precedent for using the postal laws to regulate free speech. Blair personally confiscated mailed material that he determined was disloyal to the Union and/or might aid the Confederacy. Near the end of the war, Congress again addressed the obscenity issue and on February 8, 1865, the Senate and House passed a bill that stated

[t]hat no obscene book, pamphlet, picture, print, or other publication of a vulgar and indecent character, shall be admitted

into the mails of the United States; any person or persons who shall deposit or cause to be deposited, in any post-office or branch post-office of the United States, for mailing or for delivery, an obscene book, pamphlet, picture-print, or other publication, knowing the same to be of vulgar and indecent character, shall be deemed guilty of a misdemeanor, and, being duly convicted thereof, shall for every such offense be fined not more than five hundred dollars, or imprisoned not more than one year, or both, according to the circumstances and aggravations of the offense.[9]

Since Congress never defined what constituted "vulgar," "indecent," or "obscene," the determination was left up to judges, who, like most nineteenth-century Americans, believed obscenity could be easily recognized. Victorian Americans thought that obscenity was linked to drinking, gambling, masturbation, and all other social ills. And despite the fact that citizens had constitutionally protected First Amendment rights, prudish Victorians were in favor of moral censorship and suppression of "whatever outrages decency and is injurious to public morals."[10]

THE NEW YORK SOCIETY
FOR THE SUPPRESSION OF VICE

After the Civil War, Christian moralists began an aggressive campaign to censor literature as a way to control American society. In 1873, the same year Bennett started the *Truth Seeker*, the New York Society for the Suppression of Vice was incorporated by the New York State Legislature. The society was America's version of the organization that had originated in London and prosecuted Charles Bradlaugh and Annie Besant, the English freethinkers who published a birth control pamphlet. Anthony Comstock, a twenty-nine-year-old failed traveling salesman and member of the Young Men's Christian Association (YMCA), was responsible for the formation of the society. Samuel Colgate, the wealthy soap manufacturer, was president; Comstock served as secretary and chief vice hunter. In this capacity, and subsequently as the United States Post Office Department's "special agent," Comstock, a devout Christian, waged war on publishers of "obscene" literature, who he believed were poisoning the minds of America's children. The "three great crime-breeders in America," Comstock declared, were "intemperance, gambling, and evil reading, and the greatest of these is evil reading."[11]

With blessings from New York's Christian leaders and financial support from Colgate and the YMCA, Comstock made frequent trips to Washington where he lobbied members of Congress to induce them into believing that America's youth were at great moral risk. His dogged determination and satchel full of lewd pictures and devices, which he spread out for the congressmen to examine, convinced his fellow Republicans that the children of America were receiving such material in their mailboxes. Subsequently, on March 3, 1873, in the closing hours of the 42nd Congress, the Republican majority recklessly passed a series of acts while the House was in a state of confusion and some members, according to D. M. Bennett, were under the influence of alcohol. Two hundred and sixty acts were passed without inquiry or consideration of merit and summarily signed into law by President Grant, whose administration was mired in corruption scandals. Using the same tactics, Comstock had a similar set of laws passed by the New York Legislature. Two sections of the laws read:

Sec. 3893. No obscene, lewd, or lascivious book, pamphlet, picture, paper, print, or other publication of an indecent character, or any article or thing designed or intended for the prevention of conception or procuring of abortion, nor any article or thing intended or adapted for any indecent or immoral use or nature, nor any written or printed card, circular, book, pamphlet, advertisement, or notice of any kind giving information, directly or indirectly, where or how, or of whom, or by what means either of the things before mentioned may be obtained or made, nor any letter upon the envelope of which, or postal card upon which indecent or scurrilous epithets may be written or printed, shall be carried in the mail; and any person who shall knowingly deposit, or cause to be deposited, for mailing or delivery, any of the herein before-mentioned articles or things, shall take or cause to be taken, from the mail any such letter or package, shall be deemed guilty of a misdemeanor, and shall, for every offense, be fined not less than one hundred dollars, or imprisoned at hard labor not less than one year, nor more than ten years, or both.

Sec. 5389. Every person who, within the District of Columbia, or any of the Territories of the United States, or other place within the exclusive jurisdiction of the United States, sells, or lends, or gives away, or in any manner exhibits or offers to sell, or to lend, or to give away, or in any manner to exhibit, or otherwise publishes or offers to publish in any manner, or has in his possession, for any such purpose, any obscene book, pamphlet, paper, writing, advertisement, circular, print, picture, drawing, or other representation, figure, or image on or of paper or other material, or any cast, instrument, or other article of an immoral nature, or any drug or medicine, or any article whatever, for the prevention of conception, or for causing unlawful abortion, or who advertises the same for sale, or writes or prints, or causes to be written or printed, any card, circular, book, pamphlet, advertisement, or notice of any kind, stating when, where, how, or of whom, or by what means, any of the articles in this section herein before mentioned can be procured or obtained; or manufactures, draws, or prints, or in anywise makes any of such articles, shall be imprisoned at hard labor in the penitentiary for not less than six months, nor more than five years for each offense, or fined no less than one hundred dollars, nor more than two thousand dollars, with costs of court.[12]

"There were four publishers on the 2nd of last March; to-day three of these are in their graves, and it is charged by their friends that I worried them to death. Be that as it may, I am sure that the world is better off without them," Anthony Comstock crowed in January 1873. "This is clearly the spirit that lighted the fires of the inquisition," Ezra Heywood, a publisher arrested by Comstock, wrote in his book *Cupid's Yokes*. Comstock, America's self-appointed censor, would eventually boast of driving fifteen persons to suicide, some of them freethinkers. In 1873 the fires of the American Inquisition were only getting started.[13]

Anthony Comstock was by all accounts massive, intimidating, and humorless. The uniform he wore at his station in the "swamp at the mouth of a sewer" (as he called it) consisted of dark clothes and utilitarian shoes popular with cops on the beat. He routinely wore a starched white shirt, black bow tie, and a long black alpaca coat even during the scorching New York City summer. Beneath his somber exterior, red flannel underwear also covered his corpulent body—all year long. The only time Comstock ever changed his drab outfit was when he annually donned his white tie in observance of Christ's birthday. When speaking, he drew down his upper lip, giving an earnest and pious appearance. Comstock called his crusade a "fight for the young," and was overly fond of the old Christian saw "Man proposes but God disposes."[14]

Because of his special agent commission from the post office, Comstock was allowed free, unlimited transportation on railroads. He assisted or influenced the formation of vice societies in Cincinnati, Chicago, St. Louis, and Boston. Although he traveled extensively in America in the discharge of his "official" duties, the purity crusader was ignorant of other countries and culture. To him, cities like Berlin, Paris, and Rome were the places where "dirty" postcards originated. He detested any nudity in art but avowed that *nobody* revered the female figure more than he did. "In my opinion there is nothing else in the world so beautiful as the form of a beautiful maiden woman—nothing," he exclaimed in an interview. "But the place for a woman's body to be—denuded—is in the privacy of her own apartment with the blinds down." It is unknown, however, if he was referring to his wife, the daughter of a Presbyterian elder, as the "maiden" whose female "form" he so adamantly adored. (The only thing friends of the couple could recall about the dimwitted homebody was that she always wore black, never spoke, and weighed only eighty-two pounds.)[15]

Regardless of his reverence for the female form, Comstock railed against the public exposure of statues and paintings of nudes that were exhibited in the prestigious Paris Salon or the "Saloons of Paris," as he reportedly referred to them. "Comstockery is the world's standing joke at the expense of the United States," George Bernard Shaw said in 1905. "It confirms the deep-seated conviction of the old world that America is a provincial place, a second-rate country town civilization after all." When Comstock was asked to respond to the Irish dramatist's remarks, he asked: "Who is he?" He later called the world-renowned writer an "Irish smut-dealer." (Three decades earlier, the editor of the *Truth Seeker* christened the vice hunter Saint Anthony.)[16]

Two of Anthony Comstock's earliest victims were sisters Victoria Woodhull and Tennessee Claflin, who brazenly exposed the adulterous affair of Reverend Henry Ward Beecher in their weekly. While details of the Beecher-Tilton love triangle and blackmail trial were mentioned in nearly all the major newspapers, the sisters were thrown in jail because Comstock did not *approve* of their lifestyle and advocacy of free love. To those like Comstock who denounced her, Woodhull replied: "Yes, I am a Free Lover. I have an inalienable, constitutional and natural right to love whom I may, to love as long or as short a period as I can; to change that love every day if I please, and with that right neither you nor any law you can frame have any right to interfere." Since church hypocrisy was one of Bennett's primary concerns, he naturally covered the Beecher-Tilton case along with other licentious escapades by "men of God." These articles became so popular with readers that he eventually published a compilation in a pamphlet called *Sinful Saints and Sensual Shepherds.*[17]

In 1877 a party of Ku Klux Klan members lured a freethinking physician from his home in Bell County, Texas. After they stripped him naked and tied him to a tree, the Christian terrorists proceeded to give him one hundred lashes. The doctor had been found guilty of giving infidel lectures. After righteously administering their punishment, the whipping party left a placard warning that they would return and burn out or hang any other lecturers who dared to utter blasphemies in the neighborhood. In the nineteenth century, the public expression of antireligious views could result in ostracism, financial ruin, and occasionally imprisonment. Speaking or publishing ungodly sentiments in urban areas was not for the timid and could also be dangerous. Bennett was not only speaking and publishing antireligious material—he was openly attacking the Christian institutions and their powerful leaders. "Comstock is virtually a Ku Klux," Bennett fearlessly declared, "and his Christian clique is a Ku Klux Klan."[18]

Bennett routinely reported and ridiculed the activities of Anthony Comstock, who was becoming a serious threat to free speech. The editor was not alone in printing accounts of the vice fighter's movements, but his attacks were by far the most forceful and relentless. And while personal attacks could cause Comstock to be revengeful, it was a "letter" that Bennett wrote that enraged the Christian crusader. Comstock's private diaries were rife with praises and supplications addressed to his personal savior Jesus Christ. Bennett's *An Open Letter to Jesus Christ* was thus a personal affront to Comstock, and in his eyes, the most blasphemous, egregious, and unforgivable act that Bennett had ever performed.[19]

AN OPEN LETTER TO JESUS CHRIST

D. M. Bennett's *An Open Letter to Jesus Christ* was first published in the November 1875 issue of the *Truth Seeker* and subsequently printed in booklet form. It is doubtful the editor had any fear of being arrested for blasphemy in New York in 1875. There were, however, blasphemy laws still on the books in some states, New Jersey among them, and the "crime" remained punishable in several states well into the twentieth century. (In New York the last prosecution for blasphemy was in 1811.) Nevertheless, Bennett had to be aware that his letter would be considered one of, if not *the*, most heretical documents ever published in America. *An Open Letter to Jesus Christ* was a facetiously written theological tract with a series of over two hundred questions that he posed "To His Excellency, Immanuel J. Christ, other-wise called 'Prince of Peace,' 'Sun of Righteous-ness,' 'Lion of the Tribe of Judah,'

'Wonderful,' 'Counsellor,' 'The Messiah,' 'The Redeemer,' 'The Sav-
iour,' 'The Bridegroom,' 'The Lamb of God,' 'Captain of Our Salvation,' 'Son of God,' 'Son of Man,' etc. etc."[20]

Bennett begins his letter by confessing that he used to pray four
or five times a day, but because his appeals were never answered he
discontinued the practice more than twenty-five years earlier. He
did not wish to be "impertinent," but since two of America's most
popular evangelists (Dwight Moody and Ira Sankey) were currently
appearing at the skating rink in Brooklyn and scheduled soon at
the Hippodrome, Gilmore's Concert Garden, and a local beer
saloon, he felt it was an appropriate time.[21]

The letter begins chronologically; Bennett asks questions
regarding Christ's infancy and childhood: "How is it that the
'Evangelists,' who are said to have been divinely delegated to
write your life and teachings, should have been so silent in reference to this interesting portion of your existence? Were these
items purposely suppressed, or was it simply accidental?" As to
how Jesus was "begotten," Bennett asks: "Was your mother psy-
chologized or mesmerized, or otherwise rendered insensible, or
did she retain her consciousness?" Did love have anything to do
in the "transaction" and "was it an example of free-love"? Christ's
school days were of special interest and the editor was curious to
know if Jesus Christ liked studying or if he ever skipped school.
He asks Christ about the "carpenter business" and if he used his
supernatural powers to stretch boards, etc., for his "stepfather
when he made them too short." He wonders if it was a good trade
and *why* he quit. "Did you like preaching and performing miracles better? Have you ever doubted whether your first miracle
changing water into wine was well advised," since the wedding
guests "were already drunk"? The editor inquires about Christ's
and his father's (God) relationship with the devil, asking:

> Did it please your loving Father better that you should die, than
> his old enemy and creature, the Devil? What was the Devil ever
> made for? Was it not the greatest mistake, the greatest folly that
> was ever committed? Why is it you still suffer him to live? Could
> your sixty thousand clergymen in this country get along without

a devil? Is there not really a tacit, secret, understanding—a partnership in fact—between the Devil, your Father and yourself? Were those Devils that you sent into the swine the same kind as the seven Devils which you extracted from Mary Magdalene? What was the size of those seven Devils? Where did they enter, and where did they make their exit?

Is not all this business devilish strange anyway? Really, after all, considering how much the Devil has done towards carrying out the divine plan concocted by your father and yourself; how much he has done for the human race by introducing education, science, inventions, innovations, and Freethought, while your clergymen and your church have been doing all they could to keep them out, is he not after all, a pretty good fellow?[22]

As the letter progresses, Bennett's questions become more pointed. He refers to Christianity as the "youngest mythology" and asks if Christ considers it "wholly a plagiarism." Regarding all mythologies, man-made gods, senseless creeds, and superstitions: "Are not Truth, Science, Reason, Fraternal Love and Human Brotherhood vastly superior to all these?" He wonders if Christ participated in the Crusades or approved of the "Holy Inquisition" and asks, "Has not the religion called after your name caused more bloodshed, more persecution, and more suffering than all the other religions of the world?" He asks Christ,

Have you been mindful of the villainous popes . . . [and] clergymen who have been guilty of dark and damning crimes and debaucheries? How did you like John XXIII in the fifteenth century, who was proved to have been guilty of seventy different kinds of crimes, among which were sodomy, simony, rape, incest and murder, and having illicit intercourse with over three hundred nuns? Do you not remember Alexander the Sixth . . . guilty of incest . . . who seduced his own daughter . . . who was the father of many illegitimate children, and reeked in the most abominable crimes, and among the rest murder? Was John XII, in the tenth century a favorite of yours, who was an unscrupulous libertine, gambler, debauchee and murderer, and who turned the Vatican into a brothel?[23]

Bennett concludes his interrogatories with the summation:

> Finally, as you now view the field, the past, the present and the
> future, would it not, in your opinion, be better to wipe out from
> the face of the earth all the priestcraft, superstition, sectari-
> anism, falsehood, all the absurdities and monstrosities which
> have so preyed upon mankind, and to inaugurate an era of
> truth, reason, common sense, science, education, simplicity,
> fraternity and humanity; discarding false gods, base devils, use-
> less saviors and degrading creeds, and to devote our time and
> attention to the improvement of this world and to the happi-
> ness of the human race?[24]

THE FIRES OF THE INQUISITION

In 1875 one of Bennett's fellow freethought publishers, John A.
Lant, was arrested for selling his *Toledo Sun* periodical, which contained Ingersoll's *Oration of the Gods*, a lecture Bennett had also previously reprinted and sold. The editor defended Lant in the pages
of the *Truth Seeker* in an article titled "Sectarian Intolerance":

> This, to make the best of it, is a piece of petty Christian tyranny,
> in this boasted land of freedom, and in view of the far greater
> obscenity of the Beecher adultery case, which for months filled
> most of the papers in the country, is simply contemptible. The
> United States authorities must have little to occupy their atten-
> tion and the pious Mr. Comstock must be spoiling for a fight to
> meddle with such small fry. Why does he not attack *The Herald,
> The Sun* or *The Graphic*?
>   Are they too powerful, and is it safer to pounce upon a
> defenseless, impoverished, struggling little sheet? Are the
> morals of the people, the welfare of society or the peace of the
> government endangered by the existence of such a paper?[25]

In 1876, amid the swelling climate of media persecution, the
Truth Seeker became a weekly, and Bennett published his first
book, *The World's Sages, Infidels, and Thinkers*. That summer,

Morris Altman, his close friend and generous benefactor, died unexpectedly. Altman supported Bennett financially since he relocated to New York. George Macdonald described Altman as strikingly handsome and fondly remembered the dapper Jewish merchant who "wore his clothes and his high hat so well, and flashed across his pleasant smile to us printers . . . with a bow as polite as he could have made anywhere." An innovative and humanitarian employer, Altman provided seats for his female clerks, shortened their hours, and closed his Sixth Avenue store early on Saturdays. Bennett was stunned at his friend's death at the age of thirty-nine and wrote, "He was a warm friend of the *Truth Seeker*, and more than once has he rendered us aid in the time of need."[26]

Later that centennial year, Bennett hired Hanna Josephine McNellis to sell subscriptions and contract for advertisements in the periodical. In an uncharacteristic notice in the *Truth Seeker*, the editor introduced her to the readers and trusted that "she will be generously received by those upon whom she may call." Unfortunately, she soon failed at her initial position (that he created for her), and also at proofreading, copyholding, and editing anecdotes. And while Eugene Macdonald found Miss McNellis to be utterly useless, Bennett admittedly enjoyed her "unusually agreeable" company. Nevertheless, Mrs. Bennett became unhappy with the situation, so the editor eventually discharged the woman.[27]

Although still plagued by financial problems, mostly caused by lack of subscriptions, Bennett began earning substantial revenue from the sale of books and tracts. Postal regulations allowed publishers to devote entire papers to advertising their own books, tracts, and pamphlets. Besides his own articles, Bennett printed submissions like *How Do Marsupials Propagate Their Kind?* written by A. B. Bradford, a former clergyman. Bennett wisely took advantage of the postal policy and became less concerned about increasing subscriptions. Nor did he worry about Comstock, who, under government authority, was "peeping" into the public's mail.[28]

In the mid-1870s, Comstock turned his attention to literature containing information on the prevention of conception or birth (the phrase *birth control* did not exist), which he declared "obscene." The vice hunter classified birth control advocates as "abortionists." One of Comstock's first victims was Dr. Edward Bliss Foote who was perhaps the most successful author-publisher of medical books and pamphlets in America. His *Medical Common Sense* volume sold more than a quarter million copies. Dr. Foote believed medical knowledge should be available to the masses and not monopolized by elite professionals and medical societies. "The time has come when scientific truth must cease to be the property of the few—when it must be woven into the common life of the world" was the motto of his *Health Monthly* periodical. Dr. Foote and other medical dissenters annoyed the country's powerful traditional medical profession that felt threatened and affiliated itself with the government in an effort to obtain control over the renegade and flourishing "medical freedom" movement.[29]

In the nineteenth century, a common belief was that magnetism played a key role in sexuality. Linking magnetism and electricity to sexuality did not seem to be an outlandish theory in 1876, the same year that Alexander Graham Bell transmitted words by using his "electric telephone." Dr. Foote theorized that men and women had magnetic auras, and sexual attraction was essentially an electric force similar to the attraction of magnetic poles. He postulated that sexual intercourse was an electrical procedure and varied between people according to their similarity or charge. He found that interaction between the penis shaft's acidic sheath of skin and the alkaline vagina created electricity. The electricity caused by this interaction produced a pleasurable stimulation and tingled the nerves of the genitalia. In his "Philosophy of Sexual Intercourse," Foote expounds that intercourse created "frictional," static electricity when body parts rubbed together. It was, he explained, like a glass rod or tube being rubbed with fur, "but no part of the animal organization is so susceptible to this influence as the glans-penis of the male and the clitoris of the female."[30]

Dr. Foote was a registered physician in the state of New York and a respected member in medical societies. Nevertheless, he was "eclectic" in his own medical practice and fought for the rights of Christian Scientists, magnetic healers, and other unorthodox practitioners. Dr. Foote used only botanical medicines and sometimes diagnosed patients with the aid of phrenology. He opposed the use of mineral medicines, mercury compounds, and dubious nostrum cure-alls. Dr. Foote was a pioneer in promoting birth control and invented the first cervical cap. His son Dr. E. B. Foote Jr., also a birth control advocate, coined the term *contraception*. The two doctors were responsible for laying the foundation for the birth control movement in the twentieth century.[31]

As busy as Dr. Foote was with his writing, publishing, and thriving medical practice at his three-story Lexington Avenue office, he found time to devote to the freethought movement. He was a principal member of numerous liberal and political organizations. He was a women's rights advocate and sent a check for $25 to Susan B. Anthony when she was fined $100 for voting. He contributed time and money in opposition to the Comstock Laws when they were first presented. When Bennett moved the *Truth Seeker* to New York, Dr. Foote provided monetary support for the publication and they became close friends. The orthodox medical establishment, however, did not approve of Dr. Foote's provocative theories regarding eugenics, birth control, and human sexuality. Moreover, the frank descriptive language he used in his medical books was highly offensive to bluenoses like Anthony Comstock. Furthermore, the fact that he initially opposed the Comstock obscenity legislation was the reason for the moralist's retaliation. After Comstock arrested the venerable homeopathic physician, Bennett defended his friend in the January 29, 1876, issue of the *Truth Seeker*:

> This notorious individual [Comstock] has placed himself beneath the contempt of honest and good men; but unfortunately he is vested with power from government to annoy men much his superior. We understand he has caused the arrest of

> Dr. E. B. Foote, author of *Plain Home Talk and Medical Common Sense*, than whom there is not a finer man in this city. The charge is Comstock's favorite one, obscenity, and is based on the language used in that most valuable medical work in treating physiology and the diseases the human frame is liable to. This man Comstock will keep fooling around until by and by he "wakes up the wrong passenger."[32]

Dr. Foote was convicted of violation of the Comstock Laws and was fined $3,500. (Anthony Comstock's favorite judge, Charles L. Benedict, presided.) The case compelled Dr. Foote and others to form the National Defense Association. The organization's goal was to investigate questionable federal and state Comstock Laws prosecutions and defend those who were "unjustly assailed by the enemies of free speech and free press." Dr. Foote served as secretary, and Albert L. Rawson, artist and biblical scholar, was president. John P. Jewett (Harriet Beecher Stowe's publisher) served as vice president.[33]

The following year Comstock arrested Ezra Heywood, the Boston publisher and notorious free-love advocate. Heywood had a strict Calvinistic theological background and intended to become a minister. However, his Christian faith was shattered after reading William Lloyd Garrison's antislavery periodical, the *Liberator*, and learning that the majority of the nation's clergy were hostile to reforms, including the antislavery movement. Heywood graduated from Brown University in 1856 and poured his energy into abolitionism and labor reform. In 1867 he organized the first Labor Reform League and later published the *Word*, a periodical devoted to his ideas regarding labor reform, women's rights, marriage, interest, taxes, tariffs, profits, war, and monopolies. Ezra Heywood was a remarkable and scholarly man—in many respects, one of the most advanced men of his time.[34]

Anthony Comstock detested Ezra Heywood's anarchistic social and sexual ideas. Using a fictitious name, Comstock sent a letter requesting copies of Heywood's *Cupid's Yokes* and Trall's *Sexual Physiology*. Both pamphlets were sold in the *Truth Seeker*. (*Cupid's Yokes* sold over twenty thousand copies!) After receiving the requested material in the mail, Comstock traveled to Boston where

Heywood was scheduled to give an address at a free-love convention. While sitting among the audience where he saw "lust in every face," Comstock first listened to a speech by Mrs. Angela Heywood—the "foulest address" he ever heard. "It was too vile; I had to go out." But he soon returned to the hall because "every manly instinct cried out against my cowardly turning my back on this horde of lusters." He sat there and listened to the "offensive tirade against common decency" with occasional references to "that Comstock." "You would have thought he [Heywood] was the champion of some majestic cause instead of a mob of free-lusters," the vice hunter wrote in his book *Traps for the Young*. After listening to the "stream of filth" as long as he could, the crusader decided to use the arrest warrant he carried. Comstock followed Heywood as he left the stage and proceeded to grab the slender, forty-eight-year-old writer by the neck, hustling him down a flight of stairs, into a waiting carriage—off to the Charles Street Jail.[35]

Ezra Heywood's arrest caused indignation among freethinkers, members of the press, and ordinary Americans, who were beginning to wonder about the methods used by the nation's self-appointed arbiter of morals. Jurists had questioned the constitutionality of the Comstock Laws from their inception in 1873, and now a growing number of concerned citizens were interested in how the vice hunter went about his mission. The country's press finally began printing inquiring editorials about the Post Office Department's special agent. The *New York Sun* expressed what many thinking Americans were wondering:

> Mr. Anthony Comstock has been conspicuous for several years past as a conservator of public morals, in the way of preventing the transmission of immoral matter through the mails. Now we should like to be informed how Mr. Comstock executes his delicate and difficult official duty. How does he find out what envelopes contain before he breaks the envelopes open? Who authorizes him to break open letters and sealed packages on which the postage has been paid? And who assists him in it? The work in which Mr. Comstock is engaged has been regarded by our religious teachers with much favor.

Some, however, have doubts whether the law under which he acts is in harmony with our Constitution and theory of government. They think that it is far from the purpose for which the Government of the United States was established to supervise the correspondence of citizens and see that it is not immoral. They regard his mode of proceeding as an evil or objectionable way of doing good. If Mr. Comstock himself would explain, fully and in detail, his whole system of operations then people could make up their minds with a better understanding of the subject. Let him tell how his plans are executed without infringing upon the secrecy of the mails.[36]

THE WRONG PASSENGER

A little after the noon hour on Monday, November 12, 1877, while preparing matter for the *Truth Seeker*, Bennett learned firsthand about the special agent's modus operandi. Comstock, accompanied by a deputy US marshal, entered the *Truth Seeker* office at 141 Eighth Street in lower Manhattan with a warrant for the arrest of the fifty-eight-year-old publisher.[37]

The two "obscene" tracts that caused Bennett's arrest were his *An Open Letter to Jesus Christ* and Arthur B. Bradford's *How Do Marsupials Propagate Their Kind?* a scientific article originally intended for *Popular Science Monthly*. Bradford, a former Presbyterian minister, was a direct descendant of Governor Bradford of the Plymouth Colony and one of the first clergymen to leave the church over slavery. His farm in Enon Valley, Pennsylvania, served as an Underground Railroad station for runaway slaves. President Lincoln appointed Bradford consul to China during the Civil War. Arthur Bradford's "innocent little possum tract," as he called it, was published in the *Truth Seeker* on January 15, 1876.[38]

After showing Bennett the two objectionable articles, Comstock demanded all copies on the premises. The editor submitted the tracts to Comstock, who displayed a package mailed to a person by the name of S. Bender, Squan Village, New Jersey. Bennett was also shown a registered letter receipt for the money that accompanied the order filled and signed in the *Truth Seeker* office. Bennett asked "whether the party to whom the tracts were addressed was a real party and he had opened his package, or a bogus party, and the letter ordering the tracts a mere decoy letter, such as he [Comstock] had used on other occasions." Comstock acknowledged it was a decoy letter that he wrote using an assumed name. On the way to the post office for his arraignment, Bennett asked, "Why it was, if he was so anxious to prohibit the circulation of obscene literature, that he did not indict the Bible Society?" The editor told him the Bible contained more "obscenity than any other publication" he knew of. He went on to give the purity crusader a half dozen or more "obscene" scenarios from the good book, such as Abraham and his concubine, David and Bathsheba and his other wives, the adultery of Absalom and his father's concubine, Solomon with his seven hundred wives, and so on. Comstock evaded the inquiries and said "some ladies near us might hear our remarks, thus virtually confessing that the persons and subjects named were indecent."[39]

Anthony Comstock also recorded the details of the arrest in the New York Society for the Suppression of Vice blotter. The document is filled with the vice hunter's contempt for the elderly publisher:

ALIASES: *The Truth Seeker*, RELIGION: Infidel, EDUCATION: Common, OCCUPATION: Publisher of Blasphemous & Infidel works, OFFENSE: Obscene matter through the Mail, INVENTORY OF STOCK SEIZED: Vile tracts, REMARKS: Publishes most horrible & obscene blasphemies. Also indecent tracts that purport to be Scientific. Also quack medical works . . . He is everything vile in Blasphemy & Infidelism. His idea of liberty is to do and say as he pleases without regard to the rights, morals or liberties of others.[40]

Bennett's arrest was no surprise. He published the *Truth Seeker* and sold freethought books in lower Manhattan for nearly four years under the noses of Comstock and the wealthy and powerful members of the New York Society for the Suppression of Vice.

The editor was in the vanguard of critics who attacked the society, but after his arrest, it became personal. Anthony Comstock finally "woke up the wrong passenger."[41]

Dr. Foote (the first of tens of thousands of libertarian supporters) posted Bennett's $1,500 bail. The editor chronicled his own arrest in a November 1877 article, "It Has Come at Last!" "The charge is ostensibly 'obscenity,'" he told readers, "but the real offense is that I presume to utter sentiments and opinions in opposition to the views entertained by the Christian Church."[42]

While awaiting his preliminary examination (postponed several times), the editor began an aggressive attack on Comstock and the society. The first assault was a white-hot exhaustive editorial titled "American Liberty: Is It a Sham?" Bennett addressed the vice hunter's offenses and voiced his opinion of the section on the Comstock Law restricting any mention of birth control information. He felt the law was vaguely designed and unconstitutional:

> There is a certain intelligent and virtuous class of community who believe there is such a thing as overpopulation and that some people have too many children—more than is for their good and more than they are able to properly take care of—and they believe it is perfectly right to take means to prevent such too rapid increase of children—not by producing abortions or infant-killing, but simply by using such legitimate and rational means as will control the matter and place it within the power of the mother, in part at least to govern the number of children she shall bear. There are many people who believe that information bearing upon this subject is very necessary and should be placed before the wives and mothers of our country. This Comstock Law struck a heavy blow at everything of this kind.[43]

Anthony Comstock's attack on freedom of speech was causing indignation and his persecution of Bennett and Heywood was creating a furor among freethinkers. It also increased the circulation of the *Truth Seeker*. In 1877 Bennett realized his goal and boasted the weekly would be increased to sixteen pages and "be the largest Liberal paper published in the world, having one third more reading matter than any similar journal published in Europe or America."[44]

Letters of sympathy came pouring in, and a defense fund was initiated. Bennett adopted a "we shall see what we shall see" attitude about the repetitive court postponements. He believed if the case came before a judge, Robert Ingersoll would defend him, and a conviction would be improbable. One of the reasons for the delay was that Comstock did not believe his case was strong enough, and he needed additional time to amend the complaint. Comstock planned to add another book, Dr. Trall's *Sexual Physiology* to the others Bennett sent through the mail. The vice hunter ignored or was ignorant of the fact that Dr. Trall's popular book had been republished for fifteen years, and respectable booksellers throughout the country sold forty thousand copies to inquisitive citizens.[45]

Bennett began a spirited campaign against postal legislation with a petition for the repeal of the Comstock Laws. With the impressive first signature of Robert Ingersoll, the petition soon had fifty thousand signatures. The editor and the petition were also getting notice in the New York press, which occasionally printed letters to the editor favoring Bennett. These complimentary letters routinely included a disparaging editorial comment. A letter to the *New York Tribune* with the heading "Elder Evans in a Tantrum" caused a stir among freethinkers and Shakers. It was from Frederick W. Evans, a prominent Shaker spokesman who periodically defended his fellow editor:

To the Editor of the *Tribune*:

Why do you great and powerful editors allow the God in the Constitution party to persecute unopposed D. M. Bennett, editor of the *Truth Seeker*? Are there any people more anxious to protect the youth of our nation from the corrupting influence of obscene publications than the Shakers? Yet, as my soul liveth, I would rather have the repeal of all laws for the suppression of vile publications than this robbing of the United States mail, these pious, lying, decoy letters, this interference with, and suppression of, free opinion on theological matters, where the orthodox infidel is just as good a man or woman as the orthodox Christian, as good an American citizen, and a thousand times more safe with human liberty in his custody. What pranks before high heaven are those that are being played in the name of religion, when men who are like Jefferson, Franklin, and Paine—founders of our Government—are being persecuted by officers of the Government which the founders gave their lives to establish.

—F. W. Evans
Mount Lebanon, December 27, 1877[46]

To the Editor of the *Tribune*, Sir:

Why add the expressive mark of contempt—the word "tantrum"—to my article, which I thank you for publishing, not for stigmatizing? Are not "the clergy a source of danger to the American Republic?" In its palmy days, The Tribune was not hand in hand with the clergy, but a pretty free-thinker. Has Samson fallen into the hands of the Philistines? If so, I regret it.

Twenty-five years ago I was in a "tantrum" about Spiritualism. To-day my prediction that "henceforth it is an American institution" is fulfilled. It is an institution of Christendom—of the world. . . .

I was in a "tantrum" about slavery. It cost us something to abolish it! I predict as bloody a war about Church and State theology as we have had about slavery. No danger—that is the battle cry. There was no danger about the "Comstock laws" to suppress infidelity until they were passed and doing their inquisitorial work. What have you Shakers to do about it? You are not in danger from obscenity or infidelity—blasphemy. We owe our liberty of conscience—our existence as an order to a secular government. We dread the Peace of Warsaw; what American citizens can lie quietly in jails and the editors go not into "tantrums" about it. With the Bible in public schools, chaplains in government service, all church property—except that of sixty communities of Shakers—untaxed, and Governmental subsidies to theological institutions, do you ask, "What aileth thee?"

—F. W. Evans
Mt. Lebanon, N.Y. Dec. 31, 1877[47]

The *Tribune*'s readers likely found the Shaker elder's defense of a notorious infidel peculiar. However, Evans, whose autobiography was published in the *Atlantic Monthly* in 1869, was a radical Shaker leader. As the editor of the *Shaker and Shakeress*, Evans advocated land reform, the abolition of debtor prisons, and the delivery of mail on the Sabbath. In 1873 he published an article calling for the separation of church and state written by A. B. Bradford, the author of the "criminal" *How Do Marsupials Propagate Their Kind?* Evans also publicly urged Robert Ingersoll to run for president.[48]

On January 5, 1878, Bennett learned from his attorney, Abram Wakeman, that the case had been dismissed. Wakeman was a respected lawyer and, ironically, the former postmaster general of New York. It was not entirely Wakeman's effort in the editor's behalf that got the case removed from judicial consideration. Colonel Ingersoll came to the rescue by traveling to Washington, DC, where he influenced the authorities to have the case dismissed. "I have very little respect for those men who endeavor to put down vice by lying," Ingersoll said, "and very little respect for a society that would keep in its employ such a *leprous agent.*"[49]

SAINT ANTHONY

Immediately after the dismissal of his case, Bennett turned up the heat on the Comstock Laws and the vice hunter. The entire January 19, 1878, issue of the *Truth Seeker* was devoted to anti-censorship, Comstock, his arrests, and his explanation of the nebulous Comstock Laws. Even the front page was altered to accommodate the history of the statutes. The weekly's four-column format that normally included "Notes and Clippings" and "Events of the Week" was changed to a unique three-column page. In an article titled "Comstock's Latest Exploits," Bennett chronicled a bungled undercover assignment by Joseph Britton, one of Comstock's "minions." While Britton was acting as an informer in Connecticut, the editor stated Comstock's "agent provocateur . . . played his game almost too well."[50]

Bennett reported that while Britton was staying in a New Canaan hotel, he drank, visited lewd characters including prostitutes, acted in a riotous manner, committed conspiracy, and "hired a horse and carriage and driven twice as far as he had reported and committed other acts not necessary to mention." After Britton was arrested for this behavior, Comstock came to his rescue, brandishing his pistol and loudly shouting, "I am an officer of the United States; this young man is in my charge and I will shoot the first man dead who attempts to take him from my custody!" Comstock is not an officer of the United States, Bennett asserted, "but simply a spy and informer, and he committed a most flagrant outrage in forcibly taking his accomplice from the hands of an officer, for which he deserves appropriate punishment."[51]

As a special agent (later an inspector of the US Post Office), Anthony Comstock was never timid about his authority and jurisdiction. One of his associates liked to tell a story that was illustrative of the vice hunter's braggadocio. While Comstock was swaggering across lower Broadway one rainy day, he was nearly run over by a horse-drawn wagon. Enraged, he pulled out his official US Post Office badge and waved it beneath the horse's nose: "Don't you know who I am? I'm Anthony Comstock!" The horse happened to be hitched to a mail wagon and, theoretically, a subordinate. The animal was not the only postal "employee" to experience the vice hunter's wrath; numerous mail carriers and clerks had to accommodate and withstand admonishment from this huffy superior.[52]

In March 1878 Anthony Comstock went to Washington accompanied by Samuel Colgate, his benefactor and the president of the New York Society for the Suppression of Vice. A hearing before the House Committee on the revision of the Comstock Laws was being held. Although Comstock was considered a dangerous nuisance to many Americans, Christian leaders and laymen were in strong support of their religious special agent. The solitary vice hunter's melodramatic account appears in his book *Frauds Exposed*:

Everything looked black. I was alone. As I strolled through the vestibule and rotunda of the Capitol, the Senate Chamber, and Representatives Hall, I found on each Congressman's desk a copy of the vile paper [the *Truth Seeker*], of which eight pages were devoted to a pretended account of the *"Life and Crimes of Anthony Comstock."* These papers were scattered everywhere. The Committee room was filled with them. As I entered the Committee room, I found it crowded with long-haired men and short-haired women, there to send obscene publications, abortion implements, and other incentives to crime by repealing the laws. I heard their hiss, their looks of derision and contempt.[53]

Anthony Comstock's pious plea on behalf of the country's children, who he claimed were ruined by "the most demoralizing articles," was effective. That, together with his assertion that some of the names were forged on the petitions, sealed the deal and persuaded the committee to unanimously reject any repeal or change in the laws. According to Bennett, the special agent used intimidation, forcing some of the petition signers to retract their authorization. Comstock expressed his disdain for D. M. Bennett and Ezra Heywood, writing, "And these monsters—these devil-men, or men-devils—caught in this cursed traffic, and prosecuted legally, and legally placed where they cannot longer strike their deadly fangs into the vitals of the youth, are made martyrs of, and the so-called 'liberals' of this land rally to their defence! and, at the beck and call of this band of ex-convicts and co-conspirators, a combined effort is made to repeal these laws!"[54]

Bennett continued to report Comstock's activities and often reprinted other publications' articles critical of him in the *Truth Seeker*. Comstock tried to suppress the weekly by visiting the printing shop and the American News Agency, the *Truth Seeker's* distributor. On several occasions he threatened the printers and promised prosecution if Bennett's "vile sheet" was not discontinued. Bennett described the society's official seal that embellished its stationery, writing, an unfortunate handcuffed victim is, by a minion of the law, being thrust into a dungeon, while Saint Anthony is making a bonfire of books and pamphlets, supposed to be *Truth Seekers, Open Letters*, scientific tracts on Marsupials, etc. One can easily imagine that around the benign but badly scarred face of the good Anthony, like his illustrious predecessor, Torquemada of the fifteenth century, hovers a wish that he could thrust the victim in the flames, as well as his books.[55]

After learning that Comstock was obtaining copies of the *Truth Seeker*, Bennett predicted that another arrest was imminent; a libel suit was pending. The editor challenged Comstock, writing, "Anthony of course knows where we are. . . . If we are forced there to defend a libel suit brought by Anthony Comstock we think we shall be able to prove an amount of guilt and black-hearted villainy against him that will damn his memory forever. . . . We will inform Anthony that we shall not run away. We are still and shall be at 141 Eighth Street."[56]

Comstock was not the only enemy aware of Bennett's Manhattan street address. In the spring of 1878, the editor reported that a group of out-of-town clergymen was spotted standing across the street from the publication's office. The "white-cravated gentlemen" were seen pointing with their canes at the office sign and shaking "their sanctimonious heads, doubtless with the full conviction that *The Truth Seeker* is the wickedest paper in the world, and that it ought not to be suffered to exist." Many of America's clergy prayed that the paper's "steady light" would be extinguished, Bennett reminded readers. "We hope there are large numbers of the clergy who will go down to their graves before *The Truth Seeker* shall expire."[57]

The petition for the repeal of the Comstock Laws came in front of the House Committee in May and June, and was believed by the *Tribune* and other newspapers to have a good chance of passing. Unfortunately, the bill to repeal the Comstock Laws on the grounds of its being unconstitutional, and in Bennett's opinion, often executed in a "tyrannical and unjust manner," was reversed—the laws stood in place, unmodified. The petition committee continued its efforts with voluminous briefs prepared by T. B. Wakeman, who was determined to prove that the US Post Office did not have the authority it conferred on Comstock.[58]

Some who opposed censorship questioned Comstock and his fellow moralists' assertion that "obscenity" corrupted those who view it. If it did, they argued, it meant that a person like Comstock, who saw the contents of countless examples of obscenity with his own eyes, had to be totally depraved. Or was the special agent so special in the entire world that all the unspeakable material that he alone viewed had no effect? In other words, someone quipped, "He could have his cake and suppress it, too?"[59]

"If the possession of this kind of demoralizing nastiness is sufficient to send a person to prison," Bennett argued in the *Truth Seeker*, "it would seem most fitting that those two men [Comstock and Britton] should spend the balance of their lives in a dungeon. There are probably no two individuals who can be better spared than this pair of 'foul birds' who revel in the vilest filth to be found in the country." The editor was not alone in this line of thought—and if they were right, it meant that Comstock and Britton both had lost their souls.[60]

Early that summer, Ezra Heywood was convicted for sending a copy of his twenty-six-page pamphlet *Cupid's Yokes* through the mail. After Heywood was fined $100 and sentenced to two years' imprisonment and hard labor in Dedham Jail, Bennett immediately issued a petition for his pardon. The editor was also busy that summer promoting his new *Champions of the Church, Their Crimes and Persecutions*. The four-pound book included a one-hundred-twenty-page chapter he defiantly issued in a booklet *Anthony Comstock, His Career of Cruelty and Crime*.[61]

In July Bennett sent copies to Samuel Colgate and the officers of the New York Society for the Suppression of Vice. The executives of the "Vice Society," as he labeled the organization, were some of New York's—perhaps the world's—most powerful men. In addition to Samuel Colgate, the soap tycoon, the NYSSV executive committee included Alfred S. Barnes and Birdseye Blakeman, publishing magnates, and John M. Cornell and Kiliaen Van

Rensselaer, both descendants of elite families. Other founding members were William E. Dodge Jr., the heir to an immense mining and lumbering fortune, and J. Pierpont Morgan, the wealthy financier. He also mailed the pamphlet to Anthony Comstock, the society's chief enforcer who described himself as only a humble "weeder in God's garden" and who complained in the *North American Review* that he had "neither money nor influential friends." Bennett addressed the pamphlet to the crusader's numerous aliases—a daring act of provocation that the editor knew would infuriate the vindictive vice hunter.[62]

NOTES

"purity and virtue.": D. M. Bennett (accredited)

1. "how capitoll soever.": p. 259. Leonard W. Levy, *Blasphemy: Verbal Offense against the Sacred; From Moses to Salman Rusdie.* Alfred A. Knopf (N.Y. 1993).

2. Ibid. "impurities and debaucheries.": Province Laws, 1711–1712, Quoted from Mary Lamonica, *The Liberty to Argue Freely: Nineteenth-Century Obscenity Prosecutions and the Emergence of Modern Libertarian Free Speech Discourse.* Unpublished.

3. "and profane libel.": Levy p. 414.

4. "while he lives.": Ibid. p. 419. "of the Transcendentalists.": Ibid. "Nonsense and Hypocrisy": Common Sense.

5. Ibid.

6. "the greatest magistrate.": Ibid. p. 413. "denial of God.": Ibid. p. 420.

7. "and doting biases.": Ibid. p. 419. "upon my mind.": Ibid. p. 423.

8. Garrison praise: Ibid. p. 419. "upon theological subjects.": WSIT.

9. Stein. Levy. "of the offense.": Congressional Globe, 38th Congress, 2nd Session (S. 390), cited in Lamonica.

10. "to public morals.": cited in Lamonica.

11. Broun and Leech. AC, DMB 1878 pp. 1009–1119. "is evil reading.": quoted in Lamonica.

In the nineteenth century, the Young Men's Christian Association—founded by evangelicals in England—was an influential international movement. With a mission to save souls, the YMCA provided more than one million Bibles to soldiers during the Civil War. After the war, the YMCA continued to flourish and acquire political clout.

The New York association's purpose was fourfold: "The improvement of the Spiritual, mental, social and physical condition of young men." www.ymca.net.

Christian organizations like the Salvation Army, Sunday School movement, and the YMCA were allied in the revival of righteousness in the post–Civil War period. This new "Puritanism," H. L. Mencken declared, "is not ascetic but militant. Its aim is not to lift up saints, but to knock down sinners." Broun and Leech, p. 76.

12. "costs of court.": Bennett, *Anthony Comstock: His Career of Cruelty and Crime.* pp. 1014–17.

13. Ezra Heywood, *Cupid's Yokes: or, The Binding Forces of Conjugal Life. An Essay to Consider Some Moral and Physiological Phases of LOVE AND MARRIAGE, Wherein Is Asserted the Natural Right and Necessity of SEXUAL SELF-GOVERNMENT.*

14. "of the sewer.": Broun and Leech. "but God disposes.": Comstock, *Frauds Exposed.*

Ulysses S. Grant also admired Anthony Comstock's favorite Christian maxim. The president who carelessly signed the Comstock acts into law prefaced his autobiography writing: "'Man proposes and God disposes.' There are but few important events in the affairs of men brought about by their own choice."

Personal Memoirs, Ulysses S. Grant (2 vols., New York, 1885–1886).

Despite his signing of the Comstock Laws, President Grant was against religion in the classroom. In a speech on Sept. 30, 1875, he stated: "Resolve that neither the State nor the nation shall support institutions of learning other than those sufficient to afford to every child the opportunity of good common school education, unmixed with sectarian, pagan, or atheistic dogmas. Leave the matter of religion to the family altar, the church, and the private school supported entirely by private contributions. Keep the church and state forever separate." Grant opposed teaching religion in public schools and public aid for sectarian schools. Furthermore, in a message to Congress on December 7, 1875, Grant recommended the taxation of church property. Many of the nation's most popular newspapers—except for the *Catholic World*—approved of Grant's proposal. Jean Edward Smith, *Grant* (Simon & Schuster, N.Y. 2001).

15. Broun and Leech.

16. Ibid. "Saint Anthony.": TS.

17. Broun and Leech. "right to interfere.": *And The Truth Shall Make You Free: A Speech on the Principles of Social Freedom*. Victoria Woodhull. Nov. 20, 1871.

18. Texas incident: GM v. 1 p. 193. KKK: TS Dec. 1, 1877. Infidels horsewhipped: GM.

19. Comstock's Diaries.

20. *An Open Letter to Jesus Christ*: TS Nov. 1, 1875.

21. Ibid.

Dwight Lyman Moody and Ira D. Sankey were the late nineteenth century's most popular American evangelists. The duo toured extensively in the United States and Great Britain and founded seminary schools and the Chicago Bible Institute. EB.

22. Ibid.

23. Ibid.

24. Ibid.

25. TS Aug. 15, 1875.

26. "have made anywhere.": GM. "time of need.": Altman obituary: TS July 15, 1876.

27. "unusually agreeable.": TS Nov. 22, 1879.

28. GM.

29. Hal D. Sears, *The Sex Radicals: Free Love in High Victorian America*.

30. Ibid.

31. Ibid.

32. Ibid. "the wrong passenger.": TS Jan. 29, 1876.

33. GM. Sears.

34. Blatt. GM.

35. Broun and Leech.

36. TS Jan. 6, 1877 *N.Y. Sun* reprint.

37. TS Nov. 17, 1877.

38. Ibid. "little possum tract.": TS Feb 9, 1878.

39. TS Nov. 17, 1877.

40. NYSSV arrest blotter.

41. TS Nov. 17, 1877.

42. TS Jan. 29, 1876.

43. TS Nov. 17, 1877.

44. TS Nov. 24, 1877.

45. TS Dec. 8, 1877.

46. TS Dec. 22, 1877. "lives to establish.": TS Jan. 19, 1878.

47. "'What aileth thee?": TS Jan. 19, 1878.

48. TS Jan. 19, 1878.

49. TS Jan. 5, 1878.

50. TS July 6, 1878.

51. TS Jan. 19, 1878.

Joseph Britton was Anthony Comstock's first choice as his assistant. Britton's overzealous methods employed while making arrests often embarrassed Comstock and damaged the SSV's reputation. After being accused of cruelty and misfeasance numerous times, Britton was eventually dismissed by his "superior."

Broun and Leech pp. 190–91.

52. Broun and Leech p. 145.

53. Ibid.

54. Comstock, *Frauds Exposed*.

55. TS April 27, 1878.

56. TS May 11, 1878.

57. Ibid.

58. TS June 8, 1878.

59. TS May 18, 1878.

60. Ibid.

61. Broun and Leech. TS July 6, 1878.

62. Ibid.

5

The Trinity

The charge is ostensibly "obscenity," but the real offense is that I presume to utter sentiments and opinions in opposition to the views entertained by the Christian Church.

—D. M. Bennett

In August 1878 the New York State Freethinkers' Association held their annual convention in Watkins Glen, New York. The association, organized only a year earlier, already had over twenty-six hundred members; it admitted members from all over the country and welcomed every shade of freethinker—materialists, Free Religionists, abolitionists, dress reformers, free-love advocates, spiritualists, orthodox ministers, and Shaker elders. Their first convention was held under a fair tent near Wolcott, New York, the previous summer. (The 1877 convention lasted four days and was possibly the largest gathering of freethinkers ever assembled in the world.) The organizers hoped to duplicate the previous year's success at Watkins Glen, a small town on the southern shores of Seneca Lake. The association chose the village because of its location and natural beauty. Watkins Glen, however, was also one of the most straitlaced and backward burgs in the state.[1]

The Who's Who of Freethought would be in attendance, and an impressive group of individuals were scheduled to speak: Frederick Douglass, the prominent abolitionist editor, was slated to speak about the liberty of thought and expression. "I prayed for twenty years but received no answer until I prayed with my legs," is a quote attributed to the former slave. "He knows what the word *liberty* means," Bennett declared. Veteran abolitionists Parker Pillsbury and the honorable Elizur Wright (1804–1885), president of the National Liberal League, as well as leading suffragists Matilda Joslyn Gage and Elizabeth Cady Stanton, would be there. Horace Seaver and J. P. Mendum of the *Boston Investigator* were among the several freethought publishers and editors attending. Representing the Shakers at Watkins Glen were Elder F. W. Evans and G. A. Lomas, editor of the *Shaker*. "This is about the only Christian body that believes in liberty of thought and speech," Bennett said about the Shakers (whom he and Mary continued to visit every five years since their apostasy over three decades earlier).[2]

A couple of weeks before the convention, the *Truth Seeker* announced Robert Ingersoll's rumored appearance at the Watkins Glen meeting and acknowledged that "Col. Ingersoll can be sure of an immense audience. The trouble will be that if it is announced in advance that he is to speak, the whole town will be thronged with an eager multitude, each of whom will desire to hear the most eloquent orator in America. The Colonel will be at home at this Convention."[3]

Robert Ingersoll would indeed have been at home at the upstate New York gathering of freethinkers. (He was born twenty-three miles north of Watkins Glen at Dresden, New York.) The Great Agnostic, however, would be conspicuously absent from the list of distinguished speakers because a few weeks earlier he and his family departed for a vacation in Europe.[4]

Two days before the convention, Bennett and some friends left New York City's summer heat to take an evening train to the cool, remote village of Watkins Glen. The convention did not start until Thursday, but they wanted to take in some of the area's natural beauty. Accompanying the editor were Professor Albert Rawson and G. L. Henderson, president and treasurer, respectively, of the National Defense Association.[5]

Albert Leighton Rawson was an artist and author who wrote numerous books including *The Divine Origin of the Holy Bible*, which he finished writing when he was only seventeen years old. Rawson was an enigmatic figure known as the Oriental Artist. He traveled extensively in the Middle East and chronicled his trips with drawings and paintings. Although Rawson sometimes only edited, coauthored, or illustrated books, he was prolific and averaged one book per year for decades. He wrote and/or illustrated books on religious history, linguistics, Middle Eastern geography, biblical works, and books about Masonic and occult orders. His diverse interests revealed his fascination with the world's religions, and he was extremely interested in the Islamic world and deeply involved in Freemasonry, Theosophy, occultism, and secret societies. D. M. Bennett was impressed with Albert Rawson's abilities and scholarship, and profiled him in his *The World's Sages, Infidels, and Thinkers*. The editor wrote about Rawson:

> While in Arabia he wore the costume of the country and walked with the guides rather than ride in the dusty train. The great Sheikh, Ali Diab Adwan, offered to give him his favorite daughter in marriage and adopt him as the "only son of the Sheikh," as a recognition of his "personal presence and manly abilities." The Arabs united in pronouncing him "worthy of being counted one among them," and voted by acclamation his adoption as an honorary member of his tribe. He is, therefore, a Diab [Wolf].[6]

The National Defense Association, a forerunner of the American Civil Liberties Union, was formed earlier that year on June 12, 1878. Its first meetings were held in Science Hall, the same building where the *Truth Seeker* was published. Three of Bennett's other closest friends, Dr. Foote Jr., Theron Leland, and Dr. Charles Winterburn, were on the organization's executive committee. The association's mission was to investigate questionable obscenity cases, sympathize with the unjustly prosecuted, provide legal aid, and "to employ all peaceful and honorable means to roll back the wave of intolerance, bigotry, and ignorance which threatens to submerge our cherished liberties." Their motto was: "Eternal vigilance, the price of liberty."[7]

After a pleasant fourteen-hour train ride via Albany, Syracuse, and Geneva, Bennett, Rawson, and Henderson finally arrived Wednesday morning at their destination in the scenic Finger Lakes. The three men spent Wednesday afternoon exploring the area that had become accessible only a dozen years earlier. The Glen, Bennett reported, was one of the "grandest curiosities" that he ever saw, rivaling the Mammoth Cave in Kentucky and Niagara Falls. The trio visited the Hope Art Gallery where James Hope, a Civil War landscape painter, exhibited his famous war paintings and images of the Watkins Glen area. Bennett was impressed with the "excellent artist" and noted, "some of his paintings are very large and are valued at thousands of dollars."[8]

Professor Rawson was also an artist of some fame and was popular for his biblical illustrations. He illustrated Henry Ward Beecher's *Life of Christ* and a deluxe edition of the Bible. After visiting the gallery, the three friends continued their hike through the Glen, eventually arriving at Glen Cathedral. The majestic cathedral-like amphitheater, surrounded with walls three hundred feet high, inspired Bennett to jokingly propose: "What a grand spot, thought we in this vaulted room with the sky for a dome, to hold a large Liberal meeting!"[9]

The following day the convention was called to order at 10 AM. Nearly a thousand people gathered in a large grove in the middle of the village to hear Dr. T. L. Brown, a homeopathic physician and president of the New York State Freethinkers' Association, deliver his address on materialism. His hourlong speech was followed by a full day of talks, lectures, and discussions on a

wide and controversial range of subjects that raised a few eye-
brows in the provincial village of thirty-five hundred orthodox
inhabitants. The residents of Watkins Glen did not know what
they were in for prior to the opening session of the scheduled
four-day event, but they had a good idea after the first meeting.[10]

That morning, the audience heard from Shaker elder Frederick Evans of Mount Lebanon, dress reformer Mary Tillotson,
and abolitionist and spiritualist Lucy N. Colman. Mary Tillotson,
who *wore* her reform—pants—and who often attracted crowds
and risked arrest in cities like New York, certainly received attention in the conservative village. Albert Rawson addressed the convention and opened with a critical analysis of Christian orthodoxy and followed with comments about Chaldean, Buddhist,
Greek, and Zoroastrian traditions. He spoke favorably about
Gnosticism, mentioned Madame H. P. Blavatsky (a founder of
the Theosophical Society), and lamented the ascent of the Roman
Catholic Church. His speech included his Liberal and Positivist
perspective and his prophecy of the upsurge of the new Church
of Humanity—The Liberal Church:

> The liberal idea of a church or society is, that it should be broad
> and comprehensive, embracing many diverse elements, and
> working together for the common good. . . . The position of the
> Church is fixed, defined, limited, narrow, rigid, hidebound,
> dogmatic, and formal, while the Liberal position is always
> advancing, relative, limitless, because always increasing, broad
> as humanity, flexible, growing, always accepting wise sugges-
> tions, and free from hurtful and binding forms. . . . The true
> Liberal endeavors to reveal to ordinary people the extraordinary
> attributes of their own nature by exemplifying before them the
> transcendent heights and depths of the human soul.[11]

The afternoon meeting offered an address by G. A. Lomas, followed by a talk by Ella E. Gibson, author of *The Godly Women of the
Bible, By an Ungodly Woman of the Nineteenth Century*. A vocal group
accompanied by a melodeon entertained the enthusiastic crowd.
Horace Seaver and J. P. Mendum arrived at the grove that evening,

whereupon Seaver was induced by the audience to deliver a short speech that was well received. "The day had been beautiful and everything passed off pleasantly," Bennett observed.[12]

The second day of the convention began with spiritualist Giles B. Stebbins reading selections from the teachings of Buddha and reciting the *Poems of the Beyond*. Elder Evans passionately expressed his advocacy of taxation of church property and the need for maintaining church and state separation. (At the time the Shakers were the only American religious group whose property was taxed.) The afternoon session included presentations by freethought lecturer W. S. Bell and Laura Kendrick, a spiritualist and free-love advocate. An interesting feature of these conventions was the open invitation extended to clergymen to speak. Two sermons were included in Friday afternoon's program but were immediately refuted by freethought lecturers. The evening meeting was held in the opera house, followed by a dance that lasted several hours.[13]

Saturday morning began with a few hundred people taking a steamboat ride on tranquil Seneca Lake, while others listened to Lucy Colman and Mary Tillotson, who spoke on dress reform. Several booksellers and publishers—Bennett among them—set up tables in the grove to sell books. The harmony of the convention began to sour during the debates between freethinkers and orthodox clergymen. "The convention had the fairness to allow their opponents, the orthodox clergy, to speak, two hours from their platform," Bennett reported, "thus showing far more liberality than they are in habit of receiving from the same clergymen in their public meetings." A Presbyterian minister addressed the audience, and in addition to the usual sermon, began disparaging Robert Ingersoll and condemning his agnosticism. While the Liberal audience listened to the clergyman for an hour, "the legal and ecclesiastical dignitaries of Watkins," Bennett heard, "were getting up a vile scheme to throw certain persons attending the convention into prison."[14]

By Saturday afternoon the mood of Watkins Glen both on the platform and on the streets was turning hostile. "As we walked their streets," Bennett recounted, "we more than once heard uncomplimentary and uncalled-for remarks made about us as we passed. The Watkins people are excessively pious, and they hate Freethinkers with an intense hatred. Several of them made the humane remark that we ought all to be hung."[15]

One of the booksellers who set up a table that afternoon was Miss Josephine S. Tilton, the idealistic sister-in-law of Ezra Heywood, imprisoned author of *Cupid's Yokes*. Josephine was a vivacious radical activist whose mother was Lucy M. Tilton, abolitionist, labor reformer, and free-love advocate. Josephine followed in her mother's footsteps and worked as a compositor apprentice for the *Liberator*, the antislavery periodical. (Leading abolitionist Wendell Phillips got her the job.) She took six hundred copies of *Cupid's Yokes* to the convention hoping to raise some money for the poverty-stricken Heywood children. Business was slow until the fifteen-cent pamphlet caught the attention of the local authorities.[16]

CUPID'S YOKES

Later that afternoon a police officer and constable arrived at the grove and arrested D. M. Bennett, W. S. Bell, and Josephine Tilton. The person to whom Bennett sold *Cupid's Yokes*, Warren Hurd, happened to be the brother of the Schuyler County grand jury judge. The three were arraigned, all pled not guilty, and bail was set at $1,000 each. At their arraignment someone remarked that the trio looked like "the father, son and holy-ghost." The enterprising defendants immediately had a photo taken and subsequently sold it as "The Trinity" for fifteen cents.[17]

Bennett provided his account of the circumstances leading up to the arrest in the *Truth Seeker*:

> We had a variety of books of our publication for sale, but not a copy of *Cupid's Yokes* was upon our table. Miss Tilton had a contiguous table, upon which she offered for sale several of Mr.

Heywood's pamphlets, photographs, etc. Among the pamphlets was the tabooed *Cupid's Yokes*. We are not sure that we sold a copy of it, but if we did it was to aid Miss Tilton when away or unable to attend to her customers. We put not a cent of the money for *Cupid's Yokes* in our pockets, nor did we have a cent of profit from the sale of them. Mr. Bell simply proffered his services to help us in selling our books as a matter of kindness, without remuneration of any kind. If he sold any of *Cupid's Yokes*, it was during her absence and as a matter of kindness.[18]

Cupid's Yokes was Ezra Heywood's prosaic sociological treatise—without photographs or illustrations—that contained his views on love and the institution of marriage, that he called "legalized prostitution." Even though the words "cupid's yokes" were taken from a poem by Isaac Watts, an English clergyman known for his hymns; the *Springfield Republican* newspaper editorialized that Heywood should be imprisoned for choosing such an *indecent* phrase to name a book. The pamphlet's complete title is *Cupid's Yokes: or, The Binding Forces of Conjugal Life; An Essay to Consider Some Moral and Physiological Phases of LOVE AND MARRIAGE, Wherein Is Asserted the Natural Right and Necessity of SEXUAL SELF-GOVERNMENT*. The lengthy title was illustrative of the contents of the wordy booklet wherein the former abolitionist argues against conventional church-sponsored state statutes that regulate "personal liberty and rights of conscience in love. . . . Why should priests and magistrates supervise the sexual organs of citizens any more than the brain and stomach?" Heywood also provides an overview of the "National Gag-Law" (Comstock Law) and expresses his contempt for the "lascivious fanaticism of the Young Men's Christian Association." He refers to Anthony Comstock as a "religious monomaniac." The commingling of religion and sex was anathema to moralists and religious fanatics like Comstock and it was no surprise that he found *Cupid's Yokes* to be "too foul for description."[19]

"I am proud to stand bail for the editor of *The Truth Seeker*," proclaimed seventy-five-year-old pioneer abolitionist Amy Post, one of the three women who bailed out the trio. During her antislavery days, the courageous Quaker lady harbored on average one hundred fifty runaway slaves in her home each year for more than twelve years. Her last years were spent as a suffragist and freethinker. Post was a gentle-hearted pacifist whose reprimands of Anthony Comstock were filled with sentiments of pity for her "dear" enemy's mother—Mrs. Comstock![20]

The crowd that gathered in the grove Saturday afternoon learned of the arrests and became indignant. Lucy Colman and other scheduled speakers expressed their collective anger from the platform. When Bennett and Bell finally returned to the meeting grounds, they were met with loud approval, and hundreds of people were eager to shake their hands. The evening session was again held in the opera house, and the highlight of the night was an address by James Parton, the late nineteenth century's most popular biographer. His speech was called "The Coming Man's Religion: Will He Have Any?"[21]

The arrests, along with the rain that night, dampened the spirit of the final day. The Sunday morning meeting had to be held in the opera house, and Elizur Wright read a paper titled "Creed and Religion as a Cultivator of Political Hypocrisy." The afternoon saw sunshine, and a large portrait of Robert Ingersoll was presented to the secretary of the New York Freethinkers' Association in appreciation of his labors. The last meeting held in the opera house included a heated discussion concerning the Comstock Laws. The night ended with an announcement of a defense fund for Bennett, Bell, and Tilton; a total of $133.00 was raised. James Parton provided a generous $25 donation.[22]

The woman who initially provided the bail for Josephine Tilton had a change of heart after she read Cupid's Yokes. Tilton was more than willing to go to jail, proclaiming her right to sell the booklet. She had taken six hundred copies of Cupid's Yokes to the convention and ended up selling them all. Tilton later said that because of the arrest publicity, she could have sold the fifteen-cent pamphlet for a dollar. A fourth man, George Mosher, was also arrested on Sunday for selling Cupid's Yokes. He was a Watkins Glen resident who, while walking among the crowd with about fifty copies for sale, was marched off to jail after offering one to the local district attorney![23]

On Monday, August 26, the Schuyler County grand jury convened and Judge Oliver P. Hurd instructed the members "with unusual severity to find" that the pamphlet was obscene. But after reading *Cupid's Yokes*, certain members found that it was not obscene. Nevertheless, Reverend Waldo of the local Presbyterian church conferred with the district attorney and convinced the members of the grand jury to indict the four. On Thursday at 2 PM, the defendants were formally indicted, and a portion of the indictment read: "The jurors of the People . . . present that D. M. Bennett being of the age of twenty-one years and over and being a person of a wicked and depraved mind and disposition, and most unlawfully, wickedly and feloniously devising, contriving, and intending to vitiate and corrupt the morals of the people of the State of New York and to bring them into a state of wickedness, lewdness, and debauchery, etc."[24]

Bennett facetiously commented on the formidable accusation and feigned surprise that the old formula "and instigated by the devil" had not been inserted in the complaint. "Then it could have been made clear how we came to be so wicked."[25]

The defendants, with the exception of Josephine Tilton, made bail and a court date was set for December 9, 1878. Tilton refused bail and with a "spirit of noble bravery and independence," Bennett reported, she "proudly and fearlessly marched out of the Court House," surrendered to the sheriff, and was taken to prison where the feisty anarchist was willing to stay until trial. One of Tilton's distinguished visitors in the jail was Theron Leland, the secretary of the National Liberal Association. Leland was a pioneer stenographer, George Macdonald's father-in-law, and one of Bennett's closest friends. Leland recorded his visit to Josephine Tilton in the Schuyler County Jail:

> I found her serene and happy, and as determined as ever to rent her room by the quarter and board by the season on the bounty of the Watkins' people. Her street shoes had been buried at the

bottom of her baggage, and her bonnet wrapped up and stowed away, not needed for immediate use. The Sheriff had promised to have her little room furnished and whitewashed, and she planted herself down for a three-month siege, awaiting trial . . . her friends as well as her enemies admired her grit and energy, but thought she was carrying her "spunk" too far.

Theron Leland persuaded Tilton to accept the $500 bail and reported that "the fruits and flowers that had been sent in to her were distributed among the prisoners left behind, with whom she had established herself as a friend and favorite, good-byes were said, and we all left the lock-up."[26]

In a letter to Bennett from Dedham Jail, Ezra Heywood wrote, "You [Bennett] have faced the music with intrepid heroism. . . . Your bold and timely move will help to settle this great question once and forever." Heywood also expressed his feeling about his sister-in-law. "Josephine's brave demeanor at Watkins reminded me of Joan of Arc . . . and several other 'good girls.'" Bennett echoed Heywood's sentiments, writing, "We felt proud of such a compatriot in the toils of Christian persecution. All honor to Josephine S. Tilton."[27]

Finally on Thursday, after waiting all week, the four were formally charged. At the indictment on August 29, Judge Hurd read the 1873 statute and commented on the pamphlet, "I have read the book and in my opinion it is an obscene work and contraband of the statute." The judge went on to discuss Heywood's conviction and imprisonment and was, in Bennett's view, prejudging the case.[28]

Bennett denounced Warren Hurd (the judge's brother) in an article titled "Which Is the Greater Criminal?" He also identified and rebuked the men he felt were responsible for the arrest in "The Very Moral Men Who Caused Our Arrest." Bennett began by castigating the leading citizens of Watkins Glen who disparaged the freethinkers prior to the convention. He condemned Frederick Davis, the leading man in making the complaint, who was also the head of the local Episcopal church. Bennett cited several examples of the town's hypocrisy:

He is by no means of a paragon of virtue and sobriety. He conducts a malt house, and changes the grain, adapted to the healthful food of men and animals, to a condition suited to the preparation of an alcoholic beverage that deprives his fellowmen of their reason and self-control. On occasions of picnics and parties he had been in the habit of getting grossly intoxicated and making a fool of himself generally. He has, we are informed, a reputation of being quite a ladies' man.

He had two or three upon the string at the time his late wife died, and conversation was held in her presence in reference to them the day before she died, which annoyed her exceedingly and embittered the hours of her death. One of these ladies he subsequently took for his wife.[29]

Bennett also exposed a member of the grand jury who "tried to screen his son from due punishment when he exhibited himself in a state of utter nudity in the streets of Watkins." A week later he linked all of his enemies:

We have received pretty direct information, which we deem authentic, that it was Anthony Comstock who instigated our arrest at Watkins. It would seem that our suspicions that he had written the Young Men's Christian Association at Watkins how to proceed in the matter were correct. If this information is true, we have again to thank his pious character for another arrest by the powers of the orthodox church. Frederick Davis, Dr. Thompson, Rev. Mr. Waldo, Warren Hurd, and his brother Judge Hurd, ought to feel very proud to thus be the tools and dupes in carrying out the instructions of this execrable character.[30]

The Watkins Glen freethinkers' convention evolved into a ten-day legal debacle for Bennett. While waiting for the grand jury, he took a steamboat ride on Lake Seneca and returned to the cathedral to have his photograph taken with friends. After making bail on Friday, August 30, he left Watkins for Rochester where he briefly visited his mother and sister who had already heard of his second arrest. In a personal letter written that day to Josephine Tilton, Bennett recounted their celebrated arrest at Watkins and the ensuing legal proceedings. "Few of the martyrs of the cause of human liberty have evinced grander traits of character," he declared. "May I long be worthy of such compatriots."[31]

The editor then returned to New York City and the *Truth Seeker* offices where he began an all-out assault on the town of Watkins Glen and the culprit who he believed instigated the arrest—Anthony Comstock. Bennett informed readers that the publicity generated by his first arrest ten months earlier increased circulation of the *Truth Seeker*. And now that he was arrested a second time, he would again "be glad to double its circulation." In a bold act of defiance, Bennett also announced his policy on the sale of *Cupid's Yokes*:

> We have hitherto sold but a very limited number of this now celebrated pamphlet. It does not present our views upon the subjects upon which it treats, but recognizing the right of every American citizen to express his views upon marriage and divorce as upon all other subjects and that every man has the right to buy or sell or read the same, we propose hereafter to sell the pamphlet to every person who wishes a copy of it. We do this by virtue of the right of an American citizen. If we go to prison for it, to prison it is. For every one that fails for selling *Cupid's Yokes* ten will rise in his place to sell more. When all the prisons of the country are filled with persons who dare to sell *Cupid's Yokes* more can be built. We propose for one to fight the battle out on this line. Let those who wish copies of *Cupid's Yokes* send in the sum of fifteen cents and they shall be supplied. Where one hundred copies were sold before, a thousand will be demanded now. The demand shall be supplied.[32]

NOTES

"the Christian church.": TS Nov. 17, 1877.

1. SP pp. 547–50. TS Sept. 14, 1878.
2. TS Aug. 3, 1878.
3. Ibid.

4. TS Aug. 10, 1878.

5. TS Aug. 31, 1878.

6. "a Diab (Wolf).": WSIT.

The "Wolf" denomination was bestowed on T. E. Lawrence, the famous English archaeologist, author, and soldier known as Lawrence of Arabia.

7. SP.

The National Defense Association evolved (at least in spirit) into the Free Speech League funded by Dr. E. B. Foote Jr. in 1902 and incorporated in 1911. The Free Speech League was primarily concerned with defending free-speech advocates, sexual reformers, and anarchists. Theodore Schroeder, an attorney, was also instrumental in founding the Free Speech League. He worked indefatigably to defend and publicize numerous censorship cases. Prior to the birth of the American Civil Liberties Union in 1920, Schroeder was perhaps the nation's most prolific writer and ardent defender of free speech.

GM and Sears.

8. TS Aug. 31, 1878.

James Hope (1817–1892), one of the last of the Hudson River School of painters. Dr. Larry Freeman, *The Hope Paintings*. Century House Americana Publishers, 1961.

9. TS Aug. 31, 1878.

10. Ibid.

11. GM. K. Paul Thompson.

12. TS Aug. 31, 1878.

13. Ibid.

14. "their public meetings.": TS Sept. 14, 1878. "convention into prison.": TS Aug. 31, 1878.

15. TS Sept. 7, 1878.

16. Blatt.

17. TS Aug. 31, 1878.

18. Ibid.

19. Broun and Leech.

20. "to stand bail.": TS Sept. 7, 1878. Amy Post "dear" enemy GM v. 1, p. 493.

21. EB.

22. TS Aug. 31, 1878.

23. 600 copies: Blatt. TS Sept. 7, 1878.

24. Indictment Aug. 23, 1878, facsimile in TS Sept. 7, 1878.

25. Ibid.

26. DMB letter from Watkins, Aug. 30, 1878, unpublished, University of Michigan. "'spunk' too far.": TS Sept. 14, 1878.

27. Heywood letter (dated Sept. 7, 1878) to Bennett: TS Sept. 14, 1878.

28. TS Sept. 7, 1878.

29. Ibid.

30. TS Sept 14, 1878.

Bennett learned from Comstock's father that his son had written the local YMCA: TS Sept. 14, 1878.

31. Letter, Aug. 30, 1878, unpublished, Josephine Tilton's autograph book, Denton Family Papers, Labadie Collection at the University of Michigan.

32. TS Sept. 7, 1878.

6

Crowding the Mourners

From the bottom of my heart I despise the publishers of obscene lit-erature. Below them there is no depth of filth. And I also despise those who, under the pretense of suppressing obscene literature, endeavor to prevent honest and pure men from writing and pub-lishing honest and pure thoughts.

—Robert G. Ingersoll
March 18, 1878

While awaiting trial for selling *Cupid's Yokes* at Watkins Glen, Bennett continued his war against Anthony Comstock and for the repeal of the Comstock Laws. Francis Abbot, the presi-dent of the National Liberal League, opposed the repeal that was polarizing the membership. Abbot, also the conservative editor of the Boston *Index*, was, according to Theron Leland, "against God in the Constitution—but for the devil in the post-office."[1]

Subsequently, a feud developed between Bennett and Abbot.

Abbot repeatedly asserted that the petition called for "total repeal." But no such words were used in the document. The petition asked for modification as much as for repeal and was, according to Bennett, "left to the option of Congress whether it shall be *modification* or *repeal.*" The disagreement caused the two liberal editors to begin trading bitter recriminations in the pages of their periodicals. Abbot accused Bennett's friend and fellow Liberal League officer Albert Rawson of being a bigamist and said that the organization was "corrupted by the poison of free love." He called Bennett a vampire. Bennett denounced Abbot as a Comstock supporter and derided him as the Apostle of Culture. He mocked Abbot's ostentation, remarking that the Bostonian had "a perfect right to be partial to kid gloves, patent-leather boots, and twenty-five cent cigars."[2]

Bennett continued to defiantly advertise and sell *Cupid's Yokes* even though Ezra Heywood, the author, was in jail. He began promoting Parker Pillsbury's provocative little pamphlet *Cupid's Yokes and the Holy Scriptures Contrasted*, and a compilation of the indiscretions committed by clergymen issued in a tract titled *Sinful Saints and Sensual Shepherds*. These "black collar crimes" were a popular weekly feature in the *Truth Seeker*. The advertisement for the booklet stated, "Infidelity and vice are by many Christian bigots considered synonymous terms. With them a Freethinker is necessarily a 'bold bad man' in popular parlance. Christianity, on the other hand, is deemed another word for virtue, purity, holiness; and Christians, perforce, are the 'salt of the earth.'"[3]

Bennett also began advertising *The Holy Bible, Abridged*, a book "consistently, conscientiously and piously dedicated to Anthony Comstock." In October the editor became embroiled in a libel suit after publishing a sordid report that chronicled an arrest made by Comstock in a house of prostitution. Written by Albert Rawson, who was also named in the suit, the article detailed the modus operandi of one of Comstock's detectives, Frank Chapman. The account revealed that Chapman, in order to make an arrest for indecent exposure, slept with one of the girls to gain the confidence of the madam. The story revealed that three girls (for $14.50) paraded naked around the room in front of his boss—Anthony Comstock. Chapman visited the *Truth Seeker* office several times and admitted that he was in on the operation, but he only went along to have fun. Nevertheless, he challenged some of the article's details and wanted $50,000 "to make his reputation good again." In his assessment of the tumultuous fall of 1878, George Macdonald wrote, "The war against Comstock, which had not failed for a moment, 'now trebly thundering swelled the gale.'"[4]

That fall, another minor incident occurred providing the editor an opportunity to share his views on a subject not previously covered—guns. After sending issues of the *Truth Seeker* to subscribers working at the Winchester Repeating Arms Company in New Haven, Connecticut, for several years, Bennett received a terse letter from W. W. Winchester, the vice president of the country's largest gun manufacturer. Winchester wrote, "We protest against your using our name on the bundle of papers sent here weekly. . . . We never gave you permission or authority to use our address and desire it discontinued hereafter. If you have subscribers in our employ you must find a way to reach them, but not through us." The editor responded to the gun manufacturer in the *Truth Seeker*:

> We have a curiosity to know if the publishers of Christian papers are requested not to send them to the pious establishment that manufactures hundreds of thousands of rifles for shooting down human beings. Does Mr. Winchester believe that the individual by whose merits he is to be saved would have engaged in such a murderous business and have furnished the weapons for taking the lives of God's creatures because he could make money by it? Do they think he approves now of the killing business? If they really believe in him can they pursue the business which he could not approve?
>
> Consistency is a jewel.[5]

As the clamor continued over the repeal of the Comstock Laws, Robert Ingersoll was drawn into the feud between Abbot and Bennett. Although he signed the petition for repeal of the

Comstock Laws, he wanted to make it clear that he was not in favor of repealing *all* obscenity laws. Ingersoll stated his position on obscenity laws in a letter to the editors of the *Boston Journal*. He wrote, "Certain religious fanatics, taking advantage of the word 'immoral,' in the law, have claimed that all writings against what they are pleased to call orthodox religion are immoral, and such books have been seized and their authors arrested." The only objection he had to the law of 1873 was "that it has been construed to include books and pamphlets written against the religion of the day, although containing nothing that can be called obscene or impure."[6]

Bennett's defense costs were considerable and in early December he again asked subscribers to forward pledged funds. Making matters worse was a slight misunderstanding between Bennett and Ingersoll. The colonel complained that the editor was selling his lectures in "cheap form." Bennett agreed to discontinue publishing Ingersoll's lectures and announced the decision in the *Truth Seeker*. A weary Bennett commented on his upcoming trial, saying he had to be ready to receive the penalty a "Christian court and a Christian jury in a bitterly Christian community see fit to deal out to us."[7]

The embattled editor received a sympathetic letter from Ezra Heywood who was in the Dedham Jail where he languished for nearly six months in declining health. "I am stretched between hope and fear," Heywood wrote. He felt he was about to be pardoned in a few days. Heywood compared Bennett to Benjamin Franklin Butler, a courageous Civil War general and distinguished politician. He wished the editor well at the upcoming Watkins trial, writing, "I look upon you as the general Butler of Freethought, whose headquarters should be in the saddle rather than in jail. Still, your prison cell would become an executive mansion to 'sway the future.' No man living has done more for human redemption from Christian sin than you since Comstock laid his unclean hand on your person one year ago this last November."[8]

The Third Arrest

As the *Truth Seeker* was about to go to press at 3:45 PM on Tuesday, December 10, 1878, Bennett was sitting at his desk, and Fritz Bernhard, the deputy US marshal, entered the office with a warrant for the editor's arrest. Bernhard was as courteous as he had been thirteen months earlier, Bennett reported, and the marshal expressed his regret at having to carry out the duty. While the editor looked over the warrant charging him for depositing *Cupid's Yokes* in the mail, Joseph Britton, Comstock's first lieutenant, waited outside at the entrance of the *Truth Seeker* office.[9]

Bennett was taken to the courthouse where he was joined by his lawyer, Thaddeus B. Wakeman, and friends Dr. E. B. Foote and his son, Dr. Foote Jr. After Wakeman convinced the district attorney to reduce his client's bail from $5,000 to $2,000, and while they were preparing the papers, Comstock strolled into the room "as happy as a clam at high water," Bennett noted, and "gently whistled the pious tune, 'The Sweet By and By.'" Two of the editor's employees were present and observed the legal proceedings. "There goes old Comstock," one of them whispered. The vice hunter abruptly stopped and asked, "What is that you say, sir?" The employee replied, "It is none of your business what I said." "But you spoke my name," the vice hunter snarled. "I will speak it again if I see fit, and you cannot prevent me." "None of your impudence here," Comstock admonished. "If you have any more of it I will kick you out into the hall, you dirty loafer."[10]

As he had always kept subscribers apprised of his activities, Bennett wrote extensively of his third arrest and included a facsimile of Comstock's semiliterate decoy letter requesting *Cupid's Yokes*:

GRANVILLE, N. Y.

Sir: I am a constant reader of your paper that I get each week from a friend. So you see I keep up with the trials you have gone through I have not much ready money but perhaps in an indirect way I might be able to help you by getting subscriptions for some of your works. I dont feel able to give outright but it may help you in ready money if I send my might for some of your books. I thought to use about $5.00 but cant spare quite all today. Knowing that you have appealed several times for help I have a little sum to send you. As I say I cant afford to give outright but so you may send me books in place and accept the will for the deed. I would like to get a copy of cloth bound Champions of the Church $3.00 a copy of the Bible abridged for 30 cents and a copy of that Heywood book you advertise Cupid's something or other you know what I mean. I send three and a half dollars and if that aint enough I will send the balance when I get the books. I wish I only had three hundred times the amount but I haint.

Please address plainly so no thief will steal, you know who I mean.

G. BRACKETT, Box 202,
Granville N. Y. Washington Co.[11]

The editor described how he filled the book order—and more importantly *why* he believed he had the right to sell *Cupid's Yokes*:

The books ordered were duly wrapped and mailed. This falsehood and hypocrisy on Comstock's part was unnecessary, for had he written like a man in his own name, or visited us in person, he would have been served just as well. We have not been selling any of our books "on the sly," but openly and above board. We have sold *Cupid's Yokes* because our patrons wished it and because, as an American citizen, we considered we had a perfect right to sell it. We do not think it is in any sense an obscene publication, and to this opinion tens of thousands of the best men and women of our country will give their sworn testimony. It is simply an earnest and honest argument in favor of a change in the existing order of things in the relations of the sexes. The views advanced may not be the true theory that is to elevate the race, and the publication may not, according to the judgment of many, be, in all respects, in the best possible taste; but it was written by an intelligent, upright, moral gentleman, and is couched in proper, well-selected language, and does not contain an indecent or improper word. Nor is it calculated to inflame the passions of the young. It is a dry dissertation, uninteresting and unattractive to young people.[12]

Bennett also continued his attack on Anthony Comstock and expressed his opinion concerning freedom of the press, writing,

> It has never been deemed a necessity in authors and dealers that the works they write or sell should just correspond with the views of any particular class or any particular church. A writer has been thought to be perfectly free in this country to advocate and defend any theory or doctrine in theology, philosophy, morals, politics, or any other field, whether it was in keeping with popular opinion or not. And it is simply an outrage upon the rights and liberties of an American citizen to arrest him, throw him into prison, deprive him of his liberty, despoil him of his property, and rob him of his good name among his fellow-men because his views are in advance of or divergent from other thinkers or writers.[13]

A week later Bennett, accompanied by Josephine Tilton, took the train to Watkins Glen for their trial scheduled for December 17, 1878. After waiting nearly three days for their case to be heard, they learned that the judge changed the venue to the Court of Sessions. The defendants were required to furnish new bail and their trial was rescheduled for February. While Bennett was still in Watkins Glen, Ezra Heywood was pardoned by President Rutherford B. Hayes and was a free man on December 19. The long-awaited pardon was unconditional, and the specific reasons Hayes gave for his decision were the "great number of Massachusetts citizens seeking Heywood's release and that Heywood's health was suffering." President Hayes wrote, "I entertain as little doubt as those who assail me" that Heywood was wrong about marriage. But, he added, "It is no crime by the laws of the United States to advocate the abolition of marriage." In his private diary, Hayes expressed his objection to *Cupid's Yokes* but maintained that it was "not obscene, lascivious, lewd, or corrupting in the criminal sense."[14]

Ezra Heywood was home for Christmas. "Hope my release will settle your cases in advance," he wrote to Bennett who was still facing two criminal cases that were of much concern. The beleaguered editor expressed his distress in an article titled "Crowding the Mourners":

> Too much of a good thing is too much, and of a bad thing a little only is too much. Of arrests for obscenity we are decidedly of the opinion that we have had too much. Three arrests in a year, or a little over, is three more than we want. And to have two indictments hanging over us at the same time, and being required to put in an appearance at two different courts, hundreds of miles apart at the same time, or at one on one day and the other on the next seems like demanding too much of an old man. We are so constituted that we cannot be in two places at the same time, and with all the vileness which A. Comstock Esq. and the Hon. S. L. Woodford seem to think we are cursed with, we cannot attend two courts at once nor occupy two prisons at once. Come one at a time gentlemen, and we can attend to you the better, and the fun for you will last longer. . . . Gentlemen, the eyes of many are upon you. What is now being done in our case will be inscribed on the pages of history, and we conjure you, for the love of justice and righteousness, to give us a fair and dispassionate trial, and not to "crowd the mourners" by unseemly haste.[15]

THE HEYWOOD RECEPTION

On January 2, 1879, Bennett traveled to Boston, where he attended a reception in honor of Ezra Heywood. The rousing meeting, held at Paine Hall, was filled with Heywood's fellow libertarians and decorated for the occasion. Above the stage hung an evergreen inscription that read *Free Speech and a Free Press Forever*. Suspended from the motto was a white dove with poised pinions and bearing in its beak an olive branch. After the meeting was called to order, several letters were read from supporters, including Stephen Pearl Andrews and Parker Pillsbury. The letter by Pillsbury was a scathing attack on the Comstock Laws and an indictment of the American Bible Society. In the thrilling letter, as Bennett described it, Pillsbury wrote, "They have published and disseminated in many lands, many languages, more pages of unclean, lewd, lascivious, and obscene literature than any other pen, press, or association from Sodom and Gomorrah away down here almost to the bottom of the nineteenth century of Christian grace. The abomination of actual obscenity cannot be too severely punished; no matter in what way, nor by whom committed—in brothels, or Bible houses."[16]

During the reading of the Pillsbury letter, which drew loud applause, Heywood, his wife, and two children entered the hall and were welcomed with long, enthusiastic acclaim. Appearing pale and emaciated from his six-month imprisonment, Heywood received three cheers followed by three more as he and his family ascended the platform. The chairman of the reception praised Heywood's antislavery work on behalf of the "once downtrodden race." The chairman stated it was only fitting that two members of the race should be present when their friend was "welcomed back to liberty." The two provided the music for the reception. "Miss Helen Sawyer, a young lady of color, was presented and sang beautifully the Marseillaise Hymn, which was vigorously encored," Bennett reported. "She was accompanied upon the piano by a companion, another young lady of color."[17]

Speakers included Moses Hull, Albert Rawson, Laura Kendrick, Bennett, and Heywood. Rawson and Kendrick spoke about the National Defense Association. Kendrick, who traveled to Washington, DC, to present the Heywood petition to President Hayes, thanked the NDA for paying the expenses. Ezra Heywood told the audience, "Liberty is as dear to me as to any other; home, family, and the dear form of friends present are as precious to me as to any other individual. But there is something dearer even than those; it is the right to think, the right to speak, the right to acquire and impart knowledge. I therefore thought it better to be an exile from my home and from society for years even, rather than surrender the right of a citizen to acquire and impart knowledge."[18]

Bennett's speech included details regarding his confrontations with Comstock and Colonel Ingersoll's influence on the Hayes administration. This influence was successful in getting the first criminal case dropped and "was a snub to Comstock and angered him not a little," he said, adding that the vice hunter "almost swore (for it is asserted that he sometimes uses bad words) that he would yet 'get that Bennett!'"[19]

In his speech, Bennett included the specifics of his second arrest at Watkins. The crowd applauded when he admitted to have subsequently sold nearly two thousand copies of Heywood's *Cupid's Yokes*. Feeling assured that his most recent arrest was not very serious, Bennett acknowledged President Hayes's "good sense" in pardoning Heywood. He concluded his speech by reaffirming his intention that no matter what the result might be, he would continue "to advocate the right of free speech, a free press, and free mails so long as he had strength to do so." The evening ended after the audience joined in the chorus of Miss Helen Sawyer's rendition of "John Brown's Body Lies Mouldering in the Grave."[20]

In a letter to Elizur Wright dated January 13, 1879, US Attorney General Charles Devens explained that President Hayes pardoned Heywood because of the prisoner's health. The attorney general's comments might have provided solace to Bennett regarding his pending cases. Charles Devens wrote, "In regard to the book itself, while it seems to me a publication not desirable to be made, I am aware that there may be much difference of opinion upon the subject, and do not confound it with those obscene publications the effect and object of which is to excite the imagination and inflame the passions."[21]

BIRTH CONTROL—COLGATE STYLE

Despite two criminal cases pending in the early part of 1879, Bennett continued to assail the enemies of a free press. The pages of the *Truth Seeker* burned with editorials critical of Anthony Comstock and supporters, especially Reverend Joseph Cook, the famous Boston religious lecturer, moralist, and Comstock cheer-leader. Cook was Boston's most respected and popular reverend-lecturer, but in the editor's opinion, he was nothing more than another sanctimonious charlatan. After Cook came to the defense of Comstock in a lecture published in the *Boston Daily Advertiser*, Bennett responded with an editorial titled "Joseph Cook, the Liar." Freethinkers found the commingling of science and religion by members of the orthodoxy unethical and intellectually dishonest. After all, science was the foundation on which unbelievers could argue their claims of evolution. It is no wonder that Cook, the apologist for Comstock, who promoted his own brand of Christian science, drew Bennett's intense animosity.[22]

When Cook addressed the annual meeting of the New York Society for the Suppression of Vice at the local YMCA, *Truth Seeker* employees handed out copies of the "Joseph Cook, the Liar" editorial at the building's entrance. This action, along with the editor's repeated typeset attention to the reverend, whom he called a "wild-mouthed blatherskite," resulted in a legendary feud between the two men that would continue around the world and last until well after Bennett's death.[23]

Another enemy the editor made during this period was Samuel Colgate, the soap manufacturer and president of the New York Society for the Suppression of Vice. Colgate was one of America's most influential, wealthiest, and most religious citizens. Colgate's father-in-law was Richard C. Morse, a member of the socially and religiously conservative New England Morse family. Richard and his brother Sidney founded the country's oldest Christian newspaper, the *New York Observer*. Their brother Samuel F. B. Morse invented the Morse telegraphic code. "What hath God wrought!" was the first message sent.[24]

A devout Baptist, Colgate had a magnificent personal library of Baptist books and pamphlets, the most complete historical collection of that denomination in the world. The soap magnate was the founder of Colgate University, a Sunday school superintendent, and a member of the finance committee of the American Tract Society, the nation's leading distributor of religious tracts.

Samuel Colgate's company was the largest soap manufacturer in America; his mammoth Jersey City plant occupied two city blocks and had hundreds of employees.[25]

Samuel Colgate and company were also agents for Vaseline. The uses of Vaseline were printed in an advertising booklet with detailed, albeit prohibited, information for its uses in birth control—an act which was in direct violation of the Comstock Laws. Although the mixture was proven to be ineffectual, Colgate was guilty at least of fraud. The pamphlet first came to the attention of the general public when Bennett printed a statement in the June 8, 1878, issue of the *Truth Seeker*: "It seems that a complaint was made against Mr. Samuel Colgate, president of the Society for the Suppression of Vice, for sending through the U.S. mails a pamphlet in regard to vaseline wherein it was spoken of favorably as a preventive when combined with a certain other drug. It is stated, however, that Mr. Colgate pleaded ignorance of the contents of the pamphlet, and the complaint was dismissed."[26]

A month before going to trial for his third arrest, Bennett wrote his *Open Letter to Samuel Colgate* that appeared in the *Truth Seeker*. The irreverent diatribe was approximately eighty-five hundred words and filled four pages. The monumental missive—a combination history lesson and criminal indictment of Colgate—was also printed as a booklet of nearly one hundred pages. The editor mailed a copy of the open letter along with a few other controversial and "obscene" items, including *Cupid's Yokes*, to Samuel Colgate. "I trust you have read the little pamphlet I sent you," Bennett wrote in the postscript and added, "I will be glad to furnish the pamphlet to all who wish it."[27]

Bennett began the letter with the things the two men have in common, followed by their differences. He attempted to enlighten Colgate as to the unbelief of America's Founding Fathers and declared, "The Government of the United States is not in any sense founded on the Christian religion. Among our later Presidents some have been unbelievers or Infidels, notably Abraham Lincoln." The letter continued with details of the editor's arrests by Comstock, and Bennett asked,

Have you realized, Mr. Colgate, what a serious thing it is to be arrested on a charge of selling obscene literature? There is scarcely another charge in the whole catalogue so disgraceful, so odious, and so utterly ruinous to a man's character among his friends and acquaintances. How would you like to be arrested on an accusation of selling obscene and lascivious publications? How would you like to have your wife, your daughters, your near relatives and friends, and your numerous acquaintances read in the daily papers that you had been arrested on this charge by United States officers? How would you like it telegraphed all over the country that Samuel Colgate had been arrested and held to bail for dealing in obscene literature? . . . I think not. But remember this has been done to me three times within the last fifteen months, and I think as much of my character as you do of yours. I have not dealt in nor handled obscene literature, and have been no more a violator of the law than yourself; in fact, not so much so as I will proceed to show you and any person who may read this.[28]

The editor included a copy of the federal obscenity statute that "your [Colgate's] society, and especially your agent [Comstock] caused to be passed. A similar law he also caused to be passed by the Legislature of this state." After citing the obscenity statute thus, italicized for emphasis, "*and every article or thing designed or intended for the prevention of conception*," Bennett accused Colgate of *violation* of the obscenity law. He quoted a few lines from a brochure written by a doctor who advised:

Physicians are frequently applied to, to produce abortion. Recently, on the same day, two women came to me; the reason assigned in the one case was that the husband was syphilitic; in the other, that pregnancy brought on violent attacks of spasmodic asthma. Of course I explained that the child had rights as well as the mother, but it was all I could do to prevent one of these cases from going to a professed abortionist. In some cases of this kind prevention is better than cure, and I am inclined to think, from some experiments, that *vaseline, charged with four or five grains of salicylic acid,* will destroy spermatozoa, without injury to the uterus or vagina.[29]

"Here are explicit directions for preventing conception, if not for procuring abortion," Bennett declared, "and you published definitely where the preparation could be obtained." The editor charged Colgate with sending the brochures containing the doctor's advice out by the thousands. "To my personal knowledge," he wrote, "the pamphlets have come from your house and they were sent by mail. They were ordered from your house, they were sent pursuant to order, the envelope having your business card printed upon it."[30]

"You violated the law, as I said, in the most positive manner," Bennett asserted, "yet you escape, while you are trying to send me to prison for not breaking the law at all. If this is justice, it must be Christian justice, or Colgate justice, which will not bear investigation." He mentioned a speech that Colgate gave at his society where the soap manufacturer said that reputable physicians, druggists, or booksellers never complain about the Comstock Laws. The reason why they did not complain, Bennett contended, was because Colgate's agent does not harass "regular" physicians, druggists, and wealthy booksellers. "The 'regular,' aristocratic physicians may prevent conceptions, produce abortions, or do anything else they choose, and your agent will not disturb them."[31]

Though it was clear that Colgate violated the law, the editor knew nothing could be done other than to expose Colgate for what he was—a hypocrite. "But your society was not organized to punish such violators of the law as yourself," he gibed, "nor for the rich and influential, nor for prominent Christians, but for poor, friendless devils who are unable to make a defense, and who can easily be hustled off to prison." The editor informed Colgate that the US prosecuting attorneys admitted that Colgate's brochure violated the law, but after learning the identity of the offender refused to prosecute. "It is not pleasant for me to charge any person with wrong doing," Bennett confessed, "and especially crimes that are punishable by imprisonment. But I am not, after all, afraid to speak the truth, and will not, when necessary, hesitate to do so."[32]

The postscript to *Open Letter to Samuel Colgate* was published in the *Truth Seeker* only two weeks before his trial. Bennett agreed that the violators of obscenity laws should be punished, but "when the charge is only a pretext . . . to punish unbelievers . . . the injustice is most reprehensible." The editor said that he understood the society's animus toward him after hearing Colgate publicly announce a year earlier that "Freethought publications would soon 'be *stamped out.'*" Bennett inquired if Colgate read the pamphlets that he sent him—*Cupid's Yokes* and Parker Pillsbury's *Letter to Ezra H. Heywood*—contrasting the condemned portions of *Cupid's Yokes* with selections from the Bible. "Parker Pillsbury was an able and ardent champion advocate for human liberty," he informed Colgate, "and toiled laboriously for years in behalf of the downtrodden. He is a man of unusual intelligence, perception, and honesty, and his opinions are worthy of close examination. I hope they did not escape your attention."[33]

Bennett drew attention to the unconstitutionality of the United States Postal Laws and cited numerous cases of individuals who were indicted for owning or selling Thomas Paine's books. He challenged the soap magnate or one of his "ablest divines" or any professor from his college to debate Christianity versus Rationalism. Bennett promised to print the debate, present Colgate's arguments before thirty thousand readers weekly, and publish subsequently in book form. "I will agree to be open to conviction and to embrace Christianity with all my heart—if you can convince me that [Christianity] is *true*." He concluded the postscript with a few lines of verse from a Scottish writer:

> But truth shall conquer at the last,
> For round and round we run;
> And ever the right comes uppermost,
> And ever is justice done.[34]

On February 25, 1879, D. M. Bennett's mother died. Her obituary printed in the *Truth Seeker* read, "Died at Rochester, N.Y., Mrs. Betsey Bennett, aged eighty years, the mother of the editor of *The Truth Seeker*. For many years she had been a member of the Congregational Church, but she had read *The Truth Seeker* steadily from its incipience, and the effect was to unsettle her former religious notions." Nine days later, the grieving publisher's trial was scheduled to begin. If convicted, the sixty-year-old faced spending quite possibly the remainder of his life in prison.[35]

NOTES

"and pure thoughts.": R. G. Ingersoll, TS June 8, 1878.

1. "the post-office": GM v. 1 p. 231.

After Abbot angered the opponents of the Comstock Laws (the majority of members in the NLL), he was voted out of office October 26, 1878, at the annual convention in Syracuse, New York. Elizur Wright was elected president. Bennett and numerous other anti-Comstock members were chosen as vice presidents. Among these were many of Bennett's friends and supporters, including James Parton, Parker Pillsbury, Horace Seaver, Robert G. Ingersoll, F. W. Evans, Amy Post, William Denton, and T. B. Wakeman. Albert Rawson was secretary.

2. GM v. 1 p. 232 and TS December 14, 1878.

"modification or repeal.": TS June 8, 1878. "of free love.": The *Index* May 30, 1878. Sept. 28, 1878. "Vampire.": June 8, 1878. "twenty-five cent cigars.": Ibid.

Francis Abbot accused Albert Rawson of being a convicted thief and bigamist. Rawson had an explanation for both charges. The "theft" incident happened twenty-eight years earlier in 1851, when the artist bought some clothes to help some people "who seemed to be in need." Subsequently, he was arrested and persuaded to plead guilty. However, he eventually was given a pardon. (A facsimile was printed with his explanation.) The "bigamy" accusation was also erroneous. Rawson said that twenty-three years earlier he had lived with a woman, but they never married. Four years after they parted amicably, he married his first wife. Unfortunately, his first wife and her family were Episcopalian; "but I was traveling with my *mind*," he wrote, and "found that my Christian friends had succeeded in alienating my wife's affections. I became the victim of religious bigotry, intolerance, and hate."

3. "An Open Letter to Elizur Wright": TS Nov. 22, 1879.

4. TS Sept. 28, 1878. "reputation good again.": TS Oct. 26, 1878. "swelled the gale.": GM v. 1 p. 229.

According to George Macdonald, the libel suit never went to trial. GM v. 1 p. 230.

5. Nov. 30, 1878.

6. TS June 8, 1878.

7. "cheap form."? "out to us.": TS Dec. 7, 1878.

8. "this last November.": Heywood letter (dated Dec. 2, 1878) TS Dec. 7, 1878.

9. TS Dec. 21, 1878.

10. Ibid.

11. Ibid.

12. Ibid.

13. Ibid.

14. "the criminal sense.": Hayes diary Jan. 10, 1879.

15. TS Dec. 21, 1878.

16. TS Jan. 11, 1879.

17. Ibid.

18. Ibid.

19. Ibid.

20. Ibid.

21. "inflame the passions.": Devens's letter (Jan. 13, 1879) reprinted in TS March 29, 1879.

22. TS Jan. 25, 1879.

23. TS Feb. 15, 1879.

24. DAB.

25. Ibid.

Bennett's *Truth Seeker* tracts were not published, consciously anyway, with the specific intent to rival the American Tract Society's religious publications. However, Bennett's tracts, printed lectures, books, and periodical were undoubtedly perceived by Christian publishers as a threat to their printed dogma.

26. TS June 8, 1878.

27. "who wish it.": *Open Letter to Samuel Colgate*, TS February 8, 1879.

28. Ibid.

29. Ibid.

30. Ibid.

31. Ibid.

32. Ibid.
33. TS March 1, 1879.
34. "is justice done.": Charles Mackay, TS March 1, 1879.
35. Betsey Bennett obituary in TS March 8, 1879.

7

THE UNITED STATES
V. D. M. BENNETT

The United States is one great society for the suppression of vice.
—William P. Fiero, Assistant District Attorney

D. M. Bennett's trial for depositing prohibited matter in the mail (*Cupid's Yokes*) began in New York on March 18, 1879. If convicted, the sixty-year-old publisher-editor faced a possible $5,000 fine and a ten-year prison sentence. While Bennett did not write the pamphlet (or necessarily agree with its contents), he believed that as an American citizen he had the right to sell it. After three arrests on similar charges, Bennett was eager to have his cause for free speech, a free press, and mails free from espionage and Comstockism put to the test.[1]

The press (especially the New York dailies) covered the trial of the country's most notorious infidel accused of selling obscenity by the US Post Office Department's fearless special agent. The *New York Sun* declared, "The trial of Dr. Bennett for sending obscene matter through the mails is one of the most important of the day." A remarkably prophetic statement considering the impact Bennett's trial would have on American jurisprudence for the next half century. The four-day trial and sensational standing-room-only press reports for the prosecution of the blasphemous publisher sold newspapers—including the *Truth Seeker*.[2]

The trial, held in the United States Circuit Court in lower Manhattan, attracted a number of famous people, "all of whom are, more or less, identified as disciples of the school of 'free thought,'" the *New York Times* reported, revealing its bias against freethinkers. A *Tribune* writer sarcastically noted, "Scattered through the crowd of long-haired men and 'strong-minded' women were a number of well-known persons who have been summoned as witnesses for the defense."[3]

Standing behind Bennett was a diverse group of distinguished reformers and National Liberal League luminaries who ardently shared the defendant's free speech advocacy. His close friends Prof. Albert Rawson, Dr. Foote Jr., and Theron Leland were present. Elizur Wright, the veteran abolitionist, came down from Boston to support the editor, as did Ezra Heywood, the recently imprisoned and pardoned author of the prohibited *Cupid's Yokes*. Heywood was accompanied by his wife, Angela Tilton Heywood, a women's rights advocate and sister of Josephine Tilton. Andrew Jackson Davis, the famous spiritualist physician, was also in the courtroom as was Reverend Octavius Brooks Frothingham, biblical scholar, author, and lecturer.[4]

Bennett and his wife were grateful for the many devoted friends in attendance at the trial. But the influential men conspicuously sitting in the courtroom, providing moral support for the prosecution, caused anxiety. If the members of the jury were unfamiliar with the defendant and his scholarly and freethinking fellow libertarians, they undoubtedly recognized the names of Anthony Comstock, New York's most celebrated vice hunter; his assistant, Joseph Britton; and their powerful patrons. Reverend Joseph Cook, the famous lecturer, described as looking "like a cross between a pugilist and a cattle-drover," traveled from his home in Boston to lend his support to Comstock and the prosecution. Samuel Colgate, the soap tycoon, took time out from his busy schedule to attend. Outside of his business, most of Samuel Colgate's activities were devoted to *only* religious work. Although he was president of the New York Society for the Suppression of Vice, Colgate did not attend every trial that his organization prosecuted, but the Bennett case was personal.[5]

Samuel Colgate had his own reasons for attending the Bennett trial. One of the pamphlets that would be entered into evidence during the trial was Bennett's *An Open Letter to Samuel Colgate*. The letter, published only a month earlier, was not only causing embarrassment for the devout Baptist, but was also costing him money. The defendant's exposé charging the soap baron with publishing illegal birth control information was inciting freethinkers throughout America to avoid Colgate's products—a boycott that would continue for years.[6]

Presiding over the trial was Judge Charles L. Benedict, the man who concerned the defendant and his anxious wife the most. It was, after all, in Judge Benedict's courtroom that Bennett's friend Dr. E. B. Foote was convicted. Even more troubling was the fact that Anthony Comstock often boasted that he never failed in Judge Benedict's court. Prosecuting the government's case was Assistant District Attorney William P. Fiero, a thirty-six-year-old political aspirant and Shakespeare aficionado.[7]

Defending D. M. Bennett was Abram Wakeman, a respected jurist who had been a friend of Abraham Lincoln and close confidant of Mary Todd Lincoln. Although this was the first case of its kind for Abram Wakeman, he had the assistance of his brother T. B. Wakeman. Thaddeus Burr Wakeman (1834–1913) was also a prominent New York attorney who graduated from Princeton with honors at the age of twenty. Wakeman was one of America's principal free-speech proponents and devoted to Bennett's cause. When T. B. Wakeman was elected president of the National Liberal League, his predecessor Elizur Wright exclaimed, "Now you have the right man in the right place. He does not fear gods or the devils or the consensus of the competent." T. B. Wakeman authored the petition to Congress for the repeal of the Comstock Laws, an articulate and widely supported argument. James Parton said of him, "He has the truth; he is the coming man."[8]

Part of the defense strategy was to use standard books to contest the charge against Bennett. The defense team positioned a large collection of popular books by well-known authors, along with books and pamphlets written by the defendant, on a separate table directly in front of the defense table. Among the books were

- *Leaves of Grass* by Walt Whitman
- *Droll Stories from the Abbeys of Tourraine* by Balzac
- *Queen Mab* by Percy Shelley
- *Decameron* by Boccacio
- *The Relations of the Sexes* by E. B. Duffey
- *The Queen versus Charles Bradlaugh and Annie Besant* (trial transcript)
- *An Open Letter to Jesus Christ* by D. M. Bennett
- Assorted works by Shakespeare

Judge Benedict did not permit the books to be presented. He also disallowed the defense attorneys' plan to employ the freethought argument of comparing alleged obscene passages in *Cupid's Yokes* with certain sections from the Bible.[9]

"Are you a member of the Society for the Suppression of Vice?" the potential jurors were asked by Abram Wakeman during jury selection on the first day of the trial. "Have you ever read or heard read the pamphlet, 'Cupid's Yokes'? Assuming the defendant to be a Freethinker and an unbeliever in the Christian religion, are you under the influence of any religious views or prejudices which will tend to prevent your acting impartially as a juror in the trial of this case?" After reading the indictment against Bennett, William P. Fiero assured the jury that the prosecution was not "religious or sectarian" and it did not matter what the defendant's views were or "whether he was a believer or an unbeliever."[10]

The prosecution called only one witness—Anthony Comstock. Despite Comstock's notoriety, his physical appearance was unknown to the general public. Because of the paucity of photographs in the press during the 1870s, jurors likely got their first look at the crusader in the courtroom. The gentle giant who meekly swore on his favorite book that morning in front of his favorite judge seemed different from the vigilante who terrorized authors, booksellers, doctors, and publishers. The humble, dark-dressed "secretary" sitting in the witness box hardly resembled the fearless "Roundsman of the Lord" whose signature ginger-colored muttonchops hid a long scar caused by a stab wound inflicted during his well-publicized "fight for the young." The obsequious prosecution witness who answered Fiero's questions, while earnestly drawing down his upper lip, was unrecognizable as the brute who grabbed Ezra Heywood and threatened to kick D. M. Bennett's employees into the hall.[11]

The special agent testified that he sent the letter requesting *Cupid's Yokes* and received the booklet in the mail. Under an intense cross-examination by Wakeman, Comstock denied ever threatening Bennett or his printers. The vice hunter was evasive when asked if he knew where the defendant's place of business was located. Wakeman reminded him that he had arrested Bennett there a year before. "If he had that book in his possession at his place of business," Wakeman asked, "hadn't you authority, under your state statute, to have taken steps for its seizure?" The question was objected to and sustained. Wakeman was, however, eventually able to argue the important point that Comstock should have acted properly and used the state statute, wherein the maximum punishment would not have exceeded two years of imprisonment and a $100 fine. The first day of the trial ended with copies of the *Truth Seeker* entered into evidence by the prosecuting attorney. The issues included the defendant's defiant declaration to sell *Cupid's Yokes* and his *Open Letter to Samuel Colgate*.[12]

The trial continued the second day only after the marshals were able to restore order in the packed courtroom. The proceedings began with Abram Wakeman's opening argument—an impassioned appeal for civil liberty for the defendant. He described Bennett as "a quiet, peaceable citizen . . . of unblemished character . . . known to a great many of our people . . . as the publisher of a newspaper . . . in which he speaks every week to perhaps 40,000 or 50,000 people, scattered all over this country." Wakeman also praised Ezra Heywood, calling him "a very reputable and worthy citizen . . . burning with a desire to do what he thinks is the right thing towards the reformation of society and mankind."[13]

Ezra Heywood was the first witness called on behalf of the defendant. The author chose the secular alternative to affirm rather than swear an oath. Benedict ruled against Wakeman's every attempt to show Heywood's intentions for writing *Cupid's Yokes*. The next witness was a New York bookseller whose testimony was as thwarted by the court and as brief as Heywood's. Benedict blocked the defense team's strategic attempt to present the pamphlet as a "philosophical treatise" that was openly sold. Octavius B. Frothingham, another witness for the defense, was also denied the opportunity to testify concerning the character and availability of the booklet. A frustrated Wakeman addressed the judge, informing him of his intention to call several "distinguished philologists . . . some 38 or 40 of our best book dealers and sellers in this city." Growing increasingly impatient, Benedict ruled out the point.[14]

D. M. Bennett took the stand in his own defense and, like Heywood, affirmed to tell the truth rather than invoke the name of God. He testified that as proprietor of the *Truth Seeker* he published books and pamphlets and stated, "I have brought out some two hundred; I believe in all." He added that he lived in New York City for approximately five or six years and was happily married for thirty-three years. Wakeman: "You may state whether your wife is still living?" Bennett: "She is; she is in this room."[15]

Fiero repeatedly objected, and Judge Benedict sustained, a series of questions by Wakeman—all nine of them. Every effort made by the attorney to show Bennett's motive for selling *Cupid's Yokes*, and the fact that booksellers and news dealers openly sold the pamphlet, was stifled. "Have you ever been charged with any crime or offense of any sort, kind, or class, or character in your life other than what has been made by Anthony Comstock?" Wakeman asked. "I have not, except I was arrested last August in Watkins," Bennett responded. "But not at the instance of Mr. Comstock?" Fiero said. "I understood it was," Bennett stated.[16]

An attempt by Wakeman to introduce a letter written by Elizur Wright and signed by "at least one thousand good citizens" defending Bennett was refused. Bennett's testimony was brief and followed by several character witnesses. Dr. Charles Winterburn, the homeopathic physician and close friend, testified that he knew Bennett for nineteen years and six months. He described the defendant as " a kind, sober, honest, intelligent, loving, and lovable man; no bad act have I known him to commit during that whole period of time; benevolent, truthful." Fiero limited his cross-examination to inquisitorial questions—not regarding *Cupid's Yokes*—but *only* about Bennett's *Open Letter to Jesus Christ*. He asked each defense witness if they saw or heard of the incendiary pamphlet. The second day of the trial ended with a testimony of a printer who worked for Bennett. Wakeman called the printer to the witness stand to rebut Comstock, who testified that he did not visit or threaten Bennett's printers. Every time the defense attorney asked a question regarding Comstock, Fiero objected and the judge sustained. Judge Benedict, however, permitted Fiero to ask the printer: "Did you ever print the 'Open Letter to Jesus Christ' for Mr. Bennett?" The printer's response was, "I cannot say as to that."[17]

"This is the first occasion in my professional experience that I have ever appeared in this class of cases," Abram Wakeman told the court at the start of his closing argument on the third day of the trial. "I should not be here to address you to-day, or to take any part in this proceeding," he said, "did I not religiously believe in the right of this defendant to sell and mail this pamphlet in question." After a "scrutinizing examination" of *Cupid's Yokes*, he declared, "I have no more doubt of the character of this particular pamphlet than I have of any other of the hundred standard works that are published in your city."[18]

Abram Wakeman made an attempt to read *Cupid's Yokes* in its entirety, in order to put purported obscene passages into context. Benedict limited the reading only to the obscene passages as marked by the district attorney. The defense lawyer hoped that reading the whole booklet would enlighten the jury of the author's literary argument. Since much of the text in *Cupid's Yokes* was quotes from books available in public bookstores and libraries, the defense wanted to inform the jury of their general availability. Wakeman argued that many of the quotes in *Cupid's Yokes* were by some of the most respected men of the day, including Charles Darwin, Henry James, John Stuart Mill, Sir Isaac Newton, and Alexis De Tocqueville. "These are the great men, the great philosophers, who are responsible for the doctrines of this text," he asserted.[19]

The defense team's extensive knowledge of the contents of *Cupid's Yokes* and the work of the writers who were quoted in the pamphlet, was evident during Abram Wakeman's argument. He quoted passage after passage with elegant and persuasive points as to why Bennett should not have been arrested. Wakeman read a section from *Scarecrows* by Victoria Woodhull, who wrote about a beautiful woman married to a New York clergyman, who, by demanding "indulgence six or eight times a day, actually killed her by his lecherous excesses." The attorney asked, "Why did not my learned friend indict the 'Scarecrows'? Why didn't he indict that book?" Wakeman quoted a passage concerning Claudius Caesar's wife, who "often required the services of the strongest and most vigorous men to satisfy her lusts." He inquired, "What is the use of selecting my good old friend and consigning him to the penitentiary, and leaving your boys and girls to go to the library and get hold of this book and read it?" The judge denied Wakeman's attempt to submit other books and the attorney had to limit his defense to *only* the marked passages.[20]

If *Cupid's Yokes* was obscene, Wakeman asked, why did its author and everyone else who read it hold it up "before the face of the world"? He contended that obscene books were always "mailed secretly" and kept out of sight. "Vice loves darkness: virtue loves light." The defense attorney inquired, "Why do such distinguished men as Elizur Wright of Boston, one of the wisest, most sagacious, and foremost citizens of the republic, openly claim the right to own and read it?" Wakeman argued that Bennett was persecuted because of his "particular doctrines." Bennett published a "great newspaper" the attorney declared. "Great because of the ability displayed in its management and the auditory which is addressed through it every week, numbering more than 50,000 readers."[21]

Nearing the conclusion of his passionate argument, Wakeman reminded the court as to the testimony of "three good citizens" who attested to Bennett's "unquestioned character." The only response from Fiero to all that Wakeman said was, "Did you know that Mr. Bennett was the author of 'An Open Letter to Jesus Christ'?" What reason did Fiero have for doing that, he wondered aloud. "Why did he jump to his feet and ask that question unless there was something besides the question of obscenity in this book?" Fiero's motive, Wakeman explained, "was to show—and it did show—the motive of this prosecution."[22]

Wakeman also addressed Anthony Comstock's obsession with Bennett and *Cupid's Yokes*. Judge Benedict admonished the defense attorney and stated: "I could not allow you to argue if the book was obscene they must acquit the prisoner because Mr. Comstock was malicious." Wakeman's declaration that "[i]t is a charge under the cover of this statute to punish heterodoxy" did not convince Judge Benedict. Still exploring motive, Wakeman commented that Comstock had to do something to earn his $4,000 annual salary. The attorney did not believe *Cupid's Yokes* "injured or corrupted" Comstock's feelings. Unless, the lawyer said, "his sense of the obscene is so acute that he can't keep a looking glass in his room, or is obliged to undress in the dark, and sleeps in an ice-house."[23]

At this point in the trial, Wakeman read a passage from *Cupid's Yokes* that he believed "may furnish a reason why this special agent can think he discovers indecency where none exists." It could also provide a possible explanation for Comstock's "excessive zeal" with this particular case. The excerpt was a letter written by Anthony Comstock at the beginning of his vice-hunting career. On January 18, 1873, the young crusader boasted, "There were four publishers on the 2nd of last March; to-day three of these are in their graves, and it is charged by their friends that I worried them to death. Be that as it may, I am sure that the world is better off without them."[24]

In an effort to appeal to the jury's sense of justice, Abram Wakeman pleaded for their impartiality toward the defendant: "He [Bennett] believes that to suppress any such paper is an invasion of the great constitutional right of printing and writing and circulating a man's views as he believes, and he proposes to stand by that right, just as heroes have stood by it before, just as martyrs have done." Wakeman ended his argument imploring the jury to place themselves "in his position, realizing and bringing home to your hearts his case as your own, and then doing justice though the heavens fall."[25]

OBSCENE, LEWD, LASCIVIOUS, AND *DANGEROUS*

William Fiero began his closing address by defending his friend Anthony Comstock and his own Christian-sanctioned marriage that he felt was under attack by Bennett and Heywood. He bemoaned the fact that he had to listen to Abram Wakeman read passages from *Cupid's Yokes* and gave a melodramatic account of his sleepless night. Fiero claimed he was personally offended after hearing an extract read aloud during Wakeman's "impossible defense." He said that he was offended to learn that his marriage, performed by a Christian clergyman, "was a life of prostitution." Fiero thought that having just learned "that the five little branches that murmur around my hearthstone were but the offspring of a prostituted right" was the reason for his lack of sleep.[26]

The prosecutor proceeded to point out to the jurors that the Holy Bible had been characterized as obscene in *Cupid's Yokes*, and also in the *Truth Seeker*. "Now, what sort of a heart can a man have who can deliberately set himself down to write a book of that character?" Fiero asked. "And what sort of a heart can a man have," he continued, "who will send that sort of literature through the mails in this community?" He characterized the defense witnesses as so-called experts and asked the jury, "Do you need Doctor Frothingham, or any other ham, to tell you what that means?"[27]

Fiero acknowledged Samuel Colgate as "one of your most respectable citizens" who "appears in court as evidence that he does most fully endorse Mr. Comstock's actions." He called the jurors' attention to the defendant's *Open Letter to Samuel Colgate* that he introduced into evidence. Fiero denied that Comstock had anything to do with the editor's arrest at Watkins. "Now, gentlemen, this case is not entitled 'Anthony Comstock against D. M. Bennett'; this case is not entitled 'The Society for the Suppression of Vice against D. M. Bennett,'" he assured the jury. "Yes, it is; it is the United States against D. M. Bennett, and the United States is one great society for the suppression of vice."[28]

As the trial progressed, Bennett became increasingly disillusioned with the judicial system. Sitting and taking notes, he recollected Dr. Foote's trial in the same courtroom in front of the same judge. The editor recalled Dr. Foote describing the legal proceedings like a "huge, crushing mill, cog after cog, mesh after mesh, fitting into each other and crushing or grinding to powder everything drawn to it." Bennett concurred with his close friend's appraisal and found the experience a mockery and travesty of justice.[29]

Bennett appreciated the prosecuting attorney's admonition to the jury that his religious views or what he believes or does not believe should not be held against him. But he was stunned by Fiero's repetitive reference to his authorship of *An Open Letter to Jesus Christ* "with a view to prejudging the minds of the Christians on the jury against us." He wondered why the court permitted Joseph Cook to sit with Anthony Comstock in plain view of the jury, reading *An Open Letter to Jesus Christ*? And how could the great forces of this so-called free government be set into motion and manipulated by such men as Comstock and Fiero? Bennett wrote in dismay,

Is this free America? Can this be a United States Court? Is this the institution established by the swords of Washington, Ethan Allen, and Israel Putnam, and by the pens of Benjamin Franklin, Thomas Paine, and Thomas Jefferson? Is this, indeed, United States justice, where every man is guaranteed the liberty of conscience and the freedom of speech, and where the state and the Courts were not to know or favor any form of religious creed? No; it is the American Inquisition! No wonder that Anthony Comstock is so fond of bringing his dirty cases into this court.[30]

"I defy any man to find a book in the English language," Fiero told the jury, "that contains, within so small a space, so much that is obscene and indecent." He went on to proclaim he was a Christian father who was properly married and standing "not as a prostitute, but as a Christian." This prosecution, he assured the jury, "struck at the head-centre of all this obscene literature." Fiero concluded his remarks, informing them that *Cupid's Yokes* had already been declared "obscene, lewd, lascivious, and dangerous" by the twenty-three "good men" of the grand jury. The prosecutor's melodramatic final declaration exemplified what Bennett described as "gush and mush"—a style that the editor thought was "more fitted to the stage of the Bowery Theatre than a United States court of justice." Fiero exclaimed, "Let the Freelovers of the country embrace their ideas; let them, if they like, roll vice as a sweet morsel under their tongue; we spit it out of our mouths to-day, once and forever."[31]

The third day of the trial ended with Judge Benedict's instructions to the jury regarding the charge against Bennett. Benedict assured them it was "not a question of religion, nor a question of the freedom of the press. There is no such question involved in this prosecution. This defendant may entertain peculiar and improper notions on the marriage relation; he may be a Freethinker; he may be whatever he pleases; that should have no effect upon your deliberations. . . . Freelovers and Freethinkers have a right to their views, and they may express them, and they may publish them, but they cannot publish them in connection with obscene matter and then send that matter through the mails." Each member of the jury received a copy of *Cupid's Yokes* and instructions to confine their "attention to the marked passages. . . . It is upon those passages alone that this case must turn."[32]

There was, understandably, confusion in the jury room as to the definition of "obscenity." There were also inaccurate press reports regarding one of the jurors who voted for conviction after holding out for Bennett's innocence for fifteen hours. Later, in a letter to the *New York Herald*, the juror wrote,

> Now it is quite true that I was tired of confinement, and that another juror was extremely anxious to get home to a sick wife; but it is not true that I changed my vote for those reasons . . . one reason for changing my vote was to enable some appeal to be taken so that the true meaning of the words "obscene" and "indecent" as used in the statute in question might be determined by some higher court. After the jury retired for deliberation, there was doubt about the meaning of those words upon which the whole case hung.[33]

GUILTY!

D. M. Bennett was pronounced guilty on March 21, 1879. He accepted the verdict calmly and remained free on bail pending an appeal. Bennett immediately invited his supporters and fellow journalists to the Astor House Hotel for a meeting "on a matter of vital interest to the press of the city and country." At the hotel, he and his defense team discussed the legal aspects of the trial and the possibilities for an appeal. Several New York newspaper and journal representatives huddled around the beleaguered publisher, who continued to proclaim his innocence. Reporters opined:

> Again the axe of the Comstockian guillotine has descended. And again an honest and conscientious head has rolled into the basket. . . . Great is the indignation which swells the breasts of thousands of high-minded and clean-hearted people as the

intelligence goes forth over the telegraphic nerves of the nation that Mr. Bennett has been convicted. Shame! Shame on the society for the manufacture of vice, which claims to be an association for the suppression of vice!

—*Dr. Foote's Monthly*[34]

If the daily reports of the New York Herald were anything like the truth, the whole proceeding was a farce, and the case one of clear persecution.

The trial was characterized by the same spirit that ruled in the case of the Government against Susan B. Anthony for offering to vote, and was like nearly all endeavors to enforce cruel laws against individual liberty and the freedom of conscience. Talk about justice in a court of law!

—*Evening Gazette*[35]

A writer for the *Telegram* asserted, "Mr. Anthony Comstock has been granted by a stupid Legislature powers with which he should never have been trusted, simply because he is not intellectually and morally competent to use them right." The *Washington Capitol* echoed the *Telegram's* sentiments about Comstock and declared Judge Benedict's ruling "surpassed anything of the sort since Pontius Pilate, and would make it dangerous to mail a Bible or a copy of Shakespeare to any one." The *New York World* criticized Comstock, Bennett, *and* freethinkers: "We presume there is not much doubt among sensible people that if such power is to be conferred upon anybody, Mr. Anthony Comstock is not absolutely the most proper person in the world to be clothed with it. And that a dangerous power does not cease to be dangerous because it is only put in motion at present against long-haired and empty-headed persons."[36]

Despite some negative press, Comstock's crime-fighting legend grew during the trial. The day after testifying against Bennett, he was involved in an arrest that was reported in glowing fashion. The *New York Times's* melodramatic account of Comstock's "desperate struggle" sounded suspiciously as though it came directly out of the Vice Society's arrest blotter. Sensational accounts of Comstock's heroic efforts often appeared in the *Times* and, a historian suspected, "appeared to come verbatim from Comstock's own pen." These "new reports" convinced the historian that the *New York Times* "served as a mouthpiece for Comstock and the Vice Society."[37]

In a letter to the editor of the *Sun*, Bennett wrote about his arrest by an agent [Comstock] of a "theological society" and "theological prosecution." He stated his case regarding what constituted obscenity and how his attorney was prepared to prove that *Cupid's Yokes* was "written with good intention, as a philosophic or polemic essay." Even the Bible, he contended, could be considered "obscene" if sentences were taken out of context. "Mr. Samuel Colgate himself has positively violated the same statute under which I am convicted," he declared, "by sending through the mail certain information which is as much a violation of the law as mailing obscene literature."[38]

Bennett considered the daily press reports very fair and truthful—with the exception of a few unnecessary snide remarks about long-haired men and short-haired women. "The men among Liberals wear no longer hair, and the women no shorter hair, than other people," he said. "Even should they do so, it would be no crime." The majority of his supporters were satisfied with the press coverage of the trial. George Macdonald wrote, "The secular press almost unanimously condemned the conduct of the trial, the conviction, and the sentence that followed."[39]

Macdonald found Abram Wakeman to be as great a man as he was a lawyer. "His presence and his eloquence made Judge Benedict on his bench look like a child in a high-chair taking a scolding and occasionally saying 'I won't.'" Fiero's abrasive manner during his closing address (that he bragged would take only nine minutes) elicited Bennett's ridicule: "His style is a kind of raving not often seen, it is hoped in the United States courts. He reached very high and squat[ted] very low, something in the style of a jumping-jack. He whispered very soft, and shouted very loud, and swung himself around with great effort."[40]

William P. Fiero's bigoted prosecutorial style and unjustifiable

condescending remarks toward the defendant and defense witnesses angered Bennett's loyalists. George Macdonald described
Fiero, who subsequently became a New York state senator—likely
because of his prosecution of Bennett—as "one of those vain fel-
lows whom for his incorrigible conceit and impudence you feel
the desire to kick." In a lull in the trial's proceedings, Fiero
approached O. B. Frothingham and offered an apology for his
insolent "ham" comment. Octavius Brooks Frothingham, who
was an abolitionist and leading Unitarian clergyman whose scholarly discourses drew large crowds of cultivated New Yorkers,
ignored the attorney and replied with dignity: "Your insults and
your apologies alike fail to reach me or affect me."[41]

As was his custom, Bennett reprinted many of the newspaper
reports, both negative and complimentary. The transcript of the
trial appeared in three weekly installments in the *Truth Seeker* and
was eventually published and promoted as a "memento to Christian and legal justice." Disapproving of the editor's publication of
the transcript, Comstock visited the American News Company,
which distributed the *Truth Seeker*. In an article titled "Another
Turn at the Wheel," Bennett reported that Comstock, "with a
copy of our paper in his hand, and by his arrogant, intimidating
manner, bulldozed the manager."[42]

ONE MORE TURN AT THE MACHINE

A few weeks before the court date for his appeal, Bennett heard
that Judge Benedict might be one of the three judges to review the
trial. "It would seem that a judge in this city, in cases of appeal,"
he wrote, "should not be one of the three to pass judgment upon
his own acts. Good taste and good sense equally forbid." He
thought it was enough that he was tried in front of Anthony
Comstock's favorite judge; but for the same judge to rule on his
own rulings was unjust, unconscionable, and patently absurd.
"Any other judge than C. L. Benedict," he demanded.[43]

On May 15, 1879, Bennett's case came up in the United States

Circuit Court before Judges Blatchford, Choate, and, to the defendant's dismay, Charles L. Benedict. Abram Wakeman introduced nineteen points of exception he had taken during the trial and argued for nearly three hours. Nevertheless, the court upheld the conviction against Bennett. About the three judges and their decision Bennett wrote,

> It will be borne in mind that the three are Calvinistic Christians, and how easy it is for them to deal impartial justice to an Infidel arraigned before them the reader can decide for himself. The fact need not be lost sight of that Judge Benedict was on trial as much as the editor of *THE TRUTH SEEKER*, and who the other two Judges would naturally feel partial to can be easily imagined.[44]

Judge Samuel Blatchford wrote the important decision based on the *Hicklin* standard for obscenity, formulated in England by Lord Chief Justice Sir Alexander Cockburn in the *Regina v. Hicklin* case in 1868. Under the equivocal *Hicklin* formula, obscenity was determined if the material tended to "deprave and corrupt those whose minds are open to such immoral influences." The vague *Hicklin* standard also permitted that *only* isolated passages could be judged and not the intention of the author. Samuel Blatchford's landmark decision in the D. M. Bennett case—based on a sole British baronet's interpretation of obscenity—would serve as the foundation for obscenity laws in America until the mid-twentieth century. (Adding insult to injury to lovers of free speech, Blatchford was subsequently nominated—and swiftly confirmed by the Senate—to the US Supreme Court.)[45]

The *Hicklin* standard's ambiguity caused concern for most justice-loving Americans but not for Anthony Comstock. In 1879 Comstock had numerous "obscenity" convictions under his belt. He probably knew more about *his* laws and their capabilities and qualifying factors than the nation's lawmakers, lawyers, and judges. Comstock was convinced of the *Hicklin* standard's judiciousness and prudent effectiveness. In his book *Frauds Exposed* Comstock grumbled, "If this law is good enough for Great Britain and the United States of America, it ought to be good enough for a handful of mongrels calling themselves Liberals!"[46]

Indignation meetings in honor of Bennett were held in Boston and New York. "When the defense in this case proposed to prove Comstock a liar, and a very spiteful liar at that," Elizur Wright told the gathering in Boston, "the Judge ruled out the evidence on the ground that Comstock's mendacity was of no consequence." Wright considered this "the most relevant and pertinent positive fact in regard to this whole persecution and the law on which it is founded, which could not move an inch without a liar for a locomotive. Judge Benedict rules the moral qualities of the locomotive of no consequence."[47]

"About 100 persons, of whom six were women" attended the New York meeting, the *New York Times* reported in an article called "Indignant Free Thinkers." An effort to have the editor pardoned was announced, and the protest included harsh criticism of the judges and the Young Men's Christian Association. The *Times* reported that speakers spoke very irreverently of Christianity: "One man said he would like to see a Joss-house at one end of Broadway and a Mosque at the other, because the Christians were becoming too strong and power always begot tyranny."[48]

On June 5, 1879, Bennett appeared in Judge Benedict's courtroom prepared to read an article titled, "What I Have to Say Why Sentence Should Not Be Passed Upon Me." His request was denied twice by the judge who proceeded to pronounce the sentence—*a fine of $300 and confinement at hard labor for thirteen months to be executed in the Albany Penitentiary*. A twelve-month sentence would have allowed the elderly editor to remain incarcerated in New York City where friends and family could have visited. The judge also denied Bennett's request to have the sentence deferred until the Supreme Court could hear the case. "There was *malice* in that thirteen months," George Macdonald declared.[49]

After the sentencing, friends crowded around the editor to shake his hand, express their love and sympathy, and assure him that they would passionately pursue a pardon. Their tearful farewell was interrupted several times by Anthony Comstock, who entered the room beaming with satisfaction. Eugene Macdonald observed that many in the crowd were overwhelmed with emotion. But not Mr. Bennett, who remained the calmest person among them. After all, Macdonald maintained, "He had the right on his side, and with this to sustain him, he said, [Bennett] should not shrink from even prison walls."[50]

NOTES

"suppression of vice.": *Trial of D. M. Bennett*, Da Capo Press, N.Y. 1973

1. TS June 7, 1879.
2. *Trial of D. M. Bennett.*
3. Ibid.
4. Ibid.
5. "a cattle-drover.": GM v. 1 pp. 255–56.
6. DAB.
7. SP.
William Pierson Fiero was elected New York state senator in 1910. *The National Cyclopaedia.*
8. GM.
9. *Trial of D. M. Bennett.*
10. Ibid.
11. Broun and Leech.
12. *Trial of D. M. Bennett.*
13. Ibid.
14. Ibid.
15. Ibid.
16. Ibid.
Bennett learned that Comstock was responsible for his arrest at Watkin's Glen after befriending the vice hunter's estranged father. The father told Bennett that his son had written to the Watkin's Glen YMCA and alerted them of the editor's arrival. TS January 11, 1879.

In the same issue that Bennett reported his third arrest, he wrote an editorial aimed at Anthony Comstock titled "Oh, For Better Employment!" He criticized Comstock for letting his poor father and his wife and children starve. Thomas Anthony Comstock moved to England before the Civil War, where he remarried and had four sons. The elder Comstock moved back to America and estranged from his famous son who did not like his stepmother. The old man was impoverished and living in Brooklyn when Bennett befriended him. The editor reported that the old man was walking the streets with his "toes protruding from his shoes, without a mouthful to put in his stomach," while his children were starving at home. All this, Bennett wrote, "while his pious son was receiving $4,000 per year besides the other fat pickings he is able to gather into his voracious maw." He said that he had the "pleasure" of giving the old man $5 to keep the Comstock family from starving. He stated that several of his Liberal friends also felt charitable toward the old man and that one of them gave him $200. "If the son would spare a little of his surplus strength and piety that he now bestows upon those he seeks to ruin, and have a trifle more sympathy and kindness for his own suffering kindred," Bennett commented. "It would be much better for all parties concerned."

TS Dec. 21, 1878 and also Broun and Leech p. 59. TS Sept. 14, 1878.

17. *Trial of D. M. Bennett.*
18. Ibid.
19. Ibid.
20. Ibid.
21. Ibid.
22. Ibid.
23. Ibid.
24. Ibid.
25. Ibid.
26. Ibid.
27. Ibid.
28. Ibid.
29. TS March 29, 1879.
30. Ibid.
31. Ibid.
32. Ibid.
33. Ibid.
34. Ibid. *Dr. Foote's Monthly.*
35. Ibid. *Evening Gazette,* March 22, 1879.
36. Ibid.
37. "desperate struggle.": *New York Times* March 20, 1879. "news reports.": Sears.

38. TS March 29, 1879.

39. GM.

40. TS March 29, 1879.

41. GM.

Octavius Brooks Frothingham graduated with honors from Harvard College in 1843. A former radical Unitarian pastor and second-generation transcendentalist, he wrote *Transcendentalism in New England* (1876), the most comprehensive, objective, and indispensable historical account of the idealistic movement.

"Transcendentalism," wrote Frothingham,

> was an important factor in American life. . . . It affected thinkers, swayed politicians, guided moralists, inspired philanthropists, created reformers. The moral enthusiasm of the last generation, which broke out with such prodigious power in the holy war against slavery; which uttered such earnest protests against capital punishment, and the wrongs inflicted on women; which made such passionate pleading in behalf of the weak, the injured, the disfranchised of every race and condition; which exalted humanity about institutions, and proclaimed the inherent worth of man,—owed, in larger measure than is suspected, its glow and force to the Transcendentalists.

Frothingham evolved from transcendentalism—the belief that divinity was latent in every man—to what he described as Rationalism in his book *The Religion of Humanity*. He was a founding member of the Free Religious Association and president from 1867 until 1878. Frothingham was a great orator, and his sermons at the New York Masonic Temple were attended by large audiences averaging one thousand listeners.

EB.

42. TS April 19, 1879.

43. Ibid.

44. TS May 24, 1879.

45. DAB.

46. Anthony Comstock, *Frauds Exposed*.

47. TS April 12, 1879.

48. *New York Times* June 4, 1879.

49. GM.

50. TS June 7, 1879.

The Trial of D. M. Bennett, Upon the Charge of Depositing Prohibited Matter in the Mail, United States Circuit Court, New York, March 18–21, 1879. The court transcript (reported by S. B. Hinsdale) was initially published in the *Truth Seeker* and reprinted a century later by Da Capo Press in 1973. A Da Capo Press Series Civil Liberties in American History, General Editor: Leonard W. Levy, Claremont Graduate School.

8

BEHIND THE BARS

A great many ladies have written to Mrs. Hayes setting forth that you are an extremely bad man, and begging that you be allowed to go to the penitentiary. I had no idea hardly of the bigotry of this country until I read some of these letters.
        —Letter to D. M. Bennett from Robert G. Ingersoll,
                                                    July 22, 1879

On June 5, 1879, after being convicted of distributing obscenity through the mail by selling *Cupid's Yokes*, Bennett was incarcerated in the Ludlow Street Jail before being sent to the Albany Penitentiary to serve a thirteen-month sentence of hard labor. Because Ezra Heywood, the author of *Cupid's Yokes*, had already received a presidential pardon, many believed a pardon for Bennett was imminent. And it was hoped the sixty-year-old editor would be permitted to remain in the lower Manhattan jail close to his anguished wife and employees until the pardon was granted. While his friends were optimistic, Bennett predicted that his enemies would likely "devise something contemptible and unjust."[1]

At one time or another, the Ludlow Street Jail held some of New York's most notorious citizens. Victoria Woodhull, America's first female candidate for president, and her sister, Tennessee Claflin, also victims of the Comstock Laws, spent time in Ludlow. While incarcerated, the beguiling sisters were visited by another onetime presidential candidate, George Francis Train, the eccentric genius who came to their defense and who himself was subsequently thrown in jail for obscenity by Anthony Comstock. Train, who periodically wrote for the *Truth Seeker*, was a frequent visitor to the sisters' prison cell where he scrawled his odd epigrams on their cell wall. "I am satisfied the cowardly Christian community will destroy you, if possible," Train wrote, "to cover up the rotten state of society."[2]

William "Boss" Tweed, New York's most corrupt and ruthless political leader, was also a former resident of Ludlow, having died in the jail less than a year prior to Bennett's incarceration. Anthony Comstock never expressed any sympathy for the countless "criminals" whom he had incarcerated in Ludlow for "obscenity," but he was surprisingly compassionate to the thief who robbed every taxpayer in New York. "The way of the transgressor is hard," Comstock wrote after Tweed was sentenced to twelve years' imprisonment. "Who makes me to differ? My temptations were not equal to this poor man."[3]

After being consigned to a cell that was little more than a dungeon, Bennett accepted an offer to pay for better accommodations. While his $15-per-week 8' × 10' room was spartan compared to "Boss" Tweed's richly furnished luxurious suite, he was able to have visitors and allowed writing privileges. Armed with a noble cause and a clear conscience, the irrepressible editor promptly began bitterly venting his feelings in the *Truth Seeker*. He accused Judge Benedict of being only a dupe and carrying out "the behests of the aristocratic clergymen of the uptown pulpits, who really were the power behind the bench." The prisoner's meals were delivered by "Boss" Tweed's African American servant, who was still working in the jail. Employing nineteenth-century prejudice to help express his utter contempt for his persecutors, Bennett wrote, "I am free to say I think more highly of the dark-skinned Luke than I do of Anthony Comstock or his pious employers. The same remarks will apply to his Honor (?) Charles L. Benedict."[4]

Thousands of citizens—many prominent Americans among them—shared Bennett's advocacy of free speech and began writing letters to President Rutherford B. Hayes. Elizur Wright, the president of the National Liberal League, wrote a sincere appeal to Hayes. G. Albert Lomas, the editor of the *Shaker Manifesto* periodical, wrote on behalf of three thousand Shakers, asking the chief executive to "save one we love." Fifteen thousand personal letters would eventually reach the president's desk.[5]

The successful petition effort to free Ezra Heywood, spearheaded by the National Defense Association, had collected six thousand names. And while the Heywood effort was very substantial for the nineteenth century, it paled in comparison to the monumental Bennett campaign. Bennett's loyalists were aiming at one hundred thousand names to be sent to the president by the end of June—but two hundred thousand signatures ended up being collected by the end of the summer of 1879. Another encouraging development occurred when Bennett and his friends learned that Charles Devens, the attorney general, was convinced that *Cupid's Yokes* was undesirable—but *not* obscene.[6]

Several distinguished Liberals visited the editor while he was in jail. B. F. Underwood, one of freethought's most popular lecturers, stopped by, as did Benjamin R. Tucker, also a lecturer and publisher. At the age of four, Tucker detected that the Bible was misquoted in the Episcopal Prayer Book. He decided to devote the remainder of his life to correcting all mistakes theological, sociological, and philosophical. Now at only twenty-five, the individualist-anarchist had founded and published his own reform periodical, the *Radical Review*. Another visitor to Ludlow was Laura Kendrick, the free-love advocate and spiritualist who was instrumental in securing Heywood's pardon and personally convincing the attorney general to declare that *Cupid's Yokes* was not obscene. By far the most colorful character to come to Bennett's defense and visit him in jail was George Francis Train.[7]

In 1879 George Francis Train was no longer the wealthy shipping magnate, respected financier, and world-renowned promoter of railways that he was decades earlier. After running unsuccessfully for president in 1872—he later declared that he preferred the post of dictator—Train challenged Anthony Comstock. He published certain passages from the Bible with sensational headlines and was arrested by the young vice hunter and thrown into New York's dark and dank Tombs Prison. While awaiting his trial, Train agreed to plead guilty to an obscenity charge—but *only* if he could add "based on extracts from the Bible" to his plea.[8]

Citizen Train, as he called himself, cut a curious figure in Manhattan, wearing his full-length sealskin overcoat, flower in his buttonhole, and curly gray hair, that according to the *Herald*, he wore in "a distractingly talented manner." New York journalists were intrigued with the adventurer who had gone around the world in eighty days (inspiring Jules Verne) and had been on friendly terms with Louis Napoleon, Empress Eugenie, and the queen of Spain. The press covered his trial daily and the proceedings were so entertaining that they became known as the Train matinées. The case against Train was eventually dismissed after his attorney convinced the judge that Train was insane—not a difficult argument to make.[9]

George Francis Train claimed to have a "psycho" force that he used to control people and exert power over life and death. He became increasingly irrational and was eventually diagnosed by doctors as having an "unsound mind, though harmless." Nevertheless, the famous knight-errant, who had once consorted with European royalty, was still able to obtain publicity and generate interest in his causes. Although Train was an outspoken atheist with communistic views, he was able, because of his extraordinary achievements and notoriety, to get his opinions—always radical and often outrageous—published in the city's major newspapers. Bennett, on the other hand, was having a difficult time accomplishing the same from his Ludlow cell. So when America's most flamboyant albeit erratic former presidential candidate came to his defense with his blazing words and eccentric epigrams, the prisoner welcomed the publicity.[10]

After learning that Bennett was "Bastiled" in the Ludlow Street Jail, Train agreed to be interviewed by the *Truth Seeker*. A series of article-interviews with Train appeared in the weekly that can only be described as very entertaining and curious colloquies. From Train's park bench in Madison Square, where he spent most of his time talking to children and feeding the squirrels from his diet of peanuts, he shared his quirky tirades about the Bennett case. The subjects of Train's rants ranged from "Comstock's Lying Brigade" and "Colgate's Crime" to "Protestant Torquemadaism [*sic*]."[11]

Bennett responded to Train in a letter addressed facetiously from the *Hotel de Ludlow*. He thanked Train for coming to his defense in the city's newspapers and his supportive articles in the *Truth Seeker*. "You flatter me most too much," Bennett wrote, "but I can take that kind of medicine in pretty large doses." The prisoner lamented his own inability to get the New York press to mention his case. "There is a great amount of unfairness and meanness in the whole business," he declared.[12]

The embattled editor had someone else working on his behalf, someone as equally famous as Train but exceedingly more rational: Robert Ingersoll, the friend of three presidents of the United States and the man who was able to get Bennett's first indictment quashed. And while Robert Ingersoll was America's most famous agnostic, his personal philosophy concerning matters of marriage and sex were orthodox and even puritanical. He was not comfortable being linked to radical free-love advocates who were a small but vocal contingent of the National Liberal League. Ingersoll refused to assist in Ezra Heywood's pardon effort even though he did not believe *Cupid's Yokes* was obscene but only "simply silly . . . a foolish argument against marriage." But, after reading Bennett's trial transcript, he felt that the editor had not violated any law and was wrongly convicted. As to Judge Benedict's conduct at the trial, Ingersoll remarked that he displayed "all the prudery of a prostitute turned nun."[13]

Robert Ingersoll, a personal friend of Hayes, knew it would be difficult getting a pardon from his fellow Republican who had received harsh criticism for the Heywood pardon. Another challenge would be to persuade Hayes to override Samuel L. Blatchford, the Second Circuit Court of Appeals judge who wrote the landmark decision on *Cupid's Yokes*. Hayes admired Blatchford, who would become a Supreme Court justice a few years later in 1882. Ingersoll was also cognizant of Bennett's powerful adversaries. On June 7, only two days after the editor entered Ludlow, Ingersoll wrote, "I am very busy, going from one dept. to another; that poor Bennett is in jail; that I am trying to get him pardoned; that all the pious frauds in the country are writing to the President asking him to keep Bennett in prison."[14]

FORCES OF RIGHTEOUSNESS

While Bennett's supporters worked zealously in every direction for his release, Anthony Comstock mounted his own campaign to prevent a pardon. The vice hunter went to Washington to see Hayes whom he found to be "a thoroughly upright man, and a most conscientious and faithful President." "One thing impressed me," Comstock wrote, "he desired to know *facts*: and then, whatever was right and consistent he would do at all hazards." Besides traveling to Washington to personally appeal to Hayes, Comstock incited what Bennett called the "forces of Christian bigotry" to send him on to Albany Penitentiary. The forces included religious publications that were popular and influential in the nineteenth century. These pious periodicals that the prisoner had plenty of time to read in his cell applauded the sentence, vehemently opposed a pardon, and scurrilously attacked his character. Three of them were the *New York Observer*, the *Christian Union*, and Comstock's favorite, the *Daily Witness*. Bennett

left: DeRobigne Mortimer Bennett circa 1873, the year he founded the *Truth Seeker* in Paris, Illinois. (*George E. Macdonald. Fifty Years of Freethought: Story of The Truth Seeker from 1875, 1931. By permission of the Truth Seeker Company*)

Mary Wicks Bennett circa 1873. (*George E. Macdonald. Fifty Years of Freethought: Story of The Truth Seeker from 1875, 1931. By permission of the Truth Seeker Company*)

The United Society of Believers in Christ's Second Appearing, more commonly known as Shakers. *(The Shakers in Niskayuna [i.e., Mount Lebanon]—Religious Exercise,* Frank Leslie's Popular Monthly *20, December 1885: 664. Private collection)*

The editor featured himself on the front page of the *Truth Seeker* in 1876.
(Library of Congress)

The William Sharp engraving (1793) after the portrait of Thomas Paine by English painter George Romney. *(Photo by permission. Copyright 2004 Kenneth W. Burchell. All rights reserved)*

Robert G. Ingersoll circa 1890, the attorney and orator known as "The Great Agnostic." *(Roger E. Greeley [ed.],* The Best of Robert Ingersoll: Selections from His Writings and Speeches, *1983)*

Eugene M. Macdonald circa 1870s, editor/publisher of the *Truth Seeker* from 1883 until his death in 1909. *(George E. Macdonald,* Fifty Years of Freethought: Story of The Truth Seeker *from 1875, 1931. By permission of the Truth Seeker Company)*

George E. Macdonald circa 1870s, editor/publisher of the *Truth Seeker* from 1909 to 1937. *(Samuel P. Putnam,* 400 Years of Freethought, *1894)*

Anthony Comstock circa 1870s, founder and secretary of the New York Society for the Suppression of Vice, at the onset of his crusade against obscenity. *(Heywood Broun and Margaret Leech,* Anthony Comstock: Roundsman of the Lord *[New York: Albert & Charles Boni, 1927])*

The official seal of the New York Society for the Suppression of Vice. *(Heywood Broun and Margaret Leech,* Anthony Comstock: Roundsman of the Lord *[New York: Albert & Charles Boni, 1927])*

D. M. Bennett circa 1876, at the time he began his fight for "free speech, a free press, and mails free from espionage and Comstockism." *(Frontispiece, D. M. Bennett,* The World's Sages, Infidels, and Thinkers *[Liberal and Scientific Publishing House, 1876])*

Ezra H. Heywood circa 1870s, the free-love advocate and author of *Cupid's Yokes. (Samuel P. Putnam,* 400 Years of Freethought, *1894)*

Dr. Edward Bliss Foote circa 1870s, author and birth-control pioneer. *(Samuel P. Putnam, 400 Years of Freethought, 1894)*

from left: D. M. Bennett, Josephine Tilton, and W. S. Bell posed for "The Trinity" photograph in 1878. *(George E. Macdonald, Fifty Years of Freethought: Story of The Truth Seeker from 1875, 1931. By permission of the Truth Seeker Company)*

Elizur Wright circa 1880s, the abolitionist and actuary who served as the president of the National Liberal League. *(Samuel P. Putnam, 400 Years of Freethought, 1894)*

Stephen Pearl Andrews circa 1880s, the reformer who developed his own language and philosophical system. *(George E. Macdonald, Fifty Years of Freethought: Story of The Truth Seeker from 1875, 1931. By permission of the Truth Seeker Company)*

The Albany Penitentiary, circa 1880s, was called "the castle on the hill" and considered a "Christian institution." *(By permission of the Albany County Historical Association)*

D. M. Bennett dressed in prison garb at the Albany Penitentiary in 1880. *(Frontispiece, D. M. Bennett,* The Gods and Religions of Ancient and Modern Times, *1881)*

Albert Lomas circa 1880s, a Shaker elder and editor of the *Shaker Manifesto*. *(Private collection)*

Henry Steel Olcott circa 1883, the cofounder and first president of the Theosophical Society. *(By permission of the Theosophical Society in America)*

Albert L. Rawson circa 1870s, the author and artist who accompanied D. M. Bennett to Europe in 1880. *(Author's collection)*

The last known photograph of D. M. Bennett, circa 1882. *(Samuel P. Putnam, 400 Years of Freethought, 1894)*

below:
The bronze medallion designed by renowned sculptor Wilson Macdonald, who also created the Thomas Paine bust in New Rochelle, New York. Beneath the image of D. M. Bennett appears the sword of persecution, cracked by the pen. Coiled around the sword is the serpent of superstition, also broken by the weapon of thought. The hilt of the sword is adorned with a cross and the ornamentation contains a pope's tiara. The unique design symbolizes the might of the church shattered by the forces of freethought. *(Photo by author)*

above:
The D. M. Bennett Monument "erected by one thousand friends" in Brooklyn's Green-Wood Cemetery.
(Photo by author)

instructed Eugene Macdonald to reprint the articles in their entirety along with editorial comments by the prisoner. If subscribers of the *Truth Seeker* were unfamiliar with "godly papers" prior to his imprisonment, they surely became better acquainted with them after they read the July 5, 1879, issue of the weekly.[15]

From his cell, Bennett attacked these "specimens of this Christian spirit of charity and brotherhood." The *New York Observer* (the publication that slandered Thomas Paine when they maliciously asserted that he recanted his unbelief on his deathbed and died a debauched drunkard) declared the editor's sentence "light when compared with the enormity of the crime." Bennett's style of writing—especially while incarcerated—could be vituperative. Bennett threatened to expose the editor of the *Observer* with "damaging proofs" that he had been involved with a girl "nearly grown."[16]

The vitriolic columns of the *Christian Union* especially incensed the prisoner. The *Union* called the *Truth Seeker* "an immoral Infidel journal," and blamed Heywood's and Bennett's "free-lust literature" for causing serial murder. The *Union* opposed a pardon and declared, "There ought to be no clemency to the man who breeds moral malaria in the community for personal profit." A Connecticut pastor's virulent tirade in the *Union* denounced Bennett as a "scoundrel" and "cancer planter" whose petition campaign was "A Conspiracy Against Society." The pastor added, "There is a sort of nervous communication among the ganglia of vicious Infidelity scattered through the country that constitutes them one system—a church of Antichrist or synagogue of Satan."[17]

One of the editors of the *Union* was Henry Ward Beecher, who only a few years earlier had been involved in a scandalous affair. If the famous Brooklyn preacher was trying to forget the sordid details of his own trial that had nearly destroyed his prestigious reputation, the imprisoned editor of the *Truth Seeker* was more than willing to remind the reading public:

> It is, perhaps, very fitting that the old lecher who is capable of committing adultery with half of the females of his large con-

gregation, and then coming into court and for thirteen consec-
utive days perjuring himself . . . slander and defamation are
poor weapons for those to use who set themselves up as
teachers and guides of morality for the world. But "they all do
it." The more purity they profess, the more false and hypocritical they are.[18]

The *Daily Witness* assault provoked Bennett to express his dis-
gust with a touch of humor. The article praised Comstock as a
brave and "worthy agent" who they hoped would "cage many
more serpents." The *Witness* opined, "If Lucifer himself were
editor-in-chief, the contents could not well be more venomous."
Judging from the article's style, the editor thought "the pure-
minded young-lady inspector, St. Anthony himself," penned it.
As to the reference to Lucifer, Bennett admitted knowing little of
him—but was willing

to bet four dollars and a half—the proceeds of the bet to go
towards putting a new coat of paint on the image of the Blessed
Virgin mother of God in Saint Patrick's Cathedral—that if there
is such a fellow as Lucifer and the data can be surely arrived at,
he is more of a gentleman than either Anthony Comstock or
the editor of the *Daily Witness*.[19]

As Bennett was lashing out in print at his opponents from his
prison cell, Robert Ingersoll was taking a more diplomatic
approach. The eminent attorney was meeting with President
Hayes who he believed was "wavering" on the Bennett pardon.
"While I am satisfied that Bennett ought not to have been convicted," the president wrote in his diary July 1, 1879, "I am not
satisfied that I ought to undertake to correct the mistakes of the
courts consistently persisted in by the pardoning power. There is
great heat on both sides of the question. The religious world are
against the pardon, the unbelievers are for it."[20]

While Ingersoll was fighting hard for Bennett and freedom of
speech, Comstock was engaged in his crusade to "save the
young." Ingersoll worked out of a sense of duty. Comstock

believed he was on a mission from God. Ingersoll relied on common sense, memoranda, and personal interviews with the president. Comstock flooded the White House with letters, petitions, and newspaper articles. In marshaling his "forces of righteousness," Comstock drafted into service the nation's bishops, ministers, and their relatives. Joining the vice hunter's crusade were nine of New York's most prominent pastors, most notably Howard Crosby, the city's leading Presbyterian preacher. In a petition, they urged Hayes to refuse Bennett's pardon on the grounds that it "would be the signal for him and others to flood the country with vile and obscene books and thus greatly increase the immorality of the land."[21]

From the entries in his diary, it is obvious that President Hayes was in turmoil over the pardon. During July he continued "turning it over carefully, trying to see all of its bearings." He received an avalanche of letters of support *and* protest. Hayes was aware the booklet was sold "by the thousand" and was widely circulated. Ingersoll gave Hayes a list of New York booksellers who openly sold *Cupid's Yokes*. He also received a four-page letter of protest from the New York Society for the Suppression of Vice signed by eleven members, including Samuel Colgate and Anthony Comstock. The letter implored the president to deny pardon and that *Cupid's Yokes* advocated

> indiscriminate intercourse between the sexes, indecent and unfit for the youth to read; and destructive alike to the sacredness of the House, the sanctity of Marriage, and the moral, physical and spiritual life of the youth. Its whole tendency is to create vice and licentiousness, where they do not exist, and foster them where they do exist. This book has been used to educate the youth, and induct in them, the practices of Free-love, or more properly speaking *Free-lust*.[22]

As a companion piece, Comstock included an article from the *Daily Witness* titled "Fifteen Reasons Why D. M. Bennett Should Not Be Pardoned by the President."[23]

In addition to the pressure Hayes was getting on both sides of the Bennett question, the commander-in-chief was also feeling heat at home in the White House. From the outset, Lucy Hayes was against any pardon and was not about to let her "Ruddy" be accused again of acquiescing to free-lovers, liberals, infidels, and smut peddlers. Mrs. Hayes was the first to be called First Lady by the press. She was a devout Methodist and called Lemonade Lucy because of her no-alcohol policy at White House social occasions. Someone remarked that during the Hayes administration, "Water flowed like wine in the White House." Mrs. Hayes was also known to have considerable influence over her husband. The First Lady had the last word after receiving "advice" from her pastor and a long petition from Sunday school children opposing a pardon.[24]

The final mention of the Bennett case in the Hayes diary was on July 19, 1879, when he wrote, "I have after very careful consideration, reached the conclusion that I ought not to pardon Bennett." He felt that the case should not have been prosecuted, but that to pardon Bennett would "nullify the law" and would be an "abuse" of his "pardoning power." He asserted that Heywood had added passages to *Cupid's Yokes* so the pamphlet could be advertised as "spicy; as rich, rare and racy," and, "in short, obscenity to make money may be truthfully alleged of it." Hayes, pious and politically prudent, pardoned the man who wrote the pamphlet—but *not* the man who sold it.[25]

"I have seen the President again today," Ingersoll wrote to Bennett on July 22, "and I believe that he has concluded not to interfere in your behalf." Considering the enormous influence the country's religionists had on Hayes, Ingersoll wondered if he had been the right man for the job and if a Christian lawyer might have achieved better results. Although Robert Ingersoll had campaigned for Hayes in 1876, he and his fellow Republican leaders were less than enamored with their president whom they were ready to return home to Ohio after his first term in office.[26]

A Damned Outrage

Bennett's readers learned in the August 2 issue of the *Truth Seeker* about the president's decision. Hayes would not intercede on Bennett's behalf; there would be "no liberation, no release, no pardon." The same issue sarcastically noted the president's attendance at a religious gathering in the Events of the Week column: "President Hayes is visiting the Ocean Grove Camp-Meeting. He ought to pray for a backbone."[27]

The editor spent his last few days in Ludlow reading, writing, and trying to retain his sense of humor during an oppressive heat wave. "The prisoners," he reported, are "asking the memorable and ever impertinent question, 'Well, is it hot enough for you?'" He penned a tribute to his eight employees, who had visited him in a group. "They entertain a high regard for me, and I assuredly do for them." Of his wife, whose health was failing, he wrote, "The injustice that has been done me has nearly broken her heart. The punishment has fallen more severely on her than on myself, and so it will be when I am far away."[28]

On the eve of his departure to Albany, Bennett wrote to Colonel Ingersoll thanking him for the time and energy that he spent on his case. He informed him that he had directed Eugene to send a check for $100 in part payment. Ingersoll, whose annual income from his law practice and lectures was $150,000 to $200,000 a year, later returned the check to Mary Bennett. The letter's tenor reflects the reverence Bennett and all freethinkers had for the Great Agnostic. He said he had just finished writing probably his last "long letter" for his paper and admitted to have given way to the spirit. "I felt and said more than I fear you will approve," he confessed, "but it was in me and it had to come out. I hope it will not offend you." As to President Hayes, he expressed his contempt: "I feel so little respect for Hayes, that I hate to have you ask him again for any kind of favor. I can stand it 8 or 9 months up in the penitentiary. Let him go to hell with his pardons, I say."[29]

The thirteen-month prison sentence meant that Bennett would have to be transferred to the Albany Penitentiary, a prison with a reputation of being the worst in the country. In a final attempt to have the sentence commuted, Ingersoll appealed to the president's personal secretary on the same day that Bennett was transferred to the Albany Penitentiary:

Dear Friend:

Think you would speak to the President this morning about changing the sentence in Bennett's case, so that the poor old man may be allowed to remain in Ludlow street jail. It seems to me a crime to put that man in the penitentiary.

Yours Truly
Robert G. Ingersoll
Letter to W. K. Rogers
July 28, 1879[30]

On July 28, 1879, D. M. Bennett, accompanied by his wife and in the custody of two US marshals, took the elevated train to Grand Central Station. The Bennetts were met at the station by the *Truth Seeker* staff and Albert Rawson, Theron Leland, Samuel Putnam, and Josephine Tilton. The prisoner was allowed a private moment with friends, Eugene Macdonald reported, before being taken away to serve a sentence "imposed on him by Christian hate and perpetuated by executive cowardice." During the sad gathering one of the marshals was overheard saying that sending the old man to the penitentiary was a damned outrage. After a final round of handshakes the prisoner boarded the train for the five-hour ride to Albany. "Mr. Bennett knew by the firm pressure and heartfelt words, that although he was consigned to a felon's cell he had friends who would stand by him to the last."[31]

NOTES

"of these letters.": Robert Ingersoll, Letter, July 22, 1879.

1. TS June 7, 1879.

2. Broun and Leech p. 109.

3. Ibid., p. 180.

4. TS June 14, 1878.

5. Wright letter: TS July 5, 1878. Lomas letter TS July 5, 1879.

6. GM. Devens letter to Wright dated Jan. 13, 1879: TDMB.

7. TS June 21, 1879.

8. Broun and Leech.

9. Ibid.

10. GM. Broun and Leech.

11. TS July 5, 1879.

12. "the whole business.": TS July 12, 1879.

13. Larson and Frank Smith, *Robert G. Ingersoll: A Life.* Prometheus Books, Amherst, N.Y., 1990.

14. Smith.

15. "at all hazards.": Comstock, *Frauds Exposed.* "godly papers.": TS July 5, 1879.

16. TS July 5, 1879.

Two years earlier in August 1877, Robert Ingersoll challenged the *New York Observer* to prove their claim that Thomas Paine recanted his freethought philosophy on his deathbed. Ingersoll offered $1,000 if the religious publication could substantiate its assertion. Not only was the *Observer* unable to prove its accusations against the beloved author of *The Age of Reason,* Ingersoll forced the periodical's editor (Reverend Irenaeus Prine) to admit that Paine *never* recanted.

Warren and Eva Ingersoll Wakefield, *The Letters of Robert G. Ingersoll.* Philosophical Library, N.Y., 1951.

17. Ibid.

18. Ibid.

19. Ibid.

20. "wavering.": Smith. "are for it.": *Hayes: The Diary of a President 1875–1881,* Edited by Harry T. Williams, David McKay Company Inc., N.Y. 1964.

21. "forces of righteousness.": Broun and Leech. NYSSV papers at Library of Congress.

Howard Crosby (1826–1891) was the chancellor of the University of the City of New York and one of the revisers of the English version of the New Testament.

22. Hayes Diary July 11, 1879. "speaking Free-Lust.": NYSSV letter July 7, 1879.

23. Ibid.

24. Arthur M. Schlesinger Jr., *The Almanac of American History*, B & N Books, 1993.

25. Hayes Diary July 19, 1879.

26. Larson and Smith.

27. TS Aug. 2, 1879.

28. Ibid.

29. "pardons, I say.": letter to RGI, July 27, 1879, L. C. and Smith. Larson.

30. Letter to R. K. Rogers: R. B. Hayes papers.

31. TS Aug. 2, 1879.

9

THE CASTLE ON THE HILL

*The past has witnessed many brutal deeds done in the name of God,
but it was reserved for the nineteenth century to witness in the freest
land under the sun, one which, in infamy and refinement of cruelty,
rivals them all. The Protestant Church has striven hard to make her
record equal in blackness the Catholic, and at last she has succeeded.*
—Eugene Macdonald

After the solemn five-hour train ride from New York, Bennett, in the custody of a deputy marshal, took a carriage
for the twenty-minute trip to the Albany Penitentiary, located
southwest of the city. The Albany Penitentiary, opened in 1846,
had a dark history of overcrowding, water torture, and even death
as a form of punishment. During the Civil War, the penitentiary
held Confederate prisoners who fell victim to plague and were
buried in the prison yard. Known to locals as the "castle on the
hill," the prison was home to about nine hundred inmates in the

fall of 1879. "It looked as though it might be a college or some other institute of learning," Bennett observed as they neared the bleak fortress sitting at the end of a wide tree-lined avenue. "But the lessons taught here are not pleasant to take."[1]

The new inmate's first lesson in Albany Penitentiary was that it was a Christian institution. He was commanded to hand over the books, newspapers, and pamphlets that he brought and hoped to read during his incarceration. Confiscated were Greg's *Creed of Christendom, Christian and Deist, Supernatural Religion,* pamphlets by Annie Besant, weekly papers, and copies of the *Truth Seeker.* When asked whether he was a Protestant or Catholic, he responded, "Neither." The puzzled official inquired, "What are you, then, if you are neither a Protestant nor a Catholic?" Bennett declared, "I am an unbeliever, commonly called an Infidel, and that is why I am here."[2]

Bennett was once again informed the prison was a Christian institution and conducted upon *Christian* principles. After being shaved and having his hair cut close by the barber (he was allowed to keep the clippings), the new inmate was issued prison garb and taken to his cell, where he was served his supper. "Having had no breakfast but two slices of toast and a cup of tea at Ludlow, and no dinner," he confessed, "the slice of bread and molasses which was handed in for supper I ate with a fair relish."[3]

The next day Bennett was taught how to march and was assigned to a special overseer who made him stand for hours facing "the corner of the room like a little criminal in school." After suffering a few painful hours, the elderly prisoner asked the man if he could sit down. "Do as you are told!" he was instructed. Weighing nearly two hundred pounds and with a lame foot from a childhood accident, he complained to the overseer who told him that he would "have to put up with it." Later that day Bennett was assigned a job in the shoemaking shop where for the first two days he had to stand for the duration of his shift. Only after his feet became inflamed and blistered was he allowed a stool. Because of his bad eyesight he was given the task of applying cement to the soles of the shoes. Considering that he was sentenced to hard labor, the work was comparatively light, he thought. "Perhaps [Judge Benedict] and Comstock had better look into it and see that I have harder labor to perform," he wrote. "Perhaps Mrs. Hayes might be induced to lend her influence in that direction."[4]

The prisoner was held incommunicado for the first thirty days at the penitentiary. The earliest report to his friends and anxious readers about his status was from George Albert Lomas, an old fellow Shaker from New Lebanon. The Shaker elder and editor of the *Shaker Manifesto*, a monthly publication, was able to visit Bennett in the penitentiary as it was located only a few miles south of the Watervliet Shaker village. In a rare touching letter to the *Truth Seeker*, Lomas described his brief interview with the prisoner and reported "the old hero was in a most undaunted mood" and likely to remain so. Lomas reported that the prisoner's uniform was "coarse but comfortable." The Shaker was especially gratified that the outfit was not the traditional half black and half red, but *all* one color—Confederate gray. "But it was terrible to my feelings," Lomas confessed, "when [Bennett] said, with deepest emotion: 'You know Albert, I have not been used to being treated and spoken to like a dog.'"[5]

Bennett was appreciative of the support he received from the Shakers and felt especially indebted to George Albert Lomas. In one of his letters from prison, printed in the *Truth Seeker*, he thanked the Shaker community and its leaders. And although he admittedly "fell from the faith" and became a "backslider," the Shakers stood by him and he prized their friendship, constancy, and integrity. The Shaker's undying support was not limited to only prison visits and letters to the *Truth Seeker*. Lomas went to Albany and met with one of the city's most eminent attorneys, who told him, "Bennett's trial exhibited the most audacious proceedings for a court of justice; and no greater tyranny had been exercised since the days of Jefferies [sic]." Concurring with the attorney's opinion, Lomas promised the readers of the *Truth Seeker* that he would continue his support for the editor, whom he called "an illustrious martyr, suffering from acts of the most devilish bigotry of our day."[6]

Elijah Myrick was another prominent Shaker who came to Bennett's defense. A skilled craftsman, writer, businessman, and spiritual leader, Myrick was an outspoken liberal Shaker who was a respected elder and trustee. His forceful, compassionate letters from Ayer, Massachusetts, often appeared in both the *Shaker Manifesto* and the *Truth Seeker*. In a letter to Lomas dated August 14, 1879, Myrick expressed his concern about Bennett's well-being. He inquired if Lomas was able to see the prisoner and wondered how the warden and officers were treating him. He instructed Lomas to influence them "to treat him kindly, as a noble human being which he is," and added, "Who knows but some of us will be behind the bars?" Myrick's letter, printed in the *Shaker Manifesto* under the heading "The Inquisition," also criticized the clergy, the God-in-the-constitution advocates, and Hayes. He expressed disdain for the "subsided" president "bowing reverently to the dictum of church authority." He defended Bennett's right to doubt and eloquently proclaimed, "It is not the 'faithful believers' that have advanced the world. History tells us it is to the doubters—the 'infidels'—that the world owes the greatest debt of gratitude."[7]

Eugene Macdonald, the *Truth Seeker*'s acting editor, was also fiercely defending Bennett in the columns of the weekly. He informed readers that Anthony Comstock instigated the editor's Watkins arrest. The source of the information was the vice hunter's estranged and destitute father. Eugene argued that Bennett was jailed because of his infidelism and that his pardon was denied because of Christian influence on a cowardly president who was afraid to pardon him. "Yes, *afraid* is the word," Eugene averred, "and just the word."[8]

LEGIONS OF WORDS

On August 28, 1879, Eugene Macdonald accompanied Mary Bennett to Albany for their first visit to the prison. Shaker Elder Lomas and Elder Giles B. Avery met them at the depot and escorted them to the penitentiary. Avery, a longtime friend and fellow Shaker, was now the leader of the Mount Lebanon Shaker community. It was hoped that the presence of the two Shakers would help calm a severely distraught Mrs. Bennett. Lomas had visited on several previous occasions and was familiar with the gloomy institution, but the other three visitors were not prepared for the harsh interior of the dismal and notorious castle on the hill.[9]

The prison clerk greeted the visitors and tersely asked Mary Bennett, "I suppose you want to see your husband?" Anxious and too emotional to speak, she could only motion her consent. After she was permitted to meet alone with the prisoner for a few minutes, Lomas signaled the others to enter the room. Eugene observed his imprisoned mentor and described the scene for readers:

> Sitting on the opposite side of the room was the noble old man, but so changed in appearance that we hardly knew him, although we have seen him every day till his imprisonment for the last six years. His beard was shaved, and the stubble of a week's growth rendered his face rough. His jacket was of coarse dark blue, his shirt was of the cheapest and coarsest cotton, his pants were of gray shoddy.[10]

After a firm handshake, Eugene and the others gathered around Bennett, who emotionally described prison conditions. A prison clerk who was listening to the conversation warned the new inmate that it was no use telling his grievances. Nevertheless, Bennett continued voicing his complaints without fear of reprisal. "He does not know what fear is, and he never seeks favors by fawning," Eugene reported, adding, "We never more fully realized the greatness of the man than at this interview, although it was a very sad one."[11]

Bennett poured his heart out to his friends for nearly an hour, discussing the details of the prison's indignities. Eugene witnessed that "the monstrous injustice of his conviction came over him . . . and as he saw his weeping wife, the moistened eyes of his friends, his lip quivered, his form shook, and he wept with us." Immediately following the emotional encounter, he commanded Eugene, "Don't you again ask Hayes to pardon me; I shall be out of here one of these days, and I would rather be in my place than his." Turning to the officious prison clerk, Bennett defiantly announced that he was going to write about prison conditions and tell the *truth* about the Albany Penitentiary.[12]

Concerned about the food that was being served in the prison, Mary brought along a basket of apples, peaches, grapes, and canned meats. As she was tenderly handing a peach to her husband, the clerk grabbed the fruit and said, "Excuse me, madam; we will give them to him by and by."[13]

As the prisoner was taken away, Elder Lomas advised Eugene to prevent Mary from watching her husband through the grated window. "It was a cruel sight, and one we shall never forget," Eugene lamented. "Going along the walk was Mr. Bennett, his arms folded and his eyes immovably fixed upon the ground before him. Posted at different points were armed keepers watching him to see that he did not look around. Had he done so he would have been punished. It was a humiliating spectacle and well calculated to make one curse the tyranny which seems inborn in Christianity." During the visit Eugene learned that one of the prison authorities commented after learning Bennett was an infidel, "I don't care any more for him than I do for a dog!" Some of the strong language used by Bennett and Macdonald shocked the two passive Shakers. Eugene apologized and said, "We are of the world . . . and usually say what we think."[14]

The next issue of the *Truth Seeker* contained Eugene's report of their visit. He thanked the two Shakers and invited them to visit New York, the city of magnificence and squalor. The twenty-four-year-old acting editor's increasing disdain of Christianity was expressed in a bitingly hostile attack on his and his friend's enemies:

> We do not envy the church the enemy she is making. Cruel has been her sowing, bitter will be the harvest. The locks and bars of her hate will not always shut him from the world. When he once more resumes his place his hatred of the church will be unbounded. The mental torture and physical pains he is undergoing will not tend to soften his attacks upon that religion whose judges are tyrannical prosecutors, and whose ministers gloat over the sufferings of the innocent.[15]

Eugene Macdonald's impassioned weekly editorials in defense of his "chief" generated support for the imprisoned editor. Touching accounts of Bennett's cruel imprisonment written by sympathizers appeared not only in the *Truth Seeker*, but also in various New York newspapers and the *Shaker Manifesto*. Donations streamed into the publication's office and were acknowledged weekly. James Parton, the biographer, began a defense fund that included some sizable amounts from libertarians who pledged to contribute monthly. The September 6 issue reported a hundred-dollar contribution.[16]

On September 11, 1879, Eugene and Mrs. Bennett made their second trip to the penitentiary and were again met at the depot by Elder Lomas, whom Eugene called "the staunch and indefatigable friend of Mr. Bennett." At their second visit they found the prisoner in a happier mood than on the previous meeting. Mary was pleased to learn that the apples she brought would be given to her husband. Although the editor welcomed the news that twenty-five thousand names had been added to the petition, he instructed Eugene *not* to send them to Hayes, who could *"go to the devil."*[17]

Bennett's second letter from Albany Penitentiary, written ten days later, revealed a troubling turn of events. He had suffered from an attack of vertigo and was placed in the prison hospital. Otherwise, he reported his health was fair and he was able to sleep nearly ten hours a night. In the hospital he was allowed to receive books and papers and to write a monthly letter on a single piece of paper. He wrote the words so closely with a sharpened pencil that they became almost solid black and held more than three thousand words. After a few months, with practice, he was up to 3,250 words, which occupied more than a page of the *Truth Seeker*.[18]

The editor's writing output while in prison was remarkable and included his *Behind the Bars: A Series of Letters Written in Prison* and a colossal two-volume compilation, *The Gods and Religions of Ancient and Modern Times*. James Parton generously praised the work and found it amazing that it could be accomplished under prison conditions and in only eleven months. "I should have wanted twenty-five years for it," he wrote, "and then [it] should not have been half as interesting as you have made it." Commenting on the book's frontispiece photo of Bennett dressed in prison garb, Parton teased, "The dress becomes you. It brings out your bland and benevolent traits, and gives you a kind of grand-pontiff expression." About the work Parton wrote: "Your example, I hope, will make many men not afraid to touch the idol and help level it with the dust. But when the idol is overthrown, the great problem of human happiness will remain. Never forget that."[19]

In his relentless crusade to preserve purity, Anthony Comstock forgot about the Constitution that guaranteed freedom of thought. Comstock's biographer asserted that the vice hunter made a serious mistake by attacking freethinkers like Bennett, who "had legions of words at their command." Comstock, he said, "had been so unwise as to make a few martyrs."[20]

THREE CHEERS

Bennett's second letter from the penitentiary included words of appreciation for all the supportive correspondence that he received. One especially cherished letter was printed in its entirety in the *Truth Seeker*. "It, of course, was not designed for publication," Bennett wrote, "but it is so earnest, so comforting to me, that I trust the writer will not censure me for giving it to you."

August 19, 1879

D. M. Bennett, Esq.

My Dear Friend:

I have just read your letter in *The Truth Seeker*. I have thought of you every hour that I have been awake since your imprisonment. Every man on the jury that convicted you committed a crime. Benedict committed a crime when he refused a new trial, and Hayes committed a crime when he listened to the hypocrites and religious zealots, and refused a pardon. Well, we will get even with them all some day. Superstition cannot rule the world forever, and the quicker the decisive struggle comes the better. I hope the keepers of your prison will have sense enough to treat you as you deserve, and not put you on a level with criminals. You have violated no law, committed no wrong, and made no being unhappy. You have lived an honorable, useful life, and in any country not governed by Christians you would be free and respected. Well, bear up as well as you can. Time goes on, and in a little while liberty will unlock your cell and give you back to home and friends.

Yours truly,
R. G. Ingersoll[21]

Robert Ingersoll's sympathetic letter, dated only two weeks before the National Liberal League convention, was a powerful declaration. Bennett and his fellow freethinkers were hoping to finally realize their dream of forming a new political party. The editor told Eugene that he was waiting for the outcome of the NLL Cincinnati Convention with "great solicitude . . . and he wanted some action taken to make the church bigots feel the weight of Liberalism." After all, did not Ingersoll state in his letter that Liberals would "get even with them all some day"?[22]

In 1879 the National Liberal League was at its peak and becoming a formidable political force in America. The Cincinnati congress was the third meeting since the conventions began in 1876, and the 162 auxiliaries represented a quadrupling of the forty of 1876. The invitation to the 1879 NLL convention read: "A Free People to Make a Free Land, Free Thought, Free Speech, Free Ballot, and Free Mails: Must Be Secured by a Secular Republic Emancipated from Church Domination." The invitation was issued by Elizur Wright, the president of the NLL, but reportedly written by Robert Ingersoll. The goal of the 1879 convention was to organize a Liberal Party to participate that fall in state elections and to prepare for the presidential election of 1880.[23]

That year, there were reports that Robert Ingersoll had withdrawn his allegiance to the Republican Party. Ingersoll was one of the many Republicans who, for various reasons, were dissatisfied with President Hayes. He had initially backed James G. Blaine, a senator from Maine, for president at the 1876 Republican National Convention. Blaine, like Ingersoll, was considered one of the greatest orators of his time. Both were opposed to government funding of sectarian schools, and in 1875 Blaine proposed an amendment to the US Constitution that would have prohibited the use of tax funds for church-related schools. The "Blaine amendment" passed in the House, but was four votes short of the required two-thirds majority in the Senate. Ingersoll and Blaine were compatriots in their opposition to attempts by Christian lobbyists to enact federal legislation in their crusade for "moral reconstruction." They were very much alone in the grand old party that was dominated by religionists in the nineteenth century.[24]

It was for James G. Blaine that Robert Ingersoll made his famous "Plumed Knight" speech at the 1876 Republican National Convention. The speech caused pandemonium and helped make Ingersoll the greatest voice of the Republican Party. According to the *Chicago Evening Journal*, "Never in the history of politics was there such a demand for any one speaker as there is . . . for Robert G. Ingersoll." Unfortunately, Blaine lost the nomination to Hayes, who finally won the contested presidency only after an electoral commission was appointed to decide the election. Ingersoll's disdain for Hayes was revealed when a reporter asked him if he thought that the disputed election might cause bloodshed. "Who would fire a gun for Hayes?" Ingersoll answered.[25]

Prior to the NLL convention, a rift developed between two of the league's vice presidents: Robert Ingersoll and T. B. Wakeman, the man who was instrumental in drafting the agenda for the new party. And while Ingersoll was undoubtedly the greatest orator and perhaps the most famous member of the league, Wakeman was also an accomplished liberal. He was president of the New York State Freethinkers' Association and president of the NLL for three years. Also a superb orator, Wakeman was an acclaimed convention speaker and was renowned for his poignant eulogies at funerals of prominent freethinkers. After hearing Wakeman speak at a funeral, the treasurer of the NLL remarked, "Wakeman—in intellect a sage, in heart a woman, in soul a poet—delivered the most touching funeral address I ever heard."[26]

Robert Ingersoll objected to many of Wakeman's proposed platform objectives. Ingersoll felt that the party's purpose should be limited "to secularize the government, to take the hand of superstition from the throat of progress." He made himself clear as to any inclusion of free lovers, whom he boldly warned, "Let them spend their time in examining each other's sexual organs, and in letting ours alone." As to Wakeman's concerns for the party's stand on issues concerning Mormon polygamy and European Socialism, Ingersoll did not believe it was their business or warranted the attention of the National Liberal League. He sympathized with Bennett, and called him a victim of "religious bigotry and ignorant zeal," but he especially did not want "obscenity" debates to dominate the meeting. "Let us to this high calling be infinitely true," he proclaimed. "Let us occupy the heights."[27]

The NLL meeting was held in Cincinnati, Ohio, on September 13 and 14, 1879. While the gathering was less turbulent than the previous year, once again Comstockery was in the forefront. Resolutions were unanimously passed to modify the Comstock Laws and form a new political party—the National Liberal Party. In a show of sympathy, Bennett was elected a vice president. Robert Ingersoll gave impassioned speeches and ended by exclaiming, "I think this convention has behaved splendidly. Let us give three cheers for the party."[28]

The league's show of support for Bennett offended Anthony Comstock, who later wrote, "The Cincinnati Convention, then, had this poor blaspheming convict and would-be martyr and libertine as the special object of its care and sympathy to rock the cradle of obscenity. Faithfully they have performed their part."[29]

NOTES

"she has succeeded.": TS Sept. 6, 1879.

1. TS Aug. 30, 1879.

Some of these prisoners were held in solitary-confinement dungeons decorated with iron rings for occupants to be strung up by their thumbs. When the penitentiary was finally torn down in 1931, a bulldozer operator dug up countless human skeletons. He said they were everywhere, "a dime a dozen . . . as common as old inner tubes."

William Kennedy, *O Albany! Improbable City of Political Wizards, Fearless Ethnics, Spectacular Aristocrats, Splendid Nobodies, and Underrated Scoundrels.* N.Y.: Viking Press; [Albany, N.Y.] Washington Park Press, 1983.

2. TS Aug. 30, 1879.

3. TS Aug. 30, 1879.

4. Ibid.

5. Letter dated Aug. 14, 1879. TS Aug. 23, 1879.

George Albert Lomas was the first editor of the *Shaker* or the *Shaker Manifesto* as it was renamed in 1879. Published monthly, the journal was "devoted to the exposition of religion, according to Shaker theology." The masthead had a favorite Bible passage from Hagai 2:7: "I will shake all nations, and the desire of all nations shall come; and I will fill this house with glory, saith the Lord." The periodical's mission was to represent "the plain, undraped purity and unselfishness of genuine Christian life," and impart "the pearl of great price,—Christ, or the kingdom of heaven on earth," by "explaining the peculiar testimony and life of the people, called *Shakers.*"

Stein, pp. 225, 262.

6. TS Aug. 23, 1879.

Judge Jeffreys was a cruel and infamous seventeenth-century British judge.

G. A. Lomas continued to try to persuade President Hayes to pardon Bennett.

As late as March 19, 1880, Lomas wrote:

To His Excellency, R. B. Hayes, President:

Once more my dear President, I come beseechingly, asking your kindly consideration for the pardon of my friend D. M. Bennett, in the Albany Penitentiary, now suffering the last months of more than a year's sentence, which myself and his hundreds of thousands of petitioners verily believe to have been one of the most unjust of sentences. Our friend, Mr. President, is an old man, but we have known him personally for more than thirty years to be above reproach of an intentional unprincipled act. Ere his full term expires, will you not do us, his friends, the favor of his partial pardon? He has been most severely punished, even had he been guilty of the unjust charge. We, as Shakers, cannot think of you as capable of committing an irreparable wrong purposely. We would think of you as we have of our dear personal friends—Lincoln, Seward, Stanton, and Wade, to whom we never made application in vain for executive interference. Hoping at this late day you will pass by any efforts that run counter to his friends' petitions, and that I may have the high honor of bearing to him the glad tidings of the President's pardon.

I am yours, etc. G. A. Lomas.

TS May 1, 1880.

7. The *Shaker Manifesto* Sept. 1879.
8. TS Sept. 6, 1879.
9. Ibid.
10. Ibid.
11. Ibid.
12. Ibid.
13. Ibid.
14. Ibid.
15. TS Sept. 20, 1879.
16. TS Sept. 6, 1879.
17. TS Sept. 20, 1879.
18. GM v. 1 p. 250.
19. Broun and Leech.
20. TS July 31, 1880.
21. Ingersoll letter dated Aug. 20, 1879, and reprinted in TS Sept. 27, 1879.
22. NLL info: TS September 6, 1879. "weight of Liberalism.": TS Sept. 27, 1879. "all some day.": Ibid.
23. 162 auxillaries: SP pp. 528–529.
In 1880 the number of National Liberal League auxiliaries rose to 212. SP p. 532.
24. Blaine info: Alfred J. Menendez, "Blaming Blaine: A Distortion of History," *Voice of Reason*, 2003, No. 2.

In his amendment, Blaine was attempting to clarify the implicit doctrine of the religion clauses of the First Amendment by adding a provision to paragraph 10 of Article 1 of the Constitution. It provided: "No state shall make any laws respecting an establishment of religion, or prohibiting the free exercise thereof; and no money raised by taxation in any state, for the support of the public schools or derived from any public fund therefor, shall ever be under the control of any religious sect, nor shall any money so raised ever be divided between religious sects or denominations."

25. "Robert G. Ingersoll.": Quoted in Larson p. 120. "gun for Hayes.": GM v. 1 p. 266.

26. "I ever heard.": SP p. 819.

27. Larson and TS Sept. 27, 1879.

28. GM v. 1 p. 265.

29. Comstock, *Frauds Exposed.*

10

WARFARE BY MUDBALLS

That my Christian enemies should indulge in this kind of amusement is expected. But that professed Liberals, in acrimony, vituperation, and malice, should out-Herod Herod, and go far beyond my sectarian enemies, is a fact deeply regretted.

—D. M. Bennett

I n the fall of 1879 Bennett's prediction that his enemies would devise something contemptible and unjust came to pass. But he could not have known that his defamers would include some of the nation's leading freethinkers *and* two of his fellow liberal publishers. While Bennett was recovering from vertigo in the Albany Penitentiary hospital, a collection of telltale letters purportedly written by the prisoner years earlier to a "young" lady was exposed. These "love letters" were sensationally published in two journals: the *Religio-Philosophical Journal* and the influential *Index*. The headline of the *Religio-Philosophical Journal* on October 25, 1879, read:

ANOTHER IMPOSTER UNEARTHED
The would-be Martyr a Foul-
Mouthed Libertine.
D. M. BENNETT,
The Apostle of Nastiness.

————

Professing Devotion to his Wife, he Teaches
Free-Love.

————

THE TRUE INWARDNESS OF A FILTHY CON-
CERN, NEVER BEFORE PUBLISHED, AND
NOW EXPOSED ONLY IN THE INTER-
EST OF TRUTH AND DECENCY BY
A SPECIAL AGENT OF THE
RELIGIO-PHILOSOPHI-
CAL JOURNAL.[1]

The readers of the *Journal* and the *Index* were not the only sub-scribers to see the scandalous matter; copies of the *Journal* were also sent to Bennett's readers. John C. Bundy, the editor of the *Journal*, mysteriously acquired the *Truth Seeker*'s mailing list that was stolen the previous year. The letters may well be considered innocuous in today's culture, but in the Victorian prudery of the 1870s, they could easily be construed as shocking, especially if written by a married man. The letters were printed and accompa-nied by lurid editorial comments and accusations of criminality by the *Journal*'s editor, adding to their sordid appeal. "A Vile and Obscene Letter Signed 'Humpty Dumpty'" was one of the provocative headings in the *Journal*. The editorial introducing one of the letters begins:

> The letter is so low, vile and filthy, and so utterly shocking to all sense of decency and propriety, that it is unfit for publication in detail in this paper. It could be conceived and written only by a libertine of the lowest character and of the vilest propensities. It charges the lady with illicit and indiscriminate intercourse with five men whose names are given and with criminally destroying human life, alleged to be the results of that intercourse etc.[2]

In his effort to prove Bennett's "guilt," John Bundy printed samples of the editor's handwriting in the *Journal* with an unusual "photo-electrotype" facsimile of one of his business letters and parts of two of the love letters. The writing style was similar to Bennett's, and the facsimile revealed to everybody that the letters were probably authentic.[3]

MASS OF INFAMY

Bennett was not allowed to read any liberal periodicals in prison, not even his own. Therefore, he was unable to immediately confirm or deny the material contained in the exposé. Although it would not be known for weeks if the letters were genuine, they ignited a firestorm of hasty speculation and rancorous discourse. Eugene Macdonald cautioned anxious readers to wait until the prisoner was heard from as to the authenticity of "those letters." As to Bundy, who printed copies of the letters and sensationalized the story about Bennett's alleged authorship, Macdonald railed, "The one who to gratify personal spite, would print such a villainous article about a man unable to answer, is simply a fiend. It is the most dastardly, cowardly, infamous act we ever saw in journalism."[4]

In his campaign for the repeal of the Comstock Laws, Bennett gained two sets of opponents, who, according to George Macdonald, "[a]greed in nothing else but the sacredness of these laws." On one hand were the nation's Christian leaders and laymen who stood behind Comstock and supported his Society for the Suppression of Vice. On the other hand, the combative editor also alienated the conservative wing of the freethought movement; Free Religionists and some of the Spiritualist faction. A quarter of the *Truth Seeker* readers were spiritualists and the majority of the country's spiritualists supported Bennett's fight against censorship. Ironically, it was a leading spiritualist periodical, the Chicago *Religio-Philosophical Journal*, that first published the telltale letters. George Macdonald pronounced the Chicago

editor's "downright meanness and conscienceless lying far surpassed [that of] their ecclesiastical allies."[5]

The *Index*, with Francis E. Abbot as editor, had several distinguished contributing editors, most notably Elizabeth Cady
Stanton, a leading suffragist. The *Index* also boasted that Charles
Darwin was one of its subscribers. Abbot was the editor whom
Bennett had first contacted in 1873 in an attempt to buy his subscription list. Bennett assured Abbot that the *Truth Seeker* would
be more "radical and infidelic" than the *Index*, and therefore not
a competitor. He could not have known at the time how popular
his little prairie monthly would become. By 1879 the two editors
were in direct competition—not just in publishing—but also for
the direction of the National Liberal League.[6]

For the most part, freethinkers were united on social issues,
including the question of women's rights; but they did not always
agree on *how* to achieve sexual equality. The *Truth Seeker* represented the more radical approach and attacked what it considered
the source of the problem: the Bible. Bennett argued that the Bible
had denounced women as inferior to men for centuries and,
therefore, deprived them of their rights that they were justly entitled. The *Index*, representing the Free Religionists, the moderate
wing of freethought, maintained that the Bible had been misinter-
preted, and that it in fact supported and bolstered their views on
the rights of women. Another issue that the two editors disagreed
on—vehemently—was the repeal of the Comstock Laws.[7]

Bennett's rivals within the conservative ranks of freethought
derided his reformer status and found his alleged indiscretions to
be the height of hypocrisy. One of his severest critics was Francis
Abbot who had served as president of the NLL but resigned in
1878 after losing the election to Elizur Wright, one of Bennett's
most ardent advocates. Although Abbot had authored and fought
for the Nine Demands of Liberalism and advocated separation of
church and state, many felt that the educator-philosopher was
too rigid and pedantic. Abbot shared Anthony Comstock's
opinion that anyone who was for repeal of the Comstock Laws
was a freelover or obscenist. Abbot and Bennett had been trading

recriminations for a couple of years. Bennett was never comfortable with Abbot's condescending demeanor and was suspicious of the Boston editor's conservative ideas.[8]

While anticipation continued to mount over the authenticity of the letters, most of Bennett's friends remained steadfast in their support, even if the letters *were* genuine. Old friends like Thaddeus Wakeman and Theron Leland were unwavering in their support for the *Truth Seeker* and its besieged editor. The *Boston Investigator* advised readers to suspend judgment until the prisoner could be heard from. One of Bennett's staunchest backers was James Parton, the eminent biographer who continued to send money and commented, "No offense with which he is charged implies anything like the craven depravity of the assault upon a man unjustly imprisoned." Parton called the letters a "mass of infamy" and told readers to burn them and "go out and get five new subscribers" each to the *Truth Seeker*.[9]

A few famous freethinkers were not as eager to give Bennett the benefit of the doubt. Benjamin Franklin Underwood, the inveterate lecturer, went out of his way and traveled to Chicago to authenticate the letters. Underwood was a popular writer, member of one of America's most distinguished families, and a women's rights advocate; his wife, Sara, wrote *Heroines of Freethought*. Underwood had a satisfactory publishing arrangement with the *Truth Seeker* since 1874. Nevertheless, Underwood was considered a conservative freethinker and would eventually succeed Abbot as the editor of the *Index*. "I always objected to Mr. Bennett's course as shown in the general obscenity of his journal," Underwood told a *Chicago Inter-Ocean* reporter. He also complained about the editor's "scurrilous articles against the clergy, and the coarseness he exhibited when attacking religion and its professors." Underwood visited the editor in Ludlow Street Jail, but his subsequent rush to judgment during the love-letters imbroglio infuriated Eugene Macdonald, who reprimanded Underwood in an article titled "And Brutus Is an Honorable Man."[10]

The uproar over the letters continued for four weeks. A vigorous debate between Francis Abbot and Elizur Wright appeared in the columns of Abbot's *Index*. Abbot accused Wright of representing the prisoner as a martyr. "As to Bennett," Wright wrote, "If all the letters alleged to have been written by him are genuine, it appears to me he should be released from the penitentiary and confined in a lunatic asylum." Wright admitted that he often found the *Truth Seeker* "distasteful" because of its "bluntness and want of humane charity." But, it also "said so much that needs to be said, and which almost no other paper has had the courage to say, that I have valued it highly and honored its editor as a brave and honest man." Wright confessed that he was still not sure that the imprisoned editor wrote the letters. However, if he did, he was "certainly not the man to be at the head of any public journal. . . . But let the very worst be true of Bennett, hounded as he is by a lot of Christians meaner than himself, I sympathize with him in a comparative sense."[11]

The man whose opinion carried the most weight was Robert Ingersoll who was drawn into the embarrassing fray soon after the letters were published. While on a lecture tour in Pittsburgh, Ingersoll granted an interview, later titled "Ingersoll, Bennett, Cook: What the Brilliant Liberal Lecturer Has to Say about 'Cupid's Yokes' and a Fellow Lecturer." Just as the interview was about to begin, a man approached the Great Agnostic and asked for his autograph for a girlfriend who was "a confirmed little infidel." Ingersoll said that he was happy to comply and always glad to hear of "young persons escaping from the bonds of creed and determining to reason for themselves." As Ingersoll was turning the pages in the girl's album, the first autograph he noticed was that of Reverend Joseph Cook. "I like to be opposite Cook in everything," he said, "I'll write my name on this page." He wrote, "Love is the legal tender of the soul. R. G. Ingersoll."[12]

Robert Ingersoll told the reporter that he met Bennett only twice in his life "and then only for a few moments." But he had always heard he was a good man, "and I supposed he was in all relations of life a most excellent gentleman." Ingersoll mentioned that they had "a little trouble about business matters, but that was forgotten by me." He said that he blamed Bennett for getting involved with *Cupid's Yokes* since Bennett "did not believe, as [Ingersoll] understood, in the principles." Ingersoll stated that after reading *Cupid's Yokes* and the trial transcript, he was convinced that Bennett's conviction was illegal. He said that if he thought that the editor had mailed an obscene book, he would have never asked for his pardon. Regarding the letters he said, "I cannot believe these letters are genuine, and will not until Mr. Bennett is heard from. But if it turns out that he wrote the letters, I shall be sorry from the bottom of my heart that he ever did so foolish a thing."[13]

Even if Bennett did write the letters, Ingersoll said that he would still not regret trying to get him pardoned. "These letters were unknown at the time of his trial, and he was not convicted on account of them, but, as I believed, and will believe, on a false charge." The reporter brought up Reverend Cook's accusation that the colonel was "in favor of sending obscene literature through the mails." Ingersoll said that everybody knew that he was opposed to obscenity and anyone who made that charge "knows himself to be a willful and malicious calumniator; and whoever in the United States makes such a declaration tells a willful and malicious falsehood."[14]

Robert Ingersoll was becoming increasingly annoyed with being associated with obscenity. He told the reporter that he had "made denial after denial, explanation after explanation," and still Cook persisted in making these false charges. When pressed about his opinion of Cook's intellect, he responded by calling the preacher "a pigmy masquerading as a giant." Ingersoll chastised Cook and remarked that the clergyman's "philosophy is the theology of New England, seasoned with a little of the poorest German thought—that is to say, he mixes sauerkraut with his beans."[15]

A week later Robert Ingersoll was quoted in the *Chicago Times* saying that if the letters *were* written by Bennett, he was wasting his "sympathy on the wrong man." Privately he expressed his anger toward the radical faction of the National Liberal League in letters to Elizur Wright, the league president. The colonel wrote that he hoped Bennett could sufficiently explain the letters, but "if he cannot, had he as many mouths as Hydra, that corruption will shut them all." Two days later, in a private letter to Elizur Wright, Ingersoll lashed out at three men who he felt were dominating the NLL agenda and creating all the bad press. "I wish that Bennett and Rawson had their necks broke, and that Abbot was in the same condition."[16]

Bennett was eventually permitted to see, albeit only briefly, the contentious issue of the *Religio-Philosophical Journal*. The sensational headlines were "libelous," he declared, and "the comments and statements referring to me were replete with malice, venom, falsehood and revenge." He denounced the letter exposé as "nearly fifteen columns of most unjust charges, cruel epithets, and villainous falsehoods, together with several private letters written by myself for the eye of one person only." Thus he gave the final answer to all the speculation in a letter dated November 16, 1879.[17]

THOSE LETTERS

"Well, Bundy, are you satisfied now?" was the first line on the front page of the November 22, 1879, issue of the *Truth Seeker*. Five thousand additional copies were printed of the highly anticipated issue that finally answered the readers' question as to the letters' authorship. "In this issue of his paper," Eugene Macdonald announced, "Mr. Bennett embraces the opportunity of writing, afforded him once a month, to clear up the scandal bruited abroad with such devilish persistency and malignant meanness by those two paragons of journalists—Bundy and Abbot."[18]

The young editor provided his perspective on the mudslinging caused by the letters and defended his mentor. He said that nearly everything written about Bennett was a lie. The "spotless girl" that Bundy championed had initially tried to blackmail Mr. Bennett. The reason that she was embittered was the fact that she was unsuccessful in her attempt to get her job back at the *Truth Seeker*. She first tried to sell the letters to Bennett, who refused to buy them; an act that in Eugene's opinion, showed "his consciousness of having committed no crime." So she took the letters to the *New York Times* and the *New York World*—both declined the offer. Eugene said that Bennett was not the first to be "taken in" by her and in her present occupation as a "ballet girl" she would have "more extended opportunities." After all, she had lived a life of " blackmail and general promiscuity."[19]

Eugene Macdonald printed sworn affidavits by Bennett's friends, Dr. Charles Winterburn, Moses Hull, and Sam Preston, who all denied the accusations made by John Bundy in his *Journal*. Eugene blamed the whole attack on jealousy and spite. Bundy wanted to get revenge on Bennett because he was popular with freethinkers. Abbot was still bitter over his defeat a year earlier at the Syracuse National Liberal League Convention, "which was brought about by his arrogance and insufferable insolence. . . . Snapping one's fingers in the faces of delegates is not the way to win votes."[20]

"Yes, my dear friends, I wrote those indiscreet letters which Bundy and Abbot have spread before the public," Bennett admitted in a letter from the Albany Penitentiary that contained nearly thirteen thousand words and filled four-and-one-half pages of the weekly. His admission included the circumstances leading up to the letters and identified the woman they were addressed to. (Her name had been redacted in the published articles.) The relationship occurred when he and his wife were having a minor falling-out. Subsequently, "A few words passed between myself and wife," he explained. "I thought she condemned me for my Infidel views and disapproved of the work I was engaged in and in which my whole heart and soul was interested." He said that it happened while he was under the impression that Mary was unsympathetic with his mission and while he was brooding over it—a "third party came upon the scene."[21]

In the same issue of the *Truth Seeker*, Mary Bennett (in her first and only statement ever published while her husband was editor) defended her husband and denounced the "malicious and revengeful attack" of the *Religio-Philosophical Journal* and its editor who first published the letters. Mary informed readers that she was more upset over the publicity than from the "infatuation" and letters that her husband admitted to her he wrote over two years before. "But it is all past," she assured readers, "and the most amicable feeling exists between us; and I am sorry that other persons should make it their business to arouse and spread a scandalous matter that was all settled and overlooked." She expressed her displeasure with "Mr. Colgate and his society" and her disappointment with President Hayes who refused to grant a pardon. "Oh, how my heart aches for my dear husband, and how sadly I miss him! He is all the world to me—my life, my light, my sunshine, and my joy."[22]

"The ghouls," George Macdonald wrote, "were indifferent to the feelings of Mrs. Bennett, who suffered much more from this publicity than she had from the affair when it occurred." The third party was Miss Hannah Josephine McNellis, the woman who worked briefly at the *Truth Seeker* in 1876. She was single, Irish Catholic, and although educated in a Catholic school, had become a spiritualist, Liberal, and self-described medium. Bennett found her to be "petite, lively, chatty," and charming. And contrary to editorial assertions by Bennett's enemies, Miss McNellis was a thirty-five-year-old woman and not as young as she was repeatedly characterized.[23]

The Bennett love-letter scandal was not confined to the liberal press. A *Chicago Inter-Ocean* writer opined that while the letters did not change the case against Bennett, they tore away his "mantle of martyrdom . . . and destroy[ed] the romantic glamour that many have sought to throw about it." The *New York Sunday Mercury* also printed an article regarding the letters, and some felt that the missives were worse than *Cupid's Yokes*. In his book *Frauds Exposed*, Anthony Comstock weighed in on the matter and blamed *Cupid's Yokes* for corrupting Bennett, whom he called the "Apostle of Nastiness," a "would-be-a-martyr," and the "special pet" of Robert Ingersoll. "He [Bennett] attempted to put in practice the very theories, doctrines and precepts of this book," Comstock asserted, and "in letters so gross, sent to a young lady, who was strong, pure and brave enough to repel his bestial advances."[24]

Anthony Comstock reprinted, with his own characteristically crass comments, a sensational segment from the *Religio-Philosophical Journal* that sounded more like an article out of the *Police Gazette* magazine. The passage described an incident that allegedly involved Sam Preston, one of Bennett's assistants. Although Preston denied the entire incident in a sworn and notarized statement less than a week after it was first "reported" in the *Journal*, Comstock saw fit to republish it in his book *Frauds Exposed*.

> Sam (one of Bennett's pimps) forced himself unannounced into her room at night and begged, and when refused swore that he would take [the letters]. Two women were alone with an unprincipled desperado, Bennett's "heavy" artist, general plagiarist, and man of "many parts," who swore that he would have the letters by force, if they were refused. The room was dimly lighted by a lamp, and the woman was equal to the occasion. Seizing a broken water pipe fawcet that lay on the mantel, she presented it at his head, boldly advancing upon him, and ordered him to leave the room or she would shoot him like a dog that he was. "Sam," seeing that the weapon had a large bore and must carry a terrible ball, saw nothing more, and with a bawl for mercy turned and fled. But the girl had been so harassed by Bennett's jackals that she left the city and sought refuge among friends in another State.[25]

The letters revealed a side of Bennett that his friends, readers, and critics had not been aware of. For a man who did not agree, at least publicly, with Ezra Heywood's free-love advocacy, the letters disclosed an apparent disregard for the marriage vows. "I have no reverence for the ceremony mouthed over by a priest," he admitted. He described his marriage as "a body without a soul—a union without love, or if love once existed, now unfortunately dissipated and fled."[26]

In the letters, Bennett's characterization of Hannah McNellis ranges from an angel to the "quintessence of indifference." He chronicles his visits to New York mediums who confirmed with the help from spirits that he was doing noble work and that the spirits spoke to him very clearly and instructed him to press on. The letter commotion continued in the pages of the *Religio-Philosophical Journal* for more than a month. Bennett's infatuation with Spiritualism also caused consternation among his materialist readers. While nearly all spiritualists considered themselves freethinkers, not all freethinkers were spiritualists. On the contrary, many freethinkers were skeptical and ridiculed the popular pseudoscientific quasi-religion.[27]

In one of the letters, Bennett confesses that he cannot remember that he is an old man and offers to buy books for the woman and pay her rent for nothing in return except for the privilege of visiting her once in a while to have a friendly chat. In another, he goes into detail about the bitterness he feels over being scornfully rejected. He goes on about the night they went to the Fifth Avenue Theatre where she "coldly trampled on his honest upright loving confiding heart."[28]

Why Bennett wrote the embarrassing, long letters he could not fully explain and did not understand himself. He felt he had been "exposed to a species of moral miasma" and "delirium." He was not about to lie his way out of it and proclaimed, "I have never represented myself as a saint, nor pretended to be without faults and failings. . . . Perhaps the old saying, 'No fool like an old fool' applies to me," he admitted. But he vehemently denied that he had committed adultery, saying, "I was *not* trying to seduce the woman. I did not wish to make her a prostitute. I did *not* ask her in any letter or otherwise to hold sexual relations with me."[29]

Bennett also informed his readers that McNellis was not exactly a "paragon of virtue" as she had been characterized and that she had tried to blackmail him. According to him, she ended up selling the letters to the editor of the *Religio-Philosophical Journal*, who subsequently passed them on to the *New York Sunday Mercury*, the *Boston Herald*, the *Providence Journal*, the *Cincinnati Gazette*, and numerous popular newspapers. "She has hawked my private letters about from pillar to post," he exclaimed.[30]

The woman solicited seven dollars from Bennett for medicine to treat her "cold." The cold turned out to be an unwanted pregnancy. He had been duped into paying for her abortion, the result of her association with *another* married man. As to the unidentified special agent who was responsible for exposing the entire sordid matter,

Bennett strongly suspected that it was the same special agent who worked for the US Post Office, Anthony Comstock.[31]

It disturbed Bennett, George Macdonald thought, to have to expose the woman since he felt that "the male sex very naturally feel a commendable degree of magnanimity toward the opposite sex." But what was he to do, Macdonald reasoned, since his reputation had been so "grossly and dastardly attacked"? Bennett was accused by the "loathsome Bundy of pursuing, persecuting, oppressing, and trying to starve out a virgin." And, "of importuning her to sacrifice her virtue on the altar of his lust, when there was no such person as a virgin concerned, and the letters and circumstances admitted of no such interpretation."[32]

Bennett's mea culpa dramatically concluded with his decision to tender his resignation as vice president of the National Liberal League. "I wish," he wrote, "by no means to compromise the good name of anyone or retard the good work in which we are all so deeply interested." As to his connection with the *Truth Seeker*, "I do not propose to resign unless you say so."[33]

Readers of the *Truth Seeker* welcomed the editor's honest admission and sent numerous laudatory letters to the New York office. "Mr. Bennett is too honest, too frank a man to conceal anything," Theron Leland wrote. "He has no idea of diplomacy or strategy or concealment. He does not know how to dodge. His lawyers and friends have had the greatest difficulty in managing him to keep him from saying this or blurting out that." Elijah Myrick expressed the prevailing sentiment among the editor's loyalists. "A man that confesses his guilt, or frankly owns up to true charges," the prominent Shaker commented, "is deserving of the support and esteem of all honest men." The beloved imprisoned editor's resignation was never even considered by readers.[34]

A Gross Outrage

In December Bennett's health took a turn for the worse. He diagnosed his biliousness, dizziness, vertigo, and constant ringing in his ears as the precursors of apoplexy and paralysis. Believing a presidential pardon still possible, Mary rushed to Washington with petitions bearing thirty thousand additional names. Anguished and in tears, she implored President Rutherford Hayes to pardon her husband. She reported that the president "seemed touched." Hayes instructed her to have the prison physician make a statement about her ailing husband's condition. (The physician's statement was sent to Hayes, along with similar statements from a few other doctors.)[35]

Besides the physicians' statements detailing the seriousness of the prisoner's deteriorating health, friends in Washington called upon the chief executive. Numerous letters were sent, and it was rumored that the attorney general had reported favorably on the pardon application. The couple remained, in Bennett's words, in "agony of hope, suspense, and anxiety." When Anthony Comstock learned of the renewed efforts, he reportedly telegraphed Washington to delay the proceedings until he could travel there. The prisoner reported that Comstock had taken Miss McNellis and the letters to meet with Hayes. The church influence, Bennett wrote, "was again brought to bear with such force that, combined with *home orders* [Mrs. Hayes's], a pardon was again prevented."[36]

Bennett observed his sixty-first birthday (December 23) and spent a dismal Christmas and New Year in Albany Penitentiary. He heard persistent disturbing rumors that Robert Ingersoll had abandoned him. In order to prove that the colonel was still in his corner, Bennett published a supportive letter that Ingersoll wrote to Mary. "When you write your husband," the colonel wrote, "tell him that I have not and will not join in the cry against him. I am no Pharisee."[37]

The new year—1880—brought improved health but still no pardon from President Hayes. "Was Bennett pardoned?" Comstock asked and answered in his book *Frauds Exposed.* "No, not even with the most extraordinary petition of 200,000 names. Why? We have a clean man for President. It needs no word of mine to sound his praise."[38]

The prisoner continued writing his monthly letter for publication in the *Truth Seeker*. On February 8, with less than three months remaining in his sentence and feeling better, Bennett quoted a line from the most popular Shakespeare play of the nineteenth century—"Richard is himself again." A week later, the *Truth Seeker* included his personal letter to President Hayes requesting to withdraw his petition for release "from the cruel and most unjust imprisonment." Feeling in improved health and able to endure till the end of his sentence, he expressed his true feelings about the chief executive:

> I believe you have intelligence and legal acumen to know thoroughly well that a gross outrage has been perpetrated upon me in the name of law and because of my religious opinions. I think I am correctly informed that you have admitted that you considered I have violated no law. Yes, sir, I am convinced that, in opposition to your own sense of justice, you have listened to the misrepresentations of my bitter, intolerant, and persecuting enemies belonging to the church, and you have preferred to please them to performing a simple act of justice and mercy in opening my prison doors and granting me the liberty to which I am as justly entitled as yourself. . . . In this action you have made a record for yourself which must stand upon the pages of history for ages to come.[39]

On his annual spring visit to observe prison conditions at Albany Penitentiary, Attorney General's Acting Commissioner C. K. Chase, Esq., gave Bennett an opportunity to voice any complaints during a private interview. "I had no complaint to make of the treatment I have received from the officers of the prison," Bennett stated. But, he added, "I thought our government had reached a pretty low point when it lent itself to carry out the behests of religious bigots and persecutors." Chase was familiar with the case and tried to secure the editor's release by calling the New York booksellers who had also openly sold *Cupid's Yokes* but were never arrested. He informed Bennett that Attorney General Devens, Pardon-Clerk Judge Gray, Colonel W. R. Rogers, the president's private secretary, and every man that was prominently

connected with the government had pronounced his imprisonment a "gross outrage." (President Hayes would eventually come
to the same conclusion, but unfortunately not in Bennett's lifetime, let alone while serving his single term in the White House.)
Chase told the prisoner, "Yes, that is just the way it is; every man
I know of connected with the government is in favor of your liberation, *except the president,* and him alone. The fact is, Bennett,
the church is too strong for you; that influence has secured the cooperation of the president, and it is too strong for you."[40]

The hue and cry over the letters eventually subsided. The
readers of the *Truth Seeker* became more concerned about Bennett's health, a possible pardon, and his upcoming release from
prison. The letters controversy reminded George Macdonald of
some advice that his mentor had written a year earlier to a
Michigan bishop who got caught writing letters to a girl. Macdonald thought at the time that Bennett's editorial was uncharacteristic and "strikingly sympathetic." Bennett wrote:

> It is a dangerous business for a doting old man to write soft and
> silly letters to any lady, for he knows not, though they are
> designed for the eyes of but a single person, how many may be
> invited to peruse them. . . . They may serve to amuse for an
> hour a giddy public, but it would have been far better to con-
> sign them to the flames. Were we to give advice to men of age,
> it would be: WRITE NO LOVE LETTERS.[41]

George Macdonald recognized that the editor had something
on his mind when he gave that advice. "That was the voice and
warning of experience, for even then he was feeling disquietude
over certain letters written by himself." As to the profusion of the
letters, Macdonald commented that Bennett "never undertook a
series of writings that could be read in an hour" and unfortunately the embarrassing letters "were serving to amuse a giddy
public, and for more than an hour too."[42]

While the letters had alienated some of the more conservative
liberals, such as Abbot, Ingersoll, and Underwood, they also
revealed the elderly editor's humanity and honesty. Perhaps Mac-

donald's compassionate assessment of the letters fiasco is the most fitting: "An honest man trusted the McNellis woman and she betrayed him. Except for her treachery we might congratulate Bennett on the experiencing of so pleasurable a commotion of the senses at sixty." Macdonald plainly concluded: *DeRobigne Mortimer Bennett fell for Hannah Josephine McNellis.*[43]

NOTES

"fact deeply regretted.": TS Nov. 22, 1879.

1. *Religio-Philosophical Journal,* Oct. 25, 1879.
2. Ibid.
3. Ibid.
4. TS Nov. 1, 1879.
5. GM p. 251. Percent of Spiritualists: GM. "their ecclesiastical allies.": GM.
6. Letter to Abbot: Cited in Chapter 3 note 19.

"Mr. Darwin was a subscriber of *The Index* from the first year of its publication to the time of his death [April 19, 1882]. He manifested his interest in this journal by generous donations from time to time; and when he last renewed his subscription, not many months ago, he enclosed a twenty-five pound note to be used in the support and circulation of this paper."

The *Index,* April 27, 1882.

7. Warren p. 129.
8. GM.

The following year Francis Abbot resigned from the *Index,* distanced himself from the NLL, and continued to have only a sporadic relationship with the Free Religious Association. Abbot devoted the rest of his life writing his "great work," *The Syllogistic Philosophy* that he began in 1859 and completed the year of his death. He spent his final years lonely and profoundly depressed. In 1903 Abbot thanked the "Master of Life that at last He call me home to my wife and to my mother"—swallowed a large number of sleeping pills and died upon his wife's grave.

W. Creighton Peden, *The Philosopher of Free Religion: Francis Ellingwood Abbot, 1836–1903,* p. 108. Peter Lang Publishing, Inc., N.Y. 1992.

9. TS Nov. 10, 1879.

10. "and its professors.": TS Dec. 27, 1879. Underwood Dec. 10, 1879.

11. The *Index*, Nov. 6, 1879.

12. The *Dispatch*, Oct. 27, 1878 Library of Congress Manuscripts.

13. Ibid.

14. Ibid.

15. Ibid.

16. Larson.

17. TS Nov. 22, 1879.

18. Ibid.

19. Ibid.

20. Ibid.

21. Ibid.

22. Ibid.

23. Ibid.

24. Comstock. *Frauds Exposed*.

25. Ibid.

26. TS Nov. 22, 1879.

27. Ibid.

28. Ibid.

29. Ibid.

30. Ibid.

31. Ibid.

32. GM.

33. TS Nov. 22, 1879.

34. "blurting out that.": TS Nov. 29, 1879. "all honest men.": TS Dec. 13, 1879.

35. TS Feb. 14, 1880.

36. Ibid.

37. TS Jan. 17, 1880.

38. Comstock. *Frauds Exposed*, p. 498.

39. TS Feb. 14, 1880.

40. TS April 10, 1880.

41. GM.

42. Ibid.

43. Ibid.

11

BELOVED INFIDEL

It is not the "faithful believers" that have advanced the world. History tells us it is to the doubters—the "infidels"—that the world owes the greatest debt of gratitude.

—Elijah Myrick

April 29, 1880, was D. M. Bennett's day of liberation from the Albany Penitentiary. (He served eleven months of his thirteen-month sentence.) After the prisoner packed his belongings and removed his "felon's garb," he put on a brand-new suit of "citizen's clothes" brought by his wife. In the guardroom he met his friends: Albert Lomas, Dr. Foote Sr., and Daniel Ryan, chairman of the Bennett Reception Committee. After handshakes and a little speech from Ryan, Bennett spoke a few grateful words and was then promptly taken to the private quarters of the prison superintendent where he found Mary anxiously waiting. They immediately locked in each other's embrace. After parting on good terms with the superintendent and his family, the Bennetts boarded a carriage and rolled away from the castle on the hill, never, Bennett hoped, "to enter its walls again." The prisoner dedicated his two-volume *The Gods and Religions of Ancient and Modern Times*, written while in prison, to the superintendent and his wife.[1]

Before boarding the express train for New York City, the couple visited the new Albany Capitol Building where they listened briefly to the state legislature discussing the question of taxation of church property. Of course it did not pass, Bennett reported, "though if church property is free from taxation, in justice all other property ought to be." After dining together for the first time in nearly a year, they proceeded to the station where they met Lomas and a Catholic priest whom Bennett had become acquainted with while in prison. "He is a man for whom I entertain a very high respect, and one who has less bigotry and less superstition and intolerance than almost any clergyman I have ever met."[2]

The 2:40 train from Albany arrived in New York City a little past seven in the evening. The Bennetts were met by friends and transported in a carriage to the brightly lit *Truth Seeker* office, where the embattled editor was warmly greeted by all of his employees. Speeches were made, toasts given, and songs were sung. The temperate former Shaker later confessed to imbibing some of the California wine that he observed was available in "reasonable quantity" in the composing room. "I found a wineglassful did me no harm," he confessed, adding, "it being the first drop of wine or beverage of any kind I had tasted for nearly a year."[3]

Years later, George Macdonald elaborated on the reception, which had been somewhat more raucous than the editor had reported. There were about ten men waiting in anticipation of Bennett's arrival, which occurred at about 8 PM. As to the wine, Macdonald wrote, "I believe anything in the form of a stimulant would have been powerless to increase the exhilaration already felt over the prospect of seeing the 'doctor' again." Macdonald recalled Bennett's concession to having had a glass of wine that the editor said did him no harm. "For my part," Macdonald said, "I do not believe he ever drank anything in his life that did him *more good*."[4]

After countless cheers and a few words from the elated editor, he told them to enjoy themselves and went into another room for a meeting with the Defense Committee. More wine was sent for and everyone sang renditions of "Isle de Blackwell." The party lasted until midnight, when Mr. Bennett came in to say goodnight and, "after a final cheer, all hands went home, feeling we had enjoyed a quiet and orderly meeting." The owner of the building, however, did not share Macdonald's opinion and complained about the noise.[5]

The following morning, the contented editor sat at his familiar table writing letters and meeting with old friends. "The change indeed is great from my condition for the past eleven months," he wrote. "Now, may my enemies let me alone and allow me to pursue my legitimate business in peace!" While many of his visitors that day congratulated him about his vigor and good health, prison had taken its toll on the sixty-one-year-old. Some believed that he *never* fully recuperated from the harsh conditions at Albany.[6]

———— ♦ ————

THE BENNETT RECEPTION

Honor to a Returned Prisoner,
Chickering Hall, Sunday Evening, May 2d

A GRAND OVATION

On Sunday evening, May 2, 1880, the Bennett reception was held in Chickering Hall at the corner of Fifth Avenue and Eighteenth Street. Built in 1875, the hall was one of the most fashionable venues in the city. In 1876 Thomas Huxley, the British biologist who championed Darwin's theory of evolution, lectured at Chickering Hall "in the presence of one of the largest and most brilliant audiences which has yet greeted him in his country," the *New York Times* reported. (A few years later Oscar Wilde, the flamboyant English writer and self-described *aesthete*, would give a lecture in the opulent venue.) Sponsored by the National Defense Association, the reception was, in George Macdonald's words, "an overwhelming success, only that the place was too small for the crowd." At 7:30 PM organ music began and accompanied a quintet led by Mrs. Virginia Macdonald (Eugene's wife), who "sang in excellent style" a song written for "our martyr friend" to the tune of "John Brown's Body Lies Mouldering in the Grave."[7]

Three thousand supporters attended the reception while another thousand remained outside. The seats were filled and standing room only was available to the fortunate who gained entrance to the sold-out reception. A pamphlet containing excerpts of the "love-letters, that had previously been mailed to Bennett's friends, rivals, and newspapers across the country was handed out in the street by boys hired by Anthony Comstock. Nevertheless, the stunt was 'ineffectual,'" Macdonald reported. There was nothing in the vice hunter's power that could ruin the rousing celebration that one publication called "not only one of the largest, but one of the most if not *the* most enthusiastic ever held in the city."[8]

Many of America's most influential reformers attended the reception. Sitting prominently on stage in a large armchair was Elizur Wright from Boston, who, as president of the National Liberal League, presided over the meeting and made the opening address. Some of the distinguished liberals at Chickering Hall were Ezra Heywood, Lucy Colman, Amy Post, Stephen Pearl Andrews, Moses Hull, Amelia Colby, Thaddeus Wakeman, and Eugene and George Macdonald. "We meet in the name of common sense and a common humanity—friends of law who protest against the perversion of law," Elizur Wright eloquently began the meeting and continued,

> What is law worth without liberty? What is government worth when it leaves no room for self-government? What is religion worth, which seeks to save men by faith in the unknowable, and exacts faith by penalty? What is enforced morality worth? What is man worth when reduced to a machine? Since the Dred Scott decision there has been nothing to my knowledge so dis-

graceful to the United States as the trials, or rather persecutions, of E. H. Heywood and D. M. Bennett.[9]

Elizur Wright denounced the Comstock Laws and praised Bennett as one of the exceptional men who unfortunately are not honored until death. The veteran abolitionist concluded his speech:

> This is why I like to grasp D. M. Bennett's hand before he is dead, and say: Go on, brother. By blasting falsehood in favor of the truth you seek you have made the world better, including yourself. Long may you live to continue it! If the bland and soft-speaking doctors of divinity don't like your sledge-hammer blows, let them discard their barbarous old creeds, morally abominable and demonstrably impossible; and if they must believe in a world beyond this, let them content themselves with the mild and amiable faith of our Spiritualist sisters and brothers, which all of us will be glad to entertain as fast as our brains, time, and opportunities will permit us.[10]

Telegrams and letters of regret from across America, Canada, and Europe were read aloud. Those libertarians who were unable to attend included Courtlandt Palmer, Horace Seaver and J. P. Mendum of the *Boston Investigator*, James Parton, and Charles Bradlaugh, the towering figure of English freethought. Though they were not at the reception, their letters were read.[11]

The second speaker, T. B. Wakeman, spoke at length of the danger of Calvinism and the evils that would result from the Comstock Laws. The attorney paraphrased the National Defense Association's uncompromising motto: "*Eternal vigilance, the price of liberty*, should be the watchword you carry with you from this hall to-night." He told the audience that he had hoped to introduce Bennett in his prison uniform, but "one could not be obtained for love or money." So "without martyr uniform and in plain citizen's dress," which Wakeman admitted he liked best, he continued the introduction. The attorney said of the editor, "The kind-hearted gentleman, the real 'truth-seeker,' the faithful friend and citizen, let us honor him with our sympathy for the past, and with our support in the future." During the address the applause was generous, but as the speaker took Bennett by the hand, leading him to the front of the stage, the clapping exploded forth like a perfect storm. For ten minutes a sustained thunderous noise shook the hall. The audience, one reporter noted, "appeared to be composed of the most respectable people, but they allowed their enthusiasm to master them, and men and women alike arose in their seats, waved their hats and handkerchiefs and shouted until they were hoarse." They were a "magnificent audience," Theron Leland observed, "who knew how to cheer in the right places."[12]

After a man stood in the gallery and proposed three cheers for Bennett, the cheers were given with so much enthusiasm as to almost tear the roof from the building. A touching moment occurred when a woman in the audience handed a large, beautiful bouquet of roses to Bennett that the modest editor accepted with a bow of gratitude. "He is almost an old man, certainly on the shady side of 60," a reporter for the *New York Times* commented, "and, as he stepped forward, his feelings overcame him, his lips trembled, and his eyes filled with tears." Nearly overcome by his emotions, he began his speech:

> My Dear Friends: Language is feeble to express to you the sentiment of my heart at this moment. This is the proudest moment of my life. I feel grateful to you for your kindness, for your sympathy, and for your appreciation of the feeble efforts I have made in behalf of liberty. I can well say this is the happiest moment of my life. [applause] I feel repaid, almost now, for what I endured in the lonely cell, four feet by eight, as well as when I lay upon the sick-bed in the hospital of the prison. I feel glad and thankful to unite with you in defense of the rights of American citizens, of liberty of speech, the liberty of the press, the freedom of the mails.[13]

Bennett proceeded to give a full account of his arrests, trial, and imprisonment. Although the editor was not a great orator, his speech was often interrupted by applause from the enraptured audience. The hall erupted in a roaring ovation at the mention of Thomas Paine. Hisses were heard when they recognized the names of their common adversaries like the Reverend Howard Crosby, chancellor of New York University who had told a YMCA audience that sending Bennett to prison was the greatest act ever performed. Bennett's litany included Judge Benedict and Joseph Cook—"the great so-considered scientific and ecclesiastical speaker." Anthony Comstock's name elicited the strongest hisses.[14]

Bennett assured the audience that he had no intention of violating any laws. And while admittedly "somewhat advanced in years," he was not going to be a coward and would never "be false to the principles of liberty, truth and justice so long as I know myself and have my right mind." Bennett defiantly concluded his speech with "I am resolved to be a good citizen; *I will speak the truth and I will print it.*"[15]

Stephen Pearl Andrews, Ezra Heywood, and Moses Hull also spoke. In between speeches, telegrams were read that provided some humorous moments for the audience. Other high points of the evening included two speeches made by Amelia Colby and Lucy Colman. "When you put God into the Constitution," Amelia Colby announced, "you put every American citizen out." At her "startling proposition," the *New York Times* noted, "the audience clapped its hands for nearly five minutes."[16]

"I have the reputation of being a very daring woman," Lucy Colman stated, "and certainly have proved it by presenting myself before you tonight." The abolitionist went on to admit to knowing nothing of the law and very little of logic. "But I know something of common sense," she declared, eliciting a "Hear, hear!" "I want to ask the mothers in this audience what kind of a feeling would come over them—any one of you—were you the mother of Anthony Comstock!" Her remarks drew loud cheers and applause. Leland wrote, "The audience at first shrank back in amazement, then recovering itself burst into the most tumultuous applause." Colman continued her speech with a few words about her antislavery work when the "flush of girlhood" was upon her cheeks. "I went before audiences, ignorant though I was, to plead for the redemption of the slave. I thought I had earned a right to quiet in my old age with my venerable friend, whom every one of you want to know—Amy Post." Applause and shouts of "Let's see her!" rang out as Post stood up. "The very compeers of Lucretia Mott, Amy Post and Lucy N. Colman dared to be called the 'queens of obscenity' for liberty and freedom!" Colman proclaimed. "Mr. Bennett, if others have suffered for you as I have suffered the past year, they know how to say, All honor, all honor, good and faithful servant," she stated while shaking his hand, "you have all our hearts."[17]

Noticeably absent from the auspicious occasion was Robert Ingersoll. There were several calls for the colonel and a man rose to his feet and exclaimed, "Only one thing is lacking to make this meeting a complete success. Where is Col. Ingersoll? Where is the missing link?" The reason given for Ingersoll's absence was that he had previously scheduled lecturing engagements. Theron Leland found reward in the colonel's absence. He believed it proved the independence of New York Liberals from other famous freethinkers. With Ingersoll present, he thought, "It would have been said, and we ourselves would have believed, that this great audience assembled to hear Ingersoll. We would have known *his* strength but not our own."[18]

While Bennett's reception at Chickering Hall was the most publicized, enthusiastic, and grandest, he also enjoyed several other welcome-home parties. But the meeting that he valued the most was the one given by his own New York Liberal League— the chapter that elected him president while he was still in prison. The jovial and touching event—celebrated with California wine—was described as a "literary, musical, social, and convivial" affair.[19]

GREETING AN EX-CONVICT

———— ◆ ————

D. M. BENNETT'S FRIENDS IN
CHICKERING HALL

A QUEER SUNDAY NIGHT MEETING—LISTENING
FOR TWO HOURS TO SOME PLAUSIBLE
TALK AND MORE BLASPHEMY AND FILTH—
DENOUNCING ANTHONY COMSTOCK
AND THE REPUBLICAN PARTY

Although Bennett was enjoying his freedom and his celebrity among his fellow freethinkers, not everyone was singing his praises. Several of the nation's newspapers, magazines, and religious periodicals found the publicity of the Chickering Hall reception *appalling*. The *New York Times* devoted three columns with the sensational heading "Greeting an Ex-Convict." Bennett dismissed the *Times* as a "a semi-religious panderer."[20]

The *Chicago Tribune* reported that the Chickering Hall reception was "characterized by blasphemy and obscenity throughout" and the audience "was made up of Freethinkers, Freelovers, Infidels, and radical Spiritualists, and free rein was given to the motley crowd." The *Tribune* writer opined, "It would have been in the interest of common decency if the whole crowd could have been landed at one sweep into the penitentiary." The *Cleveland Leader* called Bennett a "pet of Bob Ingersoll." The *Christian Advocate* and the *Evangelist* roundly condemned the gathering. The *Evangelist* reported that Bennett's "Infidelity is of the gross materialistic sort which would destroy Christianity and all religion, and leave nothing but animalism in their place."[21]

But it was the *Syracuse Evening Herald*'s long, malicious diatribe that irritated the editor the most. "More meanness and falsehood," he complained, "could hardly be crowded into a space of the same magnitude." The article struck a nerve:

Bennett proved by his own handwriting to be a dirty hound, set himself up as a martyr, and Elizur Wright, Stephen Pearl Andrews, and the rest of the crew who are laboring to bring disgrace upon Liberal thought, bowed down and worshipped his shrine. . . . As compared with the poor painted wretches who thronged the streets outside of the reception hall, plying the lowest of vocations, the women who sat on the platform within made but a feeble showing of respectability; for the drabs at least deserve credit for being ashamed of their trade and prosecuting it under cover of darkness, while the so called "female agitators" make a boast of theirs.[22]

Chickering Hall's Fifth Avenue location was one of New York's most prestigious areas, Bennett informed the out-of-town newspaper writers, and many blocks "from the haunts of vice and painted wretches, none of whom were attracted to the hall." As to the "ungentlemanly fling" at the female freethinkers on the stage, there "are no better women in this land," he declared.[23]

Controversy over the Bennett reception continued for months. *Scribner's Monthly* characterized the meeting as "The Apotheosis of Dirt." The influential periodical with over one hundred thousand readers was dismissive of Bennett's honesty and intellect. It disparaged the freethinkers who were bent on repeal of the Comstock Laws as the minority and reprinted a paragraph from the Boston *Index* calling the editor's attempt for repeal a "mad crusade." It lavishly praised Comstock as "one of the most useful and remarkable of the Christian workers of our time." Bennett wrote a letter, to no avail, to the monthly's editor requesting to refute the "dozen misrepresentations, falsehoods, and gross slanders in the article." The *Scribner's* screed concluded, "And may Elizur Wright live to be ashamed of the use the free-lovers have made of him!"[24]

In the pantheon of nineteenth-century freethought heroes, Elizur Wright looms large. Of all the liberal luminaries present at the Chickering Hall reception, Wright was the most venerated. He was the secretary of the American Antislavery Society and editor of the *Massachusetts Abolitionist*. Wright, the former insurance commissioner of Massachusetts, was, in Robert Ingersoll's assessment, "One of the Titans who attacked the monster, the gods of his time, one of the few whose confidence in liberty was never shaken, and who, with undimmed eyes, saw the atrocities and barbarisms of his day, and the glories of the future . . . when we received our morals from merchants, and made merchandise of our morals, Elizur Wright held principle above profit, and preserved his manhood at the peril of his life."[25]

Elizur Wright's abolitionist work "was conspicuously heroic and the black race of America owes to but few men more than to him," George Macdonald wrote. Wright was an ecologist before the word was coined and was affectionately known as the Nestor of Liberalism (in Greek legend, the oldest and wisest man of a community). Wright was deeply offended by "The Apotheosis of Dirt." In a letter to the monthly's editor, Wright criticized the "Christian" journal's choice of words. "Dirt is none the better for being really apotheosized, and there happens to be in the same book [Bible] where Moses Stuart [biblical scholar known as the "father of exegetical studies in America"] found a justification of slavery, a good deal of *dirt*," he wrote. Wright defended Bennett and his own participation in the great Chickering Hall Reception. The veteran abolitionist concluded his letter to *Scribner's* with "I have lived to be ashamed of having been used by Christians to propagate a set of dogmas which are essentially immoral, and if the 'Freelovers' have made use of me to deepen that degradation of woman which Christianity found her laboring under and attempted to perpetuate, I shall live to be ashamed of that. But I do not think they have intended to use me in that direction. If so, they have mistaken their man as much as the Christians did."[26]

NOTES

"debt of gratitude.": Elijah Myrick, The *Shaker Manifesto*, Sept. 1879.

1. TS May 8, 1880.

2. Ibid.

3. Ibid.

4. GM.

5. TS May 8, 1880. GM.

6. TS May 8, 1880.

7. Ibid.

8. Ibid. The *New York Times* May 3, 1880.

9. TS May 8, 1880.

10. Ibid.

11. Ibid.

12. Ibid.

13. Ibid.

14. Ibid.

15. Ibid.

16. Ibid.

17. Ibid.

Lucy N. Colman was the "Infidel-Abolitionist" who taught at "colored schools" and who was mobbed and pelted with eggs during her antislavery work. Colman was responsible for introducing Sojourner Truth, the African American slave, to President Abraham Lincoln at the White House. "Mr. Lincoln was not himself with this colored woman," recalled Colman. "He had no funny story for her, he called her aunty, as he would his washer-woman, and when she complimented him as the first Antislavery President, he said, 'I'm not an Abolitionist; I wouldn't free the slaves if I could save the Union in any other way—I'm obliged to do it.'" After meeting with the president, Colman was under the impression that he "was not glad that the war had made him the emancipator of four million slaves. Perhaps he came to rejoice over it, when he realized that by the logic of events his name would be immortal through that act; but at that time he did not see it. He believed in the white race, not in the colored, and did not want them put on an equality."

Lucy N. Colman, *Reminiscences*. 1891, microfilm F704 Reel 523 #4006, San Diego State University, San Diego, CA.

18. TS May 15, 1880.

19. GM.

20. TS May 22, 1880.

21. Ibid.

22. Ibid.

23. Ibid.

24. *Scribner's Monthly*, July 1880. By the mid-1880s it was renamed the *Century* magazine, it had a circulation of 250,000, and it was considered the best-edited, albeit prudish magazine in the world.

Edward G. Burrows and Mike Wallace, *Gotham: A History of New York City to 1898*. New York Oxford University Press, 1999.

25. SP pp. 828–29.

26. "than to him": GM pp. 385–86. Moses Stuart was "father of exegetical studies in America." EB Eleventh Edition, v. XXV p. 1048.

"the Christians did": Wright letter dated July 12, 1880, to editor of *Scribner's*: TS Sept. 11, 1880.

12

AN INFIDEL ABROAD

I am feeling very happy here. I feel that I am, temporarily at least beyond the reach of my enemies. The arrows of malice and the spears and darts of hate cannot reach me here.

—D. M. Bennett
Letter from Rome

S oon after the rousing Bennett reception at Chickering Hall, the National Liberal League asked the celebrated editor to travel to Europe to represent American liberals at the Congress of the Universal Federation of Freethinkers. This meeting, to be held in Brussels, Belgium, would be only the second in the international organization's history (the first was in Naples in 1860). The Brussels assembly invited many of the world's leading freethinkers and would prove to be one of the most historically significant conventions in the annals of freethought.[1]

Bennett was initially unsure whether to accept the NLL's invitation. He did not wish to represent "the Abbott-Bundy crowd," he assured readers. He decided to go only after learning that Francis Abbot and John Bundy, editors of the *Index* and *Religio-Philosophical Journal*, were in opposition to his appointment. Since, however, the congress was to be "composed of gentlemen and persons of honor and truth," he agreed to travel abroad. But, he wrote,

> whenever there is a Congress gotten up of Paul Prys, nosers into other people's private letters, meddlers, busy-bodies, mischief-makers, tell-tales, tattlers, blackmailers, suborners, falsifiers, liars, traducers, defamers, hypocrites, self-righteous howlers, Pharisees, plotters, conspirators, low-lived detectives, inform-ers, garroters, sneaks, assassins, maligners, befoulers, slanderers, and calumniators—yes, when a Congress of this is held, we shall recommend as fit delegates Abbot, Bundy, and Com-stock—the A B C of low-lived villainy and falsehood.[2]

Before departing for Europe, the Bennetts paid a visit to their old Shaker home at New Lebanon (hence renamed Mount Lebanon). The Shaker community was still thriving but with only half the number of Believers as there were forty years earlier. The editor felt honored to see his books and the *Truth Seeker* promi-nently displayed in the Shakers' bookcase. The couple had an enjoyable chat with Elder Frederick W. Evans, Oliver Prentiss (Mary's uncle), and Dolly Seaton, who was 104 years old! "She spoke strongly in favor of the virgin life," he noted. She was thankful that she had shunned the sin in the world, and that she had been "faithful to the dictates of her faith and conscience." They visited the society's cemetery and stood by the graves of many who they had known four decades earlier. "Many of those who have for years been resting quietly in their graves had done us acts of kindness, and we had done the same to them. The remem-brance of these things was not unpleasant." The Bennetts thor-oughly enjoyed their visit and returned home with their convic-tions confirmed that "if there is an industrious, temperate, frugal, virtuous, and happy people in the world, *they are the Shakers.*"[3]

A TRUTH SEEKER IN EUROPE

Three months after his release from prison, on August 4, 1880, Bennett and his fellow delegate, Albert Rawson, boarded the steamer *Gallia* for Liverpool. Numerous friends were present that rainy afternoon to see Bennett off on his first trip abroad. But because of inclement weather, the gregarious exchange with the departing delegates was limited. Ironically, many of the two free-thinkers' fellow passengers were clergymen. A serious group who never laughed, and in Eugene Macdonald's words, were

> long nosed, clean shaven, high-cravated, black-coated gentry . . . thick as bees, and buzzed as incessantly. . . . [They] had a sort of subdued, sepulchral joy about them to think that they were to get away for a while from the arduous labors of pitching sinners into hell or pulling them out as occasion and the state of their (the sinners') belief warranted. Probably if the ministers had known that their notorious Infidel enemy was among them, their feelings would have been different.[4]

As he had done when he went to prison, Bennett left the *Truth Seeker* in good hands; Mary would preside in the office, and Eugene, his faithful assistant, would again serve as acting editor. Bennett's departure that day reminded Eugene of the previous year when he and friends watched the editor leave for prison. But there was a considerable difference between the two occasions, he thought, and this time "[they] did it with a far lighter heart." As the elderly editor disappeared out of sight, Eugene observed, "He was followed by many hearty good wishes for his safe voyage, pleasant time, and speedy return, refreshed, invigorated, and ready for another campaign with the enemies of mental freedom."[5]

Bennett immediately began chronicling his trip as soon as he set sail on the ten-day voyage across the Atlantic. His letters appeared weekly in the *Truth Seeker* and were later published in a book, *An Infidel Abroad*. Bennett's process of writing letters for publication while traveling was similar to how Mark Twain, a decade earlier, wrote his book *The Innocents Abroad*. Although Mark Twain was a freethinker, read the *Truth Seeker,* and was known affectionately as the periodical's most irreverent subscriber, his travel book was practically devotional compared to Bennett's atheistic letters from Europe. In fact, *An Infidel Abroad* eventually had to be renamed *A Truth Seeker in Europe* in order to reach a wider audience.[6]

Rawson and Bennett landed in Liverpool, England, on August 14, 1880. At the Custom House they were asked if they had any cigars, whiskey, or tobacco in their possession. "It was easy for me to answer in the negative," Bennett wrote, "as I make no use of the articles named, and have no occasion to carry them." Before taking the train to London, they walked around Liverpool, taking in the sights. Bennett provided his readers with some interesting information about the bustling seaport. As late as 1764, Liverpool merchants were in the business of furnishing the ships for transporting African slaves. "It has since made good atonement in the promotion of a legitimate healthy commerce," he was pleased to report. Some of the most pleasant things about Liverpool were the art gallery, museum, and library—"they are *free,* and every well-behaved person has access to them without paying a penny."[7]

In London one of Bennett and Rawson's first activities was to find the South Place Chapel to hear Moncure Conway speak. Unfortunately, Conway, whom Bennett had listened to in Cincinnati over two decades earlier, was on tour in America. They were, however, able to spend some time with Charles Bradlaugh, the founder of the *National Reformer* and a highly controversial member of Parliament. Charles Bradlaugh (1833–1891) was a British political and social reformer who championed free speech and the rights of freethinkers. In 1877 Bradlaugh and his fellow editor, Annie Besant, challenged Great Britain's censorship laws and were arrested for publishing *The Fruits of Philosophy: The Private Companion of Young Married People,* a birth control manual by Charles Knowlton. Their prosecution was similar to Bennett's and caused a scandal in England. "The struggle for a free Press has been one of the marks of the Freethought party throughout history," proclaimed Bradlaugh, "and as long as the Party permits me to hold its flag I will never voluntarily lower it." Although

Bradlaugh and Besant were convicted, fined, and sentenced to prison, the case was ultimately dismissed on a technicality.[8]

Charles Bradlaugh was also the president of the National Secular Society, an attorney, and an uncompromising atheist. He was a great orator who gave lecture tours in America. After his election to Parliament, he insisted on affirming instead of taking the mandatory oath of allegiance and was barred from taking his seat. The incident evolved into a controversial and protracted parliamentary contest and became a cause célèbre for British freethinkers. After years of sensational legal wrangling in Parliament, Bradlaugh agreed to take a modified oath and took his seat in the House of Commons. He subsequently got a bill passed permitting unbelievers to enter Parliament by affirmation instead of taking the required oath of allegiance. The *New York Times* sympathized with Bradlaugh's constituents who, it agreed, had the right to choose him as their representative, but it was opposed to men of his ilk. In 1880 a couple of months before Bennett visited the brilliant orator in London, the *Times* opined "that [Bradlaugh] of all men should be allowed to pose as the champion of freedom of representation is unfortunate. He is an atheist of the vulgar type, who substitutes blasphemy for argument, and a republican, whose chief weapon is vituperation of the Government under which he lives, and abuse of the royal family. . . . Mr. Bradlaugh is, everything considered, an objectionable sort of person."[9]

"We found Mr. Bradlaugh in his study up to his elbows in business, examining his correspondence, etc.," Bennett reported. The famous freethinkers discussed the upcoming congress at Brussels and other subjects. Bradlaugh gave Bennett copies of the *National Reformer*, containing his first speech in Parliament, and invited the two Americans to visit Parliament and promised them good seats. He also wrote letters of introduction for the pair to present to the members of the French national legislative body. "He is doubtless destined to greatly distinguish himself in Parliament," Bennett predicted.[10]

Bennett and Rawson spent a few days taking in the sights in London before going on to France. The nineteenth-century American Liberal's perspective is informative, insightful, and often entertaining. His commentary included everything from women's fashion to art, architecture, female bartenders, and British drinking habits. While he reported London to be a quieter city than New York, he thought the British drank too much intoxicating liquor. He was startled at the sight of English women imbibing liquor, "but they certainly have the same right to drink that men have and it, perhaps, is not improper that they should be equally open about it." After witnessing a mother giving her child a taste from her bottle, he concluded, "This does not seem right, but still I see very little drunkenness here."[11]

On the way to Paris, they stopped and visited the Rouen Cathedral. "I have seen so many saintly, holy pictures that I would not care if I never saw another," Bennett remarked. His criticism of Europe's religious art would be a recurring theme throughout his letters. Instead of the mythological gods and goddesses, he said that he preferred paintings and statues of "real moral heroes, sensible, good men and women, historical paintings, landscapes, high mountains, works of a healthy imagination." After seeing the abundance of priests in Rouen, he said that he realized "the burden they are to society." Bennett visited the bronze statue of Napoleon Bonaparte and the marble statue of Joan of Arc. "Her cruel death," he wrote, "was a sad commentary on the religious folly" that prevailed during that age. Regarding the ubiquitous clergy, he complained, "It almost makes my blood boil to see these insidious, canting, ingratiating, hypocritical knaves gliding around from place to place, and the obsequiousness accorded them by the sisters and a certain portion of the brethren, in public as well as private. They have proved enemies to the human race, and I will gladly see their number grow less."[12]

"I have fully come to the conclusion that Paris is a great city— It is the prettiest city I ever saw, or ever will see." He credited Louis Napoleon with the city's improvements and compared the streets to Daniel Webster, an American politician, in that "they 'know no north, no south, no east, no west,' but they know how to run straight and to be wise and beautiful." Impressed with the City of

Light's opulent watch and jewelry stores, Bennett wrote, "They all speak emphatically. *This is a golden age.*"[13]

At the Brussels congress held between August 29 and 31, 1880, Bennett and Rawson reunited with their fellow American delegates, Dr. and Mrs. Foote and Madame Augusta Cooper Bristol, a prominent educator, author, poet, and lecturer. Charles Bradlaugh, unable to attend because of parliamentary duties, sent in his stead Mrs. Annie Besant and his daughter Miss Hypatia Bradlaugh, with whom Bennett engaged in a very pleasant conversation. While on the platform with many of the world's most preeminent free-thinkers and intellectuals, he considered himself "something like the fifth or sixth wheel of a coach." Sitting between Annie Besant and Dr. Ludwig Büchner, the eminent German philosopher, physician, and author of *Force and Matter*, Bennett remembered where he was the previous year. Tearfully he recalled "making shoes in the penitentiary with thieves, robbers, counterfeiters, burglars, and murderers, and locked up in my little stone cell at night." And now he found himself on stage in front of the world's leading liberals and alongside numerous editors and "[r]adicals of the most radical stamp." Among them, he wrote, "appeared the very peaceful and non-combative editor of THE TRUTH SEEKER," in his opinion, "the greatest paper of them all."[14]

After attending the four-day Freethinkers' Congress in Brussels, Bennett and Rawson traveled to Antwerp, Belgium, where they visited museums. "If the people had no Virgin and dead Jesus to worship, they would probably take Rubens and Vandyke into their pantheon. I am quite willing that they should make that change." At Antwerp, Albert Rawson departed for America to attend the National Liberal League Convention in Chicago. Bennett would continue his tour to Germany, France, Switzerland, and Italy before returning to Great Britain. Soon after Rawson departed, the editor traveled to the battlefield of Waterloo. "I could not think of leaving this part of the country without seeing that memorable field where the blood of 32,000 men saturated the earth, and where the destinies of nations were decided for a hundred years in the future."[15]

THE POET'S PRIVILEGE

Another Waterloo was about to take place in Illinois at the 1880 National Liberal League Convention. And while no lives would be lost at this battle, the fate of the National Liberal Party—and the role of freethought in American politics—would be at stake. Although Bennett was on the other side of the globe, he remained the most polarizing figure in freethought, and his opposition to the Comstock Laws continued to splinter the National Liberal League. Thaddeus B. Wakeman, his friend who assisted in his defense at his trial, shared Bennett's factious cause. The attorney was the nation's most ardent and articulate critic of the obscenity statutes that had wrecked so many lives. During Bennett's trial in front of Judge Benedict, Wakeman saw firsthand how the nebulous Comstock Laws were misused against his fellow freethinkers.[16]

The National Liberal Party, organized only the previous year, was hardly discussed or even mentioned at the 1880 congress in Chicago. While a resolution passed pertaining to state and congressional tickets and a National Liberal Party presidential ticket in four years, the majority of time was spent in contentious debate over the repeal or *only* modification of the Comstock Laws. A recent arrest and imprisonment of an Iowa editor by a Comstock agent caused outrage among many of the attending delegates. For the second year in a row, a battle of wills developed between T. B. Wakeman, who favored total repeal, and Robert Ingersoll, who strongly believed that moderation was the more politically prudent solution.[17]

In place of the two resolutions that urged repeal, Ingersoll proposed substitute resolutions that would "examine said laws" and if they were determined to be unjust, provide a defense for unfairly accused defendants. He could not understand how the "infernal question of obscenity ever got into the Liberal League." Ingersoll spoke often during the rancorous debates by delegates over the resolutions. He expressed his confidence in the federal courts but acknowledged that there were some incompetent judges: "There may be some bad judges, there may be some idi-otic jurors. I think there was in that case [of Mr. Bennett]."[18]

Robert Ingersoll said that he could not understand how the Comstock Laws could be held over their heads. "They can," exclaimed Wakeman, "[the churches] use this instrument to bring down a Liberal editor whenever they wish, and they do it." He argued that it happens—especially with "a semi-clerical aristocracy to punish whom they please" and "a prejudice through the religious and secular press which generally overwhelms both court and jury." The attorney thought that his "learned friend . . . seems to be in a sad state of confusion." Wakeman expressed his opposition to "decoy letters" and warned the league about "postal discrimina-tions." He agreed with Ingersoll that the government ran the mails—"but what for?" The post office can refuse to "send a horse and carriage by mail" because it is inconvenient and impractical. "But they cannot refuse to send Paine's *Age of Reason*," he argued, "because that would be unconstitutional, unequal, unpostal, and contrary to the spirit of our republican democratic government."[19]

Robert Ingersoll declared that when books were determined to be "manifestly obscene" they should be burned. "Who is to be the judge of that?" a delegate asked. "You know as well as I," Ingersoll said, "that there are certain books not fit to go through the mails—books and pictures not fit to be delivered." Further-more, Ingersoll claimed that some of the Comstock Laws were good. "I am going to do what I can to keep this League from destroying itself." His lengthy speech failed to convince the dele-gates who remained outraged over the case of the Iowa editor who was frivolously charged and jailed.[20]

"Our friend," said Wakeman, "speaks as though the federal government owned the post-offices as private property—as theirs. He has let some bad law and bad politics get hold of him." He reminded the congress to "remember the lessons of Thomas Jef-ferson and Thomas Paine. Politicians talk as though the people and states were merely the appendages of the federal government, and everything should be committed to it. This is a dangerous tendency," he warned.[21]

Parker Pillsbury, an old friend of Ingersoll's, accused the colonel of filibuster tactics. Albert Rawson, the secretary of the league, weighed in against the Comstock Laws and for repeal. He said that "instead of destroying this class [obscene] of literature," the Comstock Laws were used to oppress freethinkers. Rawson added that the "church could not afford to destroy obscene literature" because it "reaped a harvest out of it."[22]

Robert Ingersoll continued to plead with the delegates to see his side of the argument but to no avail. He threatened to leave the organization over the matter and finally concluded his speech: "I have no more to say. But if that resolution is passed, all I have to say is that while I shall be for liberty everywhere, I cannot act with this organization, and I will not."[23]

"If the Colonel cannot stand with us in our opposition to Comstockism," Wakeman declared, "we must stand alone." Wakeman knew that Ingersoll's withdrawal would be damaging to the league but felt that "this question immeasurably transcends all personal interests and affections." He was sorry over the chasm between them, and said, "[T]hough we love this man as our brother, shall we hesitate a moment on his account?" "Ingersoll is great," Wakeman proclaimed before calling a vote, "but liberty, truth, and duty are greater."[24]

In a surprising move, Robert Ingersoll rose, resigned as vice president, and walked out with several other like-minded delegates. The 1880 convention elected Elizur Wright to his third and final term as president of the NLL. (Because of his advanced years, Wright declined to run for the office the following year. "Let the young do the fighting," he advised.) Wakeman's resolutions passed and proved to be, according to George Macdonald, "an impolitic course for the organization to pursue . . . and in view of the consequences I am inclined to think it would have been better to take Ingersoll's advice."[25]

Two years later, Thaddeus Wakeman concurred with George Macdonald's opinion. At the Sixth Annual Congress of the National Liberal League in St. Louis, Wakeman was elected president. At the meeting, Wakeman acknowledged the damage that

Ingersoll's withdrawal had on the organization's influence in American politics. He expressed his disappointment in Ingersoll's departure. He told the audience,

> We can all remember him swinging his hat at the front of the plat-form calling for three cheers for the new party. He went right out and was rebaptized into the Republican party, and has been the hewer of wood and the drawer of water for it ever since. And the astonishing thing about it is that he seems to like his position. We told him when he gave three cheers for that new party that it would make him President of the United States.
>   So it would if he had but been true to it.[26]

James Parton, a vice president of the NLL, wrote a letter of con-gratulations to T. B. Wakeman and offered his unique perspective on Ingersoll's withdrawal. James Parton (1822–1891) was America's foremost biographer and had chronicled the lives of numerous important historical figures, such as Aaron Burr, Ben-jamin Franklin, Thomas Jefferson, and Voltaire. The distinguished author felt that Wakeman and his delegates had acted "nobly and bravely" in their opposition to the Comstock Laws, "which are a standing menace to every independent inquirer." Parton felt that the laws were needless and asked, "Who can define obscenity, even for a jury?" Nevertheless, he deeply lamented Ingersoll's defection and expressed his insight and offered some advice: "Colonel Inger-soll is essentially a poet—as indeed all very great orators are and must be. . . . Having the qualities of a poet, he has the limitations that belong to the character. . . . We must not complain that on this one occasion he seems to have injured the cause he has done so very much to promote. . . . Let him enjoy the poet's privilege of doing just as he likes."[27]

WANDERLUST

In Europe Bennett continued his travels through Switzerland and Italy. In Geneva he paid homage at the statue of Jean-Jacques

Rousseau and visited the residence of Voltaire at Ferney. He described in detail his visit to the Voltaire mansion, the beautiful grounds, and the little chapel erected by the French writer. While inside the house, he felt the solemnity and reverence of the moment, standing by Voltaire's chair and bed. He felt privileged to be able to touch articles once held in Voltaire's hands. "I entertain a profound respect for Voltaire." He wrote,

> He was great in many directions, and, considering the age in which he lived, the power of the church which encompassed him on every side, he exhibited remarkable moral courage and wrote that which few authors dared to write. He gave the church and old theological errors many severe blows, which they were never able to avert. While standing by his chair, his table and his bedside, I felt a desire to render myself useful in making many of his theological writings known to English readers, which have never yet been published in our language.[28]

The same day that Bennett visited Voltaire's home, he looked for the spot where Michael Servetus, the Spanish physician, was executed by the followers of John Calvin in 1553. Servetus, who some believed discovered the circulation of blood, was burned alive—with his books—for his opposition of the church doctrine of the Trinity. Bennett was surprised that many of the residents were totally oblivious of the horrific event. Nevertheless he finally found the spot and "stopped long enough to meditate upon the cursed deed." It occurred to him that his own fate had been similar to the fate of Servetus; they had both written and published their honest convictions and were arrested and imprisoned. And while the editor had escaped with his life, he felt that many followers of Calvin thought that he, too, should have been burned at the stake. He reminded his readers not to forget that the men who pursued him and threw him into prison were disciples of Calvin. The "infamous sneak [Comstock]," the "president of his persecuting society [Colgate]," and the "bigoted judge [Benedict]" had all been practicing Calvinists. He also excoriated Reverend Crosby: "The loud-mouthed Crosby, who perhaps is the biggest gun of Calvinism in America . . . who threw up his hands with joy at a meeting in the hall of the Young Men's Christian Association, because I had been arrested, convicted, and imprisoned, and declared it was worth one hundred thousand times as much as all that had been paid in to the society which pursued me . . . is a fine Calvinist."[29]

Bennett continued his journey through Germany and described facetiously some of the holy relics that he had the opportunity to see in Cologne. He was shown the "miraculously preserved" pieces of wood from the cross that was used to crucify Jesus, and portions of the scourging whips and thorns from his crown. "How can I doubt, how can you doubt any longer?" he wrote in jest. After all: "Have not the bishops and priests who have presided over the church of Ursula for seven hundred years said these things were so? Did not that German man who took three marks from us also say it was so?"[30]

While in Berlin, Bennett stayed at the Central Hotel, the largest he had seen in Europe. He found Berlin a fine city and was pleased to learn that the art galleries and museums were open on Sundays. He was delighted to hear that only a small percentage of Berliners attended worship. Bennett did not see an intoxicated person while visiting Berlin and wrote, "There are doubtless more unbelievers, more Freethinkers, here than in many other parts of the world, but this does not result in a decrease of morality."[31]

The editor strolled around Berlin, taking in the sights, including the Brandenburg Gate. After gazing at the marble statue of Goethe in Deer Park, he thought that the world had produced few greater minds than that of the German philosopher and poet. "He will continue to be appreciated more and more as the centuries pass away," he predicted. Bennett later traveled to a village outside of Berlin to meet author Bruno Bauer whose books about the origin of Christianity the editor found interesting. Known as the Hermit of Rixdorf, Bauer was critical of the authenticity of the New Testament and contended that Mark, a single evangelist, invented Christianity. He also argued that Christianity is of Greco-Roman origin and not Hebrew. The "Four Testaments"

(Gospels), which included the moral teachings of Jesus, were writings of Seneca, the Latin philosopher and dramatist. The Christian religion, the German hypothesized, was essentially "Stoicism triumphant in a Jewish garb."[32]

Bennett located the old German sage in his study, surrounded by his books and papers. They shared a bottle of wine and had a pleasant interview. Like many of his fellow freethinkers, the editor had long been searching for the origin of early religions. Bennett found the German to be scholarly and a deep thinker, but he was unsure how strong a case Bauer had made. In the past, Christianity's origins were attributed to Egyptian, Hebrew, Buddhist, and other sources. Bennett admittedly "smiled inwardly" when learning that yet *another* source had been found. Christianity, he thought, appears to have as many origins as it has reasons to be dead.[33]

The editor traveled on to Italy, which he found "the dirtiest, the most religious, and the most utterly priest-ridden country in the world." After ten days in Italy, Bennett returned to London where he visited preeminent British secularists Charles Watts, the publisher-editor of the *Secular Review*, and Edward Truelove, a veteran reformer and free-speech advocate who knew John Stuart Mill, George Jacob Holyoake, and Karl Marx.[34]

Bennett's days and nights in London far exceeded his wildest dreams. He accepted an invitation to dinner at the residence of Mrs. Annie Besant, Great Britain's most accomplished and eloquent female freethinker, women's rights advocate, editor, orator, and leading socialist. Charles Bradlaugh's two daughters accompanied Bennett, along with Dr. Edward B. Aveling, the dashing socialist author who would later marry Eleanor Marx, daughter of Karl Marx.[35]

The quartet traveled across town using the underground railway, taking about a half hour to arrive at Oatlands, Besant's pleasant residence. Bennett was especially impressed with Mrs. Besant, who two years earlier had lost custody of her only child because of her atheism. Bennett shared Besant's antivaccination and antivivisection advocacy. (Thirty years earlier, he had a bad experience with vaccination.) He marveled at Besant's intellect and wrote, "She probably has not a superior among the women of the world, if an equal." He had attended her lecture in the Hall of Science on labor conditions and the privileged classes, and wrote, "Her references to the useless royal family were in the purest and keenest sarcasm."[36]

On three occasions, the editor had the pleasure of dining with Dr. Aveling. They ate twice at the swank Criterion restaurant, richly appointed with statuary and paintings, and "one of the finest restaurants in London, and in the world." Bennett noted that dinner at the luxurious restaurant took "nearly an hour and a half to dispatch." The former Shaker-turned-freethinker was having the time of his life. Following dinner, they attended the theater. "Dr. Aveling had provided a private box for our party," he confided to his readers back home, "and to a casual observer it could hardly have been known that we were not of the aristocracy of the city."[37]

On October 30, 1880, the night Bennett was scheduled to depart England for America, he was given a banquet and reception by the National Secular Society of England in the prestigious Hall of Science. About a hundred members of the society and the Malthusian League enjoyed dinner, music, and speeches by Bradlaugh, Besant, Aveling, and their honored guest. Bradlaugh expressed his and thousands of others' respect and sympathy for Bennett, "a man who has fought bravely; sympathy to a man who has been defeated in the fight, but who has won by strengthening the tendency to liberty."[38]

Charles Bradlaugh called the *Truth Seeker* a "plucky paper" and its editor his "co-fighter." Bennett was presented with a large gilt frame with the inscribed motto of the society that read, "WE SEEK FOR TRUTH" "TO D. M. BENNETT." The editor gave a brief but heartfelt speech of acceptance that elicited cheers. He admitted that he was "nearly overcome with a deep sense of gratitude."[39]

Nine days later, Bennett was home in New York and back at his desk. Within a few weeks of his return, a subscriber from California suggested that he take a tour around the world. As George Macdonald observed, Bennett had "developed the *wanderlust*" during his excursion abroad and found the proposition amenable. The editor made a challenge to his subscribers: "If three hundred friends, by May 1, 1881, will each hand in the sum of five dollars we will undertake the circuit of the earth, to write it up, to return to each one of them two fat volumes containing descriptions of what we meet with on our journey. As politicians say, we are in the hands of our friends."[40]

NOTES

"reach me here.": TS Nov. 13, 1880.

1. SP p. 613.
2. TS July 3, 1880 p. 423.
3. Ibid.
Bennett reviewed Harvey L. Eads's book about Shakerism in the *Truth Seeker*.

"Not so much because I am specially fond of theological sermons and discussions," he explained, "but because some forty years ago I saw Elder Eads when he was a young man, and myself still younger, and because the doctrines he enunciates are the doctrines I once believed." The editor commended Eads's handling of the subjects, but found fault with the elder's "fondness for the Bible." Bennett described for readers the "peculiar" Shaker theology and their unbelief in the divinity of Jesus Christ "any further than all good persons are divine." He declared that their belief that nature was "depraved" and that celibacy was the only true way to God was wrong. "The sexual functions," he wrote, "are certainly not to be despised, not to be hated, not to be crucified." TS May 1, 1880.

After their visit, Bennett provided readers with an overview of the Shaker religion, writing:

The regular meeting room of the family is on the third floor of the T part of the building, a room about sixty by thirty feet, and perhaps twenty feet in height. Here the members of the family unite in singing, marching, and dancing, which are the favorite modes of worship. They also have a due proportion of speaking, with silent prayer. Vocal prayer is not used there save in songs of supplication, in which all unite. Their meetings continue from half an hour to one hour and a half. Sometimes they are very animated, when the dancing is very lively and the spirit is well aroused.

Involuntary physical operations of the body are not uncommon, and visions and trances were formerly of not infrequent occurrence. The Shakers are Spiritualists, and believe in the ministrations of departed friends.

The modification that has taken place in their theological notions within the last third of a century is very perceptible. Several expressed themselves as unbelievers in a personal deity, and regard him as the sum-total of the life principle of the universe, the supreme ruling power. Some imagine he possesses intelligence, while others, who do not think he has parts and organs, have no idea that he has intelligence, thoughts, or design. Deity, according to their views, is dual, being equally male and female. They are not trinitarians, and do not think father and son are equal in power and age, but are *duotarians*, and believe rather that God is the father and mother of all existences. They believe that Jesus was not begotten in any different manner from human beings, and this his only superiority was in the pure and sinless life he led. They regard him as having lived a true Shaker life, abstaining from all sexual indulgences, and setting an example that his true disciples must follow. They discard a physical resurrection and the idea of a literal hell, a troubled conscience being the hell they recognize. They have no use for a personal devil. Some of them attach much importance to the "Christ spirit," distinct from the person of Jesus, and regard it as an element next to the central deific power, and believe it is the spirit to which all must attain who become pure and godly. TS July 31, 1880.

4. TS Aug 14, 1880.
5. Ibid.
6. TS Aug. 28, 1880.

Mark Twain's unbelief and his contempt for the religious displays and activities in Europe and the Near East came through quite clearly to a discerning reader of *Innocents Abroad*. However, he did this by writing in a style quite alien to Bennett. Twain could probably write pornography that would gain Comstock's Good Housekeeping Seal of Approval! Mark Twain had been a subscriber to the *Truth Seeker* for several years and was in good standing when he died. He expressed his opinion of Christianity and orthodox religion in his book *Mysterious Stranger*. His opinions about the Bible came out at the time when one of his books was banned from a library on "moral" grounds. "The mind that has become soiled in youth can never again be washed clean," he wrote. "I know this by my own experience, and to this day I cherish an unappeasable bitterness against the unfaithful guardians of my young life, who not only permitted but compelled me to read an unexpurgated Bible through before I was fifteen years old. None can do that and ever draw a clean, sweet breath again this side the grave." Twain complained whenever his wife read the Bible to him aloud. "It is making me a hypocrite," he declared. "I don't believe the Bible. It contradicts my reason." TS Sept. 1, 1923.

   7. TS Sept. 4, 1880.

   8. "voluntarily lower it.": *Charles Bradlaugh: Champion of Liberty*, p. 304, C. A. Watts, London, England. 1933.

   9. "sort of person.": *New York Times* June 27, 1880, article quoted in Warren pp. 38–40.

Like many prominent American freethinkers, Charles Bradlaugh linked Christianity and slavery. "I am unaware of any religion in the world which in the past forbade slavery," he wrote.

> The professors of Christianity for ages supported it; the Old Testament repeatedly has no repealing declaration. . . . And it is impossible for any well-informed Christian to deny that the abolition movement in North America was most steadily and bitterly opposed by the religious bodies in the various States. . . . The Bible and pulpit, the Church and its great influence, were used against abolition and in favour of the slave-owner. I know that Christians in the present day often declare that Christianity had a large share in bringing about the abolition of slavery, and this because men professing Christianity were abolitionists. I plead that these so-called Christian abolitionists were men and women whose humanity, recognising freedom for all, was in this in direct conflict with Christianity. . . . For some 1800 years, almost, Christians kept slaves, bought slaves,

sold slaves, bred slaves, stole slaves. Pious Bristol and godly Liverpool less than a hundred years ago openly grew rich on the traffic. . . .

When William Lloyd Garrison, the pure-minded and most earnest abolitionist, delivered his first anti-slavery address in Boston, Massachusetts, the only building he could obtain, in which to speak, was the infidel hall owned by Abner Kneeland, the "infidel" editor of the *Boston Investigator*, who had been sent to gaol for blasphemy. Every Christian sect had in turn refused Mr. Lloyd Garrison the use of the buildings they severally controlled. Lloyd Garrison told me himself how honoured deacons of a Christian Church joined in an actual attempt to hang him. When abolition was advocated in the United States in 1790, the representative from South Carolina was able to plead that the Southern clergy "did not condemn either slavery or the slave trade." . . .

When the Fugitive Slave Law was under discussion in North America, large numbers of clergymen of nearly every denomination were found ready to defend this infamous law. . . .

In his essay linking Christianity and slavery, Bradlaugh quotes François Guizot, the French historian and statesman, who wrote: "It has often been repeated that the abolition of slavery among modern people is entirely due to Christians. That, I think, is saying too much. Slavery existed for a long period in the heart of Christian society, without it being particularly astonished or irritated. A multitude of causes, and a great development in other ideas and principles of civilisation, were necessary for the abolition of this iniquity of all iniquities." *Champion of Liberty: Charles Bradlaugh*.

10. TS Sept. 18, 1880.
11. TS Sept. 11, 1880.
12. TS Sept. 25, 1880.
13. Ibid.

"wise and beautiful." Bennett's attribution of the quote is a mistake. Daniel Webster, the famous American politician, was decidedly a Northerner. The words were by Henry Clay (1777–1852), a controversial American statesman and eloquent orator. Clay, known as "The Great Pacificator," sought to avoid Civil War and declared: "I have heard something said about allegiance to the South. I know no South, no

North, no East, no West, to which I owe any allegiance." Note that Bennett uses the words in a completely different context.

14. TS Oct. 16, 1880.
15. Ibid.
16. TS Oct. 2, 1880.
17. Ibid.
18. Ibid.
19. Ibid.
20. Ibid.
21. Ibid.
22. Ibid.
23. Ibid.
24. Ibid.
25. Ibid. GM.
26. TS Oct. 14, 1882.
27. TS Oct. 16, 1880.
28. TS Oct. 30, 1880.
29. Ibid.
30. TS Nov. 19, 1881.
31. Ibid.
32. Ibid.
33. Ibid.
34. TS Dec. 18, 1880.
35. Ibid.

In 1886 Aveling and his wife, Eleanor Marx, visited the *Truth Seeker* office in New York. The flamboyant and celebrated couple's entrance and exit caused quite a stir. "Dr. Aveling and his lady," George Macdonald wrote, "blew into the *Truth Seeker* office one day, or should I say blossomed. They made quite an appearance: he, the perfect stage Englishman as done by our best comedians, with his 'bowler' hat and a bit of a cane which he carried by the middle, and clothes of a pattern like a yard-square cross-word puzzle; and she in a gown conceived in the height of the Dolly Varden mode, bearing figures of bright roses nearer the size of a cabbage than anything that a rosebush could produce or support. Passers-by who saw this attractive couple enter the office waited for them to emerge, as when Dr. Mary Walker in her male attire or Mary Tillotson [dress reformers] in pantalets would call." The Avelings were accompanied by Wilhelm Liebknecht, a close friend of Karl Marx and member of the German parliament. GM v. 1 pp. 403–404.

36. Vaccination info TSAW v. 1 pp. 441–42. "and keen sarcasm.":
TS Dec. 18, 1880.

Bennett wrote extensively about Mrs. Besant's abilities and also
described her child custody case for readers. "When her mind became
settled upon the [religion] question she frankly told her reverend husband that she could no longer believe or sustain Christian claims and
theories. This, of course, produced a rupture; he was too much of a
Christian to allow her freedom of opinion, and it was not long before
he drew up papers of separation, by the terms of which he retained the
son and she was accorded the possession of the daughter. It will be
remembered, however, that he subsequently brought suit for the
daughter, and a bigoted and unjust judge gave him the possession of
the child on the ground that the mother, being an Atheist, was no
longer a fit person to attend to the tuition of her child, and she was
denied the natural rights of maternity. A greater injustice was never
committed." TSAW v. 1. p. 300.

37. TS Dec. 18, 1880. See Gertrude Marvin Williams, *The Passionate
Pilgrim: A Life of Annie Besant*, pp. 117–18.

38. TS Nov. 27, 1880.

39. Ibid.

40. TS Dec. 18, 1880.

13

POSITION OF THE PLANETS

I am well aware [An Infidel Abroad] has many defects, like all I do has. I have a long road before me to reach perfection.
—D. M. Bennett, letter to Elizur Wright, January 18, 1881

In the nineteenth century it was customary for American clergymen to travel abroad and write an account of their journey for the congregations at home. D. M. Bennett was the first freethinking American publisher-editor to travel to Europe and publish his uniquely irreverent viewpoints on a myriad of subjects, including art, history, geography, politics, social customs, and, most important, religion.[1]

Bennett's first travel book *An Infidel Abroad* was popular but sold even better after the title was changed to *A Truth Seeker in Europe*. There were some who objected to the original name because they wanted to lend the book to Christians, who "almost shudder at the name Infidel," wrote Bennett. So, in order to humor the prejudiced, he made the change.[2]

269

A Truth Seeker in Europe received some flattering notices in the press. One periodical found the book a "decidedly interesting volume . . . and saint or sinner can enjoy its perusal." The *Columbus (Ohio) Sunday Capitol* reviewed the book and reported that Bennett's writing had been "the terror of the Christian" for years—but he could not be crushed. Now the *Capitol* announced "the enterprising Infidel" has written another book and "thousands of indignant Christians are astonished with the news." The article praised the author of *An Infidel Abroad,* who "sees things as no American traveler before him has seen things, and the views he gives on them are so different, so terribly daring above anything we ever had from our travelers abroad, that the book is really a rich treat to those who are dying for something in the way of literature." The reviewer gave credit to Robert Ingersoll and Bennett for the progress of freethought in America and pronounced, "[T]he latter is, without doubt, the strongest and ablest leader of the two."[3]

THE MORMON PROBLEM

Bennett sent a complimentary copy of *An Infidel Abroad* to Elizur Wright. In a self-effacing letter, he thanked Wright for sending five dollars to keep his "little craft afloat" and agreeing to contribute an article for the weekly. Wright was seventy-seven years old, but still able to write some pretty "terribly daring" material himself. At the editor's request, the reformer contributed a spirited article titled "The Mormon Problem," deriding the half-century-old American religion. Utah was being denied statehood because of the Mormon practice of polygamy; it would be another fifteen years and a "divine revelation" that ended polygamy before it was finally allowed to enter the Union as the forty-fifth state. "Polygamy is surely abominable," Wright declared. "But it is a Bible institution. Abraham and Solomon, on the average, were deeper in it than Brigham Young." How could the country's statesmen punish polygamy, he argued, "while the Sunday-schools are teaching that

Abraham, a polygamist, and a very mean one at that, was the father of the faithful and a model of godliness?"[4]

Elizur Wright also found fault with the founders of the church of the Latter-day Saints and the "divinely inspired" Book of Mormon. He had personally known Sidney Rigdon, an early associate of Joseph Smith, the founder of the church. Rigdon was, in Wright's words, "a perfectly sincere zealot who believed every word of the Bible divinely inspired." Wright, like many opponents of Mormonism, claimed that the Mormon Bible was an adaptation of a rejected romance novel written by Solomon Spaulding in 1812. Critics accused Mormon founders Rigdon and Smith of turning Spaulding's manuscript into the Book of Mormon. In Wright's opinion, Smith was a "magnetic, natural-born liar" and his Book of Mormon "the stupidest book of the century." But he said that it was no "stupider or more monstrous or more foolish than a large part of what the Bible Society publishes." Wright stated,

> The Bible has considerable wisdom sandwiched in; so has the Book of Mormon. The Bible has the advantage of a good deal of better poetry and terser maxims. Nevertheless, but for the glamour thrown over it by superstition, and the dignity expended on it by the clergy lugging out a text every Sunday in every pulpit, the book as a whole, with its Munchausen histories, its Levitical laws, and its ridiculous, prophetical beasts with seven heads and ten horns, would sink in public estimation even below the Book of Mormon. At any rate, society would only preserve its best passages, as men would fish out diamonds from a cesspool.[5]

The Christian solution to the Mormon problem was "nothing but persecution," and "a bloody solution will be no solution at all," Wright concluded. The real solution, he said, would only come when the real comprehensible nature of things assumes its legitimate authority over the consciences of men and women. "I mean the men and women who rule society at large, creating its science and its literature—not only polygamy will cease, but the more deplorable commercial degradation of woman, which now disgraces our cities, will cease also."[6]

Robert Ingersoll was even less charitable than Elizur Wright on Mormonism. "The institution of polygamy is infamous and disgusting beyond expression," he told George Macdonald in an interview in the *Truth Seeker*. He wanted polygamy or "legalized lust," as he dubbed it, to be "exterminated by law." But it would be difficult to outlaw polygamy since it was one of the institutions of Jehovah and sanctioned by the Bible. Ingersoll said that only a few years ago, the same Bible validated the institution of slavery, and now that it was abolished "the passages in the inspired volume upholding it have been mostly forgotten." But polygamy was alive and thriving in Utah and the Mormons resolutely repeated the Bible passages in their favor. "It is hard for the average Bible-worshiper to attack this institution without casting a certain stain upon his own book."[7]

While Bennett's new *Infidel* book was doing well thanks to positive reviews and controversial appeal, his *Anthony Comstock: His Career of Cruelty and Crime* caused a minor fracas. Comstock told the New York State Committee of the Legislature that Bennett's book was written by another (an abortionist). "I wrote every word of that book myself," Bennett swore in an affidavit, "as my clerks and the printers, who often waited for copy while I wrote it, well know, and as the style will attest to any one familiar with my writings." Yet another brouhaha erupted that spring over *Scribner's* laudatory review of Comstock's book *Frauds Exposed*, which devoted over a chapter to condemning Bennett and the freethought movement. The editor of the *Truth Seeker* pronounced the *Scribner's* review "a disgrace to American literature."[8]

THE NATION'S CALAMITY

During the first few months of 1881, Bennett remained undecided whether to make the trip around the world. "I have often thought," he confessed, "that sitting here by my table in my little

Truth Seeker office, doing my best to show my fellow-beings what I believe to be truth and right, is the happiest place in all the world to me." There was still concern, mostly by others, that another arrest by Anthony Comstock was possible. (Bennett heard a rumor while in prison that he would be arrested again for publishing his own trial transcript.) Ezra Heywood, his fellow reformer and author of *Cupid's Yokes*, would be arrested five times for violating the Comstock Laws and twice sentenced to prison. Nevertheless, the editor continued undeterred to disparage the vice hunter and Comstockism.[9]

In April Bennett took pleasure in reporting that Comstock had been indicted by a grand jury for assaulting a woman he arrested for sending obscene and scandalous matter through the mails. The editor gleefully reprinted the woman's description of the vice hunter and his assistant: "This intruder was a burly fellow with beetling brows and the look of a bully. His eyes flashed ominously, and the repulsiveness of his evil countenance was heightened by an ugly scar across one cheek. He was accompanied by another man, also an evil-looking person, but who stood behind the other and seemed to be a sort of servant."[10]

The eight-month interim before departing America on July 30 was filled with activity. Bennett spearheaded a fund-raising campaign for the renovation of the vandalized Thomas Paine monument at New Rochelle. A rededication was held at the repaired monument on Memorial Day, 1881. The editor gave a speech at the ceremony and later he and a few others visited the farmhouse where Thomas Paine lived. The proprietor of the farm permitted them to enter Paine's cottage and visit the room where the author-hero sat, read, and wrote. They enjoyed a pleasant day and hoped that they could return every year.[11]

In March the Bennetts traveled by train to Washington, DC, not so much for the inauguration of President Garfield, the editor explained, but to take advantage of the low fares to visit the nation's capital, where they had never been. The couple was among a hundred thousand citizens who braved the snow-turned-to-slush to witness the swearing in of Garfield on March

4, 1881. Sitting on the platform in front of the Capitol building were the Hayes and Garfield families, the chief justice, representatives, senators, members of the Cabinet, and other distinguished guests, Colonel Robert Green Ingersoll among them. With his prison experience still fresh in his mind, Bennett expressed his displeasure with the outgoing president who had denied him a pardon: "We have no objections to R.B. Hayes retiring to private life, [but] he cannot have our respect in doing so. We shall hardly forget his very pious, very bigoted, and very cruel-hearted wife. . . . Let the pious pair retire to private life, beloved to bigots, but without the respect of the more liberal portion of the American people."[12]

That evening, the inaugural ball was held in the new museum building of the Smithsonian Institute. The enormous hall was finely decorated and the event was merry and festive, Bennett reported. However, "our dancing days being over, we did not attend the ball."[13]

The following day was spent seeing the sights and visiting many of the government buildings, including the Smithsonian Institute and the Art Gallery. The elderly couple climbed nearly three hundred steps of the Washington Monument that was still being constructed. After becoming thoroughly exhausted, the Bennetts accepted a friend's offer to tour the streets of the city in his carriage. They called on Colonel Ingersoll (who was not at home) and had a pleasant visit with Mr. and Mrs. Burr. William Henry Burr was a pioneer stenographer and official reporter in the US Senate. Burr compiled *One Hundred and Forty-four Contradictions of the Bible* and wrote *Revelations of Antichrist*. He claimed that Thomas Paine wrote the Declaration of Independence. Ingersoll called Burr the "greatest literary detective."[14]

Another sight that attracted the Bennetts' attention was Ford's Theatre and the house across the street where the "good and revered" president died. Bennett's close friend Albert Rawson had an interesting connection with the tragic event. Rawson's mother-in-law was Laura Keene, the actress performing onstage at Ford's Theatre the night of the assassination. Immediately after

Abraham Lincoln was shot, Keene rushed to the presidential box and was permitted to cradle the dying president's head in her arms. Keene's bloodstained dress (the "Lincoln Dress") became a blood relic, essentially a religious icon in America as well as a Rawson family heirloom.[15]

The assassination of James Garfield, only a few months after his inauguration, provided Bennett with a platform to denounce religious fanaticism. James Abram Garfield was the last American president born in a log cabin and the second to be fatally wounded by an assassin's bullet. On July 2, 1881, less than four months after Bennett witnessed his swearing-in as president, Garfield was shot twice by Charles J. Guiteau in a waiting room of the Potomac Depot in Washington, DC. Garfield lingered near death through the long hot summer while the country's churches prayed intensely for his recovery. "It was an orgy, a regular prayer drive," according to George Macdonald.[16]

While the country's newspapers and magazines focused on the assassin's supposed political motivation, Bennett expressed what he believed was Guiteau's inspiration in his editorial "A Sad and Shameful Deed":

> That a second president of this republic should be shot down by the hand of an assassin within the short space of sixteen years is indeed a most sad and unfortunate affair.... He appears not so much a partisan or politician as a fanatic and zealot. He gives it out that he is a theologian, a religious teacher, and a prophet. He is the author of an intensely religious work upon the coming of Christ [*The Truth*], and has also spoken in public upon the same subject in defense of orthodoxy as against Ingersollism and Infidelity. He also seems to have been connected with the Young Men's Christian Association, and he has devised a plan by which to evangelize and convert the whole world in a very expeditious manner.... These religious zealots and fanatics have done a vast amount of harm in the world, and it is desirable that their rule and influence may rapidly grow less.
>
> —D. M. Bennett, July 9, 1881[17]

On September 19, 1881, Garfield died in Elberon, New Jersey. In Europe the Royal Courts acknowledged Garfield's death and observed a day of mourning, marking the first time ever for an American citizen. "It was indeed a sad blow," Bennett wrote, "that a President should be so needlessly and wrongfully smitten down by an evil-minded person," and in the editor's opinion, "a great loss of labor in the way of prayer." He found the Christian argument that God knows best to be nonsensical. And since their prayers were unanswered, he reasoned, "It not only makes him [God] responsible for Garfield's death, but also guilty of the shooting." And since God knows everything and is all-powerful, *why* did he allow the president to suffer for eleven weeks and would it not "have been better to kill him with a fever rather than suffer such a vile wretch as Guiteau to shoot him down like a dog?" Bennett found it just another example and proof that there was no efficacy in prayer. He argued that if Garfield had recovered, the Christians would "triumphantly exclaim, 'See what prayer has done! It was we who did it.'" But now that Garfield has died they declare, "God knows best." He thought it was just another example of "Christian logic" and nothing more than "tweedledum or tweedledee."[18]

Robert Ingersoll campaigned for Garfield, attended his inauguration, and found himself in an unusual position in the aftermath of the assassination. The day after Garfield's inauguration, Charles Guiteau, a religious fanatic, began visiting Ingersoll in Washington. (Coincidentally, the same day that the Bennetts tried to visit him.) Guiteau was from Chicago, and he remembered that Ingersoll had also lived in Illinois and had considerable influence with President Garfield. He was hoping the distinguished attorney could get him a job in the government. Ingersoll refused to write a letter on his behalf or to lend him money. Later the orator learned that the man had made derogatory remarks about him while making public lectures. On the day of the assassination, Ingersoll had an appointment with the president at the White House. After oversleeping, and while rushing to get to the White House, Ingersoll passed the president driving to his destination, the Pennsylvania Railroad Station. A short while later, Ingersoll heard that Garfield had been shot. He immediately went to the station where he learned the president had been carried upstairs and stretched out on the floor. Ingersoll was admitted to the room and the injured president motioned for him to kneel down beside him. "He recognized me and I had a considerable talk with him," Ingersoll wrote to his brother. "I thought he would certainly die. He had the look of death."[19]

Conspiracy theories and wild rumors began to circulate. There was even an absurd rumor saying that the assassin purchased the pistol with some money loaned from Robert Ingersoll. Naturally some Washington and New York clerics asserted that secular liberalism had influenced Guiteau and caused him to shoot the president. "It is humiliating," Ingersoll wrote his brother, "to read the follies of the press & pulpit on this matter." In a letter to George Jacob Holyoake, the English philosopher and Father of Secularism, Ingersoll wrote, "It was fortunate for me that the assassin was a good Christian, that he had delivered lectures answering me, that he was connected with the Young Men's Christian Association, and that he spent most of his life reading the sacred scriptures."[20]

Charles Guiteau went to the gallows convinced the assassination was inspired from God. While facing the hangman, he sang a childish hymn that he composed, "I am going to the Lordy." Prior to the execution, an editorial, likely written by Eugene Macdonald, appeared in the *Truth Seeker* titled "The Nation's Calamity." Macdonald opined,

> President Garfield is dead. . . . He is the second President who has been slain by assassination. But Lincoln was killed in the heat of passion stirred up by civil war, while Garfield was shot by cold-blooded fanaticism, wrought upon by political feeling. Garfield was shot by religion, and when Guiteau is arraigned at the bar of justice religion should stand up with him. He was, he says, inspired by God to shoot the President. . . . And the lesson to be drawn is that we have still the old murderous spirit of Christianity in our zealous fanatics that must be driven out ere the life of any man is safe.[21]

PSYCHOMETRY, PROPHECY, AND THE PANTARCH

Prior to the departure for his trip around the world, Bennett became increasingly interested in the occult. In a letter to Mrs. Elizabeth M. F. Denton, he enclosed a check for two copies of William Denton's book *Our Planet*. William Denton was a free-thinking explorer, geologist, and pioneer in paranormal research. Elizabeth Denton was especially adept at psychometry. As a psychometer, she could hold a piece of quartz from Panama and allegedly comment on the climate and other physical aspects of the region. Mrs. Denton also reportedly had the ability to "fly" to the area. This talent became known as remote viewing or traveling clairvoyance. The Dentons were convinced that they could telescope into the past—using psychometry.[22]

Three months later, the editor ordered Denton's *The Soul of Things; or, Psychometric Researches and Discoveries*. The three volumes describe past ages in narrative style, with the help of psychometry. It is obvious from Bennett's letter to Mrs. Denton that he was also becoming more philosophical, writing, "I am sorry to hear that sickness has paid you so severe a visit and hope it will soon pass by. There is little doubt that the troubles and griefs of life far exceed the joys and pleasures. All we can do is to meet what fate has for us, with philosophic patience and equanimity."[23]

During this period there was widespread apprehension in the world about the year 1881. Mother Shipton, the supposed prophetess, had predicted centuries earlier that the world would come to an end in 1881. She was credited with predicting the advent of the telegraph, the steam engine, and other modern inventions. While Bennett found some of her predictions remarkable, he believed no more in Mother Shipton's prophecy than in "Father Jeremiah's, Uncle Ezekiel's, or Cousin Daniel's." And he was willing to "wager" a hundred copies of Paine's *The Age of Reason* against "a good farm or first-class house and lot that the world does not come to an end in eighteen-hundred and eighty-one."[24]

In weighing the pros and cons of taking a trip around the world, Bennett took astrology into consideration. And while widespread apprehension considered it an unlucky year, he argued the planets could hardly exert any more baneful influence on the other side of the world. Allaying fears by some friends that he would be in danger from an accident and perhaps never return, he assured them that their fears were unproven, traveling was safe, and people in the Orient were considerate. To those who thought Mary should accompany him—an agreeable idea to both of them—Bennett replied that the journey would be too long, difficult, and "improper for her to rough it" as he planned to do.[25]

Whether it was the position of the planets, his poor health weakened by prison environment, or some intuitive feeling, Bennett seemed reluctant, at least privately, to take the journey. Finally on May 7, 1881, he reached a decision to take the trip. The amount of subscriptions sent to the office would determine *when* he would leave. Within two months, seven hundred more five-dollar donations arrived—nearly fifteen hundred patrons would eventually subscribe! Encouraged by the positive reception and commercial success of *An Infidel Abroad*, he agreed to provide subscribers to his Around the World Fund with a set of two or three books that he proposed to write chronicling his journey. (In typical Bennett fashion there would be four!)[26]

On July 4, the Bennetts took six days of recreation and traveled to the New Lebanon and Watervliet Shaker communities where they called upon Elder Lomas and some of Mary's relatives. In Rochester the couple visited his mother's grave. After staying two days at his sister's Sea Breeze resort on Lake Ontario, they attended a reception in his honor at Amy Post's home in Rochester. Before returning home to New York City, they took the train to Albany and visited the place whose walls he hoped to never enter again: the Albany Penitentiary. After looking in at his former cell and the prison hospital, the Bennetts enjoyed dinner with the prison superintendent and his family in the infamous castle on the hill.[27]

As the publisher-editor of the *Truth Seeker*, Bennett was closely associated with numerous members of New York's intelligentsia, most notably Stephen Pearl Andrews. The Pantarch, as he was known, was a dynamic reformer who developed his own philosophical system and universal language. He had an extraordinary command of the philosophy of language and was familiar with thirty-two languages, some of which he spoke fluently: Chinese, Greek, Hebrew, Latin, and Sanskrit. Andrews asserted that there was a science of language, as precise as mathematics or chemistry. By applying this science that he termed Universology, Andrews devised his own scientific universal language that he named Alwato (a language that preceded Esperanto). "I have made it the business of my life to study social laws," he wrote. "I see now a new age beginning to appear."[28]

Stephen Pearl Andrews's search for a universal energy would be more accepted in the twentieth than the nineteenth century. The philosophy that evolved from his Universology was called Integralism, a concept that was beyond most nineteenth-century people's intellectual grasp. "In applying the law of metaphor to mind and matter," his biographer asserted, "he crossed almost by instinct a boundary that is today being laboriously crossed by the formulas of nuclear physicists." Andrews "might have found a larger niche in a world familiar with Einstein's work on relativity and the atomic researches of nuclear physicists. In such a world his metaphysical vaporizing might have taken on more substance."[29]

Although George Macdonald concluded that Andrews's "Universology had more contacts with the common mind than Einstein's theory of relativity," Bennett admittedly never fully understood his philosophy. But since Einstein predicted that his theory of relativity would never be comprehended by more than twelve living persons, it is no wonder that the editor could not comprehend Andrews's complex theories. Nevertheless, Bennett believed it because Andrews believed in it.[30]

The day before Bennett was scheduled to leave America, he visited Stephen Pearl Andrews and expressed his appreciation for Andrews's work. Bennett apologized for not publishing his writing in the *Truth Seeker* over the years and admitted that he found it a bit too scholarly for him and his readers. "We are a plain people, we understand common language and common ideas, and we don't understand much else," he told Andrews. The two men discussed the future and Bennett talked about his goals in the world. The visit lasted two or three hours and Andrews recollected that the editor lingered and seemed reluctant to leave. "There was a sort of . . . foreboding," he recalled, "as though in a high degree of probability, he should never return—never complete his journey; and there was a tenderness and real heartfelt friendliness manifested toward me, personally, that I had no knowledge of before."[31]

NOTES

"to reach perfection.": Elizur Wright Papers.

    1. TS May 7, 1881.
    2. TS June 18, 1881.
    3. TS March 26, 1881.
    4. "little craft afloat.": Letter to Wright, Jan. 18, 1881. "model of Godliness.": TS March 26, 1881.

Bennett and Eugene Macdonald would periodically ask Wright to contribute articles to the *Truth Seeker*. In 1884 Eugene wrote a letter to Wright asking him to contribute an article. Eugene said that he wanted the "best brains among the Liberals," and although he left the subject of the article to Wright, he suggested that "a good weapon against the church . . . would be something showing conclusively that the church was against abolition and in favor of slavery." Letter, October 28, 1884. Elizur Wright Papers.

    5. TS March 26, 1881.
    6. Ibid.
    7. TS Sept. 5, 1885.
    8. TS July 2, 1881.
    9. TS May 7, 1881.
  10. TS April 23, 1881.
  11. TS June 4, 1881.
  12. TS March 12, 1881.
  13. Ibid.
  14. GM v. 2 p. 316.

15. TS March 12, 1881.

16. TS May 7, 1881. Allan Peskin, *Garfield: A Biography*. The Kent State University Press 1978.

17. TS July 9, 1881.

18. TSAW.

19. "look of death.": Larson pp. 164–67, Letter to John, July 5, 1881, RGI Letters p. 172.

20. "on this matter." RGI letters p. 172. "the sacred scriptures.": GM v. 1, p. 301.

21. "to the Lordy.": Peskin, p. 611. "man is safe.": TS Sept. 24, 1881.

22. Letter dated March 9, 1881, Denton Family Papers, Labadie Collection, University of Michigan. Wilson pp. 30, 36.

23. "patience and equanimity.": Denton Family Papers.

24. TS Jan. 1, 1881.

25. TS May 7, 1881.

26. TSAW.

27. TS July 16, 1881.

28. Stern.

29. Ibid. p. 157. "on more substance.": GM v. 1 p. 408.

30. Ibid.

31. TS June 28, 1884.

14

A Truth Seeker
around the World

*In fact, a journey abroad may be the very thing to prevent some vile
attack being made upon me, though that is no reason for my going.*
—D. M. Bennett

The New York Liberal League held a bon voyage party for
Bennett a week before his departure. Among those present
for the evening of speeches, recitations, and songs were Dr. Foote
Sr., Albert Rawson, and Theron Leland. Several eloquent speeches
were made, one by Samuel Putnam, who was fast becoming one
of freethought's most gifted authors and lecturers. Less familiar to
those in attendance was Dr. Joseph Rodes Buchanan, who spoke
briefly and admitted that he had been observing the editor's
"course with interest for many years." A professor of medicine,
Buchanan was a pioneer in paranormal research and invented the
word *psychometry* or soul measurement.[1]

While discussing his upcoming trip, Bennett informed the

audience that he would be taking a "photograph apparatus" along to take "views" to illustrate his books, and stereoptic views for future lectures. He asked his friends to remember Mary while he was gone. He paid a poignant tribute to the woman who had faithfully stood by him "when the shafts of hatred, envy, and malice [had] been aimed at [him], and when the darts of obloquy and slander [had] fallen all around [him]. She proved true when others were false, and [he asked his] good friends all over the country not to forget her nor the struggle she is making for the good of the cause we all have at heart." Several voices exclaimed aloud, "We will not forget her!"[2]

Eugene Macdonald observed that the "Old Man" highly appreciated the earnest fellowship and kindly feeling expressed that evening and the sincere friendship "filled his heart to overflowing." The gathering was held at the residence of Daniel Ryan, who proudly informed the audience that he was the first person to shake the editor's hand when he "emerged from the prison walls a little over a year ago." He was honored to have the farewell meeting in his home and concluded his remarks with some heartfelt verse:

> If I were asked what best I'd prize,
> As sacred gifts conferred on me,
> And which I'd hold as treasures rare,
> My answer back would quickly be:
> A mind that's void of all offense,
> A heart as pure as sinless youth,
> A will to never swerve from right,
> A soul whose polar star is truth.[3]

On July 30, 1881, forty friends assembled at the foot of Dey Street to see Bennett off around the world. After seeing the editor coming down the pier, the group of well-wishers welcomed him by vigorously grabbing and shaking his hand. They accompanied him on board the *Ethiopia* and adjourned to the saloon where they discussed the journey. When the bell rang for all who were not passengers to go ashore, the reluctant group had to be gently persuaded by the ship's officers to leave the vessel. As the steam engines started and the large screw revolved, the *Ethiopia* proceeded out into the stream, and they all went to the end of the pier. Three cheers were proposed for Bennett as he stood by the rail waving good-bye. The enthusiastic cheers were so loud, the steamboat officials on the dock took notice.[4]

Since Bennett was planning to tour around the world for a year, he left Eugene Macdonald the editorial chair and power of attorney. He remained in communication with Eugene and provided his readers with his foreign forwarding addresses in London and Jerusalem. He immediately began writing during the eleven-day sail to Europe and, before arriving, completed a nine-column letter for the *Truth Seeker* and resumed his "What I Don't Believe" series of articles that had begun three years earlier. George Macdonald observed that Bennett never entirely understood the limited amount of space available in the weekly. He recalled the time his brother Eugene tried to make it clear "by pointing to the foot of the last column and expounding the incompressibility of type." Another factor making his letters so lengthy was his acquisition of some guide and travel books that George suspected he drew "upon freely."[5]

GREAT BRITAIN

The editor spent more than a month in Great Britain and attended the International Freethought Congress in London's Hall of Science. Within a few days of his arrival in London, Bennett was invited to accompany Charles Bradlaugh, the congress's chairman, to Hanley, Staffordshire, where the iconoclastic Parliament member was to speak at a trade union gathering. It was only a year earlier that the editor had met and spent time with Bradlaugh while on his first trip abroad. Bradlaugh advocated atheism, birth control, and republicanism to a nation that was pious, prolific, and royalist. Supporters, friends, and political pundits in France, Italy, and the United States confidently expected Charles Bradlaugh to become the first president of Great Britain.[6]

Like D. M. Bennett, Charles Bradlaugh was both loved and reviled. Only a month earlier on August 3, Bradlaugh had been brutally attacked by fourteen constables and prevented from taking his seat in Parliament. During the train ride to Hanley Bennett observed that "Bradlaugh travels like a prince." The two free-thinkers rode in a private compartment and discussed the attack, British politics, and the "Irish question." The editor reported that Bradlaugh favored granting "Ireland all the rights and privileges due to her people," and if he had the power, he would "grant her 'home rule.'" Bradlaugh's speech at Hanley (attended by five thousand) was his first since the violent incident in Parliament. Bennett sat on the platform and listened to the brilliant orator (still wearing his arm in a sling) speak about the "rights and obligations of the working men." The editor was impressed with Bradlaugh's eloquence and popularity among Great Britain's working men and women, and was flattered when the orator "was kind enough to allude to myself" during his speech. "He is building up a party which must ultimately have a marked effect upon the affairs of this country." Charles Bradlaugh would indeed become the most respected "back bencher" of the day, and the "member for India" after he was finally able to take his seat in 1886.[7]

Back in London, Bennett toured the Woolrich Arsenal, the largest munitions factory in the world. The visit gave the editor the opportunity to express his views on war and peace. He wrote,

> I could not help thinking, while looking over this vast establish-ment, what a sad commentary it is upon Christianity and its peaceful teachings. Here the first Christian nation in the world has expended hundreds of millions of dollars, and is employing thousands of men constantly, to construct the most ingenious implements and inventions for destroying human life—the lives of men, too, who never did aught themselves to wrong the British government or people. Premiums are offered for those who can invent guns and other apparatus that will destroy the greatest number of creatures bearing God's image, and brother Christians at that. This killing and maiming has been kept up century after century since Christianity became a

power. Although it boasts the highest civilization the world has known, its proudest achievement seems to kill the greatest number of human beings in a given time. I remarked that Christianity claimed to be a peaceful religion, but that it had proved itself to be more bloody, to provoke more hate, to take more life, than all the other religions among men. In spreading peace over the world Christianity has proved a failure. If war is ever done away with, and the nations study peace instead of war, Rationalism will have to effect it; Christianity will have to give way and a better religion take its place.[8]

In Scotland Bennett traveled to Glasgow and Edinburgh, and visited numerous points of interest including Inverness, the capital of the Highlands. He found the homes of John Knox and David Hume as well as the beloved Robert Burns house in Edinburgh. Like Robert Ingersoll, he held the poet Robert Burns in high esteem: "He was not much of a friend to royalty, nobility, and the priesthood," he noted. "When I meet his statue, as I have done both here and in Glasgow, my hat raises spontaneously." Before leaving Glasgow for Ireland, he traveled to Ayr to see Burns's birthplace cottage, monument, and the Bonny Doon River. He realized that Burns was "one of the most natural, simple, and one of the sweetest poets that ever sang, who, though he had some faults and weaknesses, was at heart a true man—really one of nature's noblemen, one of the highest works of her hand." At the storied Tam O'Shanter Inn, Bennett confessed to having a small glass of sherry for "Auld Lang Syne."[9]

Bennett spent six days in Ireland visiting Dublin, Belfast, Galway, Limerick, Killarney, and Cork. And while finding much of the country beautiful, he pronounced that Ireland was "cursed with too much Christianity and too many priests." He was disappointed to learn that the Irish were the most religious people in the world and noted that there was hardly a freethinker in Ireland. Along with a fairly comprehensive overview of the agriculture, linen manufacturing, and peat production of the island, he provided his views on social issues and, of course, religion. He found the overpopulation especially troubling and blamed the Catholic

Church and its "evil" policies. Although Bennett would not defend abortions, which he believed ruined health and were in his opinion absolutely criminal, he declared prevention legitimate and right. In a country so poor, he felt that every mother should be intelligent enough to safely control the number of children that she was able to raise properly. No one should add to the growing "number of wretched human beings to starve, suffer, and die, or at best eke out a miserable existence."[10]

The greatest evil Ireland faced was priests. "What if they do to some extent restrain the brutal passions of their ignorant lackeys?" It did not excuse them for the harm that they produce and was "assuredly not a healthy control." Bennett believed Ireland's answers lay in education and the "truths of science" for a morality both correct and independent of "priestly superstitions and falsehoods." As to the more than eight thousand priests in Ireland he wrote, "They are the best dressed, the most leisurely, and the most useless class of men that I have met with. They are the tyrants and oppressors of the country."[11]

While Bennett was less than enamored with Ireland, he was intrigued by Wales, where he spent four days. After visiting the reputed home of the celebrated Welsh prophet Merlin in Carmarthen, he proceeded to the village of Pontypridd to meet Evan Davies, the archdruid of the British Isles. Davies, whose Welsh name was Myfyr Morganwg, was a curious Welsh eccentric whose outfit consisted of a white archdruid's robe and a Druid's serpent egg hanging from a chain around his neck. A scholarly and gentle soul, Davies wrote several books on Druidism and the *Glory of Wales*. When Bennett informed the legendary old Druid that he had come all the way from America, Davies extended his hand and proclaimed—"Ah, then you are Mr. Bennett, the Bradlaugh of America!" "Yes, my name is Bennett, but I am hardly worthy to be called the Bradlaugh of America, though I have tried to do what I could in my way."[12]

The archdruid was familiar with the *Truth Seeker* and expressed his approval of Bennett's work; they agreed the Druidic faith was far superior to the Christian religion. They discussed the origin of religion and Davies made a statement that struck Bennett "with special force, and as being strictly true." The comment was, "Christianity is one of the greatest falsehoods the world has known, and an uncounted number of falsehoods have been used to sustain it." He found Davies "a man of first-class intelligence and of extensive learning." He was honored when Davies allowed him to sit on his bizarre throne, carved with symbols and used when he was acting in his official capacity as archdruid. Before leaving the archdruid's "genial fire," the editor inquired as to the location of the nearby Druidic temple. Davies pointed to a mountain and expressed his desire to accompany the editor but was too old and unable to make the excursion.[13]

Early the next morning, Bennett walked the mile or more crossing the Taff River to reach the old meeting place of the Druids. While climbing the hillside, he noticed "the sun was climbing the other, and when I reached the ancient religious temple we stood face to face." As he realized that some thousands of years earlier Druids had gathered on the same hill, a feeling of awe came over him and he had a sense that he was standing upon holy ground. Seeing the sun for the first time in several days, he confessed feeling "worshipful"; removing his hat and bowing reverently, he voiced aloud his invocation to the sun. Bennett proclaimed sun worship as rational as any other and concluded his prayer:

> Hail to thee, O Sun! I bow in reverence before thee. I own thee superior to all other existences within thy system. I devoutly acknowledge thee the supreme power that rules on high. There is none greater than thee; there is nothing superior to thee. As the ancients worshipped thee on this very spot of ground, so do I now worship thee, and the glorious universe of which thou art a part, now and here this lovely morning.[14]

Bennett visited the Druidic open-air temple and the Rocking-Stone, a circle of stones that had been placed under the direction of Myfyr Morganwg. The editor described the famous Rocking-Stone, weighing nine-and-one-half tons, as a marvel of precision. He later returned to Morganwg's home and exchanged pictures with the local bard, who asked him to give kind regards to any Brahmans he might meet in India. The editor was carrying a letter from the Druids of America that Morganwg signed as the arch-druid of Wales. The document that Bennett carried to India was probably the first of its kind and authorized him as a representative of the American Druids by stating that he "is authorized as our representative to extend to you on our behalf the offer of our cordial inter-fraternity, and to respectfully ask your co-operation in the extension of 'Knowledge, love, and truth' and in the investigation of our respective histories." The letter "attracted much notice from the learned Brahmans who have read it," Bennett wrote, "who have received me with great kindness."[15]

Later that same day, Bennett arrived by train in Salisbury, England. His long day's journey was made specifically to visit the ancient Druid temple of Stonehenge that night. After learning that Stonehenge was nine miles north of Salisbury, he bargained with a cabman to transport him out to the temple with as little delay as possible, though the cabman charged him twelve shillings ($60 in today's money) to make the trip. He finally arrived at Stonehenge, but at first glance thought that "the cathedral of the Arch-Druid" was not up to his expectations. However, when he got closer he realized that "Stonehenge is truly a wonder." Bennett was amazed at how primitive people could erect such a temple. And since he arrived as the sun was setting, he found it an appropriate place to worship as he had done that morning at Pontypridd. "I improved my opportunity," he confessed.[16]

While at Stonehenge, Bennett meditated "upon the work of men in the far past" until dark. Later that evening, he strolled around Salisbury, observing the residents before finally retiring, feeling that he had done a fair day's work. Although he would have enjoyed visiting the other stone temples at Avebury, he had to continue on to London where he made the most significant pilgrimage of his tour—to the Thomas Paine residence at No. 6 Ropemaker Street. It was there that the revolutionist reportedly invented the iron bridge and wrote his radical *Rights of Man* (1791/1792), one of the most popular, spirited, and luminous defenses of liberty, human rights, and equality ever written. Bennett wrote, "Thus the first iron bridge to carry people safely over turbulent streams and a great political work well-calculated to convey people over the stream of kingcraft and despotism were the results of the same brain, and their conception not far from the same time."[17]

Naturally, a persistent theme of Bennett's letters is his criticism of religion. While he was in England, the Methodist Ecumenical Council held a two-week session with representatives from the United States. Several of the American delegates stayed at the Essex House Hotel, where the editor had first stayed in London. "When they learned that I was an Ingersoll kind of man they turned up their eyes in holy horror and wondered why God suffers me to live."[18]

Another event that provided fodder for the irrepressible editor was the arrival of Dwight Lyman Moody and Ira D. Sankey, the popular American revival duo. They "have made another starring visit to England, with the hope, doubtless, of winning a few souls to Jesus, and taking back a thousand pounds or so of the coin of the realm," he reported. "I place the souls before the coin, but I am not sure that Moody and Sankey put them in that order in their heart of hearts. . . . It is very nice to work for Jesus when it pays well."[19]

On September 24, 1881, Bennett attended the meeting of American citizens at Exeter Hall in London to mourn the death of President Garfield. The hall was filled with about six thousand people who "all seemed to wear an air of sadness, and many were dressed in mourning," he noted. James Russell Lowell, the American minister to the Court of St. James, presided, "and seldom has any public meeting had an abler and more dignified chairman." Among the many foreign dignitaries was Moncure Conway, who remarked that the assassinations of Lincoln and Garfield had strengthened the "bonds of fellowship between England and America." He suggested that since ethnologists found fault with the expression "Anglo-Saxon," it should hereafter "be replaced by the nobler word Anglo-American." While in London, Bennett also attended a lecture by Mrs. Besant. "I must repeat what I have said before," he wrote. "Mrs. Besant is a very remarkable woman."[20]

THE *OTHER* BENNETT

From England Bennett traveled through Holland, Germany, Bohemia, Austria, Italy, Greece, Turkey, Lebanon, Syria, and finally Palestine and Jerusalem—the "promised land." There were several occasions when the language barrier caused minor difficulties for the elderly editor, and he hoped that the future would see a universal language—possibly Stephen Pearl Andrews's Alwato. On a train from Prague to Vienna, Bennett got into a heated argument with the railway porters that nearly ended in a fistfight. "I am not good at contention, especially the fistic variety, and it occurred to me that in many cases discretion is the better part of valor."[21]

In Egypt a few lighter moments occurred at a dance performance and during a donkey ride. Bennett could only describe an exhibition by native girls belly dancing as "not of a very modest character." He admittedly "cut a comical figure" while riding a donkey on the way to the tombs of the kings. "The donkey-boys close behind and hurrying them on and yelling at them and the girls running along our sides. . . . I could not help laughing at the novelty of the situation."[22]

Another amusing incident took place at the Nile River on December 23, 1881—his sixty-third birthday. Wishing to do something exceptional on his birthday and feeling it his duty to bathe in all the holy rivers, he walked for nearly a mile with soap and towel looking for a place where he could safely enter the water. But remembering the crocodiles in the Jordan, he compromised with himself and took only a partial bath, preferring to die of old age. "It may be the last time I will bathe in any river on my birthday."[23]

Less than two weeks later, after spending one of the grandest days of his life visiting the pyramids, Bennett departed Suez aboard a steamer bound for Bombay (Mumbai), India. The three-thousand-mile voyage through the Gulf of Suez, Red Sea, and Indian Ocean (in intense heat) would take twelve days. Traveling second class, he described his fellow passengers as mostly English and, like himself, as a "common sort of folks," on their way to India for the first time.[24]

There was another American passenger, ironically named Bennett, "but decidedly unlike me in several particulars." The young Missouri missionary on his way to India started his crusade as soon as the steamer left the dock at Suez. In his aggressive attempt to make converts out of the passengers, he approached nearly everyone except Bennett. "He did not commence upon me, and I rather held myself in reserve, with readiness to receive him in the spirit of Christ, but he came not. Possibly Jesus may have told him that I am a hard case, and scarcely worth the trouble of saving."[25]

The young man's revival hymns and glory hallelujahs were initially amusing, but as the long voyage in the stifling heat wore on, the novelty soon wore off. Occasionally he removed his shoes and socks and, with his pants rolled up, ran along the deck, leaping over whatever was in the way, shouting for Jesus. His endless deck harangues and loud O Jesuses were constant and quickly becoming intolerable. At night he could be heard kneeling in his stateroom, praying to Jesus, for all the passengers to hear. Everyone on board was getting increasingly annoyed, especially the editor, who found the young man "so full and overflowing with Jesus as to make himself a perfect nuisance."[26]

After hearing several of his fellow passengers complaining about the man's offensive behavior and the prospect of a long miserable voyage, Bennett decided to have a talk with the young zealot. While still in the Gulf of Suez near Mount Sinai, he confronted his young namesake on the ship's deck and spoke as follows:

> Look here, my young friend, you are making either a monomaniac or a damned fool of yourself, and annoying the passengers not a little. We have no objections to your being as happy with Jesus as you can possibly be, but we do object to your making us all wretched in the operation. We say, be as happy as you please, so long as you do not infringe upon our rights in doing so. It is our opinion that you are fast losing your good sense, if you ever were in possession of that article; and if you cannot

contain your fervor in your own breast, and cease to disturb us, we will be compelled to apply to the captain of the ship and require that you may be kept somewhere else, for we cannot be annoyed in this way.

I have seen men like you before, who claimed to be sinless and faultless, who had a great deal to say about their being so much better than other people, and I have found that they will bear very close watching, for a self-righteous man is more to be distrusted than any others. It is not safe for one to leave his pocketbook within reach of a self-righteous and over-holy zealot. I would not trust them a yard out of my sight. I have found in the course of my life that really good men are not constantly boasting of their excellence and their sinlessness, but leave it for others to discover the good qualities of their character. A braggart either in holiness or knowledge is always to be distrusted, for it is almost sure that he will turn out to be a rascal.

But as for this disturbance you are keeping up on the ship, it must be discontinued or, as I said, complaint will be entered to the captain, and we will see if the annoyance cannot be stopped. I will be frank with you, and say that for one I cannot put up with it and will not.[27]

The man stood red-faced and speechless for the duration of what Bennett described as a mild-mannered address. Nevertheless, the silence lasted only a day or so and soon the missionary was back on deck whooping and hollering for Jesus as loud and obnoxiously as before. Because the crew found the histrionics entertaining, Bennett decided to try to ignore him for the remainder of the voyage. The man eventually apologized to him. The editor found him to be a "goodhearted young man" but "Jesus-crazy." Some of the passengers who were aware of Bennett's notoriety told him that he would make more converts than his noisy namesake.[28]

NOTES

"for my going.": TS May 7, 1881.

1. GM. v. 1, p. 292. "for many years.": TS July 30, 1881, and Wilson p. 3.

2. TS July 30, 1881.

3. Ibid.

4. TS Aug. 6, 1881.

5. GM v. 1, pp. 292–93.

6. TSAW.

7. TSAW.

Bennett subsequently attended Bradlaugh's trial in London for voting in the House of Commons without having taken the mandatory oath. The editor liked Bradlaugh's "style" and wrote: "Mr. Bradlaugh took the stand as a witness and made affirmation in place of taking an oath and kissing the book, and I must say the affirmation is much more pretty and impressive than the old form of the oath." TSAW v. 1. p. 285.

8. TSAW.

9. Ibid.

10. Ibid.

11. Ibid.

12. Ibid.

13. Ibid.

Morganwg subsequently translated a series of articles for the *Truth Seeker* titled "Ecce Diabolus" (Behold the Devil).

14. Ibid. Rocking-Stone set up by Davies (Morganwg) EB v. 22, pp. 71–72.

15. TSAW.

Evan Davies (Morganwg) erected one of the most unusual megalithic monuments in the world. He built two circles of standing stones, connected by a path to a smaller circle forming a serpent's head. (The serpent is the symbol of Druid wisdom.) Two additional stones represented the serpent's eyes. The temple was used for bardic gatherings by the Pontypridd Druids. John Michell, *Eccentric Lives and Peculiar Notions*, pp. 134–35. Black Dog & Leventhal Publishers, Inc. (New York, N.Y. 1999).

16. Ibid.

17. Ibid.

Due to the paucity of biographical material about Thomas Paine at the time, Bennett might have erroneously reported that the author wrote *Rights of Man* and invented his iron bridge at the Ropemaker address.

18. Ibid.
19. Ibid.
20. Ibid.

Bennett elaborated on his impressions of Mrs. Besant, writing:

She lectures in the ablest manner upon theological subjects, Freethought topics, political questions, and scientific matters with equal facility and ability, and without notes. She readily and coolly answers all queries and objections that may be raised by persons in her audience. She seems to understand all questions, and to be able to handle them with almost unexampled ability. In addition, I will say she is a master of the German and French languages. In her discussion last winter with Rev. Mr. Hatchard, who considers himself one of the ablest advocates of Christianity, she utterly defeated him, and showed not only that his claims of Christianity are entirely false, but that she is decidedly an abler debater and speaker than the reverend gentleman. When he forgot himself and flew in a passion at his discomfiture, she remained throughout perfectly cool and self-possessed. The wife of a prominent clergyman, she assisted him in the preparation of his sermons and other theological writings, in which occupation she was led to see the defects in Christian arguments and proofs; and finding that the system is not what is claimed for it, she studied the subject thoroughly, reading all the works for and against Christian evidence that came within her reach, the result of which was she became a decided unbeliever. (TSAW v. 1. pp. 299–300.)

21. Ibid.
22. Ibid.
23. Ibid.
24. Ibid.
25. Ibid.
26. Ibid.
27. Ibid.
28. Ibid.

15

A Theosophical Odyssey

*I have learned to modify my prejudices. . . . I am ready to believe
Hamlet was right when he assured his friend Horatio that there was
in heaven and earth many things not dreamed of in his philosophy.*
                                                            —D. M. Bennett

Bennett arrived aboard the steamer *Cathay* in Bombay, India,
well after midnight on January 10, 1882. Because of the late
hour and high tide, the ship cast anchor in the bay and passengers had to wait until morning to go ashore. Soon after daybreak,
Bennett was standing on the deck, viewing the city of nearly
eighty thousand, when he received a note from Henry Olcott
instructing him to remain on board until Olcott arrived to take
him ashore. Bennett had corresponded with Olcott from Suez
and accepted an invitation to call upon him and Madame
Blavatsky, the founders of the Theosophical Society. "I, of course
was glad to meet them," Bennett wrote, "and renew our old

acquaintance and to see in India those whom I had known in America."[1]

Within a few hours Olcott, his Hindu assistant Damodar K. Mavalankar, his servants, and Kavasji M. Shroff, a prominent theosophist and leading advocate for the prevention of cruelty to animals, arrived in a boat to take Bennett ashore. As they made their way through the busy harbor, he observed some Africans unloading ships while "singing their national ditties, slapping their thighs, and giving a regular plantation 'break-down.'" It reminded Bennett of a "first-class minstrel performance" but no burned cork was necessary and he found their "exhibition . . . the genuine African article." Determining whether Theosophy was only a performance or genuine would prove more difficult for the editor of the *Truth Seeker*.[2]

In 1875 Madame Blavatsky, a Russian spiritualist, and Henry S. Olcott, an American lawyer and writer, established the Theosophical Society in New York City. The word *theosophy* is derived from the Greek *theos* (God) and *sophia* (wisdom) and is commonly translated as "divine wisdom." The three objects of the Theosophical Society in 1875 were as follows: first, to form the nucleus of a universal brotherhood of humanity, without distinction of race, creed, or color; second, to promote the study of Aryan and other Eastern literature, religions, and sciences, and vindicate its importance; and third, to investigate the hidden mysteries of nature and the psychical powers latent in man. Bennett paraphrased for readers the society's objectives as "partly of a scientific, partly of a religious, and partly of an investigating character into what is called the occult domain of nature."[3]

While the two leading "spirits" of the Theosophical Society had spiritualism in common, Blavatsky and Olcott had dissimilar backgrounds. Henry Steel Olcott was born in Orange, New Jersey, and served as a government fraud investigator during and after the Civil War. He was a respected member of the three-man commission assigned to investigate whether any conspiracy was behind Abraham Lincoln's assassination. Olcott's interrogation of Mary Suratt (the woman who ran the boardinghouse where the suspected plotters held their meetings) was considered "an exemplary illustration of 1865 police interrogation technique."[4]

A lawyer and freelance journalist, Olcott was drawn into the mysterious world of Spiritualism and séances while doing investigative reporting for New York newspapers. After investigating several mediums and cases of inexplicable phenomena, Olcott concluded that some spiritualistic activity was in fact genuine. His book *People from the Other World*, published in 1875, was commended by two renowned British scientists and was, according to a biographer, "one of the most remarkable testimonials to the powerful 'psychical phenomena' of mediums of the last century." A former Protestant who discarded his parents' Christianity early in life, Olcott admitted that he had "been travelling the path now called Theosophical" since the 1850s. But it wasn't until he met Madame Blavatsky in 1875 that he "converted hypothesis into certainty as to the nature of 'Soul' and 'Spirit.'" It was only then that he "came to know of the existence of 'Mahatmas.'"[5]

The Theosophical Society was successful from its inception and attracted a wide range of people, including many distinguished freethinkers—Annie Besant, Matilda Joslyn Gage, and Thomas Edison among them. Most freethinkers were former believers in orthodox Christianity and were searching for some form of spiritual sustenance to fill the void. Theosophy and its founders were controversial from the beginning. The genteel lawyer-author and the matronly Russian mystic (barely able to speak English) made an eccentric pair in Victorian New York City. The couple's exotically furnished and decorated Eighth Avenue apartment—the Lamasery—was considered bizarre by neighbors. Some of the influential visitors to the Lamasery were General Abner Doubleday, Thomas Edison, and Albert Rawson, who made several drawings of the residence-headquarters of Theosophy.[6]

Not everyone was as convinced as Olcott about Blavatsky's abilities or the existence of her mysterious Mahatmas; that remains a matter of controversy more than a century later. Helena Petrovna Blavatsky, or HPB as she preferred to be called, was a Russian-born occultist who came to New York in 1873. She claimed to have spent seven years living among her mentors, or Mahatmas, in Tibet before immigrating to America. She credited these brothers or masters of wisdom with writing her book *Isis Unveiled* through her in 1877. Blavatsky asserted that *Isis* was her attempt to reveal the divine wisdom and eternal truths that lie beyond the physical universe or veil. The book was allegedly written rapidly as Olcott observed her pen race across the pages. She insisted the book was not written while she was in a trance, but while fully conscious and aware of whichever adept was working through her.[7]

The massive two-volume *Isis* sold one thousand copies in ten days and included long letters by Albert Rawson and Charles Sotheran, the society's first librarian. In *Isis*, Blavatsky praises the work of Bennett and his friends and associates, including James Rodes Buchanan and William and Elizabeth Denton, the pioneer investigators in the field of psychometry. Blavatsky's controversial assertion that all knowledge and ancient wisdom is recorded was similar to Buchanan's theory that "the past is entombed in the present."[8]

Although the Theosophical Society was flourishing in New York in 1879, Olcott and Blavatsky relocated to India, where they could be closer to the mysterious brothers who purportedly lived secluded in the Himalayas. Within only three years they transformed the society into an international organization that was making considerable progress in unifying the world's spiritualists. They found Indians more receptive than Americans to their assertion that the Mahatmas or Great Ones (Great Souls) still existed. Olcott's long-range goal was to unite all human beings into "one great pan-religious and transnational Universal Brotherhood of Humanity"—not an easy mission considering that there were 250 million people in thirty different nations speaking different languages and jealous and suspicious of each other—in India alone. Moreover, Buddhism and Hinduism had been under attack and nearly completely suppressed by Christian missionaries for the past century.[9]

CROW'S NEST

Olcott's carriage was waiting on the busy dock, ready to take the party to the society's headquarters four miles from the landing. After a brief stop allowing Bennett to pick up his mail from America, they proceeded through the lively streets of Bombay. The editor was initially awestruck by the nearly naked condition of the natives, including the women, but he soon got used to the sight and decided it didn't make much difference whether people wore clothing or not. The warm weather, abundant blooming flowers, and palm trees impelled him to declare, "This truly seems a tropical country."[10]

The carriage finally arrived at the Crow's Nest, the theosophists' residence situated on a hill northwest of the city. "Madame Blavatsky and Col. Olcott occupy very commodious premises commanding a beautiful view of the bay and ocean that is not often excelled," Bennett noted. He learned that the house was rumored to be haunted, perhaps explaining why its rent was surprisingly low considering the luxurious estate with palm groves, gardens, and breathtaking vistas. But for two of the world's leading investigators of the occult—it was perfect. "They are not the kind of people to be afraid of ghosts and were not at all disinclined to live in a house where ghosts and phantoms are said to congregate."[11]

The editor from New York was cordially welcomed at the storied bungalow, where he hoped to enjoy a few days of rest. Bennett arrived in Bombay at a time when the Theosophical Society was still in its nascency and when Blavatsky's secret letter-writing "Masters" were most prolific and her alleged psychic feats were at their height. It was also a period in the history of the Theosophical movement that would subsequently be the most intensely investigated, debated, and controversial.[12]

Bennett was pleasantly surprised by the society's remarkable success in India. In only seven years Theosophy was already becoming a powerful international movement. Within days of arriving, he had conversations with native Indians, including

Hindus, Brahmans, and Parsees, who all gave similar testimony of the good work Olcott and Blavatsky were doing in gathering the diverse creeds "and especially in opposing the work of Christian missionaries" in India and Ceylon (Sri Lanka).[13]

The editor was impressed with Olcott's indefatigable work on behalf of the native population. In Ceylon the struggle for the Sinhalese to retain their Buddhist culture was of great importance to Olcott, who detested the Christian church's ubiquitous role in colonialism. At the time of Olcott's first visit to Ceylon, only four Buddhist schools existed, but by the time of his death in 1907, there were hundreds. Olcott's book *Buddhist Catechism* was published in English and Sinhalese versions only six months before Bennett arrived and was already becoming a best seller and standard textbook in Buddhist schools. The elementary handbook was similar to those used effectively by his Christian adversaries. Bennett was pleased to learn that some *Truth Seeker* tracts had been translated into Sinhalese and circulated among the natives. These publications, he proudly reported, were interfering with the Christian missionaries who "[were] doing their utmost to add this portion of the world to Christendom."[14]

In Henry Steel Olcott, or the White Buddhist as he was often called, Bennett found a brother in the fight against Christianity and for universal mental liberty. He praised Olcott and Blavatsky's magazine, the *Theosophist*, devoted to Oriental philosophy, art, literature, and occultism, embracing mesmerism, Spiritualism, and other secret societies. Bennett reported that the *Theosophist*, which began publication in October 1879, "is ably conducted and contains many interesting and original articles."[15]

One of Olcott's hobbies was reading a person's face for character. "Mr. Bennett was a medium-sized stout man, with a big head, a high forehead, brown hair, and blue eyes," Olcott recorded in his *Old Diary Leaves*. "There was a candor and friendliness about the man which made us sympathize at once." He found the editor to be a "very interesting and sincere person, a Free-thinker who had suffered a year's imprisonment for his bitter—often coarse—attacks upon Christian dogmatism."

Olcott's comprehensive description included an overview of Bennett and his wife's Shaker background and the "sham case . . . manufactured against him by an unscrupulous detective [Anthony Comstock] of a Christian Society." He depicted Bennett's forthcoming book, *A Truth Seeker around the World*, as an "interesting work." It was evident from his diary that Olcott admired Bennett and his cause.[16]

H. P. Blavatsky also had a high regard for Bennett. "Mr. Bennett's path to authorship and leadership in the Western Freethought movement did not run through the drowsy recitation-rooms of the college, nor over the soft carpets of aristocratic drawing rooms," she wrote in the *Theosophist*. "When his thoughts upon religion filled his head to overflowing, he dropped merchandising and evolved into editorship with a cool self-confidence that is thoroughly characteristic of the American disposition, and scarcely ever looked for in any other race."[17]

THEOLOGICAL CHARLATANISM

Bennett arrived in Bombay at a time when Theosophy was flourishing but also coming under increased scrutiny and criticism. In an ongoing crusade, Christian missionaries were assailing Theosophy and "heathen Buddhists." One of the most vociferous critics was Reverend Joseph Cook, the Comstock supporter who attended Bennett's trial and sat in the courtroom reading *An Open Letter to Jesus Christ* in plain view of the jury. Cook called Theosophy a "combination of mist and moonshine" and its founders "charlatans." Bennett and Olcott had a mutual enemy in Cook, whom Olcott described as "a burly man who seemed to believe in the Trinity—with himself as the Third Person." In a strange coincidence, the detested third person arrived in Bombay almost simultaneously with Bennett. The event caused additional controversy for Bennett, Theosophy, and a personal dilemma for Olcott.[18]

Flavius Josephus Cook gained notoriety in the 1870s as a minister, author, and lecturer who aggressively defended his Congregational faith. In 1882 Cook was at the pinnacle of his fame and was Boston's most popular preacher, whose Monday lectures at the city's Tremont Temple were attended by thousands of enthusiastic followers. While the *Boston Globe* praised his "abstruse knowledge and great command of language," Cook had many critics. In the March 1881 issue of the *North American Review*, John Fiske, a prominent historian and scientific writer, challenged Cook's attempts to reconcile science and religion as theological charlatanism. The *Dictionary of American Biography* found "no reason to doubt Cook's sincerity, but his learning was not accurate or profound, and he was often unfair to those whose views he opposed. Even his friends also acknowledged that his belief in his own learning and ability was exaggerated."[19]

Joseph Cook arrived in Bombay only a few days earlier than Bennett and promptly delivered a speech denouncing Theosophy and its leaders as adventurers. The "Christ-like Joseph," Olcott reported, "committed the blind folly" in front of a large Hindu and Parsee audience "who loved and knew us after two whole years of intercourse." Cook's first speech in the Bombay Town Hall was probably "to help the Lord in setting the missionary cause all right again in this heathen land," Bennett quipped.[20]

On January 10, the day Bennett arrived, Cook gave yet another lecture. Olcott and Bennett attended the lecture, together with a large audience of European missionaries and their followers, as well as "intelligent" natives who, Bennett reported, "take but little stock in Christian dogmas." He found Cook's arguments weak, but as usual, the pompous preacher "endeavored to induce the natives of India to take his noisy mouthings for the truth."[21]

The *Bombay Gazette* proposed a debate between Cook and Olcott. Two days later, during his speech at the Theosophical Society's anniversary meeting, Olcott mentioned the debate proposal to the audience but told his listeners he disapproved of controversies and had no time for such a debate. "But perhaps your friend," Olcott told the audience, "also a countryman of Mr. Cook and myself—Mr. D. M. Bennett, editor and proprietor of

The Truth Seeker, one of the greatest organs of the Western Freethought movement, who fortunately is here present. And, like Mr. Cook, is on a voyage around the world, may have a few words to say upon the subject."[22]

The editor, however, was reluctant to make a speech. He informed Olcott of his limited ability but finally consented and gave an account of his arrests, trial, and imprisonment. Bennett mentioned the private letters that he called indiscreet but not criminal and complained about the circulars bearing his name that had been distributed by Christians at the entrance of the Theosophical Society's hall that evening. He called the circulars proof that the Theosophists were doing good work and stirring up animosity "in the ranks of bigotry and intolerance." Bennett told them that he knew about that sort of opposition. "I know something of Christian love and charity—*I have had an opportunity of tasting it.*"[23]

Bennett spoke briefly, reviewing Cook's previous lecture, only because someone requested that he reply. He said that he thought it hardly seemed necessary because he did not think there was very much in Cook's lectures. The editor found Cook's hypothesis that nature is controlled by some imaginary weaver dishonest and deprives "[nature] of the credit which is justly due to her." He concluded his speech, arguing against the reverend's assertion that the doctrine of immortality originated with Christianity. Bennett told them that Christianity had nothing new to offer them and nothing superior to what they had hundreds of years before Christianity was known in the world. He added, "Probably better morals have never been taught than were in the past ages uttered by the sages and philosophers of your country. And there seems to be little use in throwing them away and taking in their place about the same doctrines revamped over, or in adopting a later system."[24]

After Bennett's speech, Olcott came forward, telling the audience that "doubtless through modesty" the editor had "suppressed the important facts." He informed them of the Chickering Hall reception and the banquet accorded Bennett given by British freethinkers "with Mr. Bradlaugh in the chair." Olcott's additional remarks were met with applause and cheers.[25]

Also making speeches that evening were Damodar Mavalankar and Kavasji M. Shroff, the two men who accompanied Olcott when he met Bennett at the steamship. Damodar was the society's recording secretary and a young intense Brahmin who discarded his wealth, abandoned his caste, left his wife and home, and devoted his life to the Theosophical Society. As an ascetic and seeker of occult knowledge, Damodar, according to Theosophical legend, developed occult powers and in 1883 began acting as an astral courier receiving messages from the masters. Shroff was a Parsee fellow and secretary of the Bombay branch of the National Indian Association and of the Bombay Society for the Prevention of Cruelty to Animals. (Seven years earlier, he had given a well-received speech before the New York Liberal Club on the Parsees.) During his speech that evening, Shroff welcomed Cook to India and said that he appreciated and admired "his high scholarship, his great oratorical power, his matchless eloquence." But, he told the audience, "we cannot accept his Christian teachings," and "the progress of science has already given a death-blow to Christianity in Europe. . . . Christianity is not the religion for India."[26]

When Cook heard about the speeches made during the society's anniversary meeting, he and his fellow missionaries became infuriated. Commotion erupted after Cook dictated a malicious article about Bennett in the *Times of India*. Cook alluded to the private letters and the "Apotheosis of Dirt" article printed in *Scribner's Monthly* that Bennett said were "replete with such malicious falsehoods as [Cook] so well knows how to use." He and Olcott immediately drafted letters challenging Cook to a debate to be held January 20, 1882. Bennett's letter dated January 18, 1882, from Crow's Nest Bungalow, reads:

> Sir: You have defamed my character, impugned my motives, and cast a slur upon the whole Freethought party who take the liberty of thinking for themselves. That the Indian public may know whether your several statements are true or false, I shall make on Friday evening, at 5:30, at the Framji Cowasji Institute, a public statement. On that occasion I invite you to meet me

face to face and answer the statements I shall make. Your failure to do so would be construed into an inability to substantiate the reckless allegations flung out under the protection of a crowd of sympathizers.

Should you plead other engagements, I may say that to meet your calumnies I have myself put off my engagement. Like yourself, I am on a voyage around the world, and have no time to waste.

For the whole truth, yours, etc.,   D. M. Bennett[27]

Joseph Cook returned Bennett's note unopened and did not attend the debate. The meeting went ahead as planned in order to refute the Cook slanders against Bennett and the Theosophical Society. Hundreds had to be turned away before the meeting started in the Framji Cowasji Hall that was packed and overflowing to hear the editor and Olcott speak. Prior to their speeches a reply from Cook was received and read to the audience:

Bombay, Jan. 20, 1882

Col. Olcott, of The Theosophical Society, Bombay, Sir: I am not open to challenges of which the evident object is to advertise infidelity. You ask me to sit on your platform with a man whose career has been described in an unanswerable article in *Scribner's Monthly* as "The Apotheosis of Dirt." No honorable man can keep company of this kind. For using this man as a weapon with which to attack Christianity the enlightened public sentiment of India will hold the Theosophical Society to a stern account. Men are measured by their Heroes. Several days before I received your communication I was definitely engaged to be in Poonah on the night proposed for your meeting in Bombay.   Yours, etc., Joseph Cook[28]

Bennett began his speech informing the audience of the history of Cook's attacks on freethinkers because they do not believe in the "system of religion" that he "advocates and attempts to build up." Cook, he told the listeners, had been his enemy for several years and "has poured upon us all the vile epithets which he was able to command." As to his unfair trial in New York and Cook's presence in the courtroom, "I may say I owe, in part, at least, my conviction to the influence of Joseph Cook."[29]

Bennett demonstrated Cook's hypocrisy by giving an overview of the "crimes of adultery and seduction" by Christian clergymen. *Why* wasn't Cook shocked at the crimes and immorality of the scandalous Henry Ward Beecher case? "He has never denounced Mr. Beecher in his lectures, and doubtless still recognizes him as a brother in Christ." Bennett responded to Cook's repeated assertion that he was a criminal by naming Socrates, Galileo, and Jesus Christ. "Does Mr. Cook, or any of his Christian friends," he argued, "think any the less of Jesus because he was arrested, tried, and convicted, and executed for expressing his religious sentiments?" He gave a litany of freethinkers, including Thomas Paine, who were imprisoned but committed no crime. "The catalogue of men who have been unjustly arrested, tried, convicted, imprisoned, or executed for exercising the right of thinking and expressing their thoughts is a very long one, and it embraces many of the best men who have lived."[30]

As to Cook's unjust remarks calling the editor a poisoner of youth and promoter of vice printed in the *Times of India*, Bennett denied ever sending a book or any immoral circulars to any Indian youth. "I have had no communication with the youth of Bombay, either to poison them or to give them an antidote for poison." As to Reverend Cook's statements regarding the decline of freethought: "I know this to be false, and I have good opportunities for knowing. Ten years ago there was but one Freethought journal published in the United States; now there are six."[31]

Reverend Cook's attempts to harmonize Christianity and science were ridiculed by Bennett who found the theories "absurd and untruthful . . . to pretend that science has any connection with either the Bible or Christianity." The editor said that not Moses, Jesus, or any writer of the Bible ever articulated a "single scientific truth or thought." They didn't even know the earth was round, "a simple fact which now every schoolboy understands."[32]

Bennett concluded his lengthy speech reviewing Christianity, using his encyclopedic knowledge of the Bible, and showing that it is nothing new or original, but only "borrowed from older systems." As to the story of Jesus in the New Testament, he found it entirely unhistorical and probably not written until the year 181 CE, by "designing and dishonest men, capable of using deception and fraud." Furthermore, Christianity had never been a loving and peaceful religion but was the "bloodiest religion in the world," fostering ignorance, retarding science, favoring slavery, and opposing women's rights. A two-thousand-year-old "perfect system" promoted by "the worst tyrants the world has known." Bennett's remarks drew abounding applause. He reported that Olcott spoke for an hour and a half, defending American spiritualists and fully vindicating the Theosophical Society, showing Cook "to be simply an untruthful and malignant slanderer."[33]

Following the meeting, Olcott went to Poonah to give a speech and was maligned again by Cook, who was also there giving lectures. Olcott challenged Cook to debate him on the same platform, but the reverend refused and went on to insult his audience by imploring them to join him in the Lord's Prayer. After they declined, the pontificating preacher made an attempt to induce the audience to repeat the prayer. Frustrated, Cook blurted out an insulting quip about "casting pearls before swine." He sarcastically advised the Indians to pray to their false gods. In assessing Bennett's battle with Cook in India, George Macdonald asserted, "Cook, coming well advertised to Bombay, charged upon the heathen like a warhorse. Bennett had no advance agent, but he got the decision." An Indian writer from the *Native Public Voice* agreed, writing,

> The native public of Bombay take this opportunity to thank Mr. Joseph Cook for the trouble he has taken to come to Bombay and preach Christianity to the English-speaking native and European residents of this great city. But at the same time they think it proper to inform the reverend gentleman that he should not leave them with the idea that his eloquent but flimsy unargumentative, and merely rhetorical lectures have produced any impression whatever on their minds with respect

to the truth of Christianity. Many flocked to his lectures merely to witness the magnificent tamasha [show]. Hence the large number of hearers he succeeded in obtaining. Let him and his colleagues rest assured that Christianity will never succeed in India. Nothing more need to be said.[34]

Joseph Cook's American bluster and inflammatory remarks alienated many, and his lecture tour of India was not as successful as his Christian benefactors had hoped. "His contemptible and malicious course has failed to have the effect he wished," Bennett wrote, "and his slanders have injured himself more than anybody else." The attempts by Cook and his fellow Christians to co-opt science to bolster their religion infuriated freethinkers. It was, after all, science that liberals believed would elevate mankind. And science had always been an arrow in their quiver against superstition.[35]

THE INVISIBLE BROTHERS

Bennett remained in Bombay considerably longer than he had planned, mostly because of the time and energy that he had to devote to publicly refuting Cook's attacks. His two-week stay at the Crow's Nest was during an oppressive heat wave and outbreak of cholera. Nevertheless, he enjoyed the company of his hosts and learning about Theosophy. He met A. P. Sinnett, the British author and distinguished Theosophist whom he found "of decided ability. . . . I am quite ready to accord him both intellect and honesty."[36]

Alfred P. Sinnett was an accomplished journalist and editor of the *Pioneer*, the most influential newspaper in India. His books *The Occult World* (published that year) and *Esoteric Buddhism* were instrumental in introducing Theosophy to the general public around the world. He would later become the head of the Theosophical Society in England. Olcott observed that Bennett read Sinnett's *The Occult World* with "avidity: in fact, he made very extensive quotations from it in his journal and in his new book." According to Theosophical lore, Sinnett, like Olcott and Blavatsky, received "direct instruction in the ancient wisdom by means of the letters from the Masters." Some of these letters provide a unique and, in some respects, uncomplimentary view of "Mr. Bennett of America."[37]

In a letter to his readers back home, Bennett explained his fascination with occultism and reprinted extracts from Sinnett's *The Occult World*. "Although hidden and mysterious," he wrote, "I like it for the reason that it does not claim to be miraculous or supernatural." He denied that he became a disciple but admitted that he was a "believer in the omnipotence of nature's forces," and entertained "not the slightest doubt that there are yet many of nature's laws to be learned, which by the masses are yet but little understood." Rather than mislead readers about the "intricate philosophy," he chose to quote extensively from Sinnett's newly published work.[38]

Admittedly eager to see some of the paranormal phenomena he had heard so much about, he was disappointed that he did not see any of the mysterious adepts or astral brothers, as they were sometimes known. "The nearest to a marvel I have had brought to my vision," he confessed, "is the writing in or upon letters received by mail by Col. Olcott." Olcott told him that some of the letters he received by mail were on occasion mysteriously marked by one of the invisible brothers who lived two thousand miles away in the Himalaya Mountains. The letters were received unopened and certain parts underlined, often in red ink, and comments and suggestions about the content and the writer. Blavatsky's prolific master, Koot Hoomi, signed most of them.[39]

The editor provided a detailed account for his readers of an occasion when, while he was sitting with Olcott, some letters arrived from the post office. Olcott handed the letters to him for his inspection and they seemed "perfectly intact, and presented not the slightest appearance of having been opened." But after Olcott opened them with his penknife in the usual way, he saw the "mysterious words in red ink" and the lengthy comments and "ever attendant mystic signature." The letters came from different parts of India and Ceylon and, while skeptical, Bennett did not think that it was possible that the same man could have written all the red marks. To him, the "chances for collusion seemed extremely remote" and while it could be said that Olcott had manipulated the letters, he knew "the gentleman too well to believe him capable of such subterfuge. I believe him a strictly honest man. He possibly may be deceived himself, but he is not a deceiver." And while the editor knew it would be "very hard for a stolid Materialist to accept," he thought it no harder than it would have been a century earlier to accept some of the scientific and technological wonders of the late nineteenth century. "I do not condemn this occult power as a fraud or an impossibility," he declared. "Because we of the Western world know nothing about it is not a sure proof that it has no existence."[40]

In Bombay he heard credible accounts by numerous persons whom he regarded as "strictly truthful" about strange phenomena, including bells, musical instruments, and brothers appearing in their astral bodies. He was told that Olcott and Blavatsky were "entirely in rapport and recognition with these 'Astral brothers.'" Olcott assured him that while he was still in New York, he saw one of the masters in his astral body, and after conversing with him was given an Indian shawl and handkerchief that he showed to the editor. He was also shown the gold ring, reportedly produced by Madame Blavatsky's occult power with the "aid of the Brothers." While he found Olcott an honest fellow seeker of truth, his assessment of Blavatsky was somewhat less enthusiastic.[41]

Bennett tried to explain Blavatsky's ability to communicate with the brothers, who seemingly regarded her as a special protégé. Unlike American spiritualistic mediums, she claimed that paranormal phenomena were not produced by the dead but by living persons aided by elementals, or elementary spirits. As nearly as he could understand, she did not believe in personal immortality—but that an individual retains her identity after death. Her "distinction between personality and individuality," he confessed, "is almost too obscure for my obtuse brain." He admitted that some of her amazing statements and claims staggered him and put his "credulity to the utmost stretch." But he admittedly learned to adjust his prejudices and thought that he would reserve his verdict and wait for more facts.[42]

The editor's skepticism concerning some of Olcott and Blavatsky's miraculous claims did not prevent him from his desire to join the Theosophical Society. He approved of their work and "to show this sympathy and a desire to cooperate with them," he "proposed to become a member of the society." After thoroughly discussing Theosophy with them, he applied for membership. But the Cook controversy and hostile attack by the press caused Olcott to hesitate in admitting his friend into the society. Bennett also thought that "it might not be advisable" for the burgeoning society to accept him as a member because of the negative publicity instigated by the "various slurs" and "foul slanders" uttered by Cook before the Bombay public and printed in the press. He expressed his concern to Olcott, who had his own reservations chronicled in his *Old Diary Leaves*.[43]

Olcott feared the publicity generated by Cook that was played out in the influential Indian press. They attacked and reviled Bennett so intensely that he confessed, "I hesitated to take him into membership, for fear that it might plunge us into another public wrangle, and thus interfere with our aim of peacefully settling down to our proper business of Theosophical study and propaganda." His reluctance, he admitted, "was an instinct of worldly prudence, certainly not chivalric altruism." Olcott discussed the issue with Madame Blavatsky who did not seem as concerned about Bennett's reputation. She wrote,

> We, who know something of his private life, and believe in the impartial judgment of some of our best friends in America, who knew him for years, maintain that he was made a martyr to, and has suffered for, that cause of freedom for which every right-minded man in America will stand up and will die for, if necessary . . . we proclaim Mr. Bennett a kind, truthful, quiet, right-minded man, imperfect and liable to err, as every other mortal, but, at the same time scrupulously honest.[44]

After Olcott and Blavatsky considered Bennett's admission, "she was overshadowed by a Master who told me my duty and reproached me for my faulty judgment." Olcott was reminded of his own imperfection and advised not to judge his "fellow-man." He said, "I knew that the applicant had been made the scapegoat of the whole anti-Christian party [Liberals], and richly deserved all the sympathy and encouragement we could give him. I was sarcastically told to look through the whole list of our members and point out a single one without faults. That was enough; I returned to Mr. Bennett, gave him the application blank to sign, and HPB and I became his sponsors."[45]

Alfred Sinnett also had reservations about admitting the editor to their ranks. He, too, was mildly chastened by the masters of wisdom. Sinnett received a letter that month in Allahabad from the "Disinherited" informing him of the editor's arrival. "If you can see your way towards giving him [Bennett] a correct idea of the actual present and potential future state of Asiatic but more particularly of Indian thought, it will be gratifying to my Master." Another letter to Sinnett, signed "Yours, M," enlightened him of the editor's value to Theosophy in no uncertain terms:

> Were he [Bennett] to die this minute—and I'll use a Christian phraseology to make you comprehend me the better—few hotter tears would drop from the eye of the recording Angel of Death over other such ill-used men, as the tear Bennett would receive for his share. Few men have suffered—as he has; and as few have a more kind, unselfish and truthful heart.[46]

M admonished Sinnett for seeing only Bennett's "unwashed hands, uncleaned nails and coarse language." And while Bennett was "not exactly an angel" he was morally superior to some "gentlemanly" members. "B—is an honest man and of sincere heart, besides being one of tremendous moral courage and a martyr to boot," M declared.[47]

D. M. Bennett was formally admitted to the Theosophical Society on January 14, 1882. He later described the matter of his admission:

It seems a conference was held upon the subject between Col. Olcott, Madam Blavatsky, and a few other members of the society who were present, and, as is the custom, Madam Blavatsky referred the matter to the Brothers for their advice. It seems that the desirability of every candidate for admission is referred to the Brothers, they approving of some and rejecting others. My case seems to have been laid before them, and they decided favorably upon it. The response was that I am an honest, industrious man, and well fitted to become a member of the Theosophical Society. I hope their opinion is well founded. At all events, I became a member.[48]

In the March 1883 issue of the *Theosophist*, Olcott corrected something that Bennett had written about his admission to the Theosophical Society. Olcott denied the editor's assertion that "every candidate for admission is referred to the Brothers." But, Olcott admitted, because of the controversy surrounding the editor of the *Truth Seeker*, "advice was indeed asked as to Mr. Bennett's admission." Decades later in 1907, Annie Besant (Blavatsky's successor), in a speech to the American Theosophical Society convention, stated that Bennett *was* "sponsored for admission" by Madame Blavatsky and her master, Koot Hoomi.[49]

MORE LIGHT

D. M. Bennett joined the Theosophical Society while the organization was in its halcyon days and a few years before it came under intense scrutiny. The society's motto: "There is no religion higher than truth" undoubtedly appealed to Bennett. Nevertheless, the truth about the early years of the society is shrouded in a labyrinth of secrets and bizarre theories that border on the surreal. Trying to determine the motives of its founders or the identity of Blavatsky's masters is as difficult to ascertain today—over a century later—as it was in 1882. Some believe that there was a hidden agenda behind the Theosophical Society's noble goals.[50]

What, if any, role Albert Rawson played in Bennett's Theosophical odyssey is one of the most intriguing remaining questions. Rawson, who traveled with Bennett to Europe only a year earlier in 1880 and illustrated *A Truth Seeker around the World*, was deeply involved with Theosophy and Madame Blavatsky. Rawson reportedly first encountered Blavatsky in Cairo in 1851, and it has been suggested that they had an intimate relationship. His contribution to Blavatsky's *Isis Unveiled* (written at her request) is a detailed account of his adoption as a brother while visiting the Adwan Bedouins of Moab and also his initiation by the Druze in Lebanon.[51]

In 1878 Rawson came to Madame Blavatsky's defense after she was criticized in a London periodical. It is obvious from his long, detailed letter to the editor of the *Spiritualist* that he admired Blavatsky. Later that year at the Watkins Glen Freethinkers' Convention (where he accompanied Bennett), Rawson spoke publicly about Blavatsky and India. In *Isis*, Blavatsky introduces Rawson as a "learned traveller and artist" who traveled to Mecca, visited Palestine four times, and spent many years in the East. Rawson "has a priceless store of facts about the beginning of the Christian Church," she writes, "which none but one who had had free access to repositories closed against the ordinary traveller could have collected."[52]

In addition to his public roles as the secretary of the National Liberal League and president of the National Defense Association, Albert Rawson was intensely involved in secret societies. In 1881 Rawson wrote in the *Truth Seeker* that he opposed Anthony Comstock's "application for membership in the order of Freemasons for good and sufficient reasons." There is no evidence that Bennett was ever a member of any secret society. As recently as February 1881, after traveling with Rawson to Europe, the editor commented in the *Truth Seeker* on a newly published book, *Knight Templarism Illustrated*. "Not being a Knight Templar, a Mason, or a member of any secret order," he wrote, "we are not able to say whether the book tells the truth or not, but we presume it is mainly correct."[53]

In 1882, the year Bennett traveled to India, Rawson went to Rochester, New York, at the request of Abner Doubleday to organize the first branch of the Theosophical Society outside of New York City. Bennett published material by pioneer Theosophists prior to joining the society. In 1877, the same year *Isis* was published, the editor reprinted Rawson's *Evolution of Israel's God.* He also published Charles Sotheran's *Alessandro di Cagliostro: Imposter or Martyr?* Cagliostro was an eighteenth-century occultist who was the final victim of the Inquisition. He became a Masonic martyr and was venerated by members of secret societies. Albert Rawson and Charles Sotheran belonged to Societal Rosicruciana and the Masonic Rite of Memphis—both secret societies. In Blavatsky's *Isis Unveiled*, Sotheran writes about Masonry and claims that there is a connection between America's founding fathers and the Illuminati. Also a friend of Blavatsky, Sotheran reportedly originated the word *Theosophy*.[54]

There is considerable evidence that the Theosophical Society founded by these high-ranking Freemasons was formed with a mission not only to revive Western occultism but also to oppose Christianity and revenge Cagliostro's church-sponsored persecution. Madame Blavatsky never hid her dislike of Christianity and lauded the "wonderful increase of the party of Freethought, the rapid growth of Infidel Societies and Infidel Literature." When Blavatsky was criticized for selling freethought literature in the *Theosophist,* she defended the right to offer the "outspoken fearless books of Paine, Voltaire, Ingersoll, Bradlaugh and Bennett." Blavatsky wrote, "It is not that Christian dogmatism is more hateful to us than any other form of obstructiveness, but because it is enjoying a wider power to prevent man's moral development and crush truth. . . . Christianity is the official creed of the masculine social energy of the generation. If it could, it would be spread at the sword's point and by the persuasiveness of tyranny and torture as in the good old days."[55]

One of the most puzzling remaining questions is who, if anybody, was responsible for introducing D. M. Bennett to Theosophy. Prior to Bennett's arrival in Bombay, Alfred Sinnett received a mystifying letter allegedly written by one of Blavatsky's masters:

I am also to tell you that in a certain Mr. Bennett of America who will shortly arrive at Bombay, you may recognise one who, in spite of his national provincialism, that you so detest, and his infidelistic bias, is one of our agents (unknown to himself) to carry out the scheme for the enfranchisement of Western thoughts from superstitious *creeds*.

Mahatma letter to A. P. Sinnett
(from the "Disinherited," January 1882)[56]

The Mahatma letter to A. P. Sinnett asserts that Bennett was unknowingly an "agent . . . to carry out the scheme for the enfranchisement of Western thoughts from superstitious creeds." Why he came to Bombay to meet the founders of Theosophy is only the first in a series of mysteries surrounding his visit to India. The letter raises numerous intriguing questions and myriad possibilities. The obvious questions are, Who were the Mahatmas? Who was the "Disinherited"? How did the "Disinherited" learn of Bennett's pending arrival in Bombay? Who told him or her? Was Bennett in fact one of their "agents" and if he was, why was he not told? No matter what the truth of the matter is, it seems as though someone made an attempt to use Bennett and/or tried to deceive Sinnett. Or at the least, the Mahatmas, whoever they were, or were not—were definitely mysterious and possibly devious.[57]

Bennett knew that his decision to join the society would elicit criticism among his skeptical Materialist friends. "I strongly incline to the opinion," he thought, "that there are forms of matter and forces of which they [Materialists] know very little, and that we all have much yet to learn. Nature is so immense, so extensive, so grand, that half her truths and glories are yet unlearned." Regarding the occult phenomena allegedly produced by the Theosophical Society's mysterious brothers, he wrote, "I have long thought it possible for science yet to be able to explain how these phenomena are produced. Occultism may be that science and it may be not. *I shall wait for more light.*"[58]

NOTES

"in his philosophy.": TSAW.

1. TSAW.
2. Ibid.
3. Ibid.
4. "police interrogation technique.": Howard Murphet, *Hammer on the Mountain: Life of Henry Steel Olcott.* Theosophical Publishing House, Wheaton, Ill., 1972.

Colonel Olcott's findings were not used at Suratt's trial. Murphet asserts that if they had been, Mrs. Suratt would not have been convicted and hanged.

5. Ibid.
6. Stephen Prothero, *The White Buddhist: The Asian Odyssey of Henry Steel Olcott,* Indiana University Press.
7. Ibid.
8. Helena Petrovna Blavatsky, *Isis Unveiled,* 2 vols., Reprint Wheaton, Ill.: Theosophical Publishing House, 1971, 1994.
9. Prothero.
10. TSAW.
11. Ibid.
12. Murphet.
13. TSAW.
14. Murphet. TSAW.
15. "white Buddhist.": Murphet p. 138. "and original articles.": TSAW.
16. "interesting work.": Henry Steel Olcott, *Old Diary Leaves* 2:328–30, Second Series, 1878–83. London: Theosophical Publishing Society, 1900.
17. The *Theosophist,* July 1882.
18. "mist and moonshine.": The *Boston Globe,* June 25, 1901. "the third person.": Olcott.
19. "ability was exaggerated.": DAB.
20. TSAW.
21. Ibid.
22. Ibid.
23. Ibid.
24. Ibid.

25. Ibid.

26. Ibid.

27. Ibid.

28. Ibid.

29. Ibid.

30. Ibid.

31. Ibid.

32. Ibid.

33. Ibid.

34. "false Gods.": Ibid. "got the decision.": GM "to be said.": TSAW.

35. TSAW.

36. Ibid.

37. "his new book.": Olcott. "Bennett of America.": The Mahatma Letters.

38. TSAW.

39. Ibid.

40. Ibid.

41. Ibid.

42. Ibid.

43. Ibid.

44. H. P. Blavatsky, *Collected Writings* 4:79–80.

45. Olcott.

46. The Mahatma Letters.

47. Ibid.

48. "became a member.": TSAW and the Theosophical Society Archives, Adyar, India.

49. "Mr. Bennett's admission.": The *Theosophist* March 1883. "sponsored for admission.": Gertrude Marvin Williams, *The Passionate Pilgrim: A Life of Annie Besant.* N.Y. 1931 Coward-McCann.

50. TS.

51. Blavatsky, *Isis Unveiled.*

52. Ibid.

53. "and sufficient reasons.": TS March 5, 1881. "is mainly correct.": TS Feb. 12, 1881.

54. Murphet.

55. Blavatsky: *Collected Writings.*

56. "from superstitious creeds.": The Mahatma Letters to A. P. Sinnett from the Mahatmas M. and K. H. in Chronological Sequence. Ed. Vincente Hao Chin Jr. Quezon City, Manila, Philippines: Theosophical

Publishing House, 1993. Letter # xxxvii Received at Allahabad, Jan. 1882 pp. 249–50, Rider & co., Paternoster House, Paternoster Row, London, E.C. 4., 1926.

57. Ibid.

In his book *The Masters Revealed*, K. Paul Johnson presents an intriguing theory as to the identity of H. P. Blavatsky's "Masters." Johnson asserts that Blavatsky's "adept sponsors were a succession of human mentors rather than a cosmic hierarchy of supermen." According to Johnson's hypothesis, two of Blavatsky's "Masters" were Charles Sotheran and Albert Rawson. Johnson presents the mysterious "Mahatma" letter that announced Bennett's impending arrival as evidence that the freethought movement was "infiltrated." His prime suspects include Sotheran and Rawson. *The Masters Revealed: Madame Blavatsky and the Myth of the Great White Lodge*. K. Paul Johnson, Albany: SUNY Press, 1994.

58. *"for more light."*: TSAW.

The Theosophical movement in Europe was damaged after an exposé was published in the *London Times* on September 20, 1884. The sensational article attacked Blavatsky and quoted letters written by her admitting that she had faked her "supernormal phenomena." The story was carried around the world. The following year an investigator from the Society for Psychical Research (SPR) traveled to India to investigate the "Mahatma" letters supposedly written by the God-like Master in Tibet. The SPR was formed in London in 1882, and their mission was to "scientifically" investigate paranormal phenomena. The investigator called Madame Blavatsky an imposter and Colonel Olcott a dupe. And while the bad publicity caused many devotees to abandon Theosophy, it survived. The SPR findings became known as the Hodgson Report, a 200-page denouncement that damaged Blavatsky's credibility and branded her "one of the most accomplished, ingenious, and interesting imposters in history. *H. P. Blavatsky and the SPR: An Examination of the Hodgson Report of 1885*, Vernon Harrison, Theosophical University Press, Pasadena, Calif., 1997. Another blow to Blavatsky came in January 1892, when Albert Rawson revealed the mystery surrounding her early years in *Frank Leslie's Popular Monthly* titled "Madame Blavatsky— A Theosophical Occult Apology." In the article, written shortly after her death, Rawson recounts his four-decade friendship with the occultist and reveals her fondness for hashish and secret societies. Although Rawson was an early member of the Theosophical Society, he expresses contempt for the alleged Mahatma letters and implies that her Masters Koot Hoomi and M were inventions.

Frank Leslie's Popular Monthly, January 1892.

16

THE FREETHOUGHT
MISSIONARY

*Mr. Bennett has been preaching the gospel of truth, as he sees it, to
the Indians. . . . He has had a grand time, and his visit will be long
remembered by both them and him.*

—Truth Seeker

Bennett departed Bombay on January 26, 1882, and began
his three-thousand-mile journey by rail across the Indian
continent. On January 29 (Thomas Paine's birthday) he visited
the old city of Ambar six miles north of Jeypore. A few days later
he saw the Taj Mahal, which he judged the most beautiful
building that he had ever seen but unfortunately built by forced
labor. And though the structure was perfect "it is the fruit of toil,
of deprivation, and sorrow."[1]

On a clear afternoon near the Tibetan border, Bennett spotted
the majestic Himalayas he had read about since childhood but
never expected to see. He described them as "grand beyond

description." The editor was traveling to Darjeeling, the village that was, according to Theosophical lore, the home of Madame Blavatsky's master, Koot Hoomi. He spent a day sightseeing in the scenic village and continued on to Calcutta and Madras where he made an unusual purchase. While admittedly not especially fond of parrots, he decided to buy four of the noisy birds because they appeared "so lively and cunning." Bennett thought that perhaps they could do all the talking in the *Truth Seeker* office.[2]

The editor characterized England's governing power over India as an anomaly. He was mystified how thirty thousand to sixty thousand Englishmen from a small country so far away could control 250 million intelligent people. It could only be explained by the fact that the English took advantage of the dis-unity among the Indian tribes. The English were bulldogs, he thought, and the Hindus were sheep. And while these overlords were oppressive, Bennett believed India was better off than if an emperor, rajahs, and maharajahs ruled the country. Even with their faults, the English had embraced education and promoted intelligence, he opined. But he also lamented the vices imported by the Europeans. And in spite of all the Christianity preached, there was an increase in intemperance, prostitution, and dishonesty. "This tells plainly how much the missionary effort is doing for India." As to the evil of the caste system, he favored abolition and reminded readers of England's and "happy" America's cruel caste system. Bennett asked, "Is not the caste of wealth more cruel, perhaps, than all other kinds of caste, rapidly growing up there to be a heartless, a soulless tyrant? Yes, even America has caste as really and as cruelly as India."[3]

Bennett found India a great country in many ways. He admired the Indian's philosophy, metaphysics, language, literature, "and in founding great systems of religion that have lived for many thousands of years." Nevertheless, Bennett concluded that the country was not as happy as he would have liked and feared that "the day is not close at hand in which your children will be as independent, as prosperous, and as happy as they and I desire."[4]

AN ORIENTAL SOJOURN

After leaving Madras, Bennett arrived in Galle, Ceylon, on February 18, 1882. He found Ceylon the most beautiful country he had ever seen and coming about as close to the garden of paradise as one could get. While still standing on the jetty, Bennett was greeted by friends who extended hospitalities. Anxious to travel to Colombo (where his mail awaited him), he had to decline an offer to stay at the home of one of the country's wealthiest and most respected natives. The editor was pleasantly surprised to find friends at the stations providing carriages, paying his hotel and railway bills, and even his washing bills before he had the chance to take care of them himself. And although he knew the *Truth Seeker* was available in Colombo, he never dreamed he was so popular on the other side of the globe. Bennett suspected that Henry Steel Olcott had written on his behalf, advising the time of his arrival and asking them to meet him. "I think," he said, "I have Col. H. S. Olcott to thank for much of this."[5]

On the stage ride to Colombo, Bennett enjoyed the invigorating sea air and had his first taste of coconut juice. In Colombo he found himself famous. He was excited to learn the popularity of the *Truth Seeker* and that his *Open Letter to Jesus Christ* had been translated into Sinhalese. He proudly reported the tract was "largely circulated among the natives to help the missionaries, or rather help against them." While in Colombo, he stayed at the Theosophical Society's hall and found that the "most comfortable quarters were furnished, with a cook to attend to getting up my meals, and a room to write in, etc." He was impressed with the local Sinhalese Theosophists who spoke English and were Buddhist believers in supernaturalism and miracles. The editor was complimented when he learned their paper published in Sinhalese contained a considerable portion of extracts from the *Truth Seeker*. "That paper must have a strong light," he thought, "which can reach to the opposite side of the globe and shine so brightly."[6]

In Colombo Bennett investigated Buddhism and was graciously welcomed by a dozen priests. After discussing the religion with one of the priests, he agreed on several points but also found fault with the ubiquitous display of images of Buddha in every medium imaginable and expressed his opinion that he did not think Buddha, who they believed was the greatest teacher ever, would approve of such idolatry. "I said the teachings of Buddha are so good that they require no image to enable you to remember them, and if you keep the import of those teachings in your hearts, or in your minds, you will not require any images."[7]

While in Ceylon, Bennett was persuaded to travel to different cities and give lectures. He tried to explain that he was not a professional lecturer and that he never addressed an audience until he was over fifty-five years old. But it was all in vain—his new friends refused to take no for an answer. Because they had been very kind, and he did not want to seem ungrateful, he agreed to speak. His speeches had to be translated into Sinhalese and lasted over two hours. Written expressly for the people of Ceylon, his talks were divided into three segments: the origin of Christianity, the truthfulness of Christianity, and Christianity compared with Buddhism. The editor pointed out the similarities and mutual goals of Buddhists and freethinkers. "Buddha was a philosopher and to a great extent a scientist" compared to Jesus, who stressed prayer and believed in miracles and superstition. He concluded his address by urging his listeners not to give up their religion for Christianity. Furthermore, Bennett advised them to cooperate with Olcott and the Theosophical Society "whose march is in the right direction." He said, "I am sure your lives will be spent in doing good, and that a rich reward will crown your efforts."[8]

On another occasion, Bennett addressed an audience on the subject of education and women's rights. He cited women's accomplishments throughout the ages and informed them of the scholarship of Annie Besant and countless American female authors, editors, physicians, and lawyers. The subject matter of his speech was chosen after he noticed the women in Ceylon households that he visited were kept in the background. He expressed the opinion that men should inaugurate a change. His new friends welcomed his reform suggestions. Bennett was asked to address his proposals to an audience of both men and women:

> I endeavored to show them that the highest state of civilization and the happiest condition of society depended upon male and female being equal, and going forward hand in hand in every good work. . . . The more the mind is improved, whether male or female, the more lovable and the more estimable they become. I said it is all a mistake that men should be learned and women ignorant. Women have brains as well as men, and they should be cultivated and improved as carefully. . . . The more intellectual women become the better companions they are, the better wives and mothers they make. The more intellectual the mother, the more intellectual the children will be.[9]

The editor's feminist remarks did not fall on deaf ears, and after his lecture a few women came over to him, including the wife of the president of the society. He regretted that the woman could not speak English because he desired to impress upon her the importance of some noteworthy women progressing in this manner. Bennett advised her, through an interpreter, to cooperate with her husband, one of the most progressive men in Ceylon, and to persuade other women to attend meetings and lectures of the Theosophical Society. "She gave me a promise that she would do so, but I fear it was rather faint," he surmised. "It seems like an immense struggle for her to throw off the customs of the past."[10]

In Galle Bennett delivered a lecture on the two main pillars of Christianity titled "A Fable and a Dream." He stated, "I think I succeeded in showing that these foundation pillars are extremely rotten" and unable to sustain a great system of religion. After spending twelve days in Ceylon, he departed for Penang, Java, and then on to Singapore. The editor hoped reform would take place in India as it had in other parts of the world, but he knew it would be difficult and a long time in coming. "The people of the East," he lamented, "are greatly the slaves of custom" and they seem unable to "show the enterprise and activity evinced in the west." It is difficult to determine how much of a lasting impact Bennett's freethought lectures had on India and Ceylon, where the struggle, sometimes violent, for hearts and souls continues well over a century later.[11]

On April 7, 1882, Bennett was aboard the steamer *Gwailor* bound for Hong Kong. "This is Good Friday, being the day appointed by the Catholic and English churches to commemorate the crucifixion of Jesus," he commented, "though if such an event ever took place there are a hundred chances to one that it was not on the seventh day of April." It was a beautiful day, even though he learned that on the same steamer was Reverend Joseph Cook—his old adversary, who had "taken pleasure in calumniating [Bennett] and the Liberals of America."[12]

During the weeklong voyage, Bennett observed Cook's new bride and wondered how this apostle of science who preached the importance of selecting "life-partners in consonance with the dictates of science" could have failed so miserably. Bennett described Mrs. Cook as

> [a] tall, gaunt, sallow, spare female of very uncertain age, who looks as though she had remained an old maid twenty-years too long, and who, I heard one of the passengers say, looks as though she had not vitality enough to draw a herring off a gridiron. (Perhaps that remark is a trifle severe; I did not make it. It is only my business to report what I see and hear.) But just imagine two hundred and fifty pounds of coarse adipose and lymph, which for over forty years has lived in a state of angelic purity and celibacy, basking in the rays of the sun of science till approaching the fiftieth mile-stone in the journey of life, then taking to his puffy and distended but scientific bosom ninety-five pounds of spare, elongated, osseous femininity with sallow cuticle and silvery locks, and you will have in your mind's eye what constitutes a true scientific marriage, and what matrimony is and should be according to the superior light of the scientific Joseph.[13]

Bennett remarked that his description of Cook's conjugal union was "for the benefit of those who do not want to pay fifty-cents to hear the Reverend Cook's scientific sermons" and to learn from Cook's matrimony. The editor never ran into Cook during the voyage. "But the world is tolerably wide, I discover and though Joseph and I are now on the same boat, we will probably generally find room enough to get through life without seriously colliding." They were nearly united in Canton where Cook delivered one of his Christian lectures. Bennett reported that Cook was currently declaring himself "a teacher of axiomatic theology"—if anyone knows what that means, he asked. If he called himself "a peddler of dogmatic absurdities and barefaced falsehoods and slander we would have understood the meaning of the words quite as well, and the assertion would have contained quite as much truth."[14]

In China Bennett visited Canton and Hong Kong before departing for Japan. As he did everywhere, he journalized extensively about the Chinese customs and provided an overview of the nation's three great systems of religion—Confucianism, Taoism, and Buddhism. He found their peaceful existence together for more than two thousand years "remarkable . . . they have not quarreled and fought as have the devotees of other religions."[15]

In the late nineteenth century, numerous sensationalized accounts of the Chinese use of opium appeared in the Western press, mainly in Great Britain and America. After personally visiting several opium dens, Bennett found the press reports extremely exaggerated. Bennett declared opium smoking a deplorable habit but "not nearly so gross an evil as the use of alcoholic beverages in Christian countries." And although he did not want to be considered an advocate or apologist for the destructive habit, he denounced alcohol "a hundred per cent worse." Who has not heard the midnight howlings of intoxicated men? he asked. Opium smoking did not cause husbands to beat their wives or cause riots as alcohol did, he contended. Bennett bolstered his argument by quoting a recent article by Sir Rutherford Alcock, a former British minister to China. Alcock identified the leaders of the antiopium movement to be the archbishops of Canterbury and ecclesiastical dignitaries financed by eminent philanthropists of ignorance.[16]

Bennett agreed wholeheartedly with Alcock's assessment that the Christian missionaries' presence in China was "a far greater eyesore than the importation of opium." In his writing, the editor repeated his assertion that he was not defending the evil of opium smoking, but if American and English Christians were to worry more about their own misdeeds, they would be better off. "Great Britain and America have really but slight grounds for throwing stones at the Chinese on account of their immoralities."[17]

With his characteristic candor and insight, Bennett found many of the Chinese customs admirable and declared the Chinese to be good laborers, good mechanics, and good businessmen. Nevertheless, he did not advocate great numbers of Chinese workers being sent to California to compete with American laborers. But he also found fault with his country's current immigration policy. "It seems un-American to discriminate between nationalities," he asserted, and allow some nations to send their workers while not permitting others.[18]

The Chinese vice that Bennett had the most trouble accepting was infanticide, a practice that was reportedly widespread. He pronounced infanticide and abortion wrong. Two of his closest friends in New York were Dr. Foote and his son Ned, both pioneer birth control advocates. Bennett agreed that mothers had the right to determine the size of their families, but it should be done by prevention and not by infanticide or child murder, before or after birth. He pointed out that it was done in America to an even greater extent than China and equally appalling. "John Chinaman has his vices and his virtues . . . is full of superstitious and absurd religious beliefs, but from my standpoint I regard him in some respects as head and shoulders above the other Asiatic nations I have met with."[19]

During his twenty days spent in Japan, Bennett visited numerous cities and provided a comprehensive overview of the nation's history and social customs. He called on Thomas B. Van Buren, the American consular-general and a relative of former president Martin Van Buren. Since they had both previously resided in Columbia County, New York (Bennett at New

Lebanon), he said a "sort of relationship was almost claimed." Although Van Buren was busy with his diplomatic duties, he found time to spend with Bennett. Van Buren was the author of three books, which he gave to Bennett, about Japan's trade, food, and labor. The editor felt that Van Buren was knowledgeable in Japanese affairs and a very cordial gentleman.[20]

In Yokohama Bennett was once again in the same city (and same hotel) as the Reverend Joseph Cook. For several days he noticed the walls and fences placarded with large posters advertising Cook's lecture "Does Death End All?" He went to listen to Cook's address, which was attended by about fifteen hundred people and lasted longer than two hours. Van Buren presided at the event and made, in Bennett's words, "a very neat opening speech" complimenting Cook as a "well-known orator." The editor heard nearly the same speech previously in Bombay. Reverend Cook's "weaver" theory was, in the editor's opinion, "the greatest and central falsehood of the world."[21]

Bennett wrote an extensive review of Cook's lecture and found it "as replete with sophistry" as anything he had heard in a long time. "Perhaps a trifle of charity should be extended to this Christian defamer," he wrote, "on the score of an unsound mind." He informed readers that Cook had spent time in an insane asylum and was probably liberated too soon. "If, however, it is true, as is asserted by those who claim to know, and able to prove, that he became insane in consequence of excessive self-abuse, there are less grounds for charity."[22]

THE ACTING EDITOR

Bennett prodigiously chronicled his trip while traveling and frequently mailed the letters to America to be printed in the *Truth Seeker*. Because of the nature of travel during the nineteenth century and the limitations of sending and receiving mail, it was impossible for him to comment on current events in a timely manner. Several important developments concerning freethinkers occurred while Bennett was on his yearlong journey around the world. Since Eugene Macdonald was sitting in the editorial chair in New York, as he had while Bennett was in prison, it was his job to address the consequential issues of the day. Bennett was, however, able from time to time to get copies of the *Truth Seeker* during his travels—Eugene's hard-hitting editorials were making his mentor proud.[23]

The burial of Charles Darwin, who had died on April 19, 1882, elicited some harsh condemnation from the acting editor. Macdonald criticized the Church of England for burying the English naturalist and author of *Origin of Species* in Westminster Abbey. Only a few years earlier the church had denounced Darwinism as atheism. *Now*, Macdonald wrote, these "so-called great and wise men [who] fought every idea of progress" as hard and doggedly as they could, planned to inter the evolutionist in *their* church. "After fighting him and his doctrines all of his life the church cannot now claim the credit of his discoveries as their own."[24]

Ralph Waldo Emerson, one of the founders of transcendentalism, the intellectual movement, also died that year. Eugene Macdonald lauded the Sage of Concord (as the author was known) for his seminal volume, *Nature* (1836). "This work marked a new era in American thought," he wrote, noting that it was "attacked with sharp criticism by conservative thinkers, and hailed with applause by the religiously free." Emerson was not a Christian, Macdonald asserted, "yet his exact religious standing would be hard to define."[25]

Another controversy emerging during Bennett's absence revolved around Abraham Lincoln's religion. A decade earlier, William H. Herndon, Lincoln's law partner, wrote a letter (published in the *Index*) stating that his deceased friend was *not* a devout praying Christian as church leaders were constantly proclaiming. "Mr. Lincoln was an Infidel, sometimes bordering on Atheism," Herndon declared. Herndon, who was not atheistic or even agnostic, was vilified in the press for his blasphemous remarks about Lincoln.[26]

In death, Abraham Lincoln was becoming a mythic figure. Leo Tolstoy, the Russian novelist, called Lincoln "a Christ in miniature." Christian writers and clergymen were constantly crediting God—and themselves—for all of the assassinated president's good works. William Herndon hoped to counter the Christian misrepresentations and eventually write a biography of Lincoln, which he was contemplating at the time. The biography would not be published until 1889, but a bitter protracted controversy erupted with its incendiary public claims. There was a lot at stake for Christians *and* freethinkers as to whether or not Lincoln was a believer. Some religionists felt the future of Christianity depended upon the answer. "Mr. Lincoln told me a thousand times, that he did not believe the Bible was the revelation of God, as the Christian world contends," Herndon said. When the biography was finally published, one reviewer suggested that the "obscenity" in the book was so "shocking" that Anthony Comstock should "give it his attention."[27]

In 1882 the *Truth Seeker* received a letter from Herndon who appealed to the "excellent Truth Seeker" to publish his article to refute the lies that were being published about himself and his former law partner. "I said it from 1866 to 1882 that Mr. Lincoln was an Infidel," Herndon maintained. "I said it, wrote it, and published it; and now I repeat it to you. Since those years I think I have been the best abused *little* man in America." Herndon's request fell on sympathetic ears. Freethinkers like D. M. Bennett and the Macdonald brothers were always glad to add an extraordinary individual to their liberal ranks, especially the Great Emancipator.[28]

William Herndon had done his research and interviewed numerous individuals from Lincoln's years in New Salem and Springfield, Illinois. The attorney said that he had known Lincoln since 1834 "thoroughly inside and outside, top side and bottom side." And he concluded that Lincoln did not believe in the "fall of man, nor miraculous conception, nor in the so-called divine revelation, nor miracle, nor in inspiration, as the Christian world contends. . . . At times in the moments of his terrible gloom, thick as a fog-bank," Herndon wrote, "there is no doubt that Mr. Lincoln bordered on Atheism—if not an out-and-out Agnostic. In Lincoln's better moments he was a *Theist*."[29]

Furthermore, Herndon asserted that Lincoln, after reading Thomas Paine's *The Age of Reason* and other liberal books, had himself written a short anti-Christian book in 1835–1836. After hearing that his friends were concerned it would damage his political career, Lincoln threw the heretical book into the fire. It was the only book that Lincoln ever authored and, according to Herndon, he never recanted his infidelity. "Mr. Lincoln was an Infidel of the radical type; he never mentioned the name of Jesus, except to scorn and detest the idea of miraculous conception." Herndon argued that the only reason Lincoln ever used the word *prayer* in his speeches was that he was a "shrewd and long-headed man." According to Herndon, Lincoln's references to religion were "merely conventional" and proved nothing. "He was a man of the deepest and profoundest policies; he knew that if he could get the Christians to pray for him he could chain them to himself and throw them against disunion; he used the Christians, *as it were*, as tools." Herndon asked his Christian adversaries, "Did not Mr. Lincoln, in his last inaugural, say this: 'The Almighty has his own purposes'?" William Herndon's honest assertions caused freethinkers to rejoice and Christians to moan.[30]

Countless books have been written about Abraham Lincoln's life and no other historical figure has been as exhaustively examined. The vast majority of unbiased writers and historians have confirmed William Herndon's assessment of Lincoln's unbelief in the stories of the Bible and the tenets of Christianity. At the time, however, Herndon's life and reputation came under intense scrutiny, and he was viciously assailed by the clergy and denigrated in the press. Newspapers reported that he was in a lunatic asylum "well chained" and/or a knave, liar, pauper, drunkard, and vile infidel. His Christian enemies started rumors that he was a drug addict and they even compared him to the assassin John Wilkes Booth![31]

William Herndon greatly admired Abraham Lincoln and felt it was his duty to set the record straight about the beloved president. "If truth will canonize Mr. Lincoln and make him a saint," wrote Herndon, "I shall favor it with all my heart; it is truth which I want

for the present and the future—for biography and general history."
He concluded one of his articles in the *Truth Seeker*:

> To condense: the inspiration of Mr. Lincoln's *political* life was
> *law* and *order*, *liberty* and *union*. Religiously, Mr. Lincoln was an
> Infidel—a Liberal. In his *philosophy* he was a realist, as opposed
> to an idealist; he was a sensationalist, as opposed to an intu-
> itionalist; and [he was] was a Materialist, as opposed to a Spir-
> itualist. As a *logician*, he lived on facts, figures, and principles. In
> short, Mr. Lincoln was a material, practical man—a wise, long-
> headed, deep-policied man, and one of the very best, greatest,
> and noblest of mankind.[32]

NOTES

"them and him.": TS April 15, 1882.

1. TSAW.
2. Ibid.

All four parrots died during the trip.

3. Ibid.
4. Ibid.
5. Ibid.
6. Ibid.
7. Ibid.
8. Ibid.
9. Ibid.
10. Ibid.
11. Ibid.
12. Ibid.
13. Ibid.

Bennett's "apostle of science" description of Joseph Cook is similar
to the disparaging appellation that the reverend used for Mary Baker
Eddy, the founder of Christian Science. In 1885 Cook and some of his
fellow orthodox divines were feeling threatened by Mrs. Eddy's popularity and her flourishing Christian "mind cure" doctrine. Also based in
Boston, Eddy was a famous lecturer, publisher, and founder of the

Massachusetts Metaphysical College. Her illustrious career would far surpass that of Reverend Cook, who from 1874 until her ascendancy was Boston's most famous religious lecturer. Cook struck back at her in his typical contemptuous fashion and, naturally, from the pulpit. Cook condemned the "lady apostle" and her version of "Christian Science" that he declared was nothing more than "Spiritualism, Pantheism, or Theosophy." Gillian Gill, *Mary Baker Eddy*. Perseus Books, Reading, Mass., 1998.

14. TSAW.

15. Ibid.

16. Ibid. Alcock article published Dec. 1881.

17. TSAW.

The analysis critical of Christian missionaries in China by Sir Rutherford Alcock and D. M. Bennett was a warning that went unheeded by the two countries. But these "unwelcome aggressors," as Bennett declared them, would run afoul with the Chinese nationalists a few decades later. The Boxer Uprising (Rebellion) in 1900 was provoked by Christian missionaries who were also looting and plundering Chinese property. Mark Twain and Moncure Conway exposed numerous shameful acts of plunder by Christians in their conquest of the Orient. GM v. 2, pp. 204–205.

18. TSAW.

In 1882 the Chinese Exclusion Act, the first substantial immigration restriction in America, was passed. The act suspended Chinese immigration for the next ten years and declared the Chinese ineligible for citizenship.

19. Ibid.

20. TS Sept. 2, 1882.

21. Ibid.

22. TSAW.

23. Ibid.

24. TS May 6, 1882.

Bennett subsequently reprinted an article about Charles Darwin that first appeared in the *National Reformer* (Charles Bradlaugh's paper). The article was an account of a visit that Dr. Aveling and Dr. Ludwig Buchner paid to Charles Darwin. "I am with you in thought, but I should prefer the word 'Agnostic' to the word 'Atheist,'" Darwin stated. "I never gave up Christianity until I was forty years of age." When asked why he gave up Christianity, he responded: "It is not supported by evidence." Bennett found Darwin's response "pregnant with meaning." The editor declared that Darwin "never had a superior in the world," and "The wise philosopher clearly had not a particle of belief in the most absurd system of Christianity. Many of us may feel more firm in knees and steadfast in back when we know that he, the greatest man that ever lived, professed the same views we do." TS Nov. 25, 1882.

25. TS May 6, 1882.

26. TS Nov. 25, 1882.

27. "Christ in miniature.": Allan Guelzo, *Redeemer President: Abraham Lincoln and the Ideas of Americans.*

Herndon's Life of Lincoln: The History and Personal Recollections of Abraham Lincoln as Originally Written by William H. Herndon and Jesse W. Weik, 1949.

Herndon's *Life of Lincoln* received praise from many newspapers and the *Atlantic Monthly* and the *Nation*. However, those Americans who continued to blindly venerate Lincoln as a Christian saint and refused to accept the truth—some newspaper reviewers among them—continued to condemn Herndon and his biography. "It is one of the most infamous books ever written and printed in the garb of a historical work to a great and illustrious man," a *Chicago Journal* reviewer wrote, his view typical of the attitude shared by Herndon's enemies.

It vilely distorts the image of an ideal statesman, patriot and martyr. It clothes him in vulgarity and grossness. Its indecencies are spread like a curtain to hide the colossal proportions and the splendid purity of his character. . . . It brings out all that should have been hidden—it reproduces shameless gossip and hearsay not authenticated by proof—it magnifies the idle and thoughtless antics of youth as main features of the man in his life and accomplishments—it degrades and belittles him. . . . The obscenity of the work is surprising and shocking. Anthony Comstock should give it his attention. It is not fit for family reading. Its salacious narrative and implications, and its elaborate calumnies not only of Lincoln himself but of his mother, and in regard to morals generally of his mother's side of the family, are simply outrageous. . . . It is indelicate, in every way in bad taste, is insulting to the memory of the dead, and calculated to mortify and lacerate the hearts of living. Equally shameful is the discussion of Lincoln's unripened religious, or rather irreligious beliefs, which he abandoned when he came to feel and know that an overwhelming Providence was his guide. In all parts and aspects—if we are a judge, and we think we are, of the proprieties of literature and of human life—we declare that this book is so bad it could hardly have been worse.

David H. Donald, *Lincoln's Herndon*. Alfred A. Knopf, N.Y., 1948.
28. TS Nov. 25, 1882.
29. TS March 10, 1883.
30. Ibid.
31. TS Nov. 25, 1882.

Herndon considered himself "a progressive and advanced little thinker . . . an altruist, believing in an infinite Energy—Universal soul—God—in universal inspiration, revelation—[all men the] sons of God." Donald p. 289.
32. TS March 10, 1883.

17

RETURN OF THE PILGRIM

We honestly believe Christianity to be false, to be the greatest sham in the world, without truth in its history, without loveliness in its doctrines, without benefit to the human race, and without anything to sustain it in the hold it has upon the world.

—D. M. Bennett

After a stormy eighteen-day sail from Yokohama, Japan, Bennett arrived in San Francisco, California, on May 30, 1882. Anxious to get a view of the Golden Gate, he got up before dawn to stand on the deck of the steamer *Oceanic*. Exactly ten months to the day since the *Ethiopia* departed New York, Bennett wrote that he was "truly glad once more to set eyes upon rock or land that belongs to America."[1]

Although the editor and his fellow passengers were anxious to go ashore, they were informed that they would have to be examined by a government physician before being permitted to disembark. Making matters worse were the eleven hundred Chinese passengers on board who might be detained several days in quarantine because of the prejudice against their immigration. Everybody on board was thoroughly disappointed and found the "unwelcome prospect . . . perfectly awful."[2]

While waiting hours before approaching the wharf, Bennett received a letter from his friend Byron Adonis, a leading California Liberal and editor of the *Jewish Times,* a San Francisco periodical. He learned from the flattering letter that Adonis had made arrangements for a suite of rooms at the Baldwin Hotel and that "[h]undreds of thousands of faithful friends and noble Freethinkers greet you, and with beating hearts await your coming. We have lighted the fires for you, and they are burning brightly all along the line from the Pacific to the Atlantic. We are pushing the priestly enemy to the wall." The letter, accompanied by a circular, was being sent across America. It announced the editor's arrival in San Francisco and attacked his detractors.[3]

While Adonis and California Liberals were lionizing the editor as a hero and the American Voltaire, his enemies were also active. In a letter to Eugene Macdonald a few weeks before Bennett's scheduled arrival in California, Adonis reported that San Francisco was "already flooded with tracts defaming Mr. Bennett, and they bear the ear-marks of the Comstock-Bundy gangs." The city's leading newspapers received the vilifying tracts and one of the dailies attacked all freethinkers in general, and Bennett in particular. "In it Freethinkers are stamped as men who are in favor of turning decent homes into brothels," Adonis noted.[4]

As the *Oceanic* approached the slip, Bennett was finally able to reach down and shake hands with members of the committee, including Adonis, who came to greet him. Within a few minutes, Bennett was on the wharf where customs officials inspected his baggage for contraband. After his box of stereopticon and views was transferred to the customs warehouse for later inspection, he accompanied his friends to the Baldwin Hotel. "The old traveler is looking hale and hearty," a friend observed, "and as smart as a whip." The editor was glad to be back on American soil and among people of his own race, who spoke his language, which he could understand without an interpreter, and to visit the "fine and flourishing city of San Francisco."[5]

That evening, Bennett enjoyed a pleasant gathering in his rooms at the Baldwin. He informed his friends that he had a set of instruments to project illuminated views of his travels in the Old World. There were so many visitors anxious to see him, he hardly found the time to write. Besides entertaining his guests, he spent time reviewing books sent from New York, and packaging the flower seeds he brought from the Holy Land. He worked well into the night packaging six kinds of seeds for the parties who wrote him while he was in Yokohama.[6]

The following day Bennett visited the *Jewish Times* office of Byron Adonis, where he found a copy of the *Truth Seeker* and nearly a hundred letters with invitations to visit almost as many places on his journey across America. And while flattered, he had to limit his excursions because of his schedule to be home exactly one year after leaving. His travels, however, especially in California, were extensive and his descriptions were in exhaustive detail. Bennett found San Francisco an extraordinary city and wondered why New York could not also adopt cable roads, which he thought more efficient than horses. He concluded his San Francisco account by praising three distinguished female lawyers, all staunch Liberals, who he declared were "brilliant, interesting and successful women." Bennett was honored when one of the attorneys called upon him at his hotel. Attorney Todd was, he reported, a bright and fascinating woman who recently won a judgment against the Geary Street Railroad Corporation and was an up-and-coming Greenback candidate for district attorney.[7]

Bennett spent twenty days exploring California and visited Oakland and Petaluma where he investigated the burgeoning wine business. He enjoyed a pleasant interview with Henry Kohler, one of the first men in California to produce wine. "He is a man of strict sobriety," he observed, "and appears like one who, if he uses wine, does so to a very limited extent." The editor predicted that the "wine business of California is destined to reach very large proportions."[8]

Receptions were held in Bennett's honor throughout California. Similar tributes were held in Sacramento, San Jose, Stockton, and Modesto. As he traveled across America by train, tributes were held in Utah, Colorado, Nebraska, Wisconsin, Michigan, and Illinois. While in Michigan, he visited E. D. Blakeman, his boyhood friend and fellow Shaker. The editor arrived in Rochelle, Illinois, July 14, 1882, the state where he started the *Truth Seeker* only a decade earlier.[9]

Bennett's letters from India were printed in the *Truth Seeker* only a few months prior and were already causing considerable controversy among those of his readers who were skeptical of Spiritualism, let alone Theosophy and occultism. Some subscribers were asking *how* he could reconcile his materialism with Theosophy. A few weeks before he arrived in Illinois, Bennett and his fascination with the astral brothers in India came under scrutiny by George Chainey, a freethought lecturer. Chainey stridently expressed his disapproval of Theosophy and hoped never to hear again "such rubbish served up as an intellectual banquet for American Freethinkers." George Macdonald subsequently revealed that Chainey, the clergyman turned freethinking lecturer, had himself explored the spiritual path. Chainey, Macdonald reported, attended a spiritualist camp meeting where he claimed to have found the "mother of his soul" and "proceeded from Spiritualism to Theosophy, and has been a mystic of one sort or another ever since."[10]

In Illinois Bennett visited Otto Wettstein (the first subscriber to the *Truth Seeker*), who had long been eager to meet the renowned Liberal. Wettstein arranged for a carriage and driver, and he and his wife greeted Bennett at the depot early that afternoon. On their ride to the Wettstein residence they drove through the heart of Illinois's vast prairies. Bennett remarked that his world tour would have been incomplete without visiting America's garden spot. The Wettsteins felt immediately at ease with the editor whose conversation was full of interesting incidents, and the ride that balmy and pleasant afternoon was, Wettstein admitted, "the most interesting ride it has ever been my fortune to experience."[11]

During an evening reception held at the Wettstein home, attended by about thirty people, the editor talked for two hours almost without stopping. This would be the first of two memorable and illustrative occasions when the publisher's friends and subscribers would witness his magnetic charisma. Everybody listened closely and would have happily listened for hours longer. "Brother Bennett was indeed a living encyclopedia of knowledge, all bubbling over with clear and sparkling information, and sound good sense." He found the editor's parlor discourse as well as his extemporary remarks infinitely preferable to that of the average first-class lecturer. Wettstein noted that everyone agreed, ladies and gentlemen alike, "that in his very simplicity and unaffectedness consisted his greatest power and fascination."[12]

Although Wettstein was a self-described enthusiastic admirer of Bennett's genius, he took issue with his spiritualistic beliefs and assertion that "when we are dead we are not dead!" At the risk of being rude, Wettstein, who was described as a hard-boiled materialist, requested an explanation. Bennett cheerfully complied, and Wettstein gave credit to the editor for his "calm, honest, and genial mode of argument, drawing out all the resources of our better nature and intellectuality without arousing anger or combativeness; presenting everything candidly, fairly, shunning all dogmatism or sophistry."[13]

A few months later in Rochester, New York, Bennett was honored at the Sea Breeze, his sister's summer resort on the shores of Lake Ontario. That evening an incident occurred typical of the response that he received from loyalists across the country. An elderly farmer arrived too late for the reception but located the editor in the crowd. "Mr. Bennett, this is the happiest hour of my life! I will not detain you," he promised while vigorously grasping the editor's hand. "I only wanted to look into your face and feel the touch of your hand—a hand that has made Comstock writhe and the churches to tremble. Keep right on. You will be sustained." As he left the reception the farmer added, "We shall probably never meet again."[14]

With the numerous receptions held in his honor across the

country, Bennett's excursion by rail took two months. After traveling around the globe nearly thirty thousand miles, the editor arrived in New York City on July 30, 1882, amazingly within fifteen minutes of exactly one year from leaving. In an article titled "Home Again," Bennett expressed his gratitude to his readers and to his wife, who had remained at home in America while he traveled abroad. He was pleased to see that the *Truth Seeker* had been splendidly conducted by Eugene Macdonald and reluctantly discussed financial matters and urged readers in arrears to remit the amounts owed, concluding, "May we all live to see many years of health, happiness, and usefulness."[15]

Bennett immediately resumed his hectic pace of writing, editing, and publishing. He also attended additional receptions held in his honor. The first was a dinner honoring the world traveler at the swank Martinelli's Fifth Avenue restaurant, where his New York Liberal League feted its president in style. The highlight of the banquet was the presence of Horace Seaver and J. P. Mendum of the *Boston Investigator*.[16]

The year 1882 was a time when many of the old-guard freethinkers were beginning to pass the Liberal activity on to younger men like Eugene Macdonald, his brother George, and Samuel Putnam. Decades later, George Macdonald fondly recalled meeting Seaver and Mendum, the venerable editor and proprietor, respectively, of the *Boston Investigator*, America's most influential freethought periodical. He was given the detail to meet the two veteran freethinkers at Grand Central Station. Macdonald found the two from Boston "standing together like children lost in the crowd, timidly regarding their surroundings in the big station. They were of the age I have now reached myself, when a man is not so sure of himself as he is at twenty-five." He guided them to the restaurant and seated them in places of honor at the speakers' table. Letters were read from some of those who could not be present, including Elizur Wright, James Parton, and Robert Ingersoll. Thaddeus Wakeman introduced Bennett to the audience of about sixty ladies and gentlemen and welcomed "the illustrious Pilgrim who has circled the earth in the search for truth." Wakeman asked, "And is not

a Pilgrim a 'religious person'—a product of the accursed old the-
ologies he is to live and die fighting."[17]

Dr. Slade

Bennett's first editorial after returning home was his response to
"The Slade Exposure." Dr. Henry Slade was a world-famous
American spiritualist medium known for his dramatic slate
writing (the ability to inscribe slate without actually touching it).
Slade reportedly possessed extraordinary powers since he was a
child—strange abilities that seemed to increase with age. He
toured the United States conducting séances and paranormal
demonstrations for over a decade before going to Europe in
1876. In Europe he created a sensation and performed for the
Russian royal family, becoming a member of the czar's house-
hold. (Blavatsky and Olcott reportedly recommended Slade to
Grand Duke Constantine of Russia.) In 1877 Slade's abilities
came under scrutiny in England where he was put on trial for
being a fake and sentenced to three months in prison. Although
he never served any time because the sentence was rescinded as a
result of a technicality, his reputation was damaged. But Dr. Slade
still had supporters, including two of America's most prominent
freethinkers, albeit in varying degrees.[18]

Bennett first visited Dr. Slade in New York City in 1875 after
some negative accounts about the medium appeared in the
Herald and other papers. The editor admitted having a warm side
for his spiritualist friends whom he felt "have done much
towards breaking down the walls of superstition and bigotry." He
hoped that their theory of life after death was true, and thought
that he would be able to give an unprejudiced and factual statement of Slade's ability.[19]

The Bennetts had participated in séances and believed they
witnessed some convincing demonstrations of spirit manifestations. They were involved with Spiritualism during their Shaker
years, long before it became the rage of the Victorian era. In 1876

the editor defended his belief in Spiritualism in an editorial titled "A Future Life." He admitted that he did not believe in all the claims of spirit communication and that there were fraudulent spiritualists. Nevertheless, he told readers that while he and Mary were alone together, they witnessed many examples of phenomena, including intelligence from Mary's dead brother and sister. The Bennetts also believed they received spirit communication from their deceased daughter.[20]

In March 1878 the couple attended a séance in New York. While they sat in the center of a circle of nineteen persons, an abundance of demonstrations took place, Bennett reported, including voices of Edwin Adams and other deceased actors. The editor said that he heard his own father's (John Bennett) voice. He felt an arm touch his neck and was firmly embraced by his father, who distinctly said, "My son, you are doing right; press on in your noble work." Mary on one side and her sister on the other also said they felt conscious of the presence of disembodied personages. Bennett's articles about his spiritualistic activity often incurred criticism in the form of letters to the editor. He explained to readers that he did not consider Spiritualism and atheism incompatible.[21]

On another occasion, Bennett and a friend visited Dr. Slade at his Twenty-first Street residence. He provided the *Truth Seeker* readers with a full account of the manifestations they witnessed. After a brief conversation with Slade, Bennett and the friend entered Slade's back parlor where a large table was located in the center of the well-lit room. After closely examining the walnut breakfast table, the editor did not detect any wires or machinery. The three men sat at the table with their feet placed upon Slade's in order to prevent him from using them. They also placed their hands in the middle of the table, touching each other. "Within a minute a sensation somewhat similar to a current of magnetism from a magnetic machine was perceptible," Bennett noted, and light and heavy raps occurred. They also heard taps promptly given in response to questions. The editor was handed a slate where he observed writing occurring several times.[22]

Bennett was positive that while visiting Slade he witnessed phenomena that were not the result of fraud or trickery. He recounted a demonstration of slate writing while he held the slate and "distinctly heard the writing . . . and felt the vibration." Even more amazing was that in broad daylight he saw a heavy marble-topped table whirling around and while placing himself "upon the table, and with the hands of Slade and my friend upon the table, I was lifted twice from the floor, table and all." Bennett did not say that the phenomenon was performed by spirits, but he felt there was some intelligence responsible that he admittedly did not understand. The editor could not state emphatically that Slade was not guilty of dishonesty at other times. He was, however, sure there was no trickery on Slade's part in his encounters with him. "I feel that simple justice demands me to say this much."[23]

In his defense of Slade, Bennett called attention to the hundreds of reliable witnesses to the Slade phenomena. He mentioned Professor Zollner, the eminent German astronomer and physicist who subjected Slade to rigid tests and came away mystified. Bennett and Professor Zollner were not the only famous rationalists who were bewildered by Dr. Slade's abilities. A few years earlier in 1874, the Great Agnostic experienced the Slade phenomena not once but twice.[24]

In 1874 Robert Ingersoll and his wife went to New York City for a business and pleasure visit. One evening, they went out for amusement and decided to call on the famous spiritualist at his 413 Fourth Avenue office. They sat down in a well-lighted room at a small walnut table. Doctor Slade showed them a pair of slates, a single one and a double one that could be opened like a book. Slade proceeded to clean the slates with a wet cloth and showed the blank slates to the couple. After placing a pencil between the leaves of the slate, he closed it, set it in the center of the table, and left it for a few minutes. The Ingersolls were admittedly astounded at the doctor's ability to make a pencil write between two slates. "We could hear it," Ingersoll wrote in a letter to his brother Clark, "scratching away as lively as you please— crossing the t's and punctuating like a schoolmaster." Ingersoll assured his brother that he was skeptical at first and checked every detail of Slade's presentation and listened carefully with his lawyer's mind.[25]

The Ingersolls were so fascinated by Dr. Slade's demonstration that they returned to his office the next day around noon. The second visit was even more incredible. They took along a friend from Illinois, Colonel Ralph Plumb. Still skeptical, Ingersoll used what he described as "various tests and precautions." Then, to their amazement, the pencil wrote a message: "The soul of man can never die.—signed F. Plumb." The Ingersolls were suspicious, as was their guest. Plumb told the Ingersolls that F was his daughter who passed away only the previous year. Plumb went on to say that when Ingersoll visited his home in Illinois, Plumb's daughter heard the Great Agnostic assert that he did not believe in immortality. As she was dying, she mentioned Ingersoll's unbelief and wondered how a person could be so wrong. "I suppose," Colonel Plumb said, "she has taken this opportunity to setting you right."[26]

Robert Ingersoll was so impressed with what he saw—or thought he saw—that he wrote to his brother and implored him to go to Dr. Slade's address. "It appears so utterly impossible that I doubt my own senses," he confessed. "My *reason* refuses to believe my eyes and ears. I neither believe nor disbelieve; but I am stumped." Ingersoll wanted his brother to "investigate the thing" and if nothing happened, he instructed him to "draw on me for time, trouble, and expenses." It is unknown whether Clark ever took his brother up on the investigation. Nearly two decades later, Robert Ingersoll acknowledged that at one time he had a passing interest in Spiritualism and that he attended séances, the most memorable being the ones of Dr. Henry Slade. He admitted that he never found an explanation for his own encounter with the Slade phenomena. "At the same time," Ingersoll wrote, "I do not believe that there is anything supernatural in the universe."[27]

FREETHOUGHT AND MENTAL LIBERTY

In the late summer of 1882 about two thousand freethinkers from across America, including Bennett, W. S. Bell, and Josephine Tilton, attended the Sixth Annual Meeting of the New York Freethinkers' Association held at Watkins Glen from August 23 through 27. The "trinity" found a significant change had taken place in the small village where they were arrested four years earlier. This time, Bennett reported, "Every person in the town treated us with respect, and a kindly spirit was generally manifested." He welcomed the change and noted that even the secular press reported the meetings fairly. The editor believed that when freethinkers were truthfully written about and the aversion of being an unbeliever was removed, the faith in ancient creeds and supernaturalism would disappear. "Thousands will be ready to declare that they long ago lost all faith in the dogmas of theology, and that they fully believe that the powers and forces of nature are quite sufficient to account for every result that has ever taken place."[28]

Because of rainy weather, the meetings were held in the Opera House, which was packed with a thousand people. Some of the distinguished freethinkers in attendance were Mary E. Tillotson, the dress reformer; A. B. Bradford; and J. P. Mendum of the *Boston Investigator*. Also on hand was Amy Post, the abolitionist who posted bail for Bennett in 1878. Matilda Joslyn Gage, the editor of the *Ballot Box*, spoke about women's rights and female suffrage. She asserted her equality and "called woman the great unpaid laborer of the world, and accused the church of being the great robber of her sex." Her complex discourse, Bennett remarked, was executed with marked ability. Gage also gave a comprehensive profile of the life and work of Ernestine L. Rose, America's first women's rights lobbyist.[29]

A banquet was given for Bennett at the Glen Park Hotel. About one hundred twenty leading freethinkers enjoyed dinner and speeches by Theron Leland and the honoree. Leland detailed the editor's legal battles and triumphs and touched briefly on the simmering Walt Whitman controversy. Leland commented that the publicity caused by Anthony Comstock and the New York Society for the Prevention of Vice increased sales and made "two *Leaves of Grass* where only one grew before."[30]

After returning home from the Watkins convention and all the lionizing celebrations on his behalf, Bennett found it hard to go back to work at the desk. While he continued to work on the fourth volume of his *Around the World* books and answer questions to freethinkers by Christian opponents that appeared in the weekly, he was planning a tour of America. The editor intended to give a series of lectures across the United States that winter with a stereopticon and the views he purchased abroad that he thought were "the finest collection of colored pictures of all the notable places of the Old World ever had by a public lecturer."[31]

On Sunday, September 3, the editor and two friends took a steamer destined for Glen Island and New Rochelle for a pilgrimage to the Thomas Paine Monument. He chronicled his Sunday excursion and shared his experiences that day with readers in a reflective article. During the excursion they passed beneath the Brooklyn Bridge, which had been under construction since 1870. Bennett observed the progress of the great suspension bridge connecting New York and Brooklyn that would be finished the following spring. "The execution of such an enterprise," he wrote, "is an honor to America, and to the age of the world in which we live."[32]

As the steamer proceeded past Blackwell's Island Prison, Bennett recalled unpleasant memories. "But this is a day for the enjoyment of pleasure; let us not indulge in saddening meditations." An Italian band of musicians onboard roused the passengers and helped take his mind off his past trials and tribulations. At Glen Island, a new pleasure resort, he took notice of the thousands of people enjoying the bowling alleys, billiard tables, refreshments, and amusements. And with thousands more visiting Coney Island, Rockaway, and other Sunday resorts, he thought it was "perhaps enough to make the pious and self-righteous howl in mental anguish to see both men and women here enjoying themselves rationally in these games on Sunday."[33]

In New Rochelle the editor visited the Thomas Paine Monument that had been repaired and dedicated the previous year. Standing in the sacred enclosure surrounding the monument, he felt as though they "were standing on a spot sacred to free thought and mental liberty." After a ride on a friend's yacht, they headed back to New York City. Bennett enjoyed his pleasant Sunday excursion and pledged to make the Thomas Paine pilgrimage every year. He felt that his day of leisure with friends was infinitely better than attending church wearing a long hypocritical face and hearing the same old "claims of supernaturalism repeated."[34]

Not everyone shared Bennett's views on how to relax on Sundays. Reverend Howard Crosby had a different conception on what was appropriate on the Sabbath. In a *New York Times* article titled "How Sunday Should Be Spent," Crosby affirmed that he observed Sundays "rather strictly" and objected to "light literature" being read—especially the Sunday newspapers. The reverend also opposed trains running on Sundays and pledged he "would not own stock in any railroad that ran trains on Sunday."[35]

That week the *New York Times* devoted as much space or more to religious leaders' activities as to world-changing scientific developments. The day after Bennett's Sunday excursion, September 4, 1882, Thomas Edison flipped a switch, lighting a block in lower Manhattan. Edison was a prominent freethinker and his inventions had been championed for years in the *Truth Seeker*. Although Edison's "electric light," as the *Times* called it, would eventually illuminate the entire city—and the world—the inauguration of the brilliant inventor's giant dynamos received less than a full column on page 8 of the *Times* in the "Miscellaneous City News" section.[36]

A few other opponents of freethought and Bennett were also active that fall. On October 10 the City Reform Club was formed by a group of concerned young men at the home of Theodore Roosevelt. Their mission was to purify municipal politics. Theodore Roosevelt would, after writing his biography of Gouverneur Morris, an American statesman, be the most stubborn, often quoted, and disliked critic of Thomas Paine. In the biography written in 1888, Roosevelt quotes Morris as characterizing Paine as that "filthy little atheist." Although it was a lie and Roosevelt could never produce the source of the quote, the scurrilous accusation made by a popular reform-minded president of the United States damaged Thomas Paine's reputation *to this day.* Roosevelt's fellow reform club member was Samuel Colgate, the organization's first president.[37]

The soap baron's protégé, Anthony Comstock, remained busy that autumn, devoting much of his efforts in the name of the Lord to going after gambling, lotteries, and the Long Island City pool halls. But gambling was not as sexy a cause for the repressed vice hunter as obscenity. He "never got quite as much enjoyment out of action against gamblers as he did in the pursuit of purveyors of obscene books and pictures," his biographer asserted. In the November issue of *North American Review,* the crusader complained that he had "neither money nor influential friends" when he began his life as a vice hunter. But records reveal that Comstock's backers were social register types, including Samuel Colgate.[38]

In the fall of 1882 Bennett began showing signs of a serious illness believed to be malaria. A year earlier while traveling abroad, he became ill and thought that he might have contracted the disease cholera morbus. While some of his fellow travelers blamed it on the grapes, Bennett believed it was due to the excessive heat. The former druggist had pills "containing a grain each of opium, camphor, and capsicum" from a village apothecary store and subsequently spent a day in a hotel resting and fasting. "I think more of these two remedies in curing many ills than of drugs or poisons," he wrote.[39]

LEAVES OF GRASS

The *Leaves of Grass* controversy that began the previous year while Bennett was still abroad was heating up. Walt Whitman was America's first world-famous poet. His most critically acclaimed and eventually popular book of poems, *Leaves of Grass,* was first published to mixed reviews in 1855 and in slightly larger editions in 1856 and 1860. (Bennett advertised and sold *Leaves of Grass* since 1874.) Although the editor did not consider himself a poetry aficionado, he deeply respected the good grey poet, as he was affectionately known. Bennett included a biographic profile of Whitman in his *World's Sages, Infidels and Reformers*.[40]

Three years earlier, Bennett attended a Walt Whitman lecture on the death of Abraham Lincoln and reviewed it in the *Truth Seeker*. At the time, Whitman was partially paralyzed and his hair and beard were white. Whitman and Bennett were about the same age, but the editor described the poet as looking seventy. "His voice is sweet and musical," he observed, "and his language poetical and beautiful." He found Whitman's lecture about Lincoln "graphic and deeply interesting . . . a perfect treat to all who heard it."[41]

The editor eventually became deeply entangled in the *Leaves of Grass* suppression imbroglio. Whitman's monumental work came under scrutiny of Anthony Comstock, who advised a Boston publishing house, about to issue another edition, that he judged portions of the book obscene. After Whitman refused to omit the allegedly offensive verses, the publisher refused to print a second edition. Ezra Heywood and his fellow free-love advocate Benjamin Tucker decided to challenge the New England Society for the Suppression of Vice, the Boston authorities, Comstock, and "all other enemies of liberty." Tucker openly advertised *Leaves of Grass* in his journal, *Liberty*. Several Boston newspapers bolstered his challenge, including the influential *Herald* and *Globe*. Comstock and his Christian cronies succeeded in making *Leaves of Grass* a financial success after six earlier editions.[42]

In June (while Bennett was on his way home) Eugene Macdonald took a strong editorial stand when he printed a letter by Whitman's friend William O'Connor, defending the poet and *Leaves of Grass*. O'Connor's letter included a letter by Ralph Waldo Emerson praising *Leaves of Grass*. Macdonald introduced the letter, writing,

What is the difference between this and Russian censorship except in degree? It sets hot blood surging to see a noble book

condemned by narrow bigots who gloat in secret over a religious volume filled with nastiness. It is a burning shame that
religion, with all its narrowness and hypocrisy, ever obtained
any political influence in this country. . . . We are heartily with
Mr. O'Connor in his remembrance of the descendants of the
woman-whippers and witch-hangers of Massachusetts.[43]

Ezra Heywood's challenge to the latest assault on free speech
and free mails became another divisive issue among freethinkers.
The controversy simmered that summer and was mentioned by
Theron Leland at the Watkins Glen convention. Bennett
remained surprisingly aloof during the dispute. His response
seemed overly cautious to some and outright cowardly to others.
But Heywood's arrest by Comstock on October 26, 1882, in
Princeton, Massachusetts, drew him into the confrontation,
albeit reluctantly. Heywood was arrested at his home to face a
four-count indictment. In addition to mailing *Cupid's Yokes*, the
reformer was charged with sending through the US mail two of
Whitman's poems from *Leaves of Grass*: "A Woman Waits for Me"
and "To a Common Prostitute." The other two counts were for
advertising a contraceptive device in his periodical, the *Word*. The
Comstock Syringe, as it was sardonically dubbed, had also been
advertised in the *Truth Seeker* with the hope of driving the vice
hunter into a frenzy—and that it did![44]

Walt Whitman was an honest and earnest man, Bennett said.
He did not feel, however, that everything that the poet wrote was
desirable to spread over the land. The editor wrote of Whitman's
poems, "As a rule they are grand, and doubtless contain the
genius of true poetry." Nevertheless, he thought that a few of the
poems should have been omitted from *Leaves of Grass* and could
not be of "special benefit to anybody." Although Bennett did not
wish to censure, he confessed that he wondered *why* Heywood
mailed the matter. "We are in favor of free mails, the same as free
thought," the editor declared, "but we are not in favor of sending
indecent matter by mail, or any other way." About "Mr. H. [who]
has been indiscreet," Bennett wrote,

He [Heywood] has seemed to us not a man with a coarse, animal nature, but naturally as free from such a tendency as one man in a thousand. We must say, however, that he chose to make himself conspicuous by mailing Walt Whitman's most objectionable poem, and by publishing some things which we most certainly would not publish. We could not see what good was to be gained by it, what principle of Liberalism is involved, or how the interests of any class of the community can thereby be served. There is no reason why any one should unnecessarily thrust his hand into the lion's mouth.[45]

Bennett's seemingly uncharacteristic reaction to Heywood's latest arrest caused astonishment and anger. Heywood expressed his displeasure in *An Open Letter to Walt Whitman* that he printed in the *Word*. Heywood complained that since his release from Dedham Jail, he was "slowly becoming comparatively 'respectable' again when lo suddenly I am 'of no reputation.'" He informed Whitman (and all those who read the *Word*) of Bennett's yearlong prison sentence in Albany Penitentiary for "alleged-mailing" *Cupid's Yokes*—then called attention to Bennett's unsympathetic editorial that he reprinted on the same page.[46]

In the same issue of the *Word*, Heywood reprinted a considerably more severe response to Bennett's editorial by Benjamin Tucker, his fellow free-love advocate. Tucker had supported Bennett's free-speech cause and visited him in the Ludlow Street Jail. Now he lashed out bitterly at what he considered the editor's complete reversal of policy on the Comstock Laws. "We must express our indignation at the cowardly conduct of D. M. Bennett, editor of the 'Truth Seeker,' who prates about Mr. Heywood's taste & methods," Tucker wrote in *Liberty*. "We do not approve of Mr. Heywood's taste and methods, but neither did we of Bennett's when we did our little best a few years ago to save him from Comstock's clutches. It is not a question of taste, but of liberty: no man who fails to see this and act accordingly can ever fairly call himself a Liberal again."[47]

Walt Whitman, the poet whose words caused the furor, was not appreciative of all the negative attention he was receiving.

Furthermore, he did not want to be identified with the free-love movement or with Ezra Heywood, its most outspoken proponent. "Heywood is certainly a jackass," Whitman declared. And while the poet's sentiment toward Heywood was not expressed in print publicly during the controversy, Bennett's words were exposed for everyone to see and judge.[48]

Initially, George Macdonald thought Bennett's remarks about Heywood were spiteful. While he was pondering what Bennett's motives might be, he heard one of the *Truth Seeker* printers comment: "Achilles had his vulnerable spot, and so has the Doctor. I'm afraid it is his vanity; he is in the limelight, and isn't encouraging any rivals in martyrdom." Macdonald found wisdom in the printer's classical explanation, but he also blamed the editor's change of heart on the illness—which was getting worse—that he had been suffering from for several weeks.[49]

In the November 25, 1882, issue of the *Truth Seeker*, Bennett responded to the "pretty lively hornet's nest" he was blamed for stirring up. He denied that he had "flopped over" or "turned a summersault" or was "guilty of cowardly conduct." The editor admitted that he still sold *Cupid's Yokes* but once again argued it *was not obscene*. If others wanted to circulate "indecent literature," that was their business but not his intention. As to publishing indecent parts of the Bible, he maintained that since the "great engine of superstition and error" was in every home, Sunday school, and the hands of every man, woman, and child, "we claim a perfect right to do so." But he did not wish to harm Walt Whitman by pursuing the same course. Bennett concluded by explaining his object and mission for readers:

> It is to oppose the errors of supernaturalism, the tyranny of priestcraft, and the absurdities of the current system of religion. We honestly believe Christianity to be false, to be the greatest sham in the world, without truth in its history, without loveliness in its doctrines, without benefit to the human race, and without anything to sustain it in the hold it has upon the world.
>
> We are in favor of advocating the truths of nature, we are glad to aid in disseminating the teachings of science. We are in

favor of extending and enlarging the rights of oppressed men and women. We are in favor, so far as possible, of an even distribution of the wealth of the world. We are opposed to a few holding immense fortunes which they never earned, while millions are suffering for the commonest necessities of life. We are opposed to the oppressions of capital and monopoly. We are in favor of all men acquiring a comfortable competence in life, and opposed to one man seizing and holding that which belongs to millions, and is indispensable for their comfort. We shall not deny to others the right to circulate erotic literature if they think that is the highest; but we shall not engage in it ourselves nor advocate it. We trust we have now defined our position so fully that we shall not again be called upon to "rise and explain."[50]

NOTES

"upon the world.": TS Nov. 25, 1882.

1. TS Oct. 7, 1882.
2. Ibid.
3. Adonis letter dated May 25, 282 (Bruno Calendar): TS Oct. 7, 1882.
4. Adonis letter dated April 8, 282: TS May 27, 1882.
5. "as a whip.": TS June 24, 1882. "of San Francisco.": TS Oct. 7, 1882.
6. Ibid.
7. TS Nov. 4, 1882.

The *Greenback Party* was a minor political party from 1876 to 1884. The party advocated an increase in the volume of greenbacks (treasury notes), prohibiting bank issues, and the paying in greenbacks of the principal of all government bonds not explicitly payable in coin. Bennett championed Greenbackism and supported Peter Cooper (1791–1883), the industrialist, humanitarian, and founder of the Cooper Union in New York City, for president in 1876. GM v. 1. p. 173.

8. TS Nov. 4, 1882.
9. Wettstein first subscriber: TS Sept. 1, 1923.
10. "for American Freethinkers.": TS June 17, 1882. "another ever since.": GM v. 1 p. 330.

11. TS April 14, 1883.

12. Ibid.

13. GM v. 1 p. 387. "dogmatism or sophistry.": TS April 14, 1883.

14. "never meet again.": TS Aug. 5, 1882.

15. Ibid.

16. TS Aug. 12, 1882.

17. Ibid.

18. Ronald Pearsall, *The Table Rappers*. St. Martin's Press, Inc. N.Y. 1972, p. 232.

19. TS July 15, 1876.

20. Ibid.

21. TS March 16, 1878.

22. TS Aug. 5, 1882.

23. Ibid.

24. Ibid.

25. Larson.

26. Ibid., p. 113.

27. Ibid.

28. "ever taken place.": Sept. 2, 1882. "Spiritualism and Atheism": TS July 20, 1878.

29. TS Sept. 9, 1882.

30. Ibid.

31. TS June 24, 1882.

32. TS Sept. 9, 1882.

33. Ibid.

34. Ibid.

35. The *New York Times* Sept. 5, 1882.
In 1878 Reverend Howard Crosby founded the Society for the Prevention of Crime, organized to combat the evils of gambling, saloons, and houses of prostitution. Crosby was also instrumental in reviving laws that prohibited leisure activity on Sundays. He incorporated the Sunday Closing League in his effort to require New Yorkers to observe the Christian sabbath. Broun and Leech p. 205 and TS Dec. 9, 1882.

36. The *New York Times* Sept. 5, 1882.
Thomas Edison was a generous benefactor of the Thomas Paine National Historical Association at New Rochelle, New York. Edison was an unremitting skeptic and outspoken freethinker. A visitor to Edison's laboratory in East Orange, New Jersey, found the inventor sitting at a long table filled with jars of chemicals. "Well, I'm reading my Bible,"

Edison told the young man. "The Bible of nature is a splendid book if one understands it," the visitor replied. "The best damn Bible in the world," Edison enthusiastically remarked. "Its laws are perfect, and grand, and all the prayers in the world can't change them. There is intelligence and law in this world, and there may be supreme intelligence and law; but so far as the religion of the day is concerned, it is all a damned fake." GM v. 1 p. 188.

37. "filthy little atheist": Fruchtman p. 442.

In Theodore Roosevelt's biography of Gouverneur Morris, he writes:

> One man had a very narrow escape. This was Thomas Paine, the Englishman, who had at one period rendered such a striking service to the cause of American independence, while the rest of his life had been as ignoble as it was varied. He had been elected to the Convention, and having sided with the Gironde, was thrown into prison by the Jacobins. He at once asked Morris to demand him as an American citizen; a title to which he of course had no claim. Morris refused to interfere too actively, judging rightly that Paine would be saved by his own insignificance and would serve his own interests best by keeping still. So the *filthy little atheist* [italics mine] had to stay in prison, "where he amused himself with publishing a pamphlet against Jesus Christ." There are infidels and infidels; Paine belonged to the variety—whereof America possesses at present one or two shining examples—that apparently esteems a bladder of dirty water as the proper weapon with which to assail Christianity. It is not a type that appeals to the sympathy of an onlooker, be said onlooker religious or otherwise.

Roosevelt wrote the biography in 1888, but the derogatory remarks about Thomas Paine did not come to the attention of freethinkers until he became president in 1901. Roosevelt's disparaging statements about Paine became a cause célèbre of freethinkers. In 1902 the *Truth Seeker* defended Thomas Paine's reputation and articulated the attitude of American freethinkers. Sidney Warren summarizes the *Truth Seeker*'s seven points of defense. He writes:

First, Paine's life was not ignoble, but on the contrary was characterized by a nobility of purpose and action. Second, the cause of Paine's arrest was not a Jacobin conspiracy; it was the result of Gouverneur Morris' action. Third, Paine *did* have a claim to the title of American citizen; Morris and Monroe had referred to him as such, and Monroe's reclamation of Paine as an American citizen was officially approved by the American Secretary of State, Edmund Randolph. Fourth, it was fallacious to state that Morris judged rightly that Paine would be saved by his own insignificance. After all, Paine was sufficiently important to have represented three departments in the Convention, would not have been imprisoned in the first place if he were not a significant person, and was immediately recalled to his seat upon his release from prison. Fifth, Paine was not an atheist, but on the contrary set forth his devout belief in a Deity in *The Age of Reason*. Sixth, the pamphlet published by Paine while in prison was not against Jesus Christ; the latter is mentioned by Paine in its pages only in the most respectful terms. And last, Roosevelt degraded his subject by introducing "a bladder of dirty water" as a weapon of theological controversy, and by availing himself of its contents in assailing the character of one of the noblest figures in American history.

Warren pp. 111–12.
38. Broun and Leech. *North American Review*, Nov. 1882.
39. TSAW.

In 1881 Bennett wrote a "Business-Personal" editorial promoting William Wilson's "magnetic garments" that were advertised and sold through the *Truth Seeker*. An unabashed capitalist until the end, Bennett prefaced his editorial-advertisement, declaring: "I wish to do what good I can, especially when I can do so with some profit to myself." He said that for several months he had carefully observed the "astonishing benefit" of Wilson's electrical healing "appliances." "Magnetism is known to be the vital principle without which life cannot exist," he declared, adding, "and with a deficiency of it health departs and pain and disease are inevitable." The editor, like many in the late nineteenth century, believed that "magnetism" could cause illness and therefore magnetism could also be the cure.

But the "magnetic goods" were not miraculous, he assured readers;

they worked "in pursuance of a simple law of nature." He admitted that he was no longer sure of the efficacy of medicines. "For forty years of my life I have been engaged in preparing, selling, and dispensing medicines," he told readers. "Probably not less than a hundred tons of drugs have been in my possession, and made up in the form of mixtures, decoctions, tinctures, powders, pills, etc., to be taken into the human stomach. I meant well in all this, but fear I was in the dark, and not pursuing the best system of imparting health." And since "sunlight, pure air, pure water, and the magnetic fluid are nature's great remedies," he reasoned, Wilson's "magnetic goods," although not miraculous, worked "in pursuance of a simple law of nature."

TS March 28, 1881. The infamous Anthony Comstock, not an admirer of Wilson, chose to meddle. He published a circular disparaging Wilson and claiming that he did business in Science Hall (where the *Truth Seeker* office was). Wilson brought a civil suit for libel against Comstock and had the vice hunter arrested. Bennett reported the details of the arrest and noted that Samuel Colgate provided bail. "He fathers all of Comstock's operations," he wrote, "and stands ready with his wealth to back him in all his questionable transactions. They are a precious pair of Christians whom the country would be better off without." TS Sept. 24, 1881.

40. WSIT.
41. TS April 19, 1878.
42. *Liberty*.
43. TS June 10, 1882.
44. Blatt.
45. TS Nov. 4, 1882.
46. "of no reputation.": The *Word* Dec. 1882. *Liberty* Nov. 11, 1882.
47. "a Liberal again.": The *Word* Dec. 1882.
48. "certainly a jackass.": Blatt p. 143.
49. GM v. 1 p. 322.
50. TS Nov. 25, 1882.

18

The Defender of Liberty, and Its Martyr

And that he was murdered, just as we were nearing age 'tis so hard to think of . . . and that professed Liberals helped to make his death martyrdom—is the worst of all to bear.

—Mary Wicks Bennett

D. M. Bennett's illness became noticeable in October 1882, after he caught a cold while the *Truth Seeker* office was being moved from Science Hall to a new location at 21 Clinton Place. After a painter he hired turned out to be a worthless fellow and suddenly quit, Bennett with his predictable disregard of self took off his jacket and finished the job. (Some believed that he was poisoned by the lead paint.) During the move, he began to hiccup uncontrollably. He was overheard saying to Dr. Foote and his son, "If you boys don't do something to stop this hiccupping, I am gone." Eugene observed that the hiccups were shaking him apart when he tried to work, speak, or eat, and thought Bennett "was enough of a physician to know what to expect."[1]

On Friday, December 1, Bennett went to the office, carrying the last three pages of his manuscript for *Around the World*. He complained of not feeling well and returned home, leaving a piece of unfinished copy on his desk. George Macdonald took the article, titled "Reviving Puritanism," to the editor's room where he dictated only one paragraph. According to Macdonald, the article was the shortest installment (to be continued) of anything Bennett ever wrote. (The article appeared in the same issue of the *Truth Seeker* that printed his obituary.)[2]

Bennett relied on his own medical experience concerning his illness until it became imperative that a doctor be consulted. Dr. E. Guernsey, considered one of the very best homeopathic physicians in New York, was summoned. The doctor diagnosed the illness as gastric fever. Mary helped her husband into bed where he stayed for the next few days suffering from intense pain. Except for mentioning his unfinished *Around the World* that he had struggled so hard to complete, and expressing concern for his wife, he never complained. Dr. Guernsey visited several times but the prognosis was grim. Although the editor was able to recognize his wife and friends, he could only respond to them in half-choked whispers. The following Tuesday at 10 PM, he suffered a stroke and sank into a coma. The physician informed Mary, who was distraught and crying, that unless a drastic change took place her husband would die. That night, Bennett remained unconscious and in the morning he was pronounced dead. DeRobigne Mortimer Bennett died on Wednesday, December 6, 1882—only seventeen days before his sixty-fourth birthday. D. M. Bennett's death was announced in the December 9 issue of the *Truth Seeker*. The following week's edition included a rare woodcut image of the deceased editor and a comprehensive biographic profile. Both issues were trimmed with traditional mourning borders. "No man ever journeyed to the end more tranquilly," the *Truth Seeker* reported. "No soldier was braver, no patriot more undaunted, no statesman more assured, no sage more untroubled."[3]

THE TRUTH SEEKER AT REST

The news of Bennett's death was telegraphed to the leading liberals across the country. Local chapters of the National Liberal League held D. M. Bennett memorial services. The New York Liberal League, of which he was president, held a Lodge of Sorrow meeting at the *Truth Seeker* office. A memorial meeting was held in Boston at Paine Hall to pay tribute to the deceased editor. Letters and telegrams poured into the *Truth Seeker* office and were printed in the periodical.[4]

"Few men since Capt. Cook ever circumnavigated the globe to better material purpose," Parker Pillsbury wrote to T. B. Wakeman. "And surely from a moral and spiritual standpoint, he stands unrivalled among all discoverers and travelers."[5]

Samuel P. Putnam paid tribute and said,

> Mr. Bennett brought to our philosophical Liberalism a smack of human nature; he poured into it the freshness and vigor of the soil. . . . He was our Thomas Paine, and he spoke words of thrilling common sense.
>
> Mr. Bennett was one of nature's noblemen. . . . He was like an oak. If he was rough it was because he had met the storm as well as the sunshine, and had wrestled the elemental forces. He had nothing of the daintiness of fashion. He boasted not of the elegance of the dilettante. He had not the smoothness of insipid culture, nor the superficial grace of inherited custom. . . . He was perfectly natural. . . .
>
> He was not only a Truth Seeker, but a truth-revealer constantly of his own being.
>
> He had no arts of concealment; not a particle of make-believe. His personality was not hid behind any "esthetic sham." He was so thoroughly in earnest that he paid no regard to appearances. . . . He saw a work to be done, and he did it, even though he used the shovel and hoe and not the silver knife and fork.
>
> He did not care for aromatic holiness, for ethical perfumery, and barber-shop morality. He was himself from head to foot. He did not have an inner and outer self at odds with one another and playing hide and seek in the masquerades of the world. His

outward form was identical with his inward desire. His speech was one with his thought. It was this absolute sincerity, this indomitable truth-seeking and truth-speaking, that made Mr. Bennett such an invaluable aid to human progress. . . .

Mr. Bennett was not afraid of the truth though it might lose him many a friend.

Truth was to him the first of all. . . . It made our Liberalism more virile. . . . This is the true glory of Mr. Bennett. He was an honest man; and he helped to make Liberalism a thoroughly honest affair. . . .

He was a steadfast friend, and because capable of a strong affection. He was a good hater. He could strike back. He did not believe in Christian meekness. His warfare, however, was open. There was no subterfuge. He did not carry concealed weapons.

He hit straight from the shoulder, and gave his enemy fair warning. . . .

The attacks made upon his character were outrageous in the extreme. In substance they were false as hell. I regard the action of those Liberals who joined in the hue and cry against Mr. Bennett with the utmost loathing and abhorrence. . . . A more devilish act was not perpetrated under the regime of the Inquisition. . . . It was the cruelty of a barbarian. . . .

The hero sleeps peacefully now. He has won the victory. He was the devotee of truth, and truth shall honor him for evermore. . . . The hypocrite is soon forgotten, no matter how splendid his name. The world does not care much for veneer. . . .

Mr. Bennett cast his lot with the truth—the plain, unvarnished truth. The storm burst upon him because he would not be otherwise than truthful. The sunshine of truth will rest upon him hereafter, for in the end the truth is the most blessed light.[6]

Elizur Wright spoke Bennett's praises:

A hero has fallen in our war. . . . It is no ordinary mortal who has now met the inevitable destiny of all. . . . He was the victim of a theologically instigated law, of which the United States will yet be ashamed—an absurd, hypocritical, contemptible, and essentially wicked law. . . . The grand work he wrote in prison will live. . . .

Like the immortal work of Thomas Paine, that was partly written in prison, and which first aroused Bennett's soul to battle with the tyranny of a sham theology, it will never be answered; it will cut its way through all the deserts and jungles of superstition to a better land in which human love and brotherhood shall prevail, and universal justice shall banish crime. It is ours to perpetuate his name by not letting his work stop.[7]

Obituaries appeared in several newspapers and periodicals with varying degrees of acclamation and accuracy. A San Francisco paper noted that Bennett did not start writing until his fifty-fourth year "and since then he has written more works of a religious character than any man who ever lived." The Sunday *Morning Mirror* wrote, "In the recent death of D. M. Bennett, in New York, the church in America loses one of its most persistent and able opponents. He was the leader of atheism in the United States."[8]

The *New York Times*: "D. M. Bennett, editor of a journal called the *Truth Seeker*, died yesterday at his residence, No. 27 Clinton-place. Mr. Bennett obtained some notoriety in 1878 by reason of his arrest upon the charge of sending indecent publications through the mails. He was tried and convicted and served 11 months of his sentence in the penitentiary. Mr. Bennett was a pronounced free-thinker. At the time of his death he was 64 years of age."[9]

The *Theosophist*: "We may note the coincidence that within a few weeks of each other, two well known journalists and authors, among our members—Mr. Bennett and Dr. Brittain—died suddenly and just after completing their most important books."—Henry Steel Olcott.[10]

The *Doylestown Democrat*: "By some, of course, he would be heretic and Infidel; by others, a great and truthful man, but too far in advance of the mass of humanity to be generally understood and properly appreciated. We viewed him as the Luther of the nineteenth century. A hundred years hence he will be known as the man falsely accused, calumniated, and persecuted, as one of the martyrs and great men of his day. His life has been one of labor and usefulness."[11]

The *Rochester Herald*: "D. M. Bennett, the author of Cupid's Yokes [*sic*], died in New York Wednesday. He has but recently returned from a tour around the world, lectured in Chicago and some other places on his way. Before he went abroad he had been imprisoned for a year in the Albany penitentiary for circulating an obscene book, or one so judged.—An ultraist on religious and social questions he courted the notoriety proceeding from his views. He had a following of course, but neither the leader nor his disciples had much reason to be proud of each other."[12]

The *Union (Oregon) Mountain Sentinel*: "The nineteenth century has produced but few more remarkable men then [*sic*] Mr. Bennett, and few more determined and devoted to the cause of combating error and upholding right regardless of cost or consequences. Entertaining the broadest views on all scientific subjects, and with a heart that throbbed for the great cause of humanity . . . and with his pen and columns of his Truth Seeker he spread consternation broadcast throughout the land by vanquishing the sophistries of the champions of the church. . . . His life was spent in breaking the shackles that enslave the human mind and he has left works that will live as long as man inhabits this planet."[13]

D. M. Bennett's funeral was held at the German Masonic Temple, 220 East Fifteenth St., New York City. Among the hundreds of mourners were Lucy Colman, Josephine Tilton, T. C. Leland, Eugene Macdonald, and George Macdonald. Dr. Foote sent a pillow of roses and camellias with "The Truth Seeker at Rest" spelled in purple flowers. There was universal sorrow among Bennett's employees, who formed a sad procession before placing flowers upon his coffin. "They were loyal to a man when Comstock was terrorizing all connected with *The Truth Seeker*," George Macdonald recalled.[14]

Thaddeus Wakeman gave an address at the funeral and spoke later at the graveside in Green-Wood Cemetery. His eulogy included an overview of Bennett's life and a speech written by the deceased editor regarding death. Wakeman's heartfelt words moved the audience to tears and touched upon one of Bennett's greatest concerns. "Death in the past has been a terror, a fear, a horror; the hobgoblins of despair have flitted through its domain and covered all with the gloom of terror," he told the mourners. "To our brother that fear of death was one of the great curses that rested upon mankind which he wished to remove. He had no fear of death." In an effort to console the mourners, Wakeman said that he could do no better than to recite Bennett's *own* words concerning death:

> Let us look upon death, not with apprehension and dread, but as it really is, a necessary change in Nature. . . . Death is essential to life and equally forms a part of the laws of the universe. Let it then be regarded not as an enemy, but rather as a friend. . . . At the close of a wearisome life we pass into such a rest, such an undisturbed repose. Cares, anxieties, toils, and troubles are superseded by a state of rest. This short word, rest, is full of meaning—full of consolation. To him oppressed with care, with distress, anguish, and pain, how sweet is rest. This word is replete with bliss; more suggestive of a perfect freedom from trouble and sorrow and ills of all kinds, than any other word in our language. Our departed brother is now at rest.[15]

Immediately after Bennett's death, spiritualist mediums reported receiving messages from the deceased editor. Some of these purported communications were printed in spiritualist publications, including the *Banner of Light* weekly from Boston. Macdonald dismissed these claims, wondering why Bennett would reach out to strangers rather than "come back to his personal intimate friends whom he loved and who loved him." Although Macdonald acknowledged that he did not entirely share Bennett's belief in a future life, his wish that it might be true was exceedingly strong. "Let others be not too hasty to rush into print with fancied wrongs," he cautioned, adding, "It is said that even angels fear to tread in certain places."[16]

Amid the mostly considerate press response to Bennett's death, there also appeared an erroneous published account of his confrontation with Reverend Joseph Cook in India. Cook resumed his abuse of the deceased editor during his Monday Lectures in Boston. Cook continued to repeat the lies about Bennett that he had been telling audiences for months. "He was the editor of the foremost Infidel newspaper rag of the continent that deserves to be handled with the tongs," he said. Once again, Cook attacked the Theosophical Society and said Bennett came to one of his lectures carrying a horsewhip under his coat. Eugene Macdonald promptly came to his deceased mentor's defense and refuted Cook's asinine story. "Mr. Bennett never thought of personally chastising the blackguard, however richly he deserved a horsewhipping," he declared. Cook's malicious remarks were published in the press, including the *Christian Advocate*. Macdonald reminded readers that Reverend Flavius Josephus Cook had spent time in an insane asylum (where he died two decades later).[17]

Anthony Comstock recorded D. M. Bennett's death at the bottom of his extensive notes about the editor in the New York Society for the Suppression of Vice arrest blotter. The brief handwritten *Died Dec. 6/1882* entry is noticeably larger than the other writing about his blasphemous archenemy. The notation's unusually festive flourish seems to express Comstock's reaction to Bennett's passing—Good riddance![18]

At the time of Bennett's death, Anthony Comstock was still a young man in his vice-hunting prime. Although Comstock never bothered the *Truth Seeker* publication over the next thirty-five years, he never forgot the founder. In 1892, a decade after the editor's death, Comstock went to Fremont, Ohio, to preach at the Presbyterian church. While in Fremont, he paid a visit to Rutherford B. Hayes, the politician he lauded as a clean man during the Bennett petition drive. Comstock again praised the former president for his decision *not* to pardon Bennett. Hayes, however, was not as confident in his decision as the obsequious vice hunter. "I was never satisfied, as I would wish," Hayes admitted in his diary, "with the correctness of the result to which I came chiefly in deference to the courts. 'Cupid's Yokes' was a free-love pamphlet of bad principles, and in bad taste, but Colonel Ingersoll had abundant reason for his argument that it was not, in the legal sense, 'an obscene publication.'"[19]

In 1913 Anthony Comstock bragged that he had personally convicted enough people to fill a passenger train of sixty-one coaches (approximately thirty-seven hundred people) and destroyed 160 tons of obscene literature. Someone remarked that Comstock never read books; he weighed them. The same year, George Macdonald (who succeeded his brother, Eugene, as editor of the *Truth Seeker*) was on a ferryboat and overheard a grouchy old man elbowing his way through the crowd and causing a commotion at the gate. As he looked closer, he recognized the man as Anthony Comstock! Macdonald decided to merge with the throng of passengers to see what might happen. But as he got nearer, he was startled at the sight of a pale, gray-haired, flabby, short-winded, bewildered old man tottering on his legs. The pathetic old bluenose was "no game for anybody but the undertaker," Macdonald concluded. America's self-described weeder in God's garden died two years later, and the *Truth Seeker* used Anthony Comstock's own words for his epitaph—*The world is better off without him.*[20]

The D. M. Bennett Monument

Soon after D. M. Bennett's death, members of the Bennett Liberal League (formerly the Fourth New York Liberal League) resolved to erect a monument in memory of their deceased league president. All had been close friends of the editor and considered the enterprise a labor of love. A committee of eminent freethinkers was appointed, including Eugene Macdonald. The Bennett Monument Fund Committee's goal appeared in the *Truth Seeker* of December 23, 1882, on what would have been Bennett's sixty-fourth birthday: "It is intended to place as fine a monument over Mr. Bennett as the amount contributed will permit; and we hope to make it an imposing memorial of the love and esteem which will worthily mark the resting place of one of the greatest Liberals of the age."[21]

Daniel E. Ryan, the committee chairman, had been the first man to grasp Bennett's hand as he came out of the Albany Penitentiary—and now, only two years later, the first of a thousand friends to contribute to the monument fund. His generous $50 donation got things off to a promising start; the committee commissioned a builder to begin construction.[22]

During the summer of 1883, while the construction was still underway, the league's plan for an imposing memorial over the editor's grave in Green-Wood Cemetery was in jeopardy. A national furor erupted after the article "Infidelity in Green-Wood Cemetery" was printed in the *Pittsburgh Daily Post*. The piece contained numerous untruths about Bennett and even went so far as to include a fictitious interview with Mary, his still-grieving widow. The writer also offered his biased prediction about rumored monument inscriptions that had not, at the time of the article's printing, even been selected: "Such is the fond expectation of the widow, and it may possibly be realized, but I think not in Green-Wood Cemetery. The quotations selected to be inscribed are violently denunciatory of Christianity, and Green-Wood is a Christian burial ground, whose authorities will not permit the diversion of sacred ground to such a use."[23]

Green-Wood was indeed a Christian burial ground. Built in the mid-nineteenth century, it was initially inspired by the Père-Lachaise Cemetery in Paris and designed for both the dead *and* the living. The Garden City of the Dead, as it was known because of its landscaped rolling hills, lakes, ponds, winding paths, and weeping statues, was an idyllic haven far from the hustle and bustle of Manhattan and was *the* final resting place for prominent New Yorkers. The world-famous Brooklyn cemetery encouraged visitors and provided horse-drawn carriages to convey tourists around the 478-acre pastoral necropolis where countless historical celebrities were buried. The Gothic Revival main entrance, with its stone spires that rose over one hundred feet toward heaven and impressive brownstone gatehouse with the facade adorned with two bas-reliefs of Jesus Christ, might seem to visitors as if they had almost reached the pearly gates. In the nineteenth century, cemeteries were considered schools of religion and philosophy where the living could learn lessons. The rumor of a monument containing blasphemous inscriptions caused immediate controversy for the cemetery filled with crosses, praying cherubs, and mourning angels. The cemetery officials began receiving letters of protest from all over the country. And although the inscriptions chosen for the monument still had not been made public by the Bennett Monument Fund Committee, it did not stop the editorial "humorist" of the *New York Times* from "reporting" in the paper's August 29, 1883, issue:

> Mr. Bennett during his life-time was the editor of an infidel paper wherein the orthodox rules of grammar and spelling were treated with almost as much contempt as the editor expressed for the Christian religion. Mr. Bennett was also addicted to obscenity as well as infidelity and served a term in prison for the offense of circulating obscene literature. If the surviving admirers of Mr. Bennett choose to erect an ordinary gravestone over his remains in Green-Wood no one will make any objection. They intend, however, to make his proposed monument an enduring expression of his peculiar views by decorating it with sentences taken from his works. The managers of the cemetery could not reasonably object to a tombstone bearing the name of Mr. Bennett, the dates of his birth and death, and perhaps the date of his commitment to jail; but they will certainly object to a tombstone bearing such sentences as "There ain't no God," "My works ain't no more obscene than Moseses," or "D—n ANTHONY COMSTOCK."[24]

In equally passionate opposition, Eugene Macdonald defended his deceased mentor and attacked what he called brutal journalism in the September 8, 1883, issue of the *Truth Seeker*. He was especially annoyed with the *New York Times* and described it as "stilted, stuffy, slushy and slanderous—and yet grammatical inaccuracy cannot be charged against it. It has several suits for criminal libel now pending against it in this state—nevertheless its orthodoxy has not been questioned. It defends monopoly, corporate powers, and political thieves—yet the atrocity of unbelief in the teachings of Christian superstition cannot be laid at its door."[25]

It came as no surprise to the committee when Green-Wood's secretary notified them that any proposed inscriptions had to first be submitted to the cemetery's board of trustees for approval. The committee complied, but was immediately informed by the cemetery official that it was unlikely the trustees would permit the selections to be engraved. With winter fast approaching, the builder was anxious to finish the monument, but the trustees were slow in meeting, and work on the memorial came to a halt. The builder was advised by the secretary that the front of the obelisk could be engraved, but the heretical sentiments could not be cut on its sides, and they added a reminder that the cemetery was Christian and *must not be desecrated*. The builder decided to place the monument in position over Bennett's grave and postponed its engraving until the matter was settled between the committee and Green-Wood's board of trustees.[26]

The cemetery trustees finally met and resolved that they could not interfere in the matter. Nevertheless, Green-Wood's secretary sent a notice demanding to speak with a committee representative. Eugene Macdonald responded on behalf of the committee. The interview, while brief, was decided. The secretary was a very nice gentleman and a "good Christian," Macdonald said, who did not want any more publicity about the monument. The secretary assured Macdonald that he could not speak authoritatively for the board, but if the committee persisted in putting heretical sentiments upon the stone, in his opinion and in spite of the resolution, the board would surely interfere. According to the secretary, the board had "power to remove any monument or erase any inscription which a majority of its members might deem offensive." The man asked Macdonald not to bother the board but rather to agree to a compromise. "This is not a Christian country, our laws do not recognize Christ," Macdonald asserted. The editor explained that the monument was on private property and the committee was within their rights to inscribe whatever they chose. He went on to say that although he could not speak for the entire committee, just as the secretary could not speak for the entire board, he believed that the inscription would be engraved on the monument as written. Macdonald's assertions terminated the interview. "The secretary might as well have asked us to join his church."[27]

Eugene Macdonald reported the outcome of the interview to the committee, who unanimously agreed to engrave the selected quotations. By this time, it was midwinter and a shed had to be constructed around the monument so the stonecutters could proceed to engrave the cold granite.

> The monument is built; the heretical sentiments are engraved upon it; and there the committee proposes they shall stay. If the cemetery authorities want it blown from one end of the land to the other then they are bigots; if they desire to have their authority questioned and their jurisdiction denied through every court in New York, they will proceed to meddle with the words cut in the granite marking Mr. Bennett's resting place. They will, however, injure themselves and Christianity much less by submitting to the inevitable.—The *Truth Seeker*, March 15, 1884.[28]

> In selecting these quotations the Committee was desirous of embodying in them as many as possible of the philosophical and humanitarian principles held by Mr. Bennett. . . . Mr. Bennett had more than one idea and was the friend of all reforms. But he was preeminently a freethinker, using the term in its sense of opposition to Christianity. He was practically an atheist, though he sometimes expounded pantheism, declaring his philosophical adhesion to that belief. . . . He was converted to spiritualism by phenomena occurring in his own household and elsewhere, and he reasoned out a philosophy covering the ground he took of "material spiritualism."
>
> Eugene Macdonald[29]

D. M. BENNETT

THE FOUNDER OF "THE TRUTH SEEKER"
THE DEFENDER OF LIBERTY, AND ITS MARTYR
THE EDITOR TIRELESS AND FEARLESS;
THE ENEMY OF SUPERSTITION,
AS OF IGNORANCE, ITS MOTHER;
THE TEACHER OF MULTITUDES,
THE FRIEND FAITHFUL AND KIND,
THE MAN HONEST AND TRUE
RESTS HERE.
THOUGH DEAD HE STILL SPEAKS TO US AND ASKS
THAT WE CONTINUE THE WORK HE LEFT UNFINISHED.

WHEN THE INNOCENT IS CONVICTED,
THE COURT IS CONDEMNED.

DEMONSTRATED SCIENCE MAY BE REGARDED AS THE
ONLY TRUE
SOURCE OF KNOWLEDGE. WHAT IS CALLED REVELATION
IS A SNARE,
A DELUSION, A FALSEHOOD. THOSE WHO CLAIM TO
SPEAK FOR THE GODS SIMPLY SPEAK THEIR OWN
THOUGHT. THE GODS DO NOT SPEAK; THEY ARE AS
DUMB AS THE ROCKS, THEY ARE AS SPEECHLESS AS THE
GRAVE. WITH NATURE IT IS NOT SO. TO KNOW HER IS TO
KNOW THE TRUTH, AND TO STUDY HER IS TO BE WISE.

THE OBJECT OF OUR LIVES SHOULD BE TO MAKE THE
WORLD AS BEAUTIFUL, AND OURSELVES AND OUR FEL-
LOWS AS HAPPY, AS IS IN OUR POWER. I CAN HARDLY
YIELD MY CONSENT THAT THIS IS THE LAST OF OUR
INDIVIDUALITY; AND I FONDLY THINK THAT FATHER AND
MOTHER NATURE ARE ABLE TO ACCOMPLISH THE BEST,
GREATEST, AND MOST DESIRABLE OF ALL PROBLEMS—A
CONTINUED INDIVIDUAL EXISTENCE. BUT I AM BOR-
ROWING NO TROUBLE ABOUT IT.

I BELIEVE IN THE ETERNAL POWERS AND PRINCIPLES OF
NATURE, IN THE SUPERIORITY OF GOOD LIVES, IN ACTS
OF KINDNESS TOWARD OUR FELLOW-BEINGS, AND IN
EFFORTS TO SPREAD THE LIGHT OF TRUTH OVER THE
DARK SPOTS OF THE EARTH. EACH PERSON MUST BE
RESPONSIBLE FOR THE GOOD OR ILL HE DOES. HERE IS
OUR DUTY, HERE IS OUR ALLEGIANCE, AND NOT IN THE
SKY ABOVE US. WE MUST MAKE OUR HEAVEN ON THE
EARTH, AND NOT IN THE AIR.[30]

At the dedication on June 13, 1884, Daniel Ryan eloquently
stated,

> There has been no pretense on the part of the committee to
> build a great monument. Such was not the purpose; the time is
> to come for that. As it stands in Mr. Bennett's generation, the fit-
> ting expression of the love and respect of his friends, and it is
> their final verdict on his virtues and deeds. It remains for future
> generations to render the justice of a great monument in the
> memory of D. M. Bennett; be it a statue, a noble shaft, a grand
> institution of learning, or a temple of liberty in the form of a
> great public hall. When the heritage of his great work has
> increased his thousand friends into millions, then on this foun-
> dation of facts and honor which we have placed for them . . . let
> them build anew.[31]

D. M. Bennett affectionately referred to Mary as his better half.
Only months before his death, he expressed his gratitude to her
in the *Truth Seeker*, writing, "More than words of thanks are due
to my faithful wife who has remained at home during my long
absence and every day applied herself to the interests of our
cause." Less than a year after Bennett's death, Mary decided to sell
the *Truth Seeker* to Eugene Macdonald. "I have not lost one iota
of love for the cause," she informed the patrons of the weekly,
"and were it not for my infirmities I would stand at the helm as
long as life lasts."[32]

A few years later, Lucy Colman visited Mrs. Bennett, who was
still living alone in the same rooms where her beloved husband

had died. Colman said that Mary looked very well and even more beautiful than the last time she saw her. The widow, Colman observed, was surrounded by the beautiful gifts he brought her from India and other exotic places that he visited during his travels. She described Mary as having what was known as a "spiritual expression." Mary expressed her belief that her husband was still *with* her. "He was the love of my girlhood, the dear husband of my matured womanhood," she confided to Colman. "And that he was murdered, just as we were nearing age 'tis so hard to think of . . . and that professed Liberals helped to make his death martyrdom—is the worst of all to bear."[33]

Mary spent her final days living at the home of Eugene Macdonald, whom she had been like a mother to since he was a young man. Mary Wicks Bennett died on July 31, 1898, only one month before the *Truth Seeker's* twenty-fifth anniversary. Thaddeus B. Wakeman gave the address at her funeral, as he had done at her husband's sixteen years earlier. Wakeman concluded his eloquent remarks with his reading of Felix Adler's poem "The City of Light."[34]

Mary Wicks Bennett's ashes rest beside her husband in the shadow of the D. M. Bennett Monument. Her obituary (likely written by Eugene Macdonald) acknowledged that Mary—like her husband—had left the creeds of the Christian religion in the past:

> She had listened somewhat to the doctrine of Spiritualism,
> and had shown a passing interest in that philosophy as modified by
> theosophy,
> but to her these were speculations and not facts, and while at times
> she expressed a hope that
> they were true, her hope did not amount to confidence, and the
> whole subject was displaced in her mind by what she regarded as
> the most important matters of this world. . . .
> She was his adviser and helpmate,
> and when it came to the founding of this paper,
> it was she who chose its name.
> —The Truth Seeker.[35]

NOTES

"all to bear.": TS March 15, 1884.

1. GM v. 1 p. 323.
2. Ibid.

In his last editorial, "Reviving Puritanism," Bennett railed against Reverend Howard Crosby's Sunday Closing League or "society of fanatics" as he called them. Bennett defended the city's population, who worked an average of ten hours per day, six days per week. "The bootblack on the corner who tried to make a few pennies was summarily consigned to a cell," he wrote, "while the preacher in the pulpits earning his hundred or more dollars, was allowed to go on, and protected by the same legal machinery that arrested the bootblack. . . . This 'Sunday Closing League' is the same kind of a society as Comstock's, and is fully as dangerous to the liberties of the people. . . . It is very dangerous to clothe ecclesiastics with power, and this last move is well calculated to alarm honest men who love liberty and personal freedom." TS Dec. 9, 1882.

In 1885 the *Truth Seeker*, together with the National Liberal League (renamed the American Secular Union), began a campaign to have New York's museums remain open on Sundays. It would, however, take until 1891 until the long hard-fought campaign to secure the opening of New York museums on Sundays finally succeeded. The Metropolitan Art Museum opened for Sunday visitors that year. And in 1892 the American Museum and Natural History Museum followed suit. In assessing the *Truth Seeker*'s pivotal role, George Macdonald wrote: "The millions who every year enjoy the treasures of art and science placed at their disposal in the two larger and the many smaller museums of the metropolis, assume that the privilege has always been theirs and few among them will ever realize that they owe to *The Truth Seeker* [and D. M. Bennett], more than to any other single agency, the priceless boon which they accept as a matter of course. Many of the worst calumniators of this paper are among those whose lives have been thus enriched as a consequence of its devoted labors in behalf of their welfare and enjoyment." GM.

3. TS Dec. 16, 1882.
4. Ibid.
5. Pillsbury to Wakeman letter: TS. Jan. 6, 1883.
6. TS Jan. 13, 1883.
7. Wright letter: TS Jan. 6, 1883.

8. TS Jan. 20, 1883. "who ever lived.": San Francisco *Universe* in TS Jan. 6, 1883.

9. The *New York Times*, Dec. 7, 1882.

10. The *Theosophist*, March 1883.

11. TS Jan. 6, 1883.

12. Ibid.

13. Ibid.

14. TS Dec. 16, 1882.

15. Ibid.

16. TS Feb. 10, 1883.

17. TS March 24, 1883.

18. NYSSV arrest blotter.

19. Ari Hoogenbloom, *Rutherford B. Hayes: Warrior President*, notes, p. 593. University Press of Kansas. 1995.

20. Broun and Leech p. 16. "but the undertaker.": GM v. 1 pp. 286–87. Anthony Comstock obit: TS Oct. 2, 1915.

Anthony Comstock died on July 21, 1915, soon after returning home from the International Purity Congress at the San Francisco Exposition, where he served as a delegate appointed by President Wilson. Comstock was proclaimed "a soldier of righteousness" at his funeral and was buried in Evergreen Cemetery in Brooklyn, New York. "In memory of a fearless witness. . . . Lay aside every weight—looking unto Jesus—despising the shame" is carved on his tombstone. Anthony Comstock's crusade had been mostly forgotten, but his name lives on in infamy and is synonymous with bigoted censorship.

21. TS Dec. 23, 1882.

22. Ibid.

23. TS Aug. 18, 1883.

24. Edwin G. Burrows and Mike Wallace, *Gotham: A History of New York City to 1898*, New York Oxford, Oxford University Press, 1999 and *American Cemetery Magazine*, January through April 1985, "Green-Wood, Brooklyn's 'Garden City of the Dead,' Frederick G. Vogel. "D—n ANTHONY COMSTOCK." *New York Times*, Aug. 29, 1883.

25. TS Sept. 8, 1883.

26. TS March 15, 1884.

27. Ibid.

28. Ibid.

29. TS June 28, 1884.

30. TS March 15, 1884.

31. TS June 28, 1884.

32. "of our cause.": TS Aug. 6, 1898. "as life lasts.": TS Oct. 13, 1883.

Eugene M. Macdonald would continue as the editor of the *Truth Seeker* until his death in 1909. During his stewardship, the periodical remained moderate on economic and political issues and avoided Populism and Socialism. In 1888 Macdonald learned firsthand the stifling effects of the alliance between church and state, when he was denied the right to vote, because of his refusal to swear on the Bible. Macdonald's tenure as editor coincided with the birth of the militant labor movement in the United States. Like Bennett, he recognized the inequities of American society and continued to promote labor reform. He spoke out against the disparity witnessed daily in New York, a city that he characterized as of magnificence and squalor.

In 1896 Macdonald published *Ingersoll as He Is*, countering the malicious lies that were circulating about "The Great Agnostic." In 1906, with the help of his brother, he published *A Short History of the Inquisition*. Macdonald was elected president of the American Secular Union (ASU) in 1901 when it had nearly fifty thousand members.

After learning that he had tuberculosis in 1908, Eugene left his brother in charge of the *Truth Seeker* and moved to the country to "take the cure." Assessing Eugene's important contribution to the *Truth Seeker*, George Macdonald stated: "Institutions have their founders, and generally their saviors, Bennett and E. M. Macdonald played those parts." Eugene Macdonald died on February 26, 1909, at the age of fifty-four. Fittingly, the man who devoted his entire life to promoting individual sovereignty and fighting for civil liberties for his fellow Americans died in a small village in upstate New York called Liberty.

George E. Macdonald was associated with the *Truth Seeker* for more than half a century and was editor for nearly three decades. In the early twentieth century, several important civil-liberties and church-and-state historical issues occurred in America and abroad. In 1909, the year of Eugene Macdonald's death, the *Truth Seeker* publicized the persecution and execution "instigated by the church" of Francisco Ferrer, the innovative and freethinking Spanish educator. During the First World War, the *Truth Seeker* remained patriotic, fiercely loyal, and beyond reproach; nevertheless, it was repeatedly suppressed for advocating secularism. Macdonald's hard-hitting editorials exposing church graft and his unwavering attacks on the ethically challenged YMCA and the Salvation Army caused the publication intense scrutiny. The *Truth Seeker* was subsequently declared "unmailable under the Espionage Act." Naturally, Macdonald extensively covered the Scopes Trial because the *Truth Seeker* had promoted Charles Darwin's theory of evolution since the publication's infancy. Not since D. M. Bennett's trial in 1879 had the periodical gone to such an extent as it did covering the Tennessee proceedings that brought the antievolution statute out in the open. When George Macdonald published his *Fifty Years of Freethought: Story of the "Truth Seeker,"* Clarence Darrow agreed to write the foreword. "It is well for us to remember these men and women who have made it safe to think," the famed attorney wrote. "The world owes an enormous debt to the fighters for human freedom, and we cannot suffer their names to be forgotten now that we are reaping the fruits of their intelligence and devotion." In 1937 George Macdonald retired as editor but continued to contribute his "Observations" column to the *Truth Seeker* until his death at the age of eighty-seven on July 13, 1944.

33. TS March 15, 1884.

In 1891 Lucy N. Colman expressed her admiration for D. M. Bennett and her gratitude in her *Reminiscences* about her courageous and daring life. She wrote:

> The editor and publisher of the *Truth Seeker* died a martyr to mental liberty, but his paper lives, and is to-day the bible of thousands of readers. . . . The *Truth Seeker* family with its supporters are very dear to me—my own family, as I have no other, I may call it. They have always treated me with kindness—with an appreciation far beyond my deserts, never having rejected anything which I have sent them. I have had more than my share of the paper. Since I came into this family of Truth Seekers we have lost by death very many valuable members. First our martyred editor and publisher, but "his soul has been marching on" through all these years, inspiring his followers to continue the work so well begun by him.

34. TS Aug. 6, 1898.

Felix Adler (1851–1933). American philosopher, reformer, and founder of the Society for Ethical Culture, a humanistic religious and ethical movement, in New York in 1876. Bennett praised Adler in the pages of the *Truth Seeker* in 1878, writing: "The society is doing good work in an unpretending way. . . . Mr. Adler has far more followers to-day than did Jesus Christ, after the first two years of his preaching, and Mr. Adler's followers are men of the highest culture—thinkers, and not ignorant boors incapable of telling right from wrong. . . . Mr. Adler preaches love instead of violence as a means of redeeming the world from sin.": TS May 18, 1878.

"The City of Light" (The Golden City)

Hail the glorious golden city,
Pictured by the seers of old.
Everlasting light shines o'er it,
Wondrous things of it are told.
Wise and righteous men and women
Dwell within its gleaming wall.
Wrong is banished from its borders.
Justice reigns supreme o'er all.

We are builders of that city.
All our joys and all our groans
Help to rear its shining ramparts.
All our lives are building stones.
Whether humble or exalted,
All are called to task divine.
All must aid alike and carry
Forward one sublime design.

And the work that we have builded,
Oft with bleeding hands and tears,
Oft in error, oft in anguish,
Will not perish with our years.
It will live and shine transfigured
In the final reign of right.
It will pass into the splendors
of the city of the light.

35. Ibid.

AFTERWORD

The *New York Times* obituary writer minimized D. M. Bennett's free-speech advocacy, writing that he had "obtained some notoriety in 1878 by reason of his arrest upon the charge of sending indecent publications through the mails . . . and was tried and convicted and served 11 months of his sentence in the penitentiary." The *Times*, like most "secular" newspapers in the nineteenth century, was Christian, conservative, pompous, and essentially a guardian of repressive Victorian morality.[1]

D. M. Bennett's 1879 obscenity trial was a travesty of justice. The *Hicklin* standard, based on a landmark British case from 1868, was an ambiguous test for obscenity that permitted work to be judged by introducing *only* isolated passages and not the intention of the author. The Bennett conviction and appeal denial was a landmark decision that became the foundation for obscenity law for more than half a century. Bennett's trial transcript (that he originally published) has been reprinted and is still studied by law students and legal scholars.[2]

During my initial research, I wondered why no one had ever written a biography of D. M. Bennett. Further along in my research, I discovered that Bennett's free-speech campaign was never fully examined and most of what was previously written about him was based largely on Anthony Comstock's biased writings. With access to archival material only recently made available, we are able to get closer to the truth about Bennett's arrests, conviction, imprisonment, and monumental petition campaign. Bennett was aware of his archenemy's hostility toward him and his beloved journal but not to the extent revealed in the twentieth century. Rutherford B. Hayes's personal diaries shed light on Bennett's unjust conviction and expose the president's prejudice and his admittedly flawed decision *not* to pardon the editor of the *Truth Seeker*.[3]

Anthony Comstock's self-righteous fight-for-the-young battle cry has often been retooled in America by self-serving moralists to fit their agenda. There have been numerous censorship campaigns and celebrated obscenity cases since D. M. Bennett's 1879 New York trial. And if the past is prologue, there will be more attacks on free speech. "No Liberals! The morals of children first," was one of Comstock's favorite edicts—an expression that sadly might always sound contemporary.[4]

A century after Bennett's death, the *Dictionary of American Biography* described him as "an amalgam of quack, crank, and idealist," and added, "The quack and crank are somewhat excused by the hard conditions of his early life; the idealist, in spite of faults of taste and mistakes of judgment, was for almost a decade an effective popular spokesman for liberal ideas in religion and ethics."[5]

The source of the quack remark is Anthony Comstock's highly biased and often-repeated notation in his arrest blotter. In the 1870s reformers like Bennett had plenty of issues to be cranky about. The editor and many of his Liberal colleagues were in the vanguard of the women's rights movement and promoting birth control. Freethinkers fought for the separation of church and state and protested against monopolies, puritanical censorship laws, and Sunday laws that prevented working people from rightfully enjoying life, liberty, and the pursuit of happiness. Bennett was certainly guilty of being an idealist—as was his hero, Thomas Paine.[6]

"Biographies are not written by neutrals," one biographer aptly asserted. I have given as complete and truthful a portrait of D. M. Bennett as I could; this is why I chose to include a great many of his own words. I found that his voice and human frailties made his story all the more compelling. I have come to greatly appreciate Bennett's courageous struggle against religious and/or state-sponsored intrusion, coercion, and censorship—a battle that is just as noble and needed today as it was over a century ago. DeRobigne Mortimer Bennett's contribution to American civil liberties has yet to be rightfully acknowledged. Hopefully this biography will help the founder of the *Truth Seeker* finally gain the recognition that he deserves.[7]

"Mr. D. M. Bennett was a man wholly extraordinary, and his career was not less so," James Parton wrote a few days after his friend's death. The biographer added,

> He was not a perfect character as he well knew and frankly acknowledged; but his merits, considering all things, were very great and very rare; and they were his own while his faults were due in great measure to the grossly false and profoundly immoral religion from which he had the courage and the mental force to escape. His wonderful labors have made the escape of others easier than he found it. He embraced an unpopular cause; he made it less difficult for others to do so.[8]

James Parton's heartfelt summation is, in my opinion, an eloquent and accurate assessment of the nineteenth century's most controversial publisher, American free-speech martyr, and quintessential *truth seeker*.

NOTES

1. *New York Times*, Dec. 7, 1882.

2. *The Trial of D. M. Bennett. Hicklin* standard: James C. N. Paul and Murray L. Schwartz. *Federal Censorship: Obscenity in the Mail.* N.Y.: Free Press of Glencoe, Inc., 1961.

3. Anthony Comstock, The New York Society for the Suppression of Vice arrest blotter, Library of Congress microfilm. Hayes Diary.

4. Anthony Comstock, *Frauds Exposed.*

5. *Dictionary of American Biography,* Edited by Allen Johnson. Charles Scribner's Sons, N.Y. 1957.

6. NYSSV arrest blotter.

Although Bennett was never a "regular" medical doctor, he was the Shaker community physician, owned drugstores, and successfully marketed patent medicines he developed from his herbal and homeopathic knowledge. Many of the Shakers' natural alternatives to primitive nineteenth-century medicine have subsequently proven to be effective, legitimate, and popular.

7. Broun and Leech.

8. TS Jan. 6, 1883.

SELECTED BIBLIOGRAPHY

Andrews, Edward Deming. *The People Called Shakers: A Search for the Perfect Society*. New York: Dover, 1963.

Bennett, DeRobigne Mortimer. *Anthony Comstock: His Career of Cruelty and Crime; A Chapter from "The Champions of the Church."* 1878. Reprint, New York: Da Capo Press, 1971.

———. *The Champions of the Church: Their Crimes and Persecutions*. New York: Liberal and Scientific Publishing House, 1878.

———. *An Infidel Abroad* [also titled *A Truth Seeker in Europe: A Series of Letters Written Home During a Ten Week's Visit*]. New York: Truth Seeker, 1881.

———. *Trial of D. M. Bennett, Upon the Charge of Depositing Prohibited Matter in the Mail*. Reported by S. B. Hinsdale. New York: Truth Seeker, 1879. Reprint, Civil Liberties in American History. New York: Da Capo Press, 1973.

———. *A Truth Seeker around the World: A Series of Letters Written while Making a Tour of the Globe*. 4 vols. New York: D. M. Bennett, 1882.

———. *The World's Sages, Infidels, and Thinkers* [also titled *The World's Sages, Thinkers and Reformers*]. New York: Truth Seeker, 1876.

Blatt, Martin Henry. *Free Love and Anarchism: The Biography of Ezra Heywood*. Urbana and Chicago: University of Illinois Press, 1989.

Broun, Heywood, and Margaret Leech. *Anthony Comstock: Roundsman of the Lord*. New York: Albert & Charles Boni, 1927.

Encyclopaedia Britannica. 11th ed. 1910.

Fruchtman, Jack, Jr. *Thomas Paine: Apostle of Freedom*. New York: Four Walls Eight Windows, 1994.

Hoogenbloom, Ari. *Rutherford B. Hayes: Warrior and President*. Lawrence: University Press of Kansas, 1995.

Larson, Orvin. *American Infidel: Robert G. Ingersoll*. 1962. Reprint, Madison, Wis.: Freedom from Religion Foundation, 1993.

Levy, Leonard W. *Blasphemy: Verbal Offense against the Sacred: From Moses to Salman Rushdie*. New York: Knopf, 1993.

Macdonald, George Everett Hussey. *Fifty Years of Freethought: Story of the "Truth Seeker" from 1875*. 2 vols. New York: Truth Seeker, 1929, 1931.

Paine, Thomas. *The Age of Reason*. With a biographical introduction by Philip S. Foner. New York: Citadel Press, 1988.

Putnam, Samuel P. *400 Years of Freethought*. New York: Truth Seeker, 1894.

Sears, Hal D. *The Sex Radicals: Free Love in High Victorian America*. Lawrence: University Press of Kansas, 1986.

Smith, Frank. *Robert G. Ingersoll: A Life*. Amherst, N.Y.: Prometheus Books, 1990.

Stein, Gordon, ed. *The Encyclopedia of Unbelief*. 2 vols. Amherst, N.Y.: Prometheus Books, 1985.

Stein, Stephen J. *The Shaker Experience in America: A History of the United Society of Believers*. New Haven, Conn.: Yale University Press, 1992.

Stern, Madeleine B. *The Pantarch: A Biography of Stephen Pearl Andrews*. Austin: University of Texas Press, 1968.

Warren, Sidney. *American Freethought, 1860–1914*. New York: Gordian Press, 1966.

INDEX

391